Scraping By

Studies in Early American Economy and Society
from the Library Company of Philadelphia

Cathy Matson, *Series Editor*

Scraping By

Wage Labor, Slavery, and Survival in Early Baltimore

SETH ROCKMAN

The Johns Hopkins University Press

Baltimore

The Johns Hopkins University Press
2715 North Charles Street
Baltimore, Maryland 21218-4363
www.press.jhu.edu

Library of Congress Cataloging-in-Publication Data

Rockman, Seth.
Scraping by : wage labor, slavery, and survival in early
Baltimore / Seth Rockman.
p. cm. — (Studies in early American economy and society from
the Library Company of Philadelphia)
Includes bibliographical references and index.
ISBN-13: 978-0-8018-9006-2 (alk. paper)
ISBN-10: 0-8018-9006-3 (alk. paper)
ISBN-13: 978-0-8018-9007-9 (pbk. : alk. paper)
ISBN-10: 0-8018-9007-1 (pbk. : alk. paper)
1. Labor—Maryland—Baltimore—History—19th century.   2. Wages—
Maryland—Baltimore—History—19th century.   3. Slavery—Maryland—
Baltimore—History—19th century.   4. Working class—Maryland—
Baltimore—History—19th century. 5.   African Americans—
Employment—Maryland—Baltimore—History—19th century.
6. Whites—Employment—Maryland—Baltimore—History—
19th century.   7. Capitalism—Social aspects—Maryland—Baltimore—
History—19th century.   8. Baltimore (Md.)—Economic conditions—
19th century.   9. Baltimore (Md.)—Social conditions—19th century.
10. Baltimore (Md.)—Race relations—History—19th century.   I. Title.
HD8085.B33R63   2008
331.109752'7109034—dc22   2008011847

A catalog record for this book is available from the British Library.

*Special discounts are available for bulk purchases of this book. For more information,
please contact Special Sales at 410-516-6936 or specialsales@press.jhu.edu.*

The Johns Hopkins University Press uses environmentally friendly book
materials, including recycled text paper that is composed of at least 30 percent
post-consumer waste, whenever possible. All of our book papers are acid-free,
and our jackets and covers are printed on paper with recycled content.

To my parents, Barbara Karp Rockman and Saul Rockman

CONTENTS

FIGURES AND TABLES

FIGURES

TABLES

Studies in Early American Economy and Society, a collaborative effort between the Johns Hopkins University Press and the Library Company of Philadelphia's Program in Early American Economy and Society (PEAES), aims to promote scholarly discussion of the early American economy and bring together people who wish to advance our understanding of the economy under the umbrella of numerous disciplines, methodologies, and subjects. In addition to this book series, PEAES sponsors seminars, fellowships, public outreach programs, conference gatherings and publication of their proceedings, and ambitious acquisition of print and manuscript sources about the early economy. PEAES also reaches across numerous scholarly disciplines, methodologies, and subjects to enlarge this ongoing enterprise.

In this fourth title in the series, Seth Rockman recovers Baltimore's remarkable rise to prominence in the new nation through the menial labor of countless men and women who strung together livelihoods at the economic margins. The bristling enterprise and commercial growth of Baltimore during the first post-Revolutionary generations relied on a huge array of unskilled and skilled immigrants, runaway slaves, and women struggling to support their families, all of them confronting the harsh realities of Baltimore's rise by "scraping by." Largely hidden from view because they left virtually no public paper trail and sank only shallow roots in the city, thousands of African Americans, European immigrants, and people coming from the countryside arrived with little means of support. Slave and free, both white and black, toiled in a common labor market and occupied the same neighborhoods of this early republic boomtown.

In the face of slim and recalcitrant sources for this great flood of human labor, Rockman has nevertheless stitched together a finely grained portrait of work sites and the people who labored at them, from manual laborers who built the city's transportation infrastructure with the amazing "mudmachine," to semi-employed men and women who left the city to perform rural farm labor at harvest time, to the dockyards where free and unfree workers struggled together to turn out Baltimore's famous clippers, to the children and peddlers scavenging in the alleyways. Employers used a variety of discursive and material means to collapse the differences of race, class, ethnicity, and age between some workers—or to enhance those differences when it was expedient—but always to affirm employer ownership and control over those who scraped by. And for those slaves who were rented out, or wage laborers who worked alongside indentured men and women, the struggle to find work or move from job to job, stringing together as many days as possible, offset the dream of earning high wages in early republican Baltimore. Rockman's study also uncovers the hidden labor markets of capitalist economies. Here unpaid and mundane (but vital) tasks like sewing, washing, feeding, provisioning, and boarding complemented the backbreaking work of building Baltimore.

Cathy Matson
Professor of History
University of Delaware
Director, Program in Early American Economy and Society
The Library Company of Philadelphia

City of Baltimore, circa 1823. Based on Fielding Lucas, Jr., *Maryland*, 1823. Courtesy David Rumsey Map Collection.

❧ City of Baltimore ❧
circa 1823

1. **Coming to Work in the City**
   Office of *Niles Weekly Register*

2. **A Job for a Working Man**
   New Bridge over Jones Falls

3. **Dredging and Drudgery**
   Mudmachinists in the Harbor

4. **A Job for a Working Woman**
   Concentration of Households
   Employing Domestic Servants

5. **The Living Wage**
   Female Union Society of
   Seamstresses Meeting Hall

6. **The Hard Work of Being Poor**
   Fells Point Market

7. **The Consequence of Failure**
   Old Almshouse

8. **The Market's Grasp**
   Slavetrading District

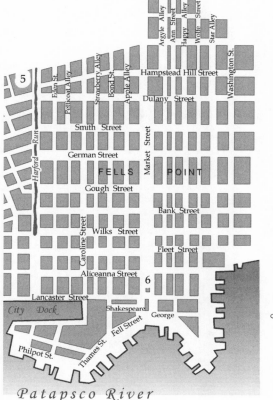

Based on Fielding Lucas, Jr.,
Maryland, 1823,
courtesy of the David Rumsey
Map Collection
www.davidrumsey.com

Digital Re-creation
L. Carlson, 2007
Brown University

Scraping By

Introduction

ecause dirty work is rarely well-remunerated work, the petition that arrived at Baltimore's city hall in February 1829 contained no surprises. Four manual laborers complained that the wages they earned as "scrapers of the streets" were too low. Perhaps men who picked up manure for a living should not have expected more, but John Thompson, Charles Burns, John Hickman, and Hugh Murphy thought otherwise. Removing street manure was no small undertaking in the age of the horse, but it was an essential matter of public health and a key source of municipal revenue. In fact, the city government maintained a manure monopoly, limiting scavenging to the handful of scrapers on the public payroll. The collected manure was carted out to the almshouse on the outskirts of town, where it fertilized the institution's farm. The 15,000 heads of cabbage and 22,000 tomatoes it helped grow annually saved the city thousands of dollars in poor relief expenditures. In the winter of 1829, however, the almshouse loomed large in the imaginations of the street scrapers for a different reason. Already poor and growing poorer "at a time when the price of the most requisite necessaries of life is considerably enhanced," they feared that they might find themselves and their families toiling at the almshouse farm—spreading manure rather than collecting it—if they did not get a raise.[1]

For the street scrapers, wage labor was not a stepping stone to landed independence, as Thomas Jefferson and other apostles of the American yeoman ideal had hoped. Rather, these adult white men were lifelong wage laborers whose ability to pay rent or clothe their children depended on stringing together as many days of employment as possible. As their petition indicated, having a job was no guarantee of making a living. For those who labored under far greater disadvantages of legal, political, and social disfranchisement, the prospects of making ends meet were even more doubtful. The circumstances of the street scrapers were enviable in comparison to those of the white women who stitched shirts by candlelight in their own apartments, the free African American men who could not take jobs that kept them out later than a curfew on people of color, or the enslaved domestic servants who waited on prosperous families while worrying about the integrity of their own. Nonetheless, what a free black sawyer, a German-born seamstress, an enslaved hod carrier, and the wage-earning street scrapers shared were lives of arduous labor that netted no economic security in return. In relating "the wants, necessities, and lowly circumstances of poor industrious Families," the street scrapers could stand for all workers struggling "to derive a tolerably sufficient subsistence from their time application and labour."[2]

This book explores the livelihoods of families whose members performed what is often called "unskilled labor." Here, the street scrapers toil alongside seamstresses, mariners, ditchdiggers, dockworkers, domestic servants, woodcutters, rag pickers, and others whose work was typically dirty and devalued. Collectively, their labor animated the cities of the new United States in the decades following the American Revolution. Whether male or female, native born or immigrant, Euro-American or African American, enslaved, indentured, or free, these working people struggled to scrape by. All "lived poor"—a hand-to-mouth existence characterized by minimal control over their own labor, periodic spells of joblessness, and severe privation. Their living situations were precarious and easily jeopardized by external forces. Most would rely on public welfare or private charity in the aftermath of an illness, during the years when children were too young to work, or in the midst of a cold winter. A charity appeal from 1805 defined this cohort as those "who perform the meaner offices of labor": women picking oakum, hawking fruit on the street corners, and finishing shirts for slopshops, as well as men "hauling wood from the wharves, and those employed in supplying masons and bricklayers with sand—scowmen—boat men—the laborers in the mud machines, and in the brick-yards—and in fact, all day-laborers of every kind."[3]

The liberal promises of the American Revolution stood beyond the reach of these workers, for whom economic failure was far more common than the upward mobility so widely associated with the era of the early republic.[4] No account of the economic insecurity of working people, however, can deny that the new nation *did* see unprecedented prosperity, unparalleled social dynamism, and rapid technological advances that allowed more people than ever before to imagine themselves as agents of their own destiny.[5] Because the celebratory accounts of prosperity and the sobering accounts of privation are usually told separately, it is easy to forget they are flip sides of the same coin. The trick is to recognize these two versions of the past as contingent on one another, rather than as mutually exclusive. At a moment of great entrepreneurial energy and social mobility, prosperity came to Americans who could best assemble, deploy, and exploit the physical labor of others. The early republic's economy opened up new possibilities for some Americans precisely because it closed down opportunities for others. This book, then, tells the story of the chronically impoverished, often unfree, and generally unequal Americans whose work made the United States arguably the most wealthy, free, and egalitarian society in the Western world.[6]

There is no better place than Baltimore to see the new promises, possibilities, and perils of the early American republic. Baltimore was an early republic boomtown, gaining municipal independence in 1797, just as it surpassed Boston to become the third largest city in the nation. With virtually no colonial-era past to set the tone of its early republic development, Baltimore embodied the ambitions and limitations of the new United States.

Imagine a scene on the docks of Baltimore in 1816, as American-born steve-dores loaded crates of ready-made shirts aboard a merchant ship bound for South America. Focusing in on the ship, one might see a rural miller haggling with the captain over the price of one of the indentured teenagers whom the ship had recently brought from Bremen, or a free black mariner signing articles to work the outgoing voyage as an ordinary seaman. Expand the view, and one might glimpse that sailor's laundress wife washing clothes in Harford Run, or the sailor's enslaved sister serving tea in the home of the merchant who owned the ship and hoping that her brother might one day accumulate enough money to purchase her freedom. A widening perspective reveals the widowed seamstresses stitching shirts at home, as well as the apprenticed boys winding thread in Baltimore's first manufactories on the outskirts of town. Along the waterfront, a middle-aged white domestic servant might be cooking breakfast in a Fells Point boardinghouse, where some of the ship's crew spent its shore leave in the company of women supporting themselves through prostitution. In the harbor, Scotch-Irish dredgers on the mudmachine were battling sedimentation to keep Baltimore's port open. From an even broader vantage, one might see the enslaved field laborers of a distant cotton plantation, whose growing market value encouraged urban slaveholders to resist liberating the men, women, and children they owned in Baltimore, or even the menial workers in Lancashire, Cap François, Ouidah, and Paramaribo— the "Atlantic proletariat" whose labor integrated an already global economy.[7]

The workers populating these snapshots did not lead interchangeable lives. They followed separate historical paths to proletarian status, crafted identities for themselves out of disparate materials, and labored under vulnerabilities specific to their social positions, be they married women, non-English-speaking immigrants, or people of color. But in searching for and explicating the significance of social difference in the survival strategies of Baltimore's stevedores, seamstresses, sailors, and servants over the half-century between 1790 and 1840, this book also stresses the commonalities in their experiences of finding and keeping work, translating labor into subsistence, and filling the inevitable shortfalls through scrounging, scavenging, and scheming. At bottom, all these workers lived and worked within a broader system that treated human labor as a commodity readily deployed in the service of private wealth and national economic development.

The obvious differences among such a diverse working population could melt away in a city like Baltimore, where the majority of common laborers were white, where enslaved men and women frequently earned wages, and where employers readily combined workers of different nativities, colors, ages, sexes, and legal conditions in the same productive enterprises. While remaining sensitive to the different lived experiences of such diverse workers, and always recognizing how larger structures like white supremacy, patriarchy, and legal slavery situated people differently in the social matrix, this study locates the widest spectrum of manual laborers in the same capitalist political economy—one designed to transform their labor into new wealth and power for those who could purchase it, whether by the hour, day, week, month, season, year, or lifetime.[8]

As Baltimore grew from a backwater in 1776 to the nation's third largest city by 1800, its common laborers lived in precarious circumstances, not merely because poverty had always been the fate of those who work with their hands, but because the city's employers found new ways to hire and fire more workers at will, to deploy slaves as tractable workers and lucrative investment properties, to seek out women and children as workers whose putative status as dependents assured their wages would stay low, to use the policing power of the state to discipline those who refused to work, and to create new social fictions around the legitimacy of market relations.

In these same years, Baltimore's merchants, manufacturers, and bankers thrived not merely because of their entrepreneurial talents, but also because they had at their disposal a diverse pool of labor that included more workers who could be hired and fired at will, more who could be bought for life and compelled through violence, and yet more who could be paid sub-subsistence wages on the assumption that others would make up the difference. Baltimore's wealthy could marshal the power of municipal and state government to enforce vagrancy statutes, to fund institutions to rehabilitate the shiftless, and to arrest workers who formed unions. Employers denounced as quaint such traditional practices as legally restricting the price of bread, and they published reports declaring poverty inconceivable in so free a nation. The emergence of this new political economy intensified economic insecurity for the overwhelming majority of urban workers. And in turn, the intensification of economic insecurity for urban workers opened new avenues to prosperity for those who were in the position to purchase labor.

This interrelated process has consequences for how scholars narrate American economic development and date the emergence of a recognizably capitalist society. Historians have generally avoided rigid theoretical definitions of capitalism but tend instead to "know it when we see it." Different historians have dated capitalism's arrival to Alexander Hamilton's program of national finance; to the technological innovations that jump-started manufacturing in places like Pawtucket and Lowell; to the immersion of rural families in an expanding consumer culture; to the intensification of commercial agriculture; and to the rise of new men liberated from the artificial hierarchies of the colonial era, from aristocratic scorn for work, and from cultural prohibitions against self-interest. The advance of capitalism in the early republic period is variously symbolized by an explosion of canal and turnpike construction linking distant regions in a common market, by the proliferation of banks and the circulation of cash as the medium of exchange, and by the reconfiguration of law to facilitate the granting of corporate charters and sanctify property rights.[9]

For all their variety, scholarly accounts of early republic economic change have been content to define capitalism by its manifestations and effects rather than by its underlying social relations. Too often capitalism appears as a synonym for market exchange and not as a political economy that dictated who worked where, on what terms, and to whose benefit. But to follow the careers of low-end laborers through an early republic boomtown like Baltimore lays bare those rules and the unequal relationships of power that propelled economic development in the decades following the American Revolution.[10]

The aspect of capitalism that took the longest to arrive was a "free market" in labor, where workers could choose their own employers, receive cash wages for their time, quit at will, and toil free of physical violence. In the Marxist tradition, this system of free labor is the sine qua non of capitalism, and its halting, inconsistent, and incomplete arrival to the American workplace has long confounded efforts to understand the economy of the early republic United States.[11]

The decades between the American Revolution and the Civil War saw substantial growth in the percentage of workers exchanging labor for a wage, but such workers were not the majority who powered national economic development. Outside the wage system stood the larger number of Americans who labored within household units of production, who performed the unpaid reproductive labor that sustained wage-earning workers, or who labored as slaves growing cotton, the nation's most valuable commodity. Complicating matters further, many workers who earned wages did so without any semblance of market freedom. Those whose skin color, sex, or age stripped them of civil rights or prevented them from traveling in search of better wages could hardly be said to meet their employers as equals in the marketplace. Even enslaved workers sometimes earned wages, though they lacked the legal power to keep them. As important, patriarchal presumptions of women's dependence limited the jobs available to female workers and set their pay so low that it guaranteed dependence on male breadwinners or on the social welfare institutions of the state. Custom set women's wages, not ebbs and flows in the labor supply. Studies of early republic enterprise have shown just how essential such workers were to production in iron forges, chemical factories, and textile mills. Attending to this reality underscores Joseph Schumpeter's observation that "the capitalist order rests on props made of extra-capitalist material."[12]

The persistence and expansion of slavery has proved especially vexing to historians trying to explain capitalism's development in the early republic. By many accounts, slavery constituted an entirely different mode of production, whose destruction was a necessary precondition for capitalism's emergence. Whether owing to Marxist models of social development, to the common depiction of the Civil War as a battle between slavery and free labor, or to the proclivity of American scholars to equate capitalism with human liberation, the general tendency has been to depict capitalism and slavery as fundamentally incompatible systems. From the standpoint of simple labor economics, slavery should disappear where free workers predominate, and vice versa. According to such arguments, employers would never invest capital in their labor force when they could instead hire and fire free workers whose self-interest motivated them to toil more diligently than hopeless slaves. In contrast, free workers would avoid places where slavery was the dominant system of labor, lest they call into question their own freedom and risk racial degradation. Slavery would also depress wages because employers would have no need to entice workers with better pay so long as profits were, in the words of one visitor to Baltimore, "pinched and screwed out of the Negro."[13]

Historians are now reconsidering the presumptive antagonism of slavery and capitalism. One approach has involved thinking about slavery less as a labor system and more as a property regime—that is, as a legally protected way of investing, storing, transporting, and bequeathing wealth. Even in locations where wage labor was more productive, slavery could remain vital because owners held on to slaves as commodities rather than as workers. So long as someone somewhere was willing to pay for that commodity, slaves retained a value that enhanced their

owners' estates, provided collateral for loans, and served as the dowries and in-
heritances that predicated generations of white prosperity on the ownership of
generations of black families. In this regard, the perpetuation of slavery in a place
like Baltimore owed less to the actual labor compelled from enslaved workers and
more to the fact that plantation purchasers in Charleston, Augusta, New Orleans,
and throughout the South were willing to pay hundreds of dollars for Baltimore
slaves. Under the "chattel principle" that facilitated the instantaneous conversion
of a person into cash, Baltimore slaveholders reaped wealth from slavery that had
little to do with urban labor itself.[14]

Other historians have suggested that the "cultural work" of slavery should be
considered alongside the actual work that enslaved men and women performed.
What slaveholders obtained from their human property was not merely labor, but
a way of conceptualizing themselves as "masters," a vehicle for performing patriarchal obligations to one's wife and children, a means of class differentiation
relative to nonslaveholding whites, a mode of social discipline to keep impoverished European immigrants grateful for their low wages, and a tool for undermining interracial solidarity of working people in general. Slavery sustained, if
not promoted, many of the values and practices associated with early republic capitalism, such as the performance of self, the attainment of middle-class standards
of respectability, and the pursuit of upward mobility. Seen in this light, slavery
appeared worth preserving as a system not merely for compelling labor and accumulating capital, but for its ability to shape the contours of a broader range of
social and cultural relations.[15]

Both a property regime and a system of cultural power, slavery was also a labor system that accelerated economic development. Payroll records and job advertisements from Baltimore reveal the ready assimilation of enslaved workers
into a fluid labor market. Through the practice of hiring slaves, employers rec-
onciled slavery with the most advantageous aspects of a "free-labor" economy,
namely the ability to hire and fire workers at will and to jettison traditional responsibilities of providing laborers with room and board. However, they were not
so committed to the free-labor ideal that they sought to abolish slavery or convert
all labor relations to a wage basis. There was no need to choose between a labor
force entirely of enslaved workers or one entirely of free, self-owned, and legally
equal workers. Instead, the system that emerged in Baltimore blurred boundaries
between categories of labor, assuring the interchangeability of different workers
along a continuum of slaves-for-life to transient day laborers—with term slaves,
rented slaves, self-hiring slaves, indentured servants, redemptioners, apprentices,
prisoners, children, and paupers occupying the space in between. Urban employers

desired the largest pool of labor at their disposal, fulfilling what Eric Wolf has called "the general tendency of the capitalist mode to create a 'disposable mass' of laborers out of diverse populations, and to then throw that mass into the breach to meet the changing needs of capital."[16]

Baltimore employers constantly adjusted their workforces, shifting between and combining laborers who were enslaved, indentured, and free; black and white; male and female; young and old; native born and immigrant. The simultaneous sale of laborers' time *and* laborers' bodies brought employers the power to choose whom to buy, hire, rent, or recapture in order to find exactly the worker they sought at any given moment. While some of the city's shipbuilders, butchers, and cabinetmakers purchased slaves, others rented slaves from their legal owners, paid wages to enslaved men and women who had responsibility for finding their own hire, or sought out recent Irish immigrants, apprenticed children, or free black wage laborers. Even within a specific field like housing construction or shoemaking, employers made divergent choices about how best to recruit, organize, and discipline labor. Baltimore employers were unlikely to deem a particular job suited only to men, only to adults, only to white people, or only to slaves.

Rather than depicting such an erratic labor market as merely a transitional moment en route to a fully developed capitalism (as the teleology of economic history has typically suggested), this study argues that early republic capitalism thrived on its ability to exploit the labor of workers unable fully to claim the prerogatives of market freedom. Baltimore's substantial population of enslaved workers illustrates this dynamic in particularly stark terms, but slavery was only one of several devices for assuring that workers and employers would not negotiate as equals. Legal coverture, alongside the presumptive dependence of women on male providers, made it impossible for female workers to bargain for better wages or, often, to control the wages they did earn. Free people of color could not testify in court against white employers, and therefore could not sue for unpaid wages. Even adult white men stood on unstable ground when it came to their ability to quit a job without forfeiting wages they had already accrued, to negotiate collectively, or to strike for better pay or a shorter workday. Even as a growing number of workers traded direct subordination to a master for indirect subordination to the marketplace (in the apt formulation of historian David Montgomery), they did not meet their employers as legal equals. The absence of negotiation, the persistence of coercion, and the disparity in power between those buying labor and those performing it were not imperfections or temporary contradictions in capitalist development; they were the very foundation of capitalism in the early republic.[17]

———

How did laboring people operate within this system? What strategies did they use to find work? To translate income into food, rent, clothing, and fuel? To navigate underground economies and social welfare programs? Finally, and most importantly, how did such strategies vary among workers whose race, gender, age, ethnicity, and legal status placed differing constraints on their choices? These are the questions this book attempts to answer.

The response of working people to the challenges of capitalist economic development has been a fundamental issue in the field of labor history and central to discussions of class formation in the United States.[18] For the early republic period, most scholars have focused on workers with far more resources—material and political—than the street scrapers, seamstresses, and servants examined in this book. Despite the centrality of casual and low-end laborers to the seaport economies of the new nation, labor historians have privileged the experiences of that minority of workers associated with the craft workshop. These artisans constructed their craft skill as a form of property and drew from it their identity as independent republican citizens, virile husbands and fathers, and in most cases, *white* Americans. Losing ground as new manufacturing processes made their skill less valuable, militant artisans redoubled their claims to a meaningful place within electoral politics and formed unions, founded newspapers, and waged strikes. Building on the pioneering scholarship of E. P. Thompson and Herbert Gutman, historians have traced the emergence of "artisan republicanism" in numerous local settings and made artisans' politicization synonymous with working-class formation in the United States.[19]

In recent years, scholars have begun to chip away at the "artisans into workers" narrative. The craft workshop could hardly have provided the experiential basis for working-class formation for the simple reason that most workers labored outside it. Feminist historians, in particular, have made this point by relocating the "quintessential worker" from the shop floor to the household and by emphasizing relations of reproduction over sites of production. Artisans were neither the majority of working people, nor the appropriate representatives of a broader working class, most of whom had no craft training, shared no common culture with their employers, and could not claim the prerogatives of white American manhood. In fact, artisan identities were typically constructed *in opposition* to the majority of laborers, who were female, black, immigrant, or enslaved.[20] While artisans met the challenges of economic change by participating in parades, militia musters, and other rituals of civic life, common laborers frequently coped with capitalism by directing violence toward fellow workers and through self-destructive behavior. A generation of unsparing and unromantic scholarship has revealed the fragmentation of working-class experience.[21]

This new scholarship has vastly enlarged the scope of "who counts" as a worker in early America, placing prostitutes, laundresses, chimneysweeps, market women, plantation healers, canal men, and all-around scoundrels alongside heroic hammer-wielding mechanics in the narrative of American labor history.[22] Including the experiences of enslaved blacksmiths and Irish canal laborers clearly complicates labor history's preference for the citizen worker. The politics of class change when the workers in question are African American, female, or immigrant. Adding categories of difference to scholarly investigations has made it commonsensical that race, gender, and class were mutually constitutive in the lives of any given cohort of workers. The next—and necessary—step is to consider capitalism's systemic dependence on these multiple, simultaneous, and overlapping forms of inequality. To do so requires situating enslaved mariners, widowed seamstresses, Irish domestic servants, and American-born street scrapers in the same capitalist political economy and tracing them through shared neighborhoods, common job sites, and a broader labor market that saw them all as functionally interchangeable.[23]

At first glance, putting such diverse workers into the same story and keeping multiple categories of difference simultaneously in play would seem an unlikely method for narrating American working-class formation. Such skepticism is warranted by the primacy given in recent scholarship to the articulation of class identity through dress, leisure, and other forms of cultural expression. In taverns and bedrooms, along avenues, and on street corners, disfranchised people socialized, sang, loved, gossiped, primped, promenaded, and fought. In countless ways, working people expressed their distaste for middle-class propriety and the standards of self-discipline and delayed gratification emerging in the dominant culture. But there were deep fissures within this plebian counterculture: white workers used minstrelsy to degrade African Americans; native-born workers paraded with "stuffed Paddies" to antagonize Irish immigrants; and laboring men caroused in a misogynist sporting culture. Perhaps more serious was the violence that workers directed against one another, violence white workers leveled on their black peers, Protestant and Catholic immigrants from Ireland brought against one another, and men used against women. If capitalist transformation produced new class solidarities, the countervailing forces of patriarchy, nativism, sectarianism, and white supremacy pulled workers apart. There is little evidence that common laborers in a city like Baltimore shared a consciousness of themselves as a social group with a distinctive identity and politics.[24]

As the search for workers' *resistance* and *agency* has turned scholarly attention toward culture, labor has fallen out of much labor history, obscuring the degree to which daily life was organized around work and the processes of getting it, keeping it, and subsisting from it. For the workers portrayed in this book, class experience was waiting every February for the harbor to thaw so that low-end jobs might resume. Class consciousness was knowing the proper pose of deference to get hired. Class struggle was trying to meet the rent and scavenging for firewood to stay warm during winter.

These perils of being poor were common to German immigrants who performed domestic service, enslaved construction workers who hired themselves out for wages, young white women who sewed clothing while caring for small children, and the petitioning street scrapers who were failing as breadwinners for their families. Although positioned in different ways by race, sex, nativity, or legal status, all these workers experienced the exigencies of the labor market, navigated underground economies, and developed inventive survival strategies that were usually more alike than different.

By considering together the full range of workers whose labor was for sale in the early republic city, this book does not find a shared consciousness, identity, or politics percolating from working people themselves, but sees class as a material condition resulting from the ability of those purchasing labor to economically and physically coerce those performing it—and to do so under the social fiction of a self-regulating market that purportedly doled out its rewards to the deserving in accordance with the laws of nature. To make such an argument is not to say that class trumped race (white supremacy) and gender (patriarchy) as the primary determinant of who worked where and owned what. These analytical categories of historical experience were not in competition, and historians need not offer one primacy over another. Rather, historians must look for the larger system constituted at the intersection of these categories and seek the overlapping "relations of ruling" that organized the lives and labors of workers of divergent subjectivities and identities.[25]

To highlight how the political economy of early republic capitalism rendered workers relatively powerless is not to suggest that laboring people were historical ciphers or without agency. Nor should the absence of a common oppositional culture be understood to mean that working people had no quarrel with the acquisitive and individualistic ethos of capitalism. But ultimately, it was not a shared ideology or a "moral economy" tradition that bound together working people. Instead, an American working class came into being through its common commodification and the ensuing circumstances of material insecurity that diligence, frugality, or industriousness could alleviate only in the most exceptional of cases. Few writers have been keener on this point than John Stuart Mill, responding to his own commonplace observation that "the really exhausting and the really repulsive labours, instead of being better paid than others, are almost invariably paid the worst of all." Of the many possible explanations, one encapsulated all others: such work was "performed by those who have no choice." The constraints and limits placed upon *choice*—that most cherished and defining characteristic of the American experience—frame the history of capitalism and its consequences for working people.[26]

The reasons to tell this story through Baltimore are many. Today, millions of Americans unknowingly conjure early republic Baltimore every time they attend a sporting event and sing the national anthem. "O say can you see" frames a Baltimore vista: Fort McHenry on September 14, 1814, the morning after the British bombardment. The flag that was still there had been sewn by a widowed Baltimore seamstress and watched over ramparts built by the city's enslaved, immigrant, and free black day laborers. Yet the War of 1812 offers just one example of Baltimore's dynamic location in the political landscape of the new nation, and only one of many moments to situate American freedom in the contingent social relations of capitalism.

The era's national newspaper of record, *Niles' Weekly Register*, was published in Baltimore, as was Benjamin Lundy's influential *Genius of Universal Emancipation*, where a young William Lloyd Garrison cut his journalistic teeth and glimpsed the truth of racial equality from his interactions with Baltimore's people of color. Baltimore was where Revolutionary War hero "Lighthorse" Harry Lee met his demise in an 1812 riot. William Ellery Channing delivered his "Unitarian Manifesto" from a Baltimore pulpit in 1819, the same year that a Baltimore bank entered the annals of American jurisprudence in the Supreme Court's *McCulloch vs. Maryland* decision. A foundational text in American economic thought, Daniel Raymond's *Elements of Political Economy* (1822), emerged from its author's longtime residence in Baltimore. Baltimore put the B in the B&O, the first railroad company in the United States. In the 1830s, William Wirt, Andrew Jackson, and Henry Clay each received the presidential nomination of his respective party in Baltimore. So captivated and disturbed by what he saw in Baltimore, Frenchman Gustave de Beaumont situated his novel *Marie* there. Not long after Beaumont's visit, the first copies of Thomas Gray's *Confessions of Nat Turner* rolled off a local press, a reminder that Baltimore was a commercial capital of the American slaveholding regime. Prominent men of politics and business made their homes in Baltimore, and so too did perhaps the most famous laborer in all of American history: Frederick Douglass.[27]

Readers of Douglass's *Narrative* will recall his wonder upon seeing Baltimore for the first time as a young boy, his account of learning to read by bribing hungry white boys with bread, and his indignation upon handing his wages over to Hugh Auld at the end of every workweek. Contending that slavery was perhaps crueler in Baltimore because freedom was so near, Douglass ruminated on the city's status at the boundary between North and South. At the time of Douglass's birth, Baltimore had the largest African American population in the United States: nearly 15,000 people of color lived in America's "Black Capital"—more than in New Orleans, Charleston, Philadelphia, or New York.[28] Baltimore's black population in 1820 was primarily free, but two of every five people of color in the city remained enslaved. The number of slaves in Baltimore might have been higher if it had included the many men, women, and children only recently sold to the cotton frontier of the Deep South. In this light, Baltimore was perched as the southernmost city in the North and the northernmost city in the South. This position on what Barbara J. Fields has called "the middle ground" makes Baltimore an ideal venue for reexamining the broader history of American race and region.[29]

Compared to the large commercial cities in the North, Baltimore had a far more diverse racial composition. African Americans accounted for roughly 10 percent of the populations of Boston, New York, and Philadelphia in the first decades of the 1800s, while the black population in Baltimore stood above 20 percent. As these cities underwent rapid development, welcomed thousands of European immigrants, and incubated a new middle-class culture, they also witnessed "community formation" among free people of color. But whereas free black churches, benevolent associations, parades, and schools provoked violence in places like Providence and New Haven (not to mention Philadelphia and New York City), the situation in Baltimore was different. Although individual people of color were subject to violence at any time, and although there were black victims in some of Baltimore's notorious riots, the city did not see the kind of collective violence to destroy black housing and institutions that took place in northern cities. Euro-American workers in Baltimore were unsuccessful in excluding people of color from neighborhoods and public spaces, while Baltimore printers turned out far fewer racist broadsides and satires than did their northern peers. Baltimore was no racial utopia, but black people were too numerous there for their impoverished white neighbors to render them invisible and too crucial to the labor market for employers to see them sacrificed on the altar of "whiteness." If historians have increasingly tied race formation (especially "whiteness") to the rapid economic development of the early republic period, then Baltimore reveals the contingency of that process, while further undermining the common belief in the South's monopoly on American racism.[30]

Of course, Baltimore was hardly a typical Southern city. Early republic Charleston, Richmond, and Norfolk each had a majority (or near majority) of black residents, most of whom were enslaved. Yet these cities were quite small. In 1810, Baltimore was twice the size of Charleston, four times as large as Norfolk, and already more populous than the Confederate capital Richmond in 1861. In the slave states, only New Orleans offered a comparable demographic diversity and complexity. Significant urban centers such as Louisville, St. Louis, and Mobile did appear in the South after 1830, but Baltimore already had forty years of experience with rapid development and a diverse population that included European immigrants, enslaved African Americans, and free people of color. From the perspective of Southern history, Baltimore complements efforts to see the region as a collection of disparate places, rather than as a monolithic society. With its wage-earning slaves and numerous other permutations on bound labor, Baltimore reveals the varieties of slavery operational in the South. At the same time, Baltimore challenges models of Southern race formation that ground white supremacy in the ability to relegate the worst tasks to enslaved African Americans. In Baltimore, where the majority of working people were of Euro-American ancestry, white skin offered no immunity from drudgery. Even in a city with slavery, low-end jobs were not easily coded as black or white. Once again, Baltimore was no racial utopia, but the particular uncoupling there of labor and the color line adds complexity to the history of race in the South.[31]

Placed in comparison with Northern and Southern cities, Baltimore could appear to be neither here nor there. Placed in the context of the urban history of industrializing Europe and the port cities of the Atlantic Basin, Baltimore could be anywhere. There was little in the struggle of Baltimore's working people to stay afloat that would have been unrecognizable to working people in London, Paris, or Mexico City. There is no "American exceptionalism" when the topic is poor people scavenging rags to sell to papermakers, forming households that extended beyond immediate kin, gaming the poor-relief system, or hoping that a lucky lottery number would change their fortunes. The relationship of seasonal economies to casual employment to hand-to-mouth existences functioned in remarkably similar ways in disparate locations, even as the depth of poverty and avenues for escaping it surely differed from place to place. Readers familiar with the "economies of makeshift" that organized poor households in eighteenth-century France or the "casual fringe" that populated nineteenth-century London will see resonances in early republic Baltimore. So too will readers familiar with social welfare practices in the Western world from 1500 onward. Questions of community responsibility for the poor and the necessity of distinguishing between the deserving and the undeserving connect Baltimore to policy and public discourse in sixteenth-century Nuremberg, seventeenth-century Lisbon, eighteenth-century Antwerp, and nineteenth-century Mexico City. Dislocations followed capitalist economies (and their new notions of industriousness and efficiency) wherever they appeared, and the efforts of working people to cope with those dislocations constitute a universal theme in modern history.[32]

To that extent, this story does not belong exclusively to the past. The gathering of African American men on a Baltimore dock for an 1830s shape-up necessarily evokes today's Central American migrants waiting for hire in the parking lots of home improvement superstores across the county. The inability of a free person of color to produce a pass for a constable in pursuit of a runaway slave could result in the same family separations that today follow random traffic stops of vehicles containing undocumented workers. A campaign to raise the piece rates of Baltimore seamstresses in 1831 likely witnessed the first American use of the slogan "living wage"; that concept now governs pay scales in a growing number of cities around the country. In many ways, the postindustrial economy of the United States looks surprisingly like the preindustrial economy of early republic Baltimore: the energy is in moving goods rather than making them; the service sector shows the fastest rate of growth and gives employment to workers whose sex, race, and legal status make them vulnerable to exploitation; the state is hostile to the efforts of labor to organize, while the labor movement faces the challenge of mobilizing a diverse workforce that comprises the politically disfranchised; working people demonstrate unimaginable resourcefulness in making ends meet, despite a pervasive public discourse that equates poverty with laziness.

A book about early republic Baltimore does not offer a remedy to the ills of globalization, but offers the possibility of using the past to ask new questions about the present, and vice versa. Critic and artist Allan Sekula has suggested that capitalism's appearance as natural, uncontestable, and inevitable depends on severing the history of capitalism from the history of labor. As he considers the wealth that moves through international ports in the age of the container ship, Sekula asks, "How do they do it without stories being told by those who do the work?" In searching for those stories, this book does not claim to speak for those silenced in the past but does heed Sekula's call for a history of capitalism predicated on the polyphony of multiple workers' voices and experiences.[33]

CHAPTER I

Coming to Work in the City

O we're hopping skipping jumping, O we're all crazy here in
    Baltimore.
Here's a road to be made, with the Pick and Spade.
Tis to reach to Ohio for the benefit of trade.
Here are mountains to be leveled, Here are vallies to be fill'd.
Here are rocks to be blown, and Bridges too to build.
And we're all digging, blowing, blasting, And we're all crazy here in
    Baltimore.

John Cole, song to honor the B&O Railroad, 1828

nthusiasm was not unusual among Baltimore's early republic boosters. The start of railroad construction in 1828 marked only the latest opportunity for proud city residents to proclaim Baltimore's glory.[1] For the previous two decades, Hezekiah Niles had sung Baltimore's praises on the pages of his *Weekly Register*, the national newspaper of record. "There is not to be found, perhaps, in the history of any country, certainly not in that of the United States, an instance of such rapidity of growth and improvement as has been manifested in the city of Baltimore," he exclaimed in 1812 from his Water Street office. Since the American Revolution, Niles continued, Baltimore moved "from absolute insignificance, to a degree of commercial importance which has brought down upon it, the envy and jealousy of all the great cities of the union." At the end of the 1810s, Niles reported that many city residents could recall when "cornfields and the native forests" stood downtown. Now "new streets, lanes, and alleys are opened, paved and built upon before one half of the people seem to know anything about them."[2]

Like the lyricist of "We're All Crazy Here in Baltimore," Niles described Baltimore's growth in the passive voice: houses were built, rail was laid, barrels were shipped. Other boosters attributed the city's development to supernatural forces: "Houses spring up almost if by magic," declared one newspaper in the 1830s.[3] Of course, new houses and roads did not magically appear, a fact that significantly complicates the story of Baltimore's amazing rise. Looking closely at how sand and clay became the bricks that lined Baltimore's new avenues reveals the disturbing social inequalities that sustained the "culture of progress" in the early republic.[4] Behind such abstractions as "improvement," "growth," and "development" was manual labor performed under difficult circumstances by those facing material deprivation or physical coercion. The toil of enslaved brick molders and immigrant street pavers did not easily lend itself to boosterism.

Creating a new commercial city required thousands of workers. "The prodigious amount of human labour that has been expended in giving to our state emporium its present aspect can be estimated only by those who remember the former appearance of its sites," observed the editor of the *Patriot* as construction began on the Baltimore & Ohio Railroad in 1828. Attributing this transformation to "the enterprise of individuals, animated by an active and intelligent spirit," such boosters did not have day laborers and domestic servants in mind. Instead, Baltimore's merchant class garnered credit for the city's boomtown growth. However, merchants did not clear stumps from prospective avenues, nor did they stand knee-deep in Jones Falls shoveling out debris. Merchants did not load and unload the ships that lined the city's wharves. Nor were merchants so numerous as to double the city's population with each decennial census.[5]

Ultimately, the story of Baltimore's rise—every city's rise—is one of menial labor. The "we" of the song proclaiming "we're all digging, blowing, blasting" to build the B&O Railroad should not obscure the division of labor between someone like Philip E. Thomas, the railroad's president, and someone like John Gladman, a worker blown up while using gunpowder to demolish rocks in the railroad's path.[6]

As Baltimore grew to be the nation's third most populous city in the early republic, fortune greeted those who could best channel other people's labor into the creation and transportation of commodities across the globe. Indeed, as Adam Smith had argued in *Wealth of Nations*, a man "must be rich or poor according to the quantity of that labour which he can command, or which he can afford to purchase."[7] But for those whose labor was itself a commodity, Baltimore's rapid expansion brought the certainty of hard work and the likelihood that someone else would reap the benefits.

Building a City

Baltimore came into being as an entrepôt, a node in a broader exchange system that linked the American hinterland to consumers and producers not only along the eastern seaboard, but also in the Caribbean, South America, the Mediterranean, West Africa, Europe, and the Pacific. Initially, Baltimore was less a place where things were made than a conduit through which things moved. Beginning in the eighteenth century, as Maryland tobacco and Pennsylvania flour sailed out of Chesapeake Bay, other boats arrived with hides from Surinam, sugar from St. Kitts, linens from England, indentured servants from Germany, and enslaved men, women, and children from Africa. Bay crafts, packet ships, rafts, carts, and eventually railcars placed Baltimore at the hub of the Chesapeake economy.

Such wide-ranging commerce generated a blur of activity. The most obvious work went into building a physical infrastructure of wharves, streets, canals, and railroads to facilitate the movement of goods. Vast amounts of labor then went into loading and unloading cargo, as well as manning the ships that left Baltimore for Atlantic and Pacific ports. Equally demanding was the service work that sustained a burgeoning population by cooking its food, washing its clothing, and sheltering its recent arrivals. An increasingly substantial manufacturing economy produced shirts, ships, saddles, and bricks in large yards, small workshops, and isolated garrets. Jobs in one segment of the economy created new jobs in others. For example, growing traffic in the harbor required more stevedores and carters to unload ships and necessitated more wharfage and additional dredging—which is to say, jobs in the construction sector. When migrants came to Baltimore to find jobs along the waterfront or berths in outgoing ships, they spurred housing construction and demanded the services of boardinghouse keepers, hucksters, and prostitutes.[8]

The commodity that drove Baltimore's commercial ascent was flour, with the city serving as a vent for the abundant surplus of the Maryland and Pennsylvania backcountry.[9] Early eighteenth-century Baltimoretown had been a tobacco inspection port, but the settlement on the Patapsco River struggled from the time of its founding in 1729. Its first thirty years were marked primarily by "battle[s] with the frogs and mosquitoes whose proper territory it had invaded." Although the population reached 6,000 by the American Revolution, Baltimore's strategic, economic, and political irrelevance saved it from British occupation or blockade.[10]

Around the time of the Revolution, Maryland planters began to replace their tobacco crops with grains, especially wheat. The European demand for tobacco had proved fickle, whereas its appetite for bread remained voracious. As Thomas

Paine quipped in *Common Sense*, American commercial farmers would "always have a market while eating is the custom of Europe." By replacing tobacco with cereals, Maryland farmers placed less stress on the soil, cut their labor costs, and kept the Chesapeake free of the Scottish and English factors whose credit had once threatened the region's independence. Baltimore merchants now had a crop easily exported to the sugar-producing islands in the West Indies. With Britain and France regularly at war with one another, Baltimore gained access to their colonies and grew wealthy provisioning Caribbean plantation societies.[11]

Situated far more inland than other Atlantic ports, near the mouth of the Susquehanna River, and protected by the Chesapeake Bay, Baltimore was prepared to sate the Atlantic market's appetite for American produce. At the convergence of three grain-producing regions, Baltimore owed its success, according to one booster, "to the spacious country surrounding it, rich by nature, and requiring but the exertion of its cultivators." Planters on Maryland's Eastern Shore floated their harvests to Baltimore's merchant millers. Growers in Maryland's western Frederick County took advantage of Baltimore's inland location to sell off their grain there. Similarly, Pennsylvania farmers sent their produce down the Susquehanna to Port Deposit or Havre de Grace, reducing overland transportation costs tremendously compared with carting grain to Philadelphia. Along the roads and waterways leading into Baltimore, upwards of fifty mills turned grain into flour. These were not neighborhood gristmills, but were capitalized commercial enterprises, owned by prominent Baltimore families like the Tysons, Olivers, and Ellicotts, and oriented toward the export market.[12]

Baltimore workers played no small role in the flourishing flour economy. The least-skilled urban workers left the city to perform farm labor at harvest time, while watermen and carters also found seasonal employment conveying grain from the countryside to the mills on Baltimore's periphery. The millers who transformed grain into flour employed common laborers to assist in the process and to move the finished product to waterfront warehouses. Next, stevedores and day laborers loaded the barrels onto the fast schooners destined for the British West Indies, Spanish South America, and Europe. Each flour barrel weighed nearly 200 pounds, and most ships could convey a load of 600 to 700 barrels at a time. Dockworkers loaded other weighty cargos: hogsheads of Maryland tobacco, casks of whiskey, barrels of salt fish, and kegs of butter. A cadre of municipal officials graded these export commodities at a staggering rate, especially as the number of barrels of flour grew from 247,046 in 1798 to 537,988 barrels in 1812. Not surprisingly, cutting wooden staves became an increasingly common task for working men.[13]

Once the cargo had been loaded, Baltimore sailors manned vessels around the

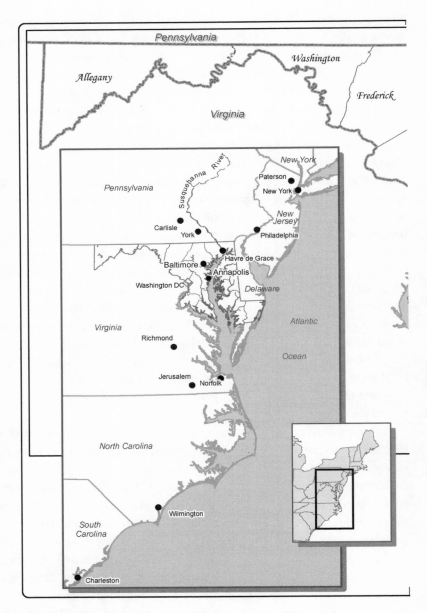

Maryland and the eastern seaboard of the United States. Created by L. Carlson,
Brown University.

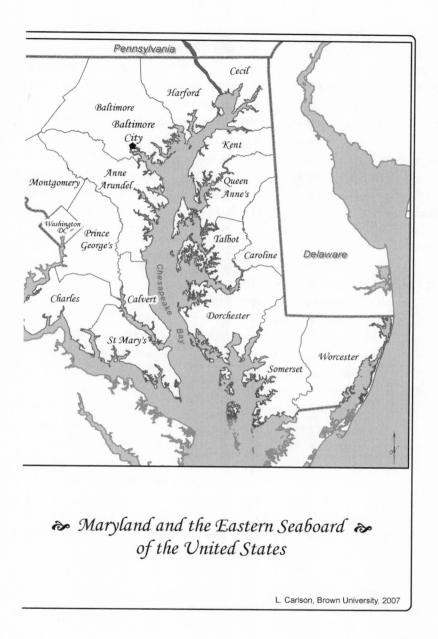

❧ Maryland and the Eastern Seaboard ❧
of the United States

Chesapeake, up and down the seaboard, and across the oceans. While the majority of Baltimore watermen plied coastal waters, over one thousand sailors left the city annually on ships bound for foreign ports. By 1795, Baltimore's shipping accounted for 95 percent of Maryland's overseas trade. In addition to carrying American produce abroad, Baltimore ships specialized in the reexport or carrying trade, brokering commodities like sugar and coffee from Caribbean and South American colonies to various European nations or other parts of the United States. Known as a particularly vibrant port for outfitting privateering ventures so long as England, France, and Spain vied for control of the Atlantic, Baltimore buzzed with the coming and going of sailors. Despite their geographical mobility, many Baltimore sailors maintained close ties with their home port, often supporting families on shore with their earnings at sea and taking jobs on land when maritime traffic ebbed.[14]

The vitality of the port reverberated into other segments of the urban economy and exerted a demand for working men and women. The city's infrastructure demanded relentless physical labor. Funded by the state and municipal governments, public works included building wharves, erecting bridges over Jones Falls (the river bifurcating Baltimore), laying roads leading out of the city, landfilling marshy lowlands, and extending avenues into the "precincts" to keep up with rapid housing construction. A ground-rent system promoted speculative homebuilding and the development of the city's famous row houses. As settlement spread outward from the waterfront, the city commissioners taxed the residents of individual streets to fund grading and paving, as well as the installation of curbstones and pumps. They then contracted specific projects to mechanics, who in turn hired their own day laborers. Similarly, the house carpenters needed laborers to dig foundations, cart supplies, and perform the least desirable, most backbreaking labor. Because creators of fire ordinances frowned on wood-frame houses, Baltimore's brickyards kept laborers busy in the arduous tasks of digging clay, carting pallets of formed bricks from the molding table to the drying area, and cutting the timber to stoke the fire of the kiln. Then, as now, the rate of new housing construction comprised an important metric of a city's economic health. Hidden within the celebrated tallies of 587 new homes in 1833, 583 in 1834, and 607 in 1835 was an astounding quantum of human labor.[15]

Keeping the port open required hundreds of manual laborers to fight the sediment that clogged Baltimore's already shallow basin, or Inner Harbor. Only eight or nine feet deep, the basin could not handle ships of significant draft, which instead had to dock in the deeper waters of Fells Point. Silting also created a perilous sandbar leading out of the harbor to the Patapsco River and into the Chesapeake

Bay. Beginning in 1790, the City funded a "mudmachine" to deepen the basin and cut a channel through the bar. This barge combined manpower and horse-power to dredge the river bottom. Oftentimes forced to stand in the shallow water, workers guided the scoop and emptied the foul-smelling muck into waiting scows, which were then unloaded to landfill the noxious cove between Fells Point and the basin. For at least nine months a year, fifty to sixty men contributed to this operation for wages of $1 a day. All told, the city spent upwards of $10,000 a year on improving the harbor, and had dedicated $600,000 to the task by 1836. Eas-ily the largest capital expense of the city government, harbor improvement was a central concern for municipal leaders. As mayor Edward Johnson explained in 1813, "the interest and future prosperity of the City of Baltimore" demanded such expenditures. A fact rarely mentioned in histories of capitalist enterprise, the abil-ity of private individuals to pursue self-interest depended on sustained public in-vestment in the infrastructure of commercial exchange.[16]

As the city grew in size, so too did the number of jobs in the service sector of the economy. With very modest capital, Baltimore residents generated indepen-dent incomes by providing new arrivals with food, recreation, and shelter. Some poor women hawked candles, cheeses, and vegetables through Baltimore's neigh-borhoods, while other women sold liquor from their basement apartments. The number of ordinaries and boardinghouses swelled, particularly in Fells Point. The transient population that passed through the neighborhood also supported an entire industry of free African American laundresses. While petty marketing and other forms of self-employment insulated many poor women and some men from working for wages, the commodification of household labor brought count-less others into the ranks of wage earners. Taverns and inns hired marginal work-ers as hostlers, cooks, and maids. Slaves and indentured servants filled many of these roles, but the demand for domestic help within public accommodations and wealthy households outpaced the supply of unfree workers. Free black, immigrant, and native-born women alike found regular employment in domestic service, es-pecially as household "help" became an important marker of status for ascendant middle-class families. With few opportunities in other segments of the economy, many adult women toiled for prosperous Baltimore families.

Common laborers also found work in Baltimore's manufacturing sector, even as skilled artisans and the traditional organization of the craft workshop governed urban production. While youthful apprentices performed much of the grunt work in the shops of saddlers, tinsmiths, and printers, adult "unskilled" workers pro-vided labor to more complex and capitalized enterprises like shipyards, forges, and breweries. In 1810, census takers located twenty-two tanneries, four sugar refineries, seven candle manufactories, and six brass foundries in the city but failed to count the number of nonartisanal workers (including slaves) who chopped firewood, cleaned hides, or carried buckets in those establishments. Much of the manufacturing in the city was decentralized, taking place "in the back shops, or on the small alleys," according to Hezekiah Niles. In shoemaking and the clothing trade particularly, master mechanics subdivided artisan handicrafts into components and then farmed out the simplified tasks to girls, women, free African Americans, and European immigrant men. By "sweating" production, relying on workers outside the craft tradition, and turning their eyes toward distant markets, artisan masters became capitalist manufacturers. Working from their own homes, adult women stitched "slop," a derisive term for cheap, ready-to-wear shirts and pants. Apprentices in the shoemaking trade lost access to the "art and mystery" of their craft and instead found themselves exploited for their labor.[17]

Early republic Baltimore did see the introduction of mechanized production, especially as the city's leading merchants pooled their capital to build textile mills along waterways leading into town. "Baltimore possesses greater facilities in water power and sites for manufactories of all kinds than any other city in the Union," declared one confident booster. Wartime disruptions to the Atlantic trade between 1807 and 1815 made "domestic production" a leading cause for the wealthy and civic minded, who petitioned Congress for protective tariffs and created such voluntary associations as the Athenian Society of Baltimore and the Maryland Œconomical Association. The Union Manufacturing Company sought republican investors for their "patriotic undertaking," which was among the largest textile enterprises in the nation before 1815.[18]

By 1816, Maryland's legislature had granted ten Baltimore manufacturing corporations the right to sell shares worth $3.6 million. The largest of these companies produced cotton yarn and cloth in the surrounding environs of Baltimore County. Families moved between the city and rural mills as employment opportunities opened and closed. By 1820, both the Union Manufacturing Company and the Powhatan Mills put 100 girls between six and thirteen years old to work tending over 4,000 spindles. Mechanized production came within the city limits after the 1820s, once steam power freed manufacturers from their reliance on waterpower. Equally important, as the city limits expanded, mills on the outskirts of town became components of the urban economy. The City Steam Sail Duck Factory, for example, employed 130 laborers in the Old Town neighborhood in 1832.[19]

Like the girls laboring in mills outside the city, Baltimore workers readily looked into the surrounding hinterland for seasonal and short-term labor. Wages for agricultural work were substantially lower than those paid for unskilled labor in the city, but farm jobs abounded at harvest time (which coincided with the yellow fever outbreaks that paralyzed the urban economy almost every August or September). Manual laborers also found employment quarrying granite, marble, and limestone, or chopping timber on woodlots in Baltimore County. This timber heated urban homes in wintertime and fed the furnaces of forges, nail manufactories, and rolling mills. Rural manufacturing also provided income to the urban women who collected rags on city streets and sold them to paper mills for pulp. Finally, internal improvement projects recruited laborers from the city. The Chesapeake & Ohio Canal, the Baltimore & Susquehanna Railroad, and the Baltimore & Ohio Railroad promised to ensure the city's commercial vitality in the 1820s. The recent immigrants who toiled on these public works usually arrived through Baltimore and often ended up back in the city once their tasks were finished.[20]

A vast outpouring of entrepreneurial energy and physical labor put Baltimore on the map in the decades following the American Revolution. "What I have seen more than equals my expectations," wrote a visitor to friends back in Hallowell, Maine, in 1813. Other than Philadelphia, Baltimore was "the most beautiful city in the U. States, and the policy of its citizens is so liberal and every thing projected upon so noble a scale, that I shall not be astonished, if in a few years it should exceed even that." Local boosters spoke in grander, if disquieting, terms, especially as railroad and canal construction intensified in the 1820s. "She can hold in servitude every port between New York and New Orleans, and even over these, she possesses power to cripple their energies," announced one celebrant of Baltimore's future prospects. He was not joking that Baltimore "possesses abundant means of self-aggrandizement."[21]

Published maps of the city attest to the capacity of urban boosters to imagine a far grander city than had yet been built. More accurately called "plans" than "maps," these projections depicted undeveloped farmland as orderly lots and broad avenues. A beautifully printed 1801 map showed Fells Point as nearly 150 square blocks, but the developed portion of the neighborhood was only one-third that size. Such representations belied the density and crowding of a city where more than 26,000 inhabitants occupied less than one square mile of urban space. The crammed blocks ringing the waterfront contain the story of Baltimore's rise, for they supplied the labor to transform the expansive vision of the maps into reality.[22]

Who Built Baltimore?

Although their toil is still visible today in Baltimore's built environment, common laborers left only faint traces in the typical sources of early American social history: city directories, tax lists, and census rolls. Such workers rarely owned enough property to meet the city's assessment minimum. For example, seven of ten white households were exempted from taxes in 1813 because they lacked the necessary $40 in property. Census takers recorded the names of household heads, but not those of adult men and women living under someone else's roof. The compilers of directories focused on those with professional or craft training, while ignoring men and women without a stable occupation or an established residence. As the docks were bustling in Fells Point, the 1796 directory listed only fifteen laborers, six hucksters, five washerwomen, and three draymen in the neighborhood. Even white men—the most "privileged" segment of the urban population—were woefully undercounted in directories; Baltimore's 1810 directory listed fewer than half the white men of working age in the city. All told, directories, census lists, and tax rolls fail to reflect the occupational or class structure of the early republic city, and by one scholarly estimate exclude "a large majority" of the urban laboring population.[23]

The transience of working people also makes it difficult to create a reliable portrait of the city's workers. Movement in and out of the city was constant. Niles estimated that one-fifth of the city's 1816 population had arrived within the previous twelve months. It is impossible to know how many of those same people would have remained in the city four years later at the time of the federal census. By Niles's count, perhaps only one in twenty of the city's adult residents had been born there. Another commentator noted that one never saw grandfathers with adult grandchildren in Baltimore, because not enough time had passed for several generations of a family to be present in the city. Just as good economic times attracted newcomers to the city at a rapid clip, declining opportunities accelerated the turnover of population. Due to the panic that had begun a year earlier, the 1820 census found perhaps 10,000 fewer people living and working in Baltimore than had been there only four years earlier. Baltimore's enslaved population also experienced massive turnover from decade to decade. As manumissions and sales of Maryland slaves to the cotton frontier reduced the city's enslaved population, natural reproduction and imports from the countryside kept the total number of Baltimore slaves growing from 1790 until just before 1820 and then constant for at least another decade. Coming and going, far more people labored in Baltimore over the course of a decade than the tally in the decennial census conveys to the modern observer.[24]

Several strategies present themselves for estimating the laboring population of a city like Baltimore. Perhaps the best starting point is to tally the number of city residents of "working age" from sixteen to forty-four years old, recognizing

Baltimore's population, 1790–1840

Year	Total	White	(% total)	Free black	(% total)	Enslaved	(% total)
1790	13,503	11,925	(88)	323	(2)	1,255	(9)
1800	26,514	20,900	(79)	2,771	(10)	2,843	(11)
1810	46,555	36,212	(78)	5,671	(12)	4,672	(10)
1820	62,738	48,055	(77)	10,326	(16)	4,357	(7)
1830	80,620	61,710	(77)	14,790	(18)	4,120	(5)
1840	102,313	81,147	(79)	17,967	(18)	3,199	(3)

Sources: Richard C. Wade, *Slavery in the Cities: The South, 1820–1860* (New York: Oxford University Press, 1964), 325; David Gilchrist, ed., *The Growth of the Seaport Cities, 1790–1825*, proceedings of a conference sponsored by the Eleutherian Mills–Hagley Foundation, March 17–19, 1966 (Charlottesville: University Press of Virginia, 1967), 34–36.

Note: Percentages do not total 100 due to rounding of figures.

that such an arbitrary category merely reflects the age brackets used in the federal census. Applying labor force participation rates for men and women (as estimated by social scientists), one is left with a figure from which can be subtracted the artisans, lawyers, shopkeepers, and merchants counted in the city directories. The resulting figure might conceivably reveal the number of common laborers in the city. Even this crude methodology is telling: the 1800 census found approximately 9,000 working Baltimore residents, but the 1802 city directory listed only 4,100 householders (and if the elderly are removed, perhaps only 3,000 of working age). The directory left perhaps 6,000 adults unaccounted for, the majority of working people in Baltimore. The problems in this methodology are apparent, but greater precision would most likely increase the number of city residents laboring at the margins. There is no reason to believe, for example, that most poor men and women stopped working at forty-five. Similarly, apprentices, enslaved children, and youngsters in poor families began contributing productive labor to their households before turning sixteen. In 1800, when the city's population stood at 26,000, potentially one-third of Baltimoreans worked cleaning houses, carting barrels, making bricks, or performing other "unskilled" tasks.[25]

The paths of migration that brought such workers to Baltimore are easier to determine. Consider the nearly six hundred African Americans who applied to the Baltimore courts for legal certificates to prove their freedom between 1800 and 1820. Most applicants came from rural Maryland, but fourteen had been raised in Virginia, three in North Carolina, and at least fifteen hailed from the West Indies. Several were freeborn Yankees: Austin Ruby from Boston, William Johnson from Connecticut, and Thomas Robinson, who had been born in Newport, Rhode Island, before the American Revolution. Negro Acoeba had been brought to Baltimore as a slave from Surinam before being freed in 1808 when he was thirty-five years old. Maria Louiza, Rosette Morel, and John Lewis had all been born as slaves in Saint Domingue and brought to Baltimore by owners fleeing the momentous revolution of the early 1790s; all three were old enough to have distinct memories of the violent overthrow of slavery in their Caribbean homeland.[26]

The admission records of the Baltimore almshouse bear similar testament to the diverse origins of city residents. Between 1823 and 1826, the pauper rolls featured six Canadians, forty-five New Englanders, fifty-seven Virginians, and four North Carolina natives. Homelands across the Atlantic included Africa, Prussia, Bohemia, Italy, Denmark, Holland, France, Poland, Sweden, Norway, Spain, Portugal, Ireland, England, and Scotland. Although most almshouse inmates came from Maryland, some from farther away had followed incredible paths to Baltimore. Standing before the almshouse clerk, forty-year-old Martin Guigar recounted his childhood in Switzerland, his stint in the British army, his desertion in America during the War of 1812, his three years in the Maryland Penitentiary for an 1816 robbery, his sojourn to Pennsylvania, his expulsion from the Philadelphia almshouse, and his return to Baltimore in 1825. Matthew Bates, a fifteen-year-old orphan, traced his passage from New York to Baltimore on "a raft of lumber." The Baptist itinerant Alexander Christian began his life in Charleston, South Carolina.[27]

These individual stories speak to broader trajectories in Baltimore's demographic growth. As Baltimore's population grew from 13,000 in 1790 to 102,000 fifty years later, three noteworthy trends explain the expansion of the city's laboring population: the massive influx of new white residents from throughout the United States and abroad; the arrival of manumitted and self-liberated slaves and freeborn people of color from throughout the Chesapeake; and the sustained importation of enslaved workers by urban slaveholders. These latter two developments gave Baltimore more people of color than any other United States city in 1820. But even as the enslaved population had nearly quadrupled and the free population of color grown more than thirty times over since 1790, the arrival of so many Euro-American migrants kept Baltimore an overwhelmingly white city. Through the early republic period, Baltimore's population was nearly four-fifths Euro-American and one-fifth African American.

Baltimore owed much of its population growth to the transformation of the rural economy. In particular, the changes in mid-Atlantic agriculture that made Baltimore a major grain center also pushed countless rural whites toward the city. Indeed, one of the major demographic trends of nineteenth-century Maryland was the dramatic decline of the white population in the southern tobacco-growing counties like Calvert, Charles, St. Mary's, Montgomery, and Prince

George's. As prosperity and increasing population density drove up land prices, the sons and daughters of small farmers found their own chances for indepen-dence constrained. These young adults could join the ranks of agricultural wage labor or seek new opportunities far from home. Many turned westward and made their way to Frederick and Washington counties, as well as to Ohio and Kentucky. Others came to Baltimore. The transition was less dramatic in northern Mary-land, but even for young whites in rural Baltimore County, there were few op-portunities to prosper as an agricultural laborer, cottager, or tenant farmer. Even with wintertime slowdowns, summertime epidemics, and unpredictable eco-nomic fluctuations, Baltimore offered more jobs and higher wages than did the countryside.[28]

This advantage also held true for the European immigrants who came to early republic Baltimore.[29] As Chesapeake grain production expanded, European agri-culture sputtered; nearly constant warfare from the 1790s through 1815 caused massive economic dislocations. Factories promised new miseries to working people, while European cities such as London, Liverpool, and Bremen threatened destitution as readily as they offered jobs to their residents. In an 1813 debate with English journalist William Cobbett, Hezekiah Niles argued that the English rate of pauperism was sixty times that in the United States. American laborers ate meat "as they please," two or three times a day, Niles boasted, whereas fifty English work-ers would wrestle in the street to pick up butchers' scraps. His newspaper con-tinued to beat this chauvinistic drum through the 1820s, publishing detailed accounts of miserable English families eager to emigrate to America. One ship captain embarking for Baltimore in 1829 reputedly found in Manchester "six or seven hundred persons all ready, not merely to tear themselves from their native soil, but willing and eager to sell themselves to a temporary slavery, in order to obtain the means of escaping to what they considered a better land."[30]

Advice manuals to prospective immigrants touted the opportunities available to workers lacking skill and capital. "Labourers are a very useful class of people in America," proclaimed John Melish in a Philadelphia publication. "In the cities, a great deal of labour is necessary at the shipping, about the wharves, on the streets, and about the buildings." Best of all, Melish concluded, "In no country of the world is labour so well paid, or labourers so much respected as in the United States." Mathew Carey echoed these rosy prospects for European emigrants in 1826: "There is scarcely any limit to the number of labourers, who are now and probably will be for twenty years to come, wanted in this country."[31]

The perceived contrast between staying in Europe and coming to America impelled many emigrants to sell themselves into servitude in exchange for passage to the United States. While indentured servants peopled the seventeenth- and eighteenth-century British North American colonies, they continued to arrive in Baltimore after the Revolution, albeit in smaller numbers. Ship captains announced cargoes of "Irish servants," such as the "Number of Healthy, Indented Men and Women Servants" who arrived from Dublin on the ship *John* in 1792. Prospective buyers were promised "reasonable terms for CASH." The Irish were not the only Europeans to choose temporary servitude in the United States. Dutch and German ship captains and their Baltimore agents announced the arrival of several hundred "strong, healthy" redemptioners each year. Once in America, such servants frequently ran away, but the advertisements for their recapture highlighted their foreignness: William Sechtling might be recognized by his "broken English," while his fellow "German servant lad" Leonard Rosabower "cannot speak English" at all. Another German servant, William Markle, had "been in the country nine months," but only "speaks bad English." Twenty-year-old Daniel Healy "speaks in the Irish dialect." As late as 1819, Louis Muller underwrote the arrival of a group of "natives of Wirtemberg and Baden." Having visited Germany and "well acquainted with the manners and customs of these people," Muller promised "general satisfaction" to those "in need of good and trusty servants."[32]

In the decades following the American Revolution, most Europeans entered the United States with their freedom intact, enticed by advertisements promising "immediate employment on landing." Although most disembarked in New York, Baltimore was an important destination especially for those intent on making their way to the interior. "If a European has previously resolved to go to the western country, near the Allegheny or Ohio rivers, he will have saved much expense and travel by landing at Baltimore," advised New York's Shamrock Society in a guidebook for Irish immigrants. The Shamrock Society implored new arrivals to leave cities like Baltimore at once for the countryside, but many never made it out of town. Of the European immigrants he saw in Baltimore in 1819, English traveler John Woods described "some without money to take them up the country; and some with no inclination to go; and some without either." Opportunities to dig canals and lay railroad track abounded in the Chesapeake countryside, but a general awareness of the harrowing working and living conditions kept many recent immigrants from leaving the city.[33]

By the end of the 1820s, civic leaders in Baltimore had concluded that too many European immigrants were staying in the city, which placed an oppressive burden on municipal resources. Most alarming, English parishes and German towns appeared to be emptying their almshouses and disgorging their feeble-minded or disabled inhabitants on American shores. In summer 1830, for example, Baltimore's health officer, Samuel B. Martin, inspected the 4,600 passengers arriving to the city on foreign vessels. As he would virtually every summer for the next decade, Martin lamented the immigrants' "deplorable" condition, their lack of financial resources, and "their infirmities, mental and corporeal, moral and physical." Amplifying Martin's point, Baltimore's mayor, Jesse Hunt, asserted that the United States would always welcome the "oppressed and distressed" of "every nation," but that European governments took advantage of American hospitality to dispose of their "surplus population." Such sentiments became more strident later in the 1830s, as a financial panic slowed the urban economy and public spending on the immigrant poor rose. "It is high time something should be done to turn back the tide of emigration which has so long been inundating Baltimore with hundreds of the worthless and depraved of other nations," a local newspaper declared in 1837.[34]

Even before ship captains were required by Maryland law in 1832 to file passenger lists with city authorities, informal counts showed the steady rate of European immigration to Baltimore. Eager to document Baltimore's rapid growth, Hezekiah Niles kept tallies for several weeks each summer. During the last two weeks of July 1817, 348 Europeans disembarked in Baltimore, including 44 from Liverpool, 65 from Belfast, 20 from Hamburg, and 126 from Amsterdam. During the same period the following year, Niles counted 331 immigrants from Liverpool, London, St. Andrews, Halifax, and Belfast. Between 1820 and 1826, one-tenth of European arrivals to the United States entered through Baltimore. During the early 1830s, Baltimore attracted more immigrants than Boston, Philadelphia, and New Orleans, trailing only New York City (which drew twice as many as the other four cities combined); some 55,000 arrived in Baltimore over the course of the decade.[35] Official tallies, however, missed those Europeans who arrived in Baltimore after disembarking in other ports, or perhaps after being discharged surreptitiously in isolated parts of the Chesapeake Bay by captains eager to skirt the head tax on immigrants. Records do not speak to the numbers staying in the city or heading westward, but health inspector Martin was convinced that "the more able part pass on to the interior, but the *pauper part* are left on our hands."[36]

The two largest groups of European immigrants were from Ireland and Germany. Subsidized with public funds in Baltimore, German and Hibernian benevolent organizations cared for newly arrived countrymen and women. These voluntary associations comprised prosperous businessmen who had arrived in the city several decades earlier and whose sympathy for new immigrants was sometimes tenuous. The Presbyterian members of the Baltimore Hibernian Society, for example, fretted for the "laborious rustic" (most likely a Catholic) who came to America without education, wealth, or connections: "Loitering about the seaport towns, for want of a better destiny in the country, he procures employment perhaps during the summer, but remains idle through the winter, wasting his hard earnings, sacrificing his time, vitiating his morals, and poisoning his health." After such a winter, the Hibernians warned, the recent immigrant "is no longer animated by health, or nerved with strength; and instead of contributing to the general fund of wealth, becomes a dronish depredator upon it." Elaborating on "the lower order of Irish," traveler John Woods commented that "Irishmen are very numerous everywhere in the States, but I am informed generally of a higher description than those in Baltimore and in the sea-ports."[37]

The Irish arrived in early republic Baltimore not as a homogeneous immigrant community, but as distinct subpopulations whose religious, political, and regional allegiances in Ireland continued to carry weight in the United States. When Baltimore Federalists and Republicans fought in the streets during the city's 1812 riots, so too did Irish Catholics and Protestants, reenacting what investigators termed "disturbances at home" between Orangemen and United Irishmen. In the following decades, Baltimore officials could scarcely understand why Irish Catholics from County Cork and County Longford might engage in violent feuds with one another, but such Old World identities mattered greatly to the immigrants whose labor would build the canals and railroads crucial to the city's prosperity.[38]

German immigrants generally arrived in Baltimore with greater resources, enabling most to avoid backbreaking manual labor. A typical ship from Germany brought a mix of young single people and families—"exactly the kind of people that we need," remarked Hezekiah Niles. For example, the Bremen ship *Gustav* arrived in Baltimore in August 1837 carrying forty families, some with as many as seven children under the age of sixteen and some with members of three generations. The ship's 229 passengers also included 57 single men and 15 single women, primarily in their twenties. Men's occupations included farmers, tailors, butchers, and shoemakers. Another German ship arriving in 1837 was reputed to bring a cargo of convicts to Baltimore, but city authorities were relieved to find instead farmers, mechanics, and artisans "packing up their goods preparatory to their departure westward."[39]

Enough Germans stayed in Baltimore, however, to have a substantial demographic impact. By one contemporary estimate, 20,000 Germans resided in Baltimore in 1839 and accounted for one-fifth of the city's total population. A group of concerned citizens called on the city to publish its ordinances in German for the 5,000 new immigrants who spoke no English. "Obliged to work hard for their daily bread, they

have neither time nor opportunity to learn" the language of their adoptive home, reported the advocates of bilingualism.[40] Yet, such diligence did not always keep German immigrants out of the almshouse, and by the mid-1830s, German-born paupers outnumbered English-born paupers among the institutionalized poor. Among
immigrants, only the Irish ended up in the almshouse with greater frequency.[41]

Many of Baltimore's new arrivals did not have to cross the Atlantic to find themselves in a new world. For the thousands of African Americans, enslaved and free,
who arrived from rural Maryland after 1790, Baltimore seemed like a foreign country. As a child on an Eastern Shore plantation, Frederick Douglass (then Frederick Bailey) listened to the boasts of his cousin Tom, who had been to Baltimore.
As Douglass recalled, "I could never point out any thing at the Great House, no
matter how beautiful or powerful, but that he had seen something at Baltimore
far exceeding [it] both in beauty and strength." Convinced that life in the city would
have to be better than that in the countryside, Douglass "had the strongest desire
to see Baltimore." Enough people of color shared that sentiment—even those like
Douglass who were sent to the city on someone else's orders—to give Baltimore
a population nearly one-quarter African American in 1820.[42]

Just as Baltimore's white population had grown with the transformation of rural agriculture, so too was the expansion of the city's free black population largely
a product of Maryland's new grain economy. As Maryland slaveholders made the
transition from tobacco to grains, they reevaluated their labor needs. Wheat farming did not require the daily tending and postharvest processing that made tobacco
such a labor-intensive crop. At the same time, Baltimore manufactures became
cheap enough to diminish the need for enslaved blacksmiths, seamstresses, and
coopers to produce goods on the plantation. The former tobacco plantations of
eastern and southern Maryland soon realized the smaller labor requirements
of grain agriculture. To be sure, Maryland planters did not abandon slavery wholesale, but their commitment to the institution wavered, especially as the transition
to the grain economy coincided with a Revolutionary-era critique of slavery as burdensome and sinful. Humanitarianism inspired a wave of manumissions, but
other owners were simply happy to free themselves of the obligations of slaveholding in the face of a new crop regime.[43]

Freed people from throughout the state migrated to Baltimore because they
were unlikely to find livelihoods in the countryside. Former slaves lacked the capital to buy their own farms, and remaining in rural areas prolonged the indignities of slavery, such as annual labor contracts to white employers and encounters
with roving patrollers. In contrast, nearby Baltimore promised better wages, personal autonomy, and the institutional resources of a growing free African Amer-

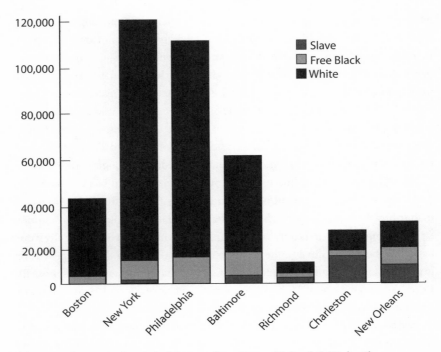

Urban populations in the United States, 1820. *Source:* Richard C. Wade, *Slavery in the Cities: The South, 1820–1860* (New York: Oxford University Press, 1964), 325; David Gilchrist, ed., *The Growth of the Seaport Cities, 1790–1825*, proceedings of a conference sponsored by the Eleutherian Mills–Hagley Foundation, March 17–19, 1966 (Charlottesville: University Press of Virginia, 1967), 34–36; Gary B. Nash, *Forging Freedom: The Formation of Philadelphia's Black Community, 1720–1840* (Cambridge, Mass.: Harvard University Press, 1988), 137, 143. Figures for Philadelphia include Moyamensing, Southwark, Spring Garden, Kensington, and Northern Liberties.

ican community, all while preserving proximity to family members still in the countryside. It helped that Maryland did not force manumitted slaves to depart the state altogether, as was the law in neighboring Virginia starting in 1806. Coming largely from the nearest counties (Baltimore, Harford, Anne Arundel, and Calvert), the city's free black population exploded between 1790 and 1840. Growing ninefold in the 1790s, the free black population doubled and redoubled in the next two decades, reaching 10,326 in 1820 and approaching 18,000 by 1840. A key milestone was passed in the first decade of the 1800s, when free people of color first outnumbered enslaved African Americans in the city, making Baltimore the only place in Maryland where most black people were free. Each of the northern Maryland counties adjacent to Baltimore City, including the surrounding Baltimore

County, had at least twice as many slaves as free people of color. In contrast, by 1820, the city was home to more than twice as many free people of color as slaves.[44]

A segment of Baltimore's black population fell somewhere between slavery and legal freedom: the rural slaves who liberated themselves and chose Baltimore as a destination where they might evade recapture, melt into the predominantly free black population, and support themselves through wage labor. Running away had long been a key strategy of slave resistance, but Maryland tobacco planters' interest in selling slaves to the lower South—a product of the new labor demands of the cotton economy—gave enslaved men and women particular incentive to flee. Beginning in the 1790s, Maryland stood second only to Virginia as a supplier to the domestic slave trade. The "second Middle Passage" ultimately carried nearly 1 million slaves from the eastern seaboard and upper South to the new territories of the Deep South. Dreading family separations, the arduous journey to market, and the reported rigors of the cotton plantation, Maryland slaves absconded to the city with enough frequency for "gone to Baltimore" to appear as a common refrain in runaway advertisements.[45]

Baltimore was an appealing destination not merely for its proximity to the free state of Pennsylvania, forty miles to the north, but also because fugitives could essentially disappear in the city. With cramped waterfront alleys, a bustling port, and a population too large to patrol, Baltimore allowed runaway slaves to assimilate into the larger free black population. "Skulking about town" or "lurking about the city" (as masters would have phrased it) was not freedom, but it did allow runaways to avoid being sold thousands of miles from family members. In fact, being reunited with a parent or sibling frequently motivated slaves escaping to Baltimore. "A free brother in Baltimore" suggested the whereabouts of Watt, who departed his Charles County plantation in 1816. Nineteen-year-old Betty fled her Montgomery County plantation for Baltimore "as she has a mother in that town by the name of Charity." When fourteen-year-old Ben Johnson escaped in 1834, Anne Arundel County slaveowner Thomas Norwood "supposed he is in Baltimore, having a free brother . . . and other relations living in Old Town."[46]

Rural slaveholders rightly imagined that Baltimore's free black population took satisfaction in assisting and sheltering runaways. "I expect he will go to Baltimore, as he has many acquaintances there," said Thomas W. Griffith of his enslaved blacksmith Robin in 1809. Delivering agricultural produce to the city gave many rural slaves a familiarity with Baltimore that proved useful when running away. According to his owner, Pompey would be easy to recapture because "he ought to be generally known about the markets in Baltimore, having been employed for a considerable time in the capacity of market man." An enslaved wagoner named Joshua Sullivan accompanied his owner to Baltimore in 1817, and then promptly disappeared into the city to find his wife, Flora, who had fled there several months earlier. While Baltimore was an obvious destination for Chesapeake runaways, slaves from farther away also made their way to the city. Writing to Baltimore's mayor in 1823, one Tennessee planter suspected that his son's slave Abednego had fled there from Franklin County, Alabama. A tall twenty-three-year-old who was "raised a waiter & can lay bricks," and who had "made a great deal by gambling with whites," Abednego would have found Baltimore a suitable refuge.[47]

Runaway advertisements highlight Baltimore's possibilities for living as free and supporting oneself through wages. In 1785, "a very dark mulatto woman, named Charity" fled her rural Maryland owner, who was still looking for her four years later: "It is asserted that she is in or near Baltimore-Town, passes for a free woman, practices midwifery, and goes by the name of Sarah Dorsey, or Dawson, the Granny." Here was a woman who took her own freedom, shed her old identity and assumed a new name, and reappropriated her own labor. In 1790, Lancaster, an enslaved ship carpenter, fled from Portsmouth, Virginia, to Baltimore, where his owner predicted "he may be employed on board vessels in the harbour as a carpenter, passing as a freeman." When sixteen-year-old Mary, a "bright mulatto woman," escaped Frederick County in 1793, her owner likewise envisioned her "on the road to Baltimore-Town, where I suspect she will endeavour to pass as free." Forty years later, Baltimore remained a destination for runaways. In 1834, Baltimore's jail warden advertised twenty-nine captured slaves, whose owners lived in North Carolina, Virginia, Delaware, and especially the counties of Maryland's Eastern Shore.[48]

But even as free people of color (whether legally so or not) developed a thriving community in Baltimore, the city's employers hardly abandoned their commitment to enslaved labor. In fact, urban producers showed a voracious appetite for slaves, as did wealthier families who desired domestic servants—so much so that white Baltimore residents bought slaves eight times more frequently than they sold them out of the city between 1790 and 1810. During those twenty years, Baltimore's enslaved population quadrupled from 1,255 to 4,672. The city's enslaved population hovered around 4,000 during the 1810s and 1820s, but then fell in the 1830s as white households found other sources for domestic labor and the high prices offered for slaves on the cotton frontier enticed urban slaveholders to answer the "Cash for Negroes" ads placed by such notorious interstate traders as Baltimore's Austin Woolfolk. As early as the 1770s, Maryland law had made it illegal to import new slaves into the state, but emigrants to the city could gain permission to resettle their slaves. Special legislation in 1792 welcomed the white refugees of Saint Domingue to bring their slaves to Baltimore, and some 168 enslaved men, women, and children found themselves far removed from Toussaint L'Ouverture's promise of liberation. In 1802, when Reverend Dr. Elijah Rattoone left a faculty position at New York's Columbia College to assume the associate rectorship of St. Paul's Episcopal Church in Baltimore, he brought an eighteen-year-old male slave with him. Not long before, Madame Jeanne Mathusine Droibillan Volunbrun had sparked a small riot in New York when she decamped for Baltimore with her twenty slaves. Once in Baltimore, Volunbrun used her slaves to operate a cigar manufactory.[49]

Other urban manufacturers and artisans relied upon enslaved workers in shipbuilding, brickmaking, and bread baking. By 1813, Baltimore artisans owned over one-third of the city's slaves and rented many more from rural planters and urban widows. For example, five of the ten slaves living under ropemaker James Neale's roof belonged to someone else, including twenty-year-old Perry (owned by a Mrs. Ward) and twenty-five-year-old Basil (owned by Judge Hanson). Domestic service was the most common labor assigned to urban slaves, which helps to explain why enslaved women greatly outnumbered enslaved men in Baltimore.[50]

The demand for slaves in Baltimore was especially high in the years preceding the federal ban on the African slave trade in 1808. Maryland's rural slaveholders, already possessed of many slaves they considered "surplus," did not legalize a last-minute scramble for new slaves, as was the case in South Carolina. Instead, they anticipated supplying Baltimore with slaves from the Maryland countryside, only at ever-rising prices. Seeing an opportunity, however, Baltimore merchants launched at least four voyages to Africa between 1804 and 1807, and delivered upwards of 750 new African slaves to buyers in Charleston. It would not be surprising if some of those survivors of the Middle Passage were smuggled into Baltimore, adding diversity to the city's growing enslaved population. John S. Tyson, the Quaker founder of the Protection Society of Maryland, alleged that illegal transatlantic importation continued into the 1810s. Slaves speaking French, Spanish, and West African languages were not uncommon in Baltimore.[51]

With the influx of white migrants, free people of color, and enslaved African Americans, Baltimore soon contained "a more various and mixed population than any other city in the U. States," according to the *Boston Repertory* in 1812. Baltimore's diversity gained attention, much of which was negative. Commentators from Philadelphia heaped abuse on Baltimore as "a new Sodom" in the aftermath of the riots that convulsed the city in the summer of 1812. Boston readers learned that Baltimore comprised "adventurers from other parts of this country, of foreigners, FUGITIVES OF JUSTICE, the OUTCASTS OF SOCIETY AND THE DISGRACE OF IT." In response, local defenders acknowledged Baltimore's lack "of that paternal or family influence, which, in older places constitutes a powerful bond of union, affection, and order." "Our manners are not fixed, as in the elder cities," Hezekiah Niles confessed to his national audience. "We labor under all the disadvantages of a newly-collected people." But as Niles would have been quick to point out, being a "newly-collected people" also had tremendous advantages for those in the market to purchase labor.[52]

Tapping New Resources

Despite their occasional complaint about a noisy Irish wake, a boisterous African American preacher, or the expense of poor relief for immigrants during a panic, Baltimore's merchants, manufacturers, bankers, and boosters welcomed the growth of the city's laboring population. Hezekiah Niles praised the value of new immigrants to the United States. "The quantity of labor here is yet inadequate to our want of it," he noted in 1816, "and as it is increased our wealth is increased."[53]

This sentiment was not merely a tenet of abstract political economy, but it informed the response of Baltimore employers to the local labor supply. As they envisioned prosperity for the new nation, for its most promising city, and for themselves, Baltimore entrepreneurs saw new opportunities in an expanding labor pool that included native-born white migrants, European immigrants, free people of color, and enslaved African Americans. With the same zeal they showed in opening new markets in China or engineering new techniques of flour milling, Baltimore businessmen calculated the virtues of some workers over others, juggled different kinds of workers within the same endeavor, and made rapid switches between types of workers when doing so seemed advantageous. Indeed, hiring decisions were among the few economic variables that Baltimore capitalists could manage directly. The city's financial fortunes stood at the mercy of British trade policy; the ebb and flow of foreign investment capital; the fickleness of Philadelphia and New York bankers; unfavorable regulation from a hostile Maryland Assembly; congressional legislation on tariffs, banks, specie, and internal improvements; and the length and intensity of winter freezes and summertime epidemics, to name only a few of the things beyond the control of Baltimore's leading men.[54] Helpless about so many of the circumstances of their economic lives, the city's employers devoted special attention to fine-tuning their labor supply.

The starting point for employers was to cast the widest possible net for workers, as a group of Baltimore manufacturers explained in an 1817 petition to Congress. The United States would soon match England in productive capacity, they argued, thanks largely to the labor resources of a city like Baltimore. For too long, the belief that "wages were too high in America" had discouraged competitive industry. Yet this made little sense in Baltimore because "women and children who perform a great part of the work can be hired nearly as low here as in England." Moreover, added the petitioners, "there is no reason to doubt that our coloured people can be extensively and advantageously employed in many manufactures." As they looked around the city, Baltimore employers saw the city's burgeoning population as an untapped resource.[55]

The hopes of American domestic industry had long hinged on marshaling labor from outside the male-dominated artisan workshop. As historian Gary Nash has noted, aspiring eighteenth-century manufacturers "saw women and children as the human material out of which a new American economy could be built." In the name of national welfare and commercial independence, Tench Coxe and Alexander Hamilton declared that "women and children are rendered more useful" by textile concerns like their "National Manufactory" in 1790s Paterson, New Jersey.[56] The 1808 Embargo and the War of 1812 reinvigorated advocates of domestic industry, who once again celebrated the potential of new classes of workers. With typical precision, Hezekiah Niles calculated that 1,500 girls between six and thirteen years old—presently "running through the streets or idling away their time"—might instead generate $359,000 annually for Baltimore's textile manufacturers. Niles lavished praise on mill owners Robert and Alexander McKim in 1817 for employing 100 "little girls" and "a few women; *who, without this employ, would earn nothing at all.*" The McKims had "transform[ed] some useless substance into pure gold."[57]

The ingredients for such alchemy were readily available in Baltimore. Like most early republic cities, Baltimore teemed with children. In 1820, over 40 percent of the city's population was younger than fifteen years old.[58] Within the free black, enslaved, and white segments of the population, boys and girls were present in roughly equal numbers, suggesting that the surfeit of children owed to natural reproduction rather than to any conscious migration strategy. Of course, different kinds of children in Baltimore had radically different futures ahead of them: enslaved boys faced a greater prospect of being sold in the domestic slave trade than did their sisters; free black girls were the least likely to serve a formal apprenticeship that might allow them a self-supporting adulthood; white boys had the greatest chance to gain a skilled trade. The majority of their apprenticeships, however, began after a their fourteenth birthdays, making younger white male children available for other modes of labor.[59]

Mobilizing child labor looked like a promising opportunity, especially for the wealthy citizens who complained about the lack of schools, truancy from the ones that did exist, and the nuisance of disorderly children in public spaces. In advocating a School of Industry for the city's working-class families in 1804, for example, a group of civic leaders proposed to employ "all proper means to induce the parents of poor children to send them to the institution as soon as they may be capable of earning any thing by their labor." Another advocate of child labor praised manufacturing establishments for providing "constant employ to a species of labor, that without them would scarcely be brought into requisition." When the Marquis de Lafayette came to Baltimore in 1824 and witnessed four orphan children at work in the city's new silk button manufactory, the newspapers dutifully reported that these little girls "work, sang, and amused themselves, not as if they were performing a labour, but as if it was part of a fete." This "most curious and pleasing exhibition" attested to the great promise of American manufactures.[60]

Women offered an even greater opportunity to potential employers. "We have several thousand respectable women that would be glad to earn even two dollars a week in any way esteemed reputable, if they could," offered Hezekiah Niles as an enticement to would-be manufacturers.[61] Boomtown growth initially gave Baltimore a preponderance of working-age men, but the number of white working-age men and women had evened out by 1820, and women had achieved a significant majority within the free black and enslaved populations.[62] Over the next two decades, Baltimore's working population became increasingly female, especially as free black and enslaved women came to outnumber free black and enslaved men by more than three to two. African American women worked primarily in domestic service, although such work was not racially exclusive in a city where demand for household labor outstripped the number of black females. Nonetheless, one consequence of black women occupying many domestic service positions was that working-class white women appeared more available for manufacturing labor. Even as the city's middle-class and elite men removed their wives and daughters from productive labor in pursuit of new standards of domesticity, they expressed no sentiment that womanhood itself protected poorer women from manual labor. The great hope of the city's poor-relief officials and moral reformers was that labor could be found to allow working-class women self-support with "the needle and thread."[63]

Baltimore's free black population also was a promising source of wage labor.

In other Southern cities, the free black population was predominantly light skinned, and manumission was frequently the result of being the son or daughter of the owner himself. In places like Charleston or New Orleans, free people of color typically formed a "black middle class," with men working in skilled trades and in a few cases even owning other African Americans as slaves (protecting their own wives and daughters from paid labor). The situation was quite different in Baltimore, where the free black population was overwhelmingly poor and dark skinned, and owed its freedom to the transformation of the regional economy, not a blood relationship. Free people of color generally entered Baltimore directly out of slavery, with no capital, tools, or training in a craft skill. Fortunate free people of color worked for themselves as carters and laundresses, but most found few job options beyond common labor and domestic service. In those capacities, however, free people of color could be seen as valuable to Baltimore's economy. "Every reasonable person will admit that he respects much more the orderly industrious African than the drunken idle white man, whether emigrant or native," explained almshouse trustee Thomas W. Griffith.[64]

Time and again, Baltimore employers resisted the opportunity to narrow the range of workers at their disposal. Take, for example, their involvement in the colonization movement, an organized effort to remove free people of color from the United States. Whereas some early advocates saw colonization as a humanitarian step toward ending slavery, others hoped to purge the nation of its free black inhabitants. In 1817, Henry Clay, the president of the American Colonization Society (ACS), touted the possibility of exiling a "useless and pernicious" population to Liberia. Baltimore's Francis Scott Key was a founding member of the ACS, but the vast majority of support in Maryland came from rural slaveholders who saw free blacks as a threat to the future of slaveholding. So invested was Maryland as a whole in the project of deporting black people (especially manumitted slaves) that the state founded its own African colony in the early 1830s. Ships transported over 600 black Marylanders to Africa in the 1830s; only eight passengers hailed from Baltimore. Free people of color in Baltimore denounced the colonization project, and urban slaveholders showed little interest in making exile a condition of manumission. Likewise, most Baltimore employers were uninterested in reducing the scope of the labor pool.[65]

White workers in Baltimore occasionally called on elected officials to rid the city of free people of color, but their pleas fell on deaf ears. The majority of manufacturers and other employers in the city expressed little sympathy for white workers who complained of job competition. When white carters petitioned for a legislative ban on black carters in 1828, for example, prominent Baltimore merchants sent a counter-petition to Annapolis arguing against any exclusionary law. Whereas proposals circulated in Charleston in the 1820s to replace all black labor with white labor, Baltimore employers felt no such imperative. As unwilling as they may have been to consider free people of color as citizens, and as wedded as they were to stereotypes that deemed free blacks lazy and irresponsible, Baltimore employers had no problem hiring them as workers.[66]

Slaves faced similar defamation in public discourse, but the prospect of removing them from the city's labor pool garnered little sustained support. Master craftsmen had much to do with the fourfold growth in the number of slaves in Baltimore between 1790 and 1810. Two-fifths of Baltimore mechanics owned slaves in 1810, and many others hired enslaved workers from urban widows, merchant *rentiers*, or rural owners. Preferred in labor-intensive industries with predictable income, slaves toiled in brickyards, ropewalks, ironworks, shipyards, chemical plants, and tobacco manufactories. Among white residents of the city, there was much hand wringing about slavery as a moral and social evil but little concerted effort to limit access to slave labor. While prominent businessmen involved in banking, insurance, and foreign commerce filled the ranks of the short-lived Maryland Abolition Society in the 1790s and the Protection Society of Maryland in the late 1810s, the majority of commercial men and manufacturers in Baltimore were not abolitionists.[67]

As Baltimore's population grew rapidly in the decades after 1790, and as the city's labor force became increasingly diverse, employers responded enthusiastically. Their interests were not in excluding certain workers from the city, but in increasing the number of available workers. Much of this impulse emerged from the desire to jump-start American manufacturing. Between the Revolutionary War and the War of 1812, the United States strove for commercial independence from Europe. The irregularities of Atlantic commerce convinced many prominent commentators and officials of the need for national self-sufficiency and the creation of an internal market. When English manufacturers flooded the United States with goods after 1815, proponents of American manufacturing called for tariffs to protect infant industries. Advocates of American industry insisted that the United States could compete with England because of the superior rewards that accompanied innovation in the young nation.[68]

The issue of labor figured prominently in the discussion of American manufacturing. A deep and diverse labor pool stocked with women, free people of color, slaves, immigrants, and children was essential to the project. Mathew Carey even advised manufacturers that one hundred slaves would prove more profitable than an equal number of white female factory operatives. Addressing Philadelphia's Franklin Institute, Thomas P. Jones explained that slaves were ideal for textile manufactories: "they are more *docile*, more constant, and *cheaper*, than freemen, who are often refractory and dissipated; who waste much time by visiting public places, attending musters, elections, &c. which the *operative slave* is not permitted to frequent." According to Jones, Carey, and their Baltimore ally, Hezekiah Niles, American economic independence required mobilizing as much labor as possible.[69]

Of course, not everyone agreed. The employment of women, children, slaves, and free people of color in industry did not receive much enthusiasm from the male craftsmen increasingly removed from the center of the manufacturing economy. By the 1820s, these artisans were likely to see their own interests at odds with those of the advocates of national industry and the erection of larger manufactories. While the white male artisans who became involved in the Workingmen's Party in the 1830s hoped to restrict the labor market (and thus reserve work and higher wages for themselves), the capitalists who owned most of Baltimore's productive resources were pleased to see a competitive, open, and diverse labor market.[70]

Many of Baltimore's leading employers continued to think of working people's labor as the property of the community as a whole. As the historian Linda Kerber has explained, one of the few "civic obligations" applying to working people within the Anglo-American political tradition was to deliver up their labor to their superiors who might best utilize it.[71] When poorer men and women withheld their labor, they should face criminal charges or forfeit freedoms inside public institutions like the almshouse. Baltimore's vagrancy statute, for instance, condemned anyone who lived "idle without employment" to a term of compulsory labor. Maryland's law fell hard upon a group of striking journeymen in 1809 who were convicted of conspiring to remove their labor from the market. Sheriffs and officers of the watch made sure that slaves and servants stayed in place. Community leaders hoped that disciplinary institutions like the almshouse, penitentiary, and a proposed (but never instituted) School of Industry would produce industrious workers for the urban economy. Although these aspirations were largely unrealized, they attest to the idea of labor as public property and the role of the state in making it so.[72]

Transforming Baltimore into a major commercial emporium required the labor of thousands of people. The burgeoning city proved alluring to workers from rural Maryland and Europe alike, and the city's population increased more than sevenfold between 1790 and 1840. For those entire fifty years, boosters predicted Baltimore's future glory and the abundant opportunities that awaited men of both capital and labor. Such optimistic prognoses invariably ignored the exact nature of the work involved. But no one would suggest that the presence of thousands of new workers in the city would alone result in prosperity; labor had to be categorized, organized, and mobilized. As the next chapters will reveal, the labor market in Baltimore had its own logic—one that used the diversity of Baltimore's population to collapse the differences between some workers, to enhance those between other workers, and always to assure that owning and controlling labor was vastly more lucrative than performing it.

CHAPTER 2

A Job for a Working Man

G etting hired as a day laborer was never an easy proposition. A man could wait a long time on the wharves for the chance to unload an arriving ship. Several intelligence offices, as employment agencies were known, offered placement services, but only to workers who came recommended by a previous employer or master. Newspaper advertisements primarily sought laborers who didn't want to work—runaway slaves and servants—rather than those who did. A kinsman or countryman might offer a lead on a position, but such informal connections were hardly a guarantee of a job. Patronage jobs on the municipal payroll would remain scarce until the expansion of the franchise transformed menial workers into voters and an organized party system emerged to claim their allegiance. Erratic demand for labor in general presented additional challenges, with financial contractions, wintertime freezes, and summertime epidemics all slowing the hiring of casual labor to a trickle. How, then, could a man get a job in Baltimore?

Knowing when and where to line up for construction labor, which of the city's newspapers published the most "help wanted" advertisements, how to cultivate one's landlord as a patron, or which ropewalks hired Irishmen—this was crucial information for a job-seeking man, whether he obtained it from patient observation or informal communication. Peter Bowen, an unemployed African American drayman, must have been pleased at his ability to get five white neighbors to recommend him as "a sober, honest, industrious man" for a city job as a privy cleaner. A recent immigrant from Glasgow might delight in seeing a newspaper advertisement calling for "European Laborers," and specifically "a Man who has been in the practice of burning clay in Scotland or Ireland." But would an out-of-work Englishman know to avoid Mr. Lambie's bootshop in early 1809, where just a few months earlier an unapologetic "Tory" foreman had been tarred and feathered?[1] Learning the ways of the city was important even to those workers who had the least choice in the matter. Jim, an enslaved man whose owner, Mr.

Poe, had rented him to a road-repair contractor in 1795, would have to toil hard enough to avoid a blow from the foreman, but not so hard as to antagonize the free workers alongside him.[2] Tacit knowledge of local mores proved valuable to male manual laborers of every sort, but it was never enough to assure a man of getting and keeping a job.

Just as it would have been for an early republic immigrant to Baltimore, the process of labor recruitment remains mysterious for historians several centuries later. The majority of urban manual labor was casual, by definition short-term, contracted orally, and unrecorded. Describing how Baltimore's free African American men found work, an 1838 missionary report noted, "There are several places where they take their positions on the wharves, or in the public streets, where they can be found by their employers as porters, or dray-men, or workmen in labour of different kinds."[3] But such accounts do not uncover the ostensible moment when employer and employee met in the marketplace. Many employers placed "help wanted" advertisements in the newspapers, but despite their stated desire to hire a white man or to rent a slave for a particular position, it remains unknown whether they found any takers. Tax lists and court documents enable historians to determine which brickmakers owned slaves and which shoemakers claimed orphan apprentices, but these same records do not go far in explaining why twelve Baltimore bakers owned slaves in 1810, but another thirty-six bakers employed legally free workers to stir batter and knead dough. Only on rare occasions did employers reveal their intentions, as tobacconist Eli Hewett did after two white teenaged apprentices and a slave escaped from his snuff manufactory in 1809. Hewitt was quick to sell off two of his remaining slaves, and then promptly advertised his intention to pay "liberal wages by the month or year" to "a steady, sober man" and "a sober, industrious and good tempered black woman." In Baltimore, no manual labor or menial work was limited exclusively to people of one racial group or legal status.[4]

Perhaps the best artifacts of early republic manual labor are the rare payrolls listing the names of men employed in shoveling, carting, or chopping. Such payrolls typically functioned as receipts to the merchant, property owner, or municipal official responsible for footing the bill. Next to the number of nails or feet of lumber that had been used, contractors indicated the amount of labor required to sink the pilings for a wharf or install curbstones on a new avenue. Lazily, but in testament to the tendency to see working people as interchangeable objects, many contractors simply listed the number of "hands" employed. But others diligently wrote the names of the five or ten or thirty men they had hired. Here one finds the names of early republic laborers who do not otherwise enter the historical record, names like Freeborn Rice, Indian Bill, John Fornandis, Matthew Dunnahew, and Commodore Budd. Recorded without distinction on the payrolls of an 1809 construction project, these names reveal the hidden history of "how work worked" in the early republic city.[5]

The most surprising aspect of manual labor payrolls is the glimpse they provide of mixed-race job sites. From street-leveling projects in the 1790s through construction projects in the 1830s, Baltimore employers hired enslaved, free black, immigrant, and native-born white workers and paid them the same wages to do the same work. Men with Irish, German, and Iberian surnames worked alongside African American men, both enslaved and free. Race, ethnicity, legal status, and nativity bore no substantive relationship to the days or weeks worked. In this light, the mobilization of manual labor in Baltimore did not conform to the same logic that upheld white supremacy in a slaveholding city, and white skin did not protect some men from backbreaking labor. Nor did it spare them the supposed indignity of working alongside men who were legally unfree or members of a denigrated racial caste. Many white workers might have preferred otherwise; with luck, some could escape the ranks of manual labor, an achievement far less likely for men of color. Yet, white men could expect no hand up from the city's employers, who relished the city's well-stocked labor pool and saw no advantage in segmenting the market for manual labor.

Employers determined how work would be recruited, rewarded, or compelled but did so unpredictably enough to leave an early republic job seeker guessing. As wage labor, legal servitude, and slavery functioned simultaneously, the heterogeneity of the city's labor force gave employers an array of choices that overwhelmed an individual man's strategies for finding and keeping work. Employers carefully considered not just one worker against another, but whole categories of workers. A laborer could do only so much to make himself desirable—or perhaps in the case of enslaved workers, undesirable—for specific kinds of work. How a given man found himself unloading a particular ship or digging a particular ditch could rarely be reduced to a good letter of recommendation, a strong back, or a premonition about where work was to be had. To follow the path that brought a man into a day's labor makes for a complex story, but it also lends itself to one of comparable simplicity: this was a system in which employers held most of the cards and prospered by their ability to access, organize, and deploy labor through the marketplace.

To tell both stories, the contingent and the structural, this chapter reconstructs the strategic considerations of five men whose labor and livelihoods converged at Jones Falls in 1809. An advertisement in September 22nd's *Baltimore Patriot* set the stage for their meeting:

Christian Baum payroll, 1809. Contractor Christian Baum paid a $1 daily wage to men like Freeborn Rice, Indian Bill, John Fornandis, Matthew Dunnahew, and Commodore Budd for work on a new bridge over Jones Falls. Manual labor payrolls offer the best evidence of mixed-race labor sites in the early republic. Courtesy Baltimore City Archives.

NOTICE TO LABOURERS

A large number of LABOURERS will be wanted by the City Commissioners, early on
Monday morning next, to work at the New Bridge in Baltimore Street—their chief
work will be at the pumps, and generous wages will be given.

Whether they read the ad, heard it read aloud, or learned about it through a social network, James Richardson, Aaron Bunton, Equillo, and William C. Goldsmith
arrived on Baltimore Street that fall. There they met the man behind the advertisement, Christian Baum, an architect and contractor commissioned to build a
bridge connecting the city proper with the Old Town neighborhood. For $17,500,
Baum agreed to procure building supplies and recruit labor for the project, paying himself $2 per day, offering similar wages to a handful of skilled carpenters,
stonemasons, and carters, and employing as many as twenty-five common laborers
at any one time for $1 per day. Here were opportunities and challenges for men
and for the owners of men.[6]

To read this advertisement required a sizeable amount of knowledge: Did
"labourers" have an implicit racial or ethnic coding? What about work "at the
pumps," the kind of labor that sailors had to be compelled to perform below deck
and that Maryland convicts had performed until only recently? Did the city allow
contractors to rent slaves and pay wages directly to their owners? Were contractors interested in hiring footloose free men who could work one day and disappear the next, or did they prefer the control gained by directing the labor of slaves?
A man in search of a job could answer some of these questions on his own, especially if he had lived in the city long enough. With other questions, however,
the answers depended on the men and women who employed and owned labor.

Two free laboring men, James Richardson and Aaron Bunton, one black and
one white, chose to pursue the "generous wages" at the New Bridge. Equillo, a teenaged slave, manned the pumps at Jones Falls because his owner, William Goldsmith, chose the job for him. Once there, little differentiated Richardson, Bunton, and Equillo from one another; their days were filled with backbreaking labor.
Meanwhile, Goldsmith pocketed Equillo's wages. The contractor, Christian Baum,
initially had more in common with the working men than the slaveholder, but
through careful management at the New Bridge, he hoped to change that.

James Richardson, a Free African American Man

For a free man of color like James Richardson, a job at the New Bridge might have
seemed promising. Richardson was unlikely to find a job in the trades or profes-

sions. This was not a matter of law, which did not limit particular occupations to white "freemen," as was the case for certain jobs in New York City.[7] As Baltimore's free black population grew in the 1800s, so too did the occupational diversity of its African American men. Black men in the city labored as blacksmiths, barbers, and carters, often using skills they had acquired while enslaved on rural plantations. But at the same time, black men in Baltimore found few avenues into the artisan trades at the heart of the city's preindustrial manufacturing economy. Coopering, cabinetmaking, and other craft occupations still relied on an apprenticeship system in which master craftsmen displayed little interest in training black boys to be independent adults.[8]

As had been custom for nearly two centuries in Anglo America, legal indentures "bound" young men to masters who would provide them with room and board, education, moral guidance, and most importantly, training in a marketable skill. Most of the Baltimore men who made careers as shipwrights, silversmiths, and shoemakers in the 1800s had served apprenticeships in a state of legal unfreedom, albeit one that ended with majority age and augured economic independence in adulthood. African American boys rarely had such opportunities, whether because their parents resisted ceding legal control of their children to white employers, or because court officials relegated black children to dead-end apprenticeships in such "unskilled" fields as housework and farming.[9] Perhaps most importantly, Baltimore employers exhibited little interest in training black apprentices for eventual freedom when they could train black slaves for eventual sale. When a black apprentice reached majority age, his master would be left empty handed. But when an enslaved boy with craft training reached majority age, he could be sold for several times his original purchase price, all on top of the unpaid labor he had provided during his years of apprenticeship.[10] In such a market, the kinds of jobs available to free men of color like James Richardson were more likely to involve shovels than leather aprons and awls.

Were Richardson unwilling to wield a pickax, his next prospect in Baltimore was in domestic service. While women constituted the bulk of the domestic labor force, many prosperous households hired black men (whether free or rented slaves) to serve as valets, waiters, drivers, and hostlers.[11] Employers desiring a male servant who was not African American usually had to state as much in their advertisements. "An attentive and smart male Servant, (a white man preferable)," requested a Harrison Street family in 1804. Most advertisements omitted mention of race, and Richardson would have been familiar with the terse notices seeking "active waiters—such as can come well recommended." Just a month before the opportunity at the New Bridge appeared, a free black man new to Baltimore advertised his desire for "a situation as a Waiter and Coachman" and promised "satisfactory recommendations" to any interested party.[12]

For many reasons, however, Richardson would have been unlikely to pursue a job as a domestic servant. As a man with his own home and family, Richardson would resist a job requiring residence in someone else's home and away from his own family. Room and board often constituted the bulk of remuneration for domestic labor, and a modest $12 monthly payment would not have allowed a man like Richardson to sustain his own household.[13] If, like so many other free people of color in Baltimore, Richardson had been enslaved at an earlier stage of his life, then a job working and living right under the nose of a white employer may have been particularly unappealing. If Richardson had been an agricultural worker in the countryside before coming to Baltimore, he might have lacked the "refinement" that urban employers increasingly sought in their domestics and he would have been unable to find a job as a servant in the first place.[14]

Free black men in Baltimore were often seafarers, and it is plausible that Richardson was one of the "black jacks" who helped bring the city's merchant marine to prominence. For most working men in the early republic, however, a career as a mariner was not an appealing prospect. Going to sea involved arduous toil, long absences from home, and the risk of capture or death. Perhaps Richardson knew the story of Clement Oakes and Daniel Cooper, two African American sailors taken captive by the Spanish in 1806 when their ship, the *Warren*, entered the waters of the Pacific. Oceangoing vessels were once known for their racial egalitarianism, but white supremacy was beginning to make shipboard labor less attractive to black men by the first decade of the nineteenth century. African American sailors were finding fewer berths and lower stations. To make matters worse, ports like Charleston, South Carolina, were imposing odious restrictions on free black sailors arriving on incoming ships. An 1806 law there mandated the whipping of any black sailor "guilty of whooping or hallooing, or of making any clamorous noise, or singing aloud indecent songs"; soon, free black sailors docking in Charleston would be forced to lodge in the city jail.[15]

Ships also remained the one place where a free man, regardless of his race, might still feel the lash for a blunder on the job. Corporal punishment was an unquestionable risk of shipboard labor, but a particularly objectionable one to a man of color whose freedom—and thus, his difference from a slave—centered on immunity from having his labor beaten out of him. In 1792, for example, a free black sailor named John Susco sued for "ill-usage" after his captain had mutilated his ear. For a free black man in need of wages, a job pumping at Jones Falls may have seemed pleasant in comparison.[16]

Still, the newspaper advertisement simply said "Labourers." What did that mean when similar advertisements called for "active and able white MEN" or "A COLOURED PERSON, to do HOUSE-Work"? Employers readily articulated the specific characteristics of the person they sought to hire, whether targeting "a middle-aged woman" or expressing that "a German will be preferred."[17] Manual labor advertisements generally lacked such specificity, and Richardson might have noticed earlier in the year that "about one hundred laborers" would be hired for a road-building project, or that "25 or 30 LABOURERS" could find employment at merchant Aaron Levering's counting house.[18] A job seeker could rightfully wonder about the implicit racial coding in an undifferentiated call for laborers. Employers who wanted or were willing to hire black men typically said as much, so advertisements without specification may have implied a preference for white men. But employers who wanted white men were also likely to be explicit, and if one presumed (as many whites did) that African Americans were suited to filling the lowest jobs, then perhaps modifying "laborers" with a racial designation was unnecessary. A straightforward classified ad could, it turns out, be quite opaque.

Getting a job required James Richardson to decode the logic of the city's employers. Had Richardson lived in Baltimore since the 1790s, he would have seen mixed-race crews at numerous job sites around the city. Or perhaps Richardson made the acquaintances of Pompey Neal and Cato Haynes, both of whom had toiled alongside Lawrence McFarling, John Sullivan, and James Doyl to clean a ditch on Howard Hill in 1795. Haynes and Neal might have recalled that they were paid the same rate as every other worker on the site and were neither last hired nor first fired as the work progressed. City commissioners hired another fifty laborers in 1797 for street cleaning, and here too, free men of color worked alongside free white men and enslaved black men, for the same $1 a day. A decade later, men like Haynes, Neal, and now Richardson were still looking for hire at a $1 a day. With uneasiness, Haynes and Neal could have noted that some of their former white workmates were now contractors, submitting bids to the city, earning twice the income, and deciding whether men like themselves would work at all.[19]

Whether to take a job alongside enslaved men might have been Richardson's final consideration. By official count, more free African Americans than slaves populated Baltimore in 1809, and as a result, the city's dominant white population could no longer presume that being a slave was the normative condition of black men. But might it seem otherwise if free men of color did the same work as slaves? No poor man looking for a job in Baltimore could dwell on the consequences of performing manual labor for wages alongside slaves. White men risked their republican credentials when they did so but could ill-afford to do otherwise. Free black men were also in no financial position to refuse such work, even as their labor might blur the thin line between African American slavery and freedom.

A decade or so earlier, freedom for black men seemed to convey a greater possibility of equality. In the 1790s, a free black man, Thomas Brown, ran for one of Baltimore's seats in the Maryland House of Delegates, and outspoken defenses of political equality appeared in the *Maryland Gazette*. The white artisans of the Mechanical Society even denounced a proposal to ban black voting as "contrary to reason and good policy, to the spirit of equal liberty and our free constitution." But not long after, the state of Maryland passed a law against black voting, office holding, and testifying against white people in court. As free people of color came to outnumber slaves, they came under increasing scrutiny for their marketing activities and public assemblies. Moreover, they became more vulnerable to being kidnapped into slavery.[20] All told, then, a free man of color like James Richardson had little to lose in going to work at Jones Falls, if only because he had already lost much. His options for more lucrative jobs were limited, and domestic service and shipboard labor were surely less appealing. Public manual labor in Baltimore had always been open to free men of color, and while Richardson might risk being mistaken for a slave while at work, this could happen at any time within the white-supremacist structure of Baltimore society.

Aaron Bunton, an Adult White Laborer

Aaron Bunton's path to Jones Falls was fraught with a different set of considerations, no less risky, no more promising. By many accounts, men like Bunton did not exist in the early republic: white career manual laborers contradicted the republican political culture of the new nation. For men to display their independence, they could not be hirelings beholden to an employer for subsistence. The promise of the early republic was that after a spell of dependent labor—whether as an apprentice, a servant, or a hireling—a white man could marshal the resources to provide for himself and his family, and thereby avoid being politically beholden to another man. Yet for all the declarations that wage labor was nothing more than a life stage for white men, Aaron Buntons were far from uncommon.[21] Even within the pages of the unreliable city directories, "labourers" appeared intermittently among the many merchants, oysterhouse keepers, and tailors. In 1802, one hundred men had become recognized householders by earning wages as day laborers. Fitting this bill, Aaron Bunton lived on East Aliceanna Street in Fells Point.[22] Residing three blocks from the waterfront, Bunton could quickly materialize on the docks when a ship arrived laden with cargo. Heading the other direction, Bunton's walk to where Baltimore Street hit Jones Falls—that is, where the New Bridge was under construction—might take about fifteen minutes.

Baltimore's substantial white majority meant that most manual laborers would be of European descent. But despite their demographic preponderance, white men's opportunities to work in more lucrative trades were narrowed by changes in the organization of craft labor. In shoemaking, for example, avaricious master craftsmen had begun to subdivide the labor into discrete parts and limit their training of apprentices to the performance of simplified piecework. This was much to the detriment of wage-earning journeymen and to the young apprentices, who no longer received the craft training that pointed to independence in adulthood. As artisan masters became manufacturers, they egregiously violated the presumed mutuality of the craft workshop and prompted journeymen shoemakers to organize in opposition. The Union Society of Journeymen Cordwainers drafted its constitution in 1806, but only a year later the state of Maryland jailed its leaders for an illegal conspiracy. For free men to associate and then collectively refuse to work until their demands were met—that is, to organize a strike—presumably violated the rights of their employers to control the structure and remuneration of labor. The conviction of the union's leaders sent a discouraging message to those craft workers hoping to rise from a journeyman's wages to a master's independence.[23]

While some white men came to manual labor as downwardly mobile artisans, others traveled to the city from the countryside to escape the low wages and dim prospects of farm labor. Historians have recently discovered the extent of poverty among white tenant-farming families in rural parts of Maryland, New York, and Massachusetts. In the decades following the American Revolution, opportunities for property ownership shrank, wage rates remained static, and many families experienced periodic privation. For many young men and women, setting out for the city appeared more promising than staying behind. These domestic migrants typically arrived in Baltimore without occupational skill and without the capital to purchase their own tools or productive property.[24] At the same time, Baltimore already attracted transatlantic migrants, poor men from Ireland, England, and Germany. Although small in comparison to the influx of Europe's poor in the 1830s and 1840s, this early immigration dramatically increased Baltimore's laboring population. Many of these immigrants had paid for their oceanic transportation with terms of bound labor in Maryland. Men who served out their contracts as indentured servants or redemptioners in the 1790s and 1800s usually faced the choice of performing seasonal farm labor for wages in the countryside or coming to the city in search of more consistent employment and better wages. Whether Aaron Bunton had found himself squeezed out of the craft economy or had fled poverty in rural Maryland or rural Europe, men like him were the most common day laborers in Baltimore.

Even if Bunton could harbor no illusion of being insulated from manual wage labor, answering the advertisement for pumping at the New Bridge required additional consideration. Labor on public infrastructure projects was closely associated with criminality in the post-Revolutionary United States. After reformers had decided to curtail whippings and disfigurements as punishments for property crimes, but before they implemented long-term confinement in penitentiaries as a suitable form of retribution and rehabilitation, American penologists saw manual labor on roads or on the waterfront as an ideal mechanism for generating a public good from crime. A sentence to a term on the roads—as Maryland prescribed for various forms of larceny and vagrancy in the 1790s and 1800s—was seen as a way to inflict shame on the convict and in the process deter spectators from criminality. The idea proved short lived, and alarmed jurists and commentators soon worried that allowing convicts to interact with free people while they worked would corrupt moral sentiment. "In the present mode in which the Criminals are employed to labour on those roads," Baltimore's grand jury reported in 1802, "the Community receive but little Benefit from their Services and that it has no tendency to bring about a reformation in themselves but the contrary." Two years later, Maryland began building its first penitentiary. When the institution finally opened in Baltimore in 1811, newspaper editor Hezekiah Niles declared his relief at the demise of the "semi-barbarous wheelbarrow law."[25]

The association of public construction labor with degradation spilled on to the specific task of manning the pumps. For several centuries, European officials had deemed pumping a particularly useful punishment for the lazy. Bunton may not have known about Amsterdam's famous "drowning cell," where idlers had been forced to pump or drown in the seventeenth century, but like any man in a seaport, he would have associated pumping with the most arduous of shipboard labor. Among the worst labor to perform on a ship was to be sent below deck to pump out the water that had seeped into the bilge. Urban laborers like Bunton likely had shipboard experience, because going to sea for part of the year was a common means of earning wages. The work of shipboard pumping had particular resonance at the time Bunton considered the job at the New Bridge. Thanks to England's policy of naval impressments against "neutral" American shipping, sailors from places like Baltimore might rightfully fear finding themselves forced to pump aboard British warships. Pumping reeked of the degraded labor of prisoners, but men in Bunton's position could ill-afford to be picky.[26]

Although Bunton might have wished that the job advertisement had specified white workers, adult white manual laborers could not count on racially exclusive job sites. Perhaps some European immigrants arrived with such aspirations, but they were quickly disabused upon arriving in Baltimore. "There is no Englishman who does not think himself above the negro," contended one such immigrant to Baltimore in 1805, "but when he comes there he will have to eat, drink, and sleep with negro slaves."[27] Working alongside or in the same occupations as black men was commonplace for white laborers. Although an employer might seek "some active and able white men," almost none could advertise the promise of a racially exclusive job site. Baltimore's privy cleaners were black and white, as were its newspaper carriers, brickmakers, and sawyers.[28] White men, free men of color, and enslaved men worked alongside one another on city construction projects. Bunton would have no reason to expect otherwise at the New Bridge.

Nonetheless, the prospect of mixed-race labor invariably challenged workers like Bunton, because they sought the prerogatives of free men in a republican political culture that frowned on paid labor and was increasingly invested in white supremacy. Early republic artisans were already articulating a white racial consciousness predicated on *not* doing the same work as people of color. For these skilled workers, hierarchies of labor and hierarchies of race were mutually reinforcing: what made African Americans inferior was that they performed the worst jobs, and what made those jobs the worst was that African Americans performed them. By that logic, performing menial labor alongside men of color was a fraught proposition for a man like Aaron Bunton. In cities with overwhelmingly enslaved black majorities like Charleston, mixed-race job sites were rare. In places like Boston or New York, the small black population assured the preponderance of white workers at any given site. Baltimore's demography offered Bunton no such security.[29]

Poor white men in Baltimore could neither opt out of manual labor nor marshal the political clout to monopolize it. Efforts to create racially exclusive job sites went nowhere. In fall 1808, a group of Baltimore "owners of hack-stages, draymen, carters, and laborers" sent a petition to the Maryland House of Delegates "stating that they are deprived of employment by the interference of slaves who engross the same." They received no legislative redress, and at no point in the early republic would state or local officials seek to curtail competition among manual laborers, whether enslaved or free, black or white.[30] Police records show little evidence in the early 1800s of workplace violence geared toward erecting a color line in manual labor, nor would employers deprive themselves of the advantages gained from a highly diverse labor pool. In short, mixed-race sites were the reality of manual labor in Baltimore, a reality Aaron Bunton likely knew full well when he answered the ad at the New Bridge.

William C. Goldsmith, Slaveholder

Least likely to fathom construction labor for himself, William C. Goldsmith was among the most likely to see the advertisement that appeared in the *Baltimore Evening Post*. With a counting house on Smith's Wharf, at the heart of the business district, Goldsmith relied on the *Post* for the latest shipping news, as well as for diplomatic updates from European capitals, word of promising investment opportunities, and notices of upcoming sheriff's sales. Flipping the pages, Goldsmith would have noted with interest an upcoming sale of a male slave. As the owner of at least five slaves already, it was always wise to keep abreast of current prices. A reader like Goldsmith might well have chuckled at some of the descriptions of runaway servants featured in the newspaper, such as Hezekiah Niles's missing apprentice, who was "not overstocked with honesty" and "capable of perverting the correct import of a plain English sentence." But perhaps most compelling would be advertisements for the opportunity to earn cash by renting his slaves to urban employers who needed additional labor. That previous spring, the merchants Enoch and Jesse Levering had sought to hire "four or five Negroes" for the entire year. A local family hoped to hire an enslaved woman "who understands plain cooking and housework generally." When the ad for laborers at the New Bridge appeared, Goldsmith was already one of those Baltimore slaveholders who invested in human property not to staff his own workshop or kitchen but to rent out slaves to city employers.[31]

The city had no small number of lawyers, doctors, bankers, and other professionals who used slaves as investment property. In tandem with employers who sought cheaper access to slave labor, they created a vibrant market in slave rentals. By one estimate, more than 15 percent of slave sale advertisements raised the possibility of hiring out instead. "Wanted to Purchase, or Hire by the Year, A good Negro Slave, or Mulatto Waggoner," read a typical 1794 advertisement that conveyed the interchangeability of renting and owning slaves for urban employers. Slave sellers frequently offered men and women "for Sale or Hire," and in some cases, the return on a year's hire could exceed the revenue of an outright sale. Thus, most slave rentiers preferred the sustained returns that came from hiring out their slaves year after year. Wealthy families could reap $100 annually by leasing a slave to a house carpenter or a shipbuilder. Such earnings supplemented a merchant's or a lawyer's annual income and allowed Baltimore's wealthy white families to attain ever-rising levels of gentility.[32]

Like investing in real estate, purchasing slaves to rent out allowed Goldsmith to establish an income-generating estate for his wife, Sarah, and their two teenaged daughters. Goldsmith's trading business would cease to be valuable upon his death, but the slave property he bequeathed to his descendants could provide wealth for decades to come, especially as enslaved women gave birth to the next generation of Baltimore slaves. Investments in rental slaves (for want of a better phrase) allowed white families to maintain their gentility—to continue to have their children's portraits painted, buy new china patterns, or take dancing lessons from a French master—after the patriarch had died and other forms of income had ceased. Many Baltimore widows depended wholly on the wages their slaves earned. Estate administrators devoted tremendous energy to managing slave rentals in order to provide surviving family members with income.[33]

Renting out one's slaves was not foolproof and came with its own set of anxieties. During slack times in the urban economy when jobs disappeared, rentable slaves brought in no income. In 1803, Thomas Derochbrune petitioned the courts for permission to sell the slaves belonging to his deceased father's estate. "At this dull time when there is no certain employment to be got," Derochbrune reported, "they are more expense to keep than they earn." Owners also worried that "going at large" or "living as free" might give their slaves an undue exposure to dangerous ideas or the corrupting influence of free people of color. Renting out slaves was also risky, insofar as slaves might be abused or injured under someone else's oversight, which would diminish the capacity for future work or the profit from future sale.[34]

Men and women who rented out their slaves created what one scholar has described as "divided mastery," or the opportunity for savvy slaves to play the interests of the master against those of the employer. Slaves used the ambiguity to expand their space. When Leaven Owings died, his slave Elizabeth was not eager to enrich the deceased man's estate. The administrator, Achsah Owings, sold Elizabeth because she "has become so ungovernable that your petitioner can not get any service from her." Likewise, Eleanor Dall wanted to sell the two slaves that her husband had deeded for her support because Moses and Charles "do not seem disposed to serve her faithfully." Mary Spence, who resided in rural Baltimore County, hoped to sell the thirty-nine slaves left to her in her husband's will. "If she hire them out, the receipts of the wages is precarious and will generally be accompanied with mutual complaint." Worse, from Spence's perspective, "there is also great danger if they are hired out and dislike their master, of their absconding from service altogether." Numerous court cases attest to the conflicts that slaves provoked between leasers and lessees.[35]

Under such precarious circumstances, slaveholders developed new methods of discipline to guarantee the return on their investment in rentable slaves. After all, the busy harbor, the crowded neighborhoods, the large free population of color, and the proximity to Pennsylvania created possibilities for enslaved workers to escape their owner's surveillance, and sometimes to escape slavery altogether. Something as basic as walking to and from a job site could tantalize a rented slave with physical mobility approximating freedom itself: stopping to chat with an associate about the weather, dropping off some food for a mother with a newborn, dipping into a tavern for a drink. From the perspective of a slaveholder, equally dangerous were the encounters at a mixed-race job site, where a misguided Irishman might spout some nonsense about freedom, or a free black man might mention something about a carriage making its way to Philadelphia late that night.

To keep slaves working in Baltimore required slaveholders to adopt disciplinary strategies suited to the city's close quarters and permeable boundaries. To be sure, Baltimore slaveholders continued to rely on their old standby, physical violence, compelling obedience by inflicting pain. One Fells Point master, for example, kept his twelve-year-old slave Mary in an iron collar. The urban setting, however, may have placed a check on the most egregious violence. Frederick Douglass recalled that abusive Baltimore slaveholders risked being ostracized by their peers, and slaveholders' pretensions of gentility may have created a social sanction against forms of physical coercion common to plantation districts. At the same time, the possibility of running away gave enslaved people in Baltimore leverage to demand better treatment. As the tobacconist Eli Hewett unwittingly revealed when he offered a reward for his runaway slave in 1809, Baltimore's demography and setting could facilitate a successful escape: "I expect he is harbored by free Negroes, as his parents are free, and he has a number of acquaintances living near the Spring Gardens." Although the man took only the clothes on his back, "it is expected he will get others, as his company has been with bad women." Finally, Hewett suspected the man would be "bound for sea," and warned "all masters of vessels against taking him away." The possibility that a runaway slave might garner assistance from family members, plebeian associates, and unscrupulous employers could have given pause to William Goldsmith as he contemplated sending Equillo to work at the New Bridge.[36]

Constrained in their recourse to physical violence, urban slaveholders created incentives for slaves to remain in the city and work diligently. But as slaveholders dangled the carrot of increased autonomy and eventual freedom to some Baltimore slaves, they wielded a heavy stick by punishing others with sale to the Deep South's cotton frontier. Taken together, these strategies gave slavery a surprising longevity in early republic Baltimore.

Most notably, slaveholders sustained the larger system of unfree labor by allowing individual slaves to obtain freedom on predetermined dates far in the future. Postdated deeds of manumission promised freedom at the end of a specified term in exchange for faithful service during the intervening period. Freedom in the long term facilitated labor exploitation in the short term. As the preeminent scholar of the practice has explained, delayed manumissions owed less to masters' humanitarianism and more to their pocketbook interest in maximizing access to a slave's labor while minimizing the risk of a slave's running away. In fact, delayed manumissions often stipulated more than simply good behavior in exchange for eventual freedom; they also required a cash payment from the slave to complete the transaction. In purchasing their own freedom, such slaves funded the purchase of their successors in bondage, because many slaveholders combined delayed manumissions and self-purchase as a method of serial labor exploitation.[37]

Although such arrangements had a longer eighteenth-century history in Maryland, they gained legal recognition in 1796. In the eyes of the law, deeds of delayed manumission were considered the exclusive will of the owner; in practice, they functioned like contracts that were legally binding once filed with the county court. When masters attempted to renege on such arrangements, or when heirs of a deceased owner tried to alter the terms, enslaved people had standing to file freedom suits and did so successfully. But when a slave who had received a delayed manumission did not uphold his or her end of the bargain, the law initially extended the term of servitude. In time, the punishment would become mandatory sale out of the state.[38]

An enslaved person who had been granted a prospective manumission became a "term slave," and an entire secondary market appeared for urban employers wishing to purchase an enslaved worker for a predetermined period in advance of their freedom. "A strong healthy mulatto Girl, about 16 years of age," began an 1809 advertisement for a slave sale, "she has 13 years to serve." "For Sale, for the term of thirteen years, a likely Negro Boy," read another. By the early 1800s, term slaves were common enough that the descriptor "for life" regularly appeared in advertisements selling slaves condemned to the normal fate of permanent servitude. Constituting as many as one-third of all slaves advertised for sale in Baltimore newspapers between 1790 and 1830, term slaves carried a lower purchase price and were presumably disinclined to run away lest they jeopardize their long-term prospect of freedom. Not surprisingly, term slaves became an attractive property for middling white families unable to afford a slave for life, and a safer investment for the widows, bankers, and merchants who sought a guaranteed income by renting slaves to urban employers.[39]

A calculating Baltimore investor might have seen a compelling opportunity in the "young mulatto woman" with eleven years to serve, who was offered for sale at the price of $150 in an 1809 advertisement.[40] If that woman could recoup more than $14 a year for the remainder of her term, the investment would be profitable. Her new owner might hire her out as a domestic servant for $50 or $60 annually, a rent comparable to that of a small house in one of Baltimore's working-class neighborhoods. Equally alluring to a slaveholder, the laws pertaining to delayed manumissions declared that the unborn children of a female term slave would be slaves-for-life unless explicitly granted their own delayed manumissions. For that reason, if at some point in her remaining eleven years of enslavement, the aforementioned woman had a baby, then her owner could hold that child in slavery long after the mother had been freed. Were that owner to sell the child, he or she could instantly recoup the $150 purchase price of the mother. Term slavery had its own perverse logic, one that turned the promise of freedom into a mechanism of greater exploitation.

As urban slaveholders converted slavery into a life stage for some, they made it vastly less escapable for others. Fast on the heels of the invention of the cotton gin, Chesapeake slaveholders became slave exporters of the first magnitude, creating an interregional market where the prices paid for slaves in Baltimore depended largely on prices paid for slaves in Charleston, Augusta, Mobile, Vicksburg, and New Orleans. Thomas Dewitt may have been envisioning such distant markets in 1804 when he placed a "Negroes Wanted" advertisement and promised "generous prices and prompt payment" for "a number of Negro Girls, from twelve to twenty years of age." In 1806, Philadelphia abolitionist John Parrish identified Maryland as the leader in the "inland trade" and informed horrified readers about Baltimore's private jails, where sold slaves were kept until transported by boat to faraway purchasers. Although it would be another decade before the infamous "Cash for Negroes" ads began proliferating in Baltimore newspapers, the city's slaveholders were already availing themselves of slave brokers to transform human beings into liquid capital.[41]

Enslaved men fetched particularly good prices farther south, and sales were brisk enough that by 1813, a sizable sex imbalance emerged among Baltimore slaves, with 56 percent of the population female. At the same time, older men had seemingly disappeared from the ranks of urban slaves, with those ages forty-five and older accounting for only 2 percent of the city's entire slave population. While slaveholders may simply have hidden older slaves from the prying eyes of the tax assessor, it seems strange that Baltimore contained a mere 52 enslaved men in their mid-forties and older in 1813. Seven years later, the census taker tallied only 165 such older men. Some older male slaves had probably moved into the ranks of free people of color, especially as delayed manumissions typically waited until a slave had completed his most productive work years before granting freedom. But the disappearance of older male slaves from the city may have owed a great deal to urban slaveholders' participation in the interstate trade in human bodies.[42]

The transformation of people into cash was the centerpiece of the American slave system, and that possibility would never be far from the thoughts of a Baltimore slaveholder like William Goldsmith. Upon learning that laborers would earn wages at the New Bridge, Goldsmith could immediately begin to calculate whether this opportunity met his family's financial needs. Whether it met the enslaved Equillo's needs was immaterial to Goldsmith: slaveholders deployed their slaves as they saw fit. On the other hand, the demography and geography of Baltimore meant that hiring out Equillo might work against Goldsmith's long-term interests, even as it might bring a short-term gain of $1 per day. The potential wealth contained within Equillo's body would evaporate if hiring out facilitated an escape from slavery altogether. Goldsmith had not availed himself of some of Baltimore's novel modes of slave discipline, and Equillo was a slave-for-life, not a term slave deterred from running away by the promise of future freedom. Perhaps Goldsmith kept Equillo as a slave-for-life to maintain his value on the interstate market, where an adult male slave could fetch upwards of $300. This potential value, however, could vanish were Equillo to sustain an injury on the job or catch a disease, something not implausible while he pumped water from a mucky stream during the height of yellow fever season.[43]

Men like Goldsmith weighed all these risks and possibilities. In the end, Equillo would pump, and Goldsmith would collect $129.62 in wages before the New Bridge was finished.

Equillo, an Enslaved African American Man

"Mr. Goldsmith's Man," "Negro Qiller," "Goldsmith Equilla," "Negrow Equila": no matter how Equillo appeared on the New Bridge payroll, he labored to create wealth for the family who owned him. It is hard to imagine being sent to the pumps was an opportunity for Equillo, just as it is difficult to conceive of the ability of enslaved workers to shape the terms of their labor. By definition, slavery involved the denial of choice, and yet enslaved workers like Equillo could make choices whose ramifications might expand personal autonomy and augur future freedom. If slaveholders had the threat of sale at their disposal, slaves held the threat of running away over their owners, who feared the loss of hundreds of dollars of valuable property. The outcome of the contest often depended on the particularities of one's owner, his or her financial priorities, community position, and physical power. Like other workers, enslaved men and women read their situations at a given moment, assessed the range of possible outcomes, and made decisions that seemed advantageous in the short run and over the long haul—while always recognizing their choices as thoroughly circumscribed and subject to violent reversal at a master's whim. Equillo's path to the New Bridge was no more straightforward than anyone else's, despite his status as a slave.[44]

Equillo was seventeen or eighteen years old in 1809. Whether he was born abroad, in the Maryland countryside, or in Baltimore is unknown. Likewise, the records do not indicate if Equillo had been born a Goldsmith slave, or if he had only recently become the family's property. The Goldsmiths owned only one slave older than Equillo—Rachel, a woman in her thirties—and six younger: Lucy, Matilda, Nancy, and Isaac (all between eight and fourteen years old), and Abraham and Zachariah (both infants). Rachel could conceivably have been the mother to all, including Equillo; Equillo and Rachel could have parented the two babies; perhaps they had no relationship at all.[45]

For Equillo, as for other enslaved people, familial relations would be important considerations in how he endured his bondage. Slaveholders turned the familial relations of slaves into leverage that could be used to compel obedience. Running away appeared less attractive when it meant never seeing one's mother, wife, or children again. Worse, running away endangered those left behind, who might bear the brunt of a slaveholder's aggression. At the same time, Baltimore slaveholders exploited family ties in conjunction with term slavery and their willingness to sell slaves into freedom for the right price. For example, when a term slave gained freedom (usually in his or her thirties), a key incentive to work diligently for wages in Baltimore was the opportunity to purchase the freedom of a spouse, son, or daughter. Maryland's laws did not prevent free people of color from buying slaves and manumitting them, nor were provisions enforced in Baltimore that required the recently manumitted to leave the state. In 1811, for example, Cornelius Cole liberated his wife, Debbie, and their children, Robert and Maria, by paying $200 to the merchant Peter Levering. Another Baltimore free man of color, James Ackerman, paid $120 to a Calvert County widow to free his wife, Susan, and their four-month-old daughter, Sarah. In 1807, Cato Haynes, a free black laborer who had worked on mixed-race city construction sites since the 1790s, had purchased his daughter, Elizabeth, and his two granddaughters, Anne and Ellen, from General Charles Ridgely of Hampton.[46]

If Equillo had found himself on the opposite side of a sawhorse from a man like Haynes, he might have imbibed important life lessons. Would the older man counsel patience to the younger one? Would the older man recount his tale with regret and advise Equillo not to make the same mistakes? As he worked alongside free men of color who had liberated their own family members, Equillo surely observed that freedom was not impossible for slaves in Baltimore. Short of running away, that prospect depended on negotiating with William Goldsmith and on whether the slaveholder could be convinced to give Equillo an incentive to work harder. For example, some slaveholders allowed slaves to keep whatever they earned above a set amount each week or month. If combined with the prospect for self-purchase, a slaveholder could reap a huge return—say, $200 a year in wages, and another $200 toward purchase price. Once free, a man or woman might continue to remit wages to the slaveholder, this time to purchase a son, daughter, or spouse remaining in servitude.

But what if the slaveholder refused to consider a self-purchase arrangement? How then could a slave like Equillo bring his owner to negotiate? One possibility was by attempting to escape, or even disappearing for a few days or weeks in Fells Point or some other crowded urban neighborhood. Knowing that a slave was contemplating escape, a slaveholder might begin to worry about incurring a large financial loss; after all, a disappeared slave was worth nothing. Selling the slave off might be prudent, but by running away the slave had already lowered his or her market value. Buyers offered far less for slaves known to be difficult. Plus, slaves typically made far bolder attempts at running away when explicitly threatened with sale.[47]

It was here that slaves found their negotiating power. They could guarantee their owner a greater financial return by working toward self-purchase. A slaveholder would reap a decent return from the slave's wages but also have a guaranteed purchaser lined up, one with the greatest self-interest in completing the deal and for whom no price was too high. Because self-purchase arrangements typically worked on installments, a slave who had already put down $100 of his $200 purchase price was unlikely to risk the half-completed deal on a tenuous escape. For these reasons, once a slave proved him- or herself capable of flight, slaveholders had an interest in protecting their investment by assenting to a self-purchase agreement or a delayed manumission (since term slaves typically did not run away either). Although it is difficult to prove that Baltimore slaves purposefully disappeared in order to gain negotiating leverage, such a sequence of events was common.[48]

Equillo probably knew other Baltimore slaves whose owners hired them out to urban employers. At the same time that Equillo was sent to the New Bridge, another teenaged slave, David Booz Duppin, was beginning to garner wages for his owner by blacking boots. Managing his own time and work schedule, Duppin cultivated his manners, became a devout Methodist, and ultimately made plans to flee from slavery altogether. When Duppin finally escaped in 1818, his owner described him as a "sensible, intelligent, and considerably educated" man. More to the point, Duppin had "plenty of money." So too did an African-born slave named John, who fled Baltimore just a few months before work began at the New Bridge. "He had money with him," reported John's owner. When slaves gained some control over the wages they earned, freedom was typically not far behind. From the enslaved blacksmith Gabriel (the supposed leader of the Richmond slave insurrection of 1800) to the enslaved ship caulker Frederick Douglass in 1830s Baltimore, access to money facilitated both a higher standard of living and a greater critique of the fundamental injustices of slavery. For Douglass, living in a manner approximating freedom made freedom's denial that much more objectionable and fed his desire to liberate himself.[49]

Within the inherently exploitative setting of slavery, hiring out might nonetheless appear to be an opportunity rather than a curse for a young man like Equillo. Perhaps he had known some of the de Volunbrun slaves from Saint Domingue, who, according to their frustrated owner, "assume the appearance and conduct of free people, although they are slaves." After a number of years of incurring debts his slaves had accumulated with storekeepers and landlords, de Volunbrun finally promised to "prosecute with the utmost rigor of the law, any person who shall enter into any agreement with them." No Baltimore slave conveyed the transformative possibilities of hiring out better than another teenager who worked in the city about a decade after Equillo went to the New Bridge. Isaac Chambers was a thin, smooth-faced nineteen-year-old, who most recently was working for a waterfront grocer. Before that, his widowed owner had hired Chambers to a nearby tavern, where he cared for patrons' horses and gained experience waiting tables and cooking. Perhaps it was here, "at the sign of the Three Tuns," that Chambers met the freckled, sandy-haired English woman who would become his companion. The two contemplated a transatlantic escape and were thought to be seeking passage to England. Chambers' owner, Susanna Bowen, was outraged, of course, but her reward advertisement allowed Isaac Chambers to speak the words that many slaves thought but few had the opportunity to put into print. Stating his intentions, Isaac Chambers had declared, "this country was not fit for a black man to live in."[50]

Being hired out was certainly not always a blessing, and many slaves suffered new indignities and greater physical danger from employers who were not their owners. Those who rented slaves could marshal all the compulsion of slavehold-ing but avoid the obligations or financial risks of actual ownership. To that extent, some slave renters proved quicker to resort to physical violence and stingier in the rations they provided. Because hiring slaves was frequently an option for em-ployers too poor to own slaves outright, some renters had no previous experience in managing slaves and brought with them delusional notions of their own mas-tery; abuse often followed. Other slave renters cheated slaves out of their wages, especially when slaves had hired their own time and collected their own earnings. A jilted slave could not sue for back wages, because Maryland law denied slaves the right to contract or the ability to testify against white citizens. Rented slaves whose owners lived outside the city were particularly vulnerable to mistreatment, while slaves with local owners had some recourse if abused on the job. If Chris-tian Baum had denied Equillo food and drink at the New Bridge, Equillo could complain to William Goldsmith, who presumably would intervene on behalf of his valuable property. Equillo could not sue Baum, but Goldsmith could. With Gold-smith likely collecting Equillo's wages directly, Baum would have been kept hon-est in his payments. But this was surely no consolation to Equillo, and may have been the worst aspect of being a hired slave—watching someone else collect the cash he had earned. A few decades later, as Frederick Douglass turned his earn-ings over to Hugh Auld, he equated a master's right to such wages with "the right of the grim-visaged pirate upon the high seas."[51]

Even though William Goldsmith consigned Equillo to the pumps at the New Bridge, there were still ways in which Equillo's choices mattered. Given the large demand for rented slaves, a seventeen-year-old slave could have been hired to clean stables, roll cigars, or serve as a deckhand on a Chesapeake Bay packet. Presum-ably, Equillo could decide when to show aptitude for certain kinds of work, or when to feign incompetence for others. By dropping a tray, Equillo could help assure that he would not be rented out again as a waiter. Because Goldsmith sought Equi-llo's wages, the slaveholder had every incentive to place his slave in a position that would maximize returns. To stress the ability of enslaved men and women to shape these outcomes is not to depict slavery as a consensual or contractual institution wherein slaves and owners negotiated as equals. But the contours of slavery in Baltimore attested to certain compromises on the parts of slaveholders, who di-vested themselves of their absolute property rights.

Consider the Baltimore slaveholder who advertised a twenty-six-year-old woman for sale in 1809 but added, "She has a husband in the city, therefore, none need apply that don't want her services at, or near this place." What accounted for this concession, if not some leverage that the woman gained over her owner in the course of their interactions? Remarkably, such advertisements became increasingly frequent in the coming years. In 1816, auctioneer Samuel Cole offered "A valuable Negro girl," but stipulated "on no account will the purchaser be permitted to carry her out of Baltimore county." After singing the praises of his two enslaved teenagers to prospective buyers, another seller warned they "will not be sold out of city." Of the sixty-nine slave sale advertisements placed in the *Baltimore Patriot* during 1816, nearly half (thirty-one) refused out-of-state buyers. Such restrictions were most often attached to slaves-for-life and were common enough that one seller of a male slave made sure to mention explicitly, "the purchaser is at liberty to take him out of the state." Perhaps the most telling advertisement came from a Baltimore slaveholder selling two enslaved women: "They will not be sold to any person who will take them out of the city, or sell them without the same, without their consent." Of all the words associated with enslavement, *consent* is not one of them, and perhaps the word is meaningless in the context of legal bondage. But the frequency of concessions in advertisements suggests that Baltimore provided a setting in which enslaved people like Equillo could nonetheless help determine the pace and place of their labor.[52]

Such room to maneuver may have done little to alter Equillo's daily routine of working to create wealth for someone else. In fact, Equillo might have been particularly anxious about being sold out of state, insofar as slave purchasers offered the highest prices for young men in their physical prime. On average, someone like Equillo might fetch over $300 in Baltimore's slave market. Slaveholders were especially prone to sell when the market for rented slaves contracted. Just a few months before Equillo went to work at the New Bridge, an enslaved teen like himself had been sold "for no fault, but for want of employ." Some of Equillo's contemporaries had already been sold to the farthest regions of the United States. Early nineteenth-century property records from New Orleans featured the enslaved butler Jacob Stephen, a *"natif des environs de Baltimore,"* and the lumberman Jacques, a *"Creole de Baltimore."* Knowing other slaves who had been sold, Equillo would have had many reasons to reassure William Goldsmith that the greatest financial returns were to be found in renting him out, rather than in selling him.[53]

For that to be true, however, Equillo would have to work diligently. This is why slaveholders always retained the upper hand. Their access to the coercive violence of the slave market proved effective in generating profit. Equillo remained working on New Bridge through the end of April 1810. He toiled under the supervision of Christian Baum for 129 days, each one bringing another dollar to the Goldsmith family.

Christian Baum, an Entrepreneurial Carpenter

Having traced the paths that brought Equillo, James Richardson, and Aaron Bunton to the New Bridge, one still faces the question why Christian Baum—or any Baltimore employer—wanted them all there. In a boomtown economy that legitimated the quest for profit, mixed-race job sites clearly served the interests of the city's employers. In an economy that offered apprenticed teens for indenture, recent European immigrants for terms of servitude, and enslaved African Americans for life or for shorter durations, employers readily invested capital in laboring bodies and then relied on coercive mechanisms to compel work from the reluctant. But that same economy offered a range of workers whose labor could be purchased on an ad hoc basis, without requiring any investment of capital whatsoever. From an employer's perspective, the ideal situation combined the coercion of bound labor with the flexibility of free labor. By utilizing diverse workers in the same setting, Baltimore employers were able to marshal the labor they desired without sacrificing the dynamism necessary to erect a new city.

Mobilizing labor in Baltimore was not merely a function of microeconomics, but was also a product of the micropolitics of difference. Employers focused on the way that legal and social differences translated into specific power over workers of varying race, sex, ethnicity, age, and legal status. Ascriptive (or socially constructed) categories like race or gender gained a concrete reality as they determined a worker's legal standing, access to economic opportunity, and ability to opt out of labor altogether. Some workers could protect their wages in the courts, limit their hours with appeals to community standards, and even punish their employers through the ballot; other workers could do none of those things. Some workers could be physically coerced to work harder or punished for quitting early or breaking a tool. Some workers had a reasonable chance of accumulating enough productive property to withdraw from wage labor, while others faced insurmountable structural barriers to economic self-sufficiency. Whether through law, culture, or social practice, some workers were "available" to be paid less and worked more. Employers could take advantage of preexisting inequalities that facilitated such distinctions; in turn, their collective hiring decisions could serve to reify and entrench those inequalities.[54]

Race, gender, age, ethnicity, and legal status structured Baltimore's labor market in unpredictable and inconsistent ways. Employers did not necessarily go straight to the least free and most vulnerable workers in the city. Instead, employers had to consider the political consequences of hiring women for a job that had previously been done by men or the financial burden of investing their capital in en-

slaved workers. Employers had to evaluate whether the greater power they possessed over enslaved workers could compensate for the risk of investing their capital in labor that could run away. They had to ask whether the ability to hire and
fire free workers at will was worth the risk that none of them might be available
at the key moment when they were needed the most.[55]

On the one hand, Baltimore had an uncommonly high number of equal-
opportunity employers (to be perverse) who labeled no work beneath the dignity
of white skin, degrading to women, insulting to a free person, or unsuited to a
child. For employers who were interested in mobilizing common labor as cheaply
and rapidly as possible, there were few advantages to a segmented job market that
declared some work fit only for women, for children, for blacks, or for slaves, and
other work as the prerogative of native-born white men. On the other hand, in
their theoretical willingness to hire any worker for any given job, Baltimore employers drew careful distinctions among workers from across the spectrum of ages,
racial designations, ethnicities, and legal statuses. Employers spent much time
thinking about the composition of their workforces but reached no consensus as
to who should work where.[56] As a result, most low-end manual labor in Baltimore
would involve workers of diverse backgrounds, with the New Bridge construction
crew in 1809 more typical than exceptional.

Efforts to change the racial composition of a particular workforce through legislation almost never came to fruition. In 1798, for example, thirteen brickyard
owners asked the city council for help in converting brickmaking to a white occupation. Black workers outnumbered white workers four to one in their brick-
yards, and white workers would stay farther away if a new ordinance enlarged the
standardized size of bricks. The owners contended that brickmaking's "extreme
hard labor" accounted for the racial imbalance of their workforce. If the toil could
be reduced, they argued, "it would encourage poor white men and boys to come
to the brickyard for implyment." They added that white-made bricks would "give
more satisfaction to buyer and seller." Converting to white labor was never so much
a priority for the brick manufacturers that they barred black workers or offered
higher wages to lure white workers. Yet their plea conveyed an interesting message about race. Rather than trying to enforce a color line to protect white workers from degraded labor, the brickyard owners hoped to entice more whites into
one of Baltimore's worst occupations.[57]

If city employers showed little interest in sparing white workers from menial
labor, they made even less effort to differentiate free men of color from enslaved
African Americans. The famed 1814 defense of the city revealed how easily free
and enslaved black men could be reduced to the same standing as available

"hands." As the British turned toward Baltimore in August 1814, Major General Samuel Smith called "all the Negroes fit to work" to build breastworks for the city. While white men trained in militia units, slaves and free blacks worked diligently to prepare the city's earthworks. There had initially been public fears that providing African Americans with spades and pickaxes was dangerous, especially in light of British enticements of freedom to slaves who fought against their American masters. Yet, military leaders in Baltimore remained optimistic that the city's African Americans would prove faithful. Colonel Lowry testified to Baltimore's Committee of Vigilance that the city's free people of color were "possessed of property and almost all zealous in their wish to preserve the city." Almost immediately, the city instituted a policy compelling free black men to work and slaveowners to hire out their slaves in exchange for 50¢ to 75¢ a day, plus rations of alcohol.[58]

The repulse of the British quickly became the most memorable event in the annals of Baltimore history. But as white chroniclers paid tribute to the bravery of Baltimore's fighting men, they denied African Americans public accolades for their role in the city's defense. In battle, the lowliest white manual laborer could proclaim his valor alongside his social superiors. In contrast, the conscription of black men of diverse talents and skills suggested that in the eyes of white Baltimore, all African Americans were fundamentally manual laborers.

Through the boom years of Baltimore's growth, employers never presumed themselves best served by a system of free labor in which all workers owned their own bodies and exchanged labor for a cash wage. To the contrary, the legal unfreedom of workers—whether apprentices, servants, or slaves—proved crucial to employers' plans. The use of such workers reflected not a premodern economy on its last legs, but a new capitalist economy's voracious demand for labor power.

Nowhere was this clearer than in Baltimore's manufacturing economy. Slaves made heavy contributions to the productive capacity of the city's artisan workshops until the late 1810s. As Stephen Whitman has found, the more capitalized an industry, the more likely it was to use slave labor. Where fixed costs were high, as in brickyards, bakeries, and shipyards, employers typically invested even more capital in bound laborers. Shipbuilder William Price owned more slaves than anyone else in the city.[59]

In industries requiring less capitalization, employers tended to increase their reliance on apprentice labor. Master cordwainers, coopers, and cabinetmakers were among the most ravenous consumers of apprentices, using them as cheap substitutes for wage-earning journeymen. Although most shoemakers took on only one or two young men, by the 1810s nearly 40 percent of apprentices in that trade labored in shops with at least five other indentured workers. Historian Charles

Steffen accuses the large-scale shoemakers like William Duncan and John Vernon of "cutting the heart out of the apprenticeship system while preserving its familiar form." Although indenture contracts retained traditional references to teaching apprentices reading, writing, and arithmetic, and providing paternal guidance, these obligations got lost in the transition to market production. Apprentices and masters negotiated cash payments in lieu of certain types of training or schooling. Advertisements for runaway apprentices suggest that masters had little invested in the traditional responsibilities of the familial craft workshop, but instead saw apprentices as a cheap and an easily replaced labor force. Whereas rewards of $40 and $50 had regularly appeared in the 1790s, token rewards became common after 1800. In 1809, Hugh Ingram's master sweetened the 6¢ reward for the twenty-year-old apprentice shoemaker by adding "a basket of leather shavens." John Davis, the president of the Washington Cotton Manufacturing Company, offered a mere 1¢ for the return of four boys who had disappeared from his establishment on the city's outskirts in 1816.[60]

Most notable in Baltimore's early republic manufacturing economy was the incorporation of diverse workers into the same productive processes. In the early 1810s, cabinetmaker William Camp had over twenty laborers in his workshop, including a dozen apprentices, several wage-earning journeymen, and three male slaves, including Ashberry, whose delayed manumission date was just five years away.[61] Owning slaves did not mean an employer excluded other kinds of workers from specific job sites, and many employers depended on a small group of slaves to provide constant labor and thus compensate for the high turnover rate among a larger cadre of free workers. This was the strategy of David McKim, whose Maryland Chemical Works proved one of the most successful endeavors in "industrial slavery" precisely because of McKim's ability to juggle free and enslaved workers in the rhythm of production. With free white workers prone to absenteeism, drunkenness, and no small sense of entitlement, McKim garnered his most productive labor from his fifteen slaves, especially those to whom he provided "overwork" opportunities to earn extra money toward self-purchase.[62]

Mixing coerced and free labor became even more common in the public works projects of the early nineteenth century. A visitor to the Chesapeake & Delaware canal in 1826 observed "2,500 men constantly at work, Irish, Dutch, Welsh, French, Swiss, and Negroes." A few years later, the managers of the Chesapeake & Ohio (C&O) canal returned to the increasingly obsolete system of indentured servitude by importing nearly 500 bound Englishmen to Maryland.[63]

One modern assumption about mixed-race labor has been its importance in keeping wages low. Employers could presumably depress wages—and especially the claims of free workers to higher wages—by holding the threat of replacement over free workers, or simply by stigmatizing the work itself by using "degraded" laborers like slaves and free men of color. However, mixed-race job sites in Baltimore did not feature wages lower than those of other kinds of employment. To the contrary, the $1 daily wage at urban construction sites was nearly double that paid for labor in the countryside, and a quarter higher than the grueling labor along the several Chesapeake canals. By the mid-1790s, common laborers were already making $1 a day. Where mixed labor may have proved advantageous to employers was in keeping that rate constant for three decades. Wages had started high but remained flat between 1790 and 1820. Because the price of labor was essentially fixed at $1 per day, the value of a day's work hinged on the prices of everything else, but especially food, housing, and heating fuel. Accordingly, real wages dropped during the first decade of the century, so the $1 a day that Cato Haynes earned in 1795 was worth about 85¢ when James Richardson was paid the same amount in 1809.[64]

Job sites like the New Bridge were not idyllic settings of racial harmony, where black men and white men, enslaved men and free men, shared an equality of last resorts and came to see themselves in common cause. As the visitor to the C&O Canal observed in 1826, "The Irish and Negroes are kept separate from each other, for fear of serious consequences." Keeping the peace required employers to make labor assignments that prevented the optimal use of worker expertise. Mixed-race payrolls indicate that although employers did not differentiate black and white common labor, they did reserve better-paying jobs for white employees. Enslaved and free African Americans did not appear on Christian Baum's New Bridge payroll among the craftsmen or carters earning higher wages. At the Northampton Iron Works, while slaves, white apprentices, and black and white free laborers all toiled in the adjacent forests cutting timber to burn in the furnace, black workers did not gain access to the more lucrative artisanal jobs as white workers did. Similarly, at the Maryland Chemical Works, David McKim put slaves and free white workers to the same unskilled tasks. Yet skilled slaves who held years more experience than transient white workers still could not hold supervisory positions.[65]

Patterns of upward mobility also attest to the barriers that kept African Americans in the lowest tasks but allowed some white workers to escape. White men sometimes moved up manual labor payrolls, starting out as common laborers, but then accumulating enough capital to purchase a horse and cart to garner a higher wage, and then eventually submitting their own bids to the city to complete new projects. Conrad Miller had gone from laborer to contractor between 1795 and 1810. In contrast, upward mobility for his initial co-workers Negro Sampson and Poe's James had meant purchasing their own freedom. But once free, they still lacked the opportunities available to a Conrad Miller. In a rare moment of sensitivity, Hezekiah Niles conceded that legal discrimination and public hostility kept African Americans from the "dreams of future independence which commonly lightens the white man's weary way and supports him in the severest drudgery and keenest privation."[66]

Christian Baum had begun pursuing those dreams long before he submitted a bid to the city commissioners to build the bridge over Jones Falls. By the time he was twenty-two in 1792, Baum was a member of the Carpenters Society of Baltimore. Having gained success as a carpenter and an architect, Baum resided on Green Street in Baltimore's Western Precincts. By 1810, eighteen people lived under his roof. Nine were white boys and young men, including his sons Christian and Samuel and a handful of apprentices and journeymen. His five daughters (Catharine, Margaretta, Mary Jane, Marian, and Jane) were surely kept busy cooking and cleaning for the men under the watchful eye of Baum's wife, Margaret. Two slaves (unidentified by sex or age in the census) rounded out the household. In 1815, Baum died "after a lingering illness," but he was able to meet his patriarchal obligations to his family even in death. His son Samuel inherited skills and tools to become a carpenter on his own account (though becoming insolvent in 1821), while the widowed Margaret lived in Baltimore for several more decades and continued to draw an income from the slaves her husband had left her. In this light, Baum, who earned his pay by the day and whose wage was only twice that of James Richardson, Aaron Bunton, and Equillo at the New Bridge, would nonetheless end his life having more in common with William Goldsmith.[67]

Baltimore employers never seemed to tire of fine-tuning their labor force and stating with ever-greater precision their desire for very specific kinds of workers. As one 1834 parody on their advertisements mocked: "WANTED—A man or youth between 17 and 40 years of age, whose hair is *Red*. Also a man not over forty five whose hair is *Grey*, or at least more grey than black—to whom a dollar a day will be given in an out door employment which will be easy." But for every advertisement that narrowed the range of possible workers, another expressed indifference: "WANTED—a good HAND, either black or white."[68]

In using mixed-race labor, Baltimore employers did not create a golden age where race did not matter. Employers had little allegiance to racial precepts that deemed certain work beneath the dignity of those with white skin, and Baltimore's demography assured that most menial tasks would fall to workers of European ancestry. Their goal was to mobilize as much labor as cheaply and rapidly as possible.

Even as Baltimore employers reached no consensus on who should work where, the crushing burden of slavery remained. While most of the men who worked on the New Bridge in 1809 soon fell out of the historical record, Equillo did not. His story offers a depressing coda to any study of the early republic labor market.

When William Goldsmith died in the early 1810s, his plans to support his wife's widowhood went into effect. Equillo and six other slaves brought Sarah a constant income. When the city assessor visited her Pitt Street residence in 1818, he valued Rachel, Equillo, Elisha, Matilda, Lucy, Abraham, and Zack at $560, although the actual market value of the six Goldsmith slaves was at least three times as much.[69]

Sarah died at the age of seventy-three in 1826, and some of her slaves then passed to her unmarried daughter. Another assessment in 1836 found Lucy and Elisha, both in their thirties, working to support Elizabeth W. Goldsmith. But not all of Sarah's slaves were passed to her daughter. In fact, the administrator of Sarah's estate, Joseph Foard, petitioned the courts in 1827 to liquidate some of the dead woman's property. The estate, according to Foard, consisted "in a considerable degree of articles perishable in their nature and of sundry negro slaves, who from their dissolute habits and ungovernable dispositions have been for a considerable time past, measurably useless to the heirs and are likely to become more so."[70]

Whether or not Equillo was "dissolute," he was a "perishable" commodity from the perspective of Foard: Equillo's value on the slave market would decline as he continued to age. Once the court granted Foard's petition, Equillo likely became one of Baltimore's disappeared black men, sold to the Deep South. The lifespan of a Baltimore slave could easily run from New Bridge to New Orleans, and this would have been a dreadful fate for Equillo. But for those he left behind, he was gone but not forgotten. Elisha and Lucy, the two slaves owned by Elizabeth Goldsmith, welcomed an infant boy in 1834. His name was Equillo.[71]

CHAPTER 3

Dredging and Drudgery

A day's work paid handsomely in Baltimore, especially relative to the daily wage for agricultural labor in the Maryland countryside or shipboard labor on vessels departing the Chesapeake Bay. But what maritime and farming jobs lacked in daily wages, they made up in the chance to string several weeks or months of continuous labor into a reasonable income. An ordinary seaman aboard a Baltimore ship might earn $22 to $35 per month. Few common laborers in Baltimore could count on twenty-two days of employment in any given month. The six-day workweek on the docks or urban construction sites rapidly dwindled to four or five when an unexpected thunderstorm descended on the city, the health inspector quarantined an inbound ship, or the building contractor called it quits at noon to attend an election picnic. Under the best circumstances, a job loading a ship or hauling bricks might last for only two or three days, after which time a laboring man would be searching for his next employer. A cold winter, a pestilent summer, a credit contraction in a distant market all brought sustained periods of forced idleness to day laborers. When stonemason John McNulty advertised for "a number of hands" in 1815, he promised "liberal wages and constant employment." This was an alluring combination—the best chance for a manual laborer to support himself in Baltimore's boomtown economy.[1]

"Constant employment" was much desired and seldom achieved in the space of any given month, let alone over the course of a year. The vagaries of the preindustrial urban economy almost assured that a wage-earning man would teeter, in the words of the nineteenth-century minister Joseph Tuckerman, "between partial self-support and constant and absolute dependence." In fact, the general understanding of wage labor in the early republic was as a temporary expedient for a young man or immigrant to earn enough money to acquire land and attain a more stable yeoman's competency. "A great object with a labourer ought to be to try and save a little out of the fruits of his labour, so as to advance him in the world," advised one guidebook for recent European immigrants. With abundant western lands presumably offering an escape to independence, day labor was not something from which men could, or should, make a life's work.[2]

Nonetheless, some men did make careers as day laborers in seaboard cities like Baltimore. Even city directories, weighted as they were toward merchants, manufacturers, and craftsmen, found some "labourers" among early republic householders. On Apple Alley in Fells Point, for instance, laborers Roger Jones and John Davis occupied small houses between those belonging to widow Mary Matson and the infelicitously named mariner Job Drown. But for every one hundred laborers included in the directories of the early 1800s, hundreds more gained no notice for their daily toil digging foundations or leveling streets. Most manual labor was short term and undocumented. On the occasion that employers kept records of their expenses, seldom did they list laborers by name. Instead, they simply specified the number of "hands" employed, alongside the feet of timber purchased or pounds of nails consumed. Accordingly, it remains difficult to find out who performed unskilled labor, let alone to gauge how regularly and for what price such men worked. Historians have found it nearly impossible to trace the free adult men who remained laborers for their entire working lives.[3]

A remarkable set of records from Baltimore provides the opportunity not only to learn the identities of one group of manual laborers, but also to assess their wage-earning ability over an extended period. The workers toiled on the mud-machine, the dredging apparatus that sustained Baltimore's commercial future. So much sediment flowed into the harbor from the expanding city that docks quickly became inoperative and ships regularly ran aground on their way in and out of the port. Only constant dredging kept Baltimore's harbor open. The mud-machine consisted of a floating barge on which horses turned a treadwheel connected to a windlass and a large scoop. Between ten and fifteen men crewed the mudmachine, guiding the scoop, driving the horses, and manning the scows that transferred hundreds of thousands of pounds of sulfurous muck to the periphery of the harbor each week. Many of the workers stood knee-deep in the water while shoveling debris in and out of the scows. The work was grueling, filthy, and unsuited to the virtuous habits of republican artisans. Without it, however, Baltimore's commercial prosperity would have ceased.

Because tax revenue funded the dredging, municipal officials kept a careful eye on expenses. Beginning in 1808, the superintendent of the mudmachine submitted a weekly payroll to the city register in order to be reimbursed for the wages he paid and the supplies he purchased. These records, 377 payrolls in total, ran from March 21, 1808, through the week of January 1, 1820. Although no records survive for 1812 and 1816, only eight weeks are missing from the existing ten years of payrolls. Whenever the mudmachine was busy, the payrolls identified the names of employees and specified the number of days each man worked and his wages. Filed week after week, these payrolls offer one of the best windows onto the world of early American wage workers.[4]

Lifelong manual laborers rarely figure in the labor history of the early republic United States. Scholars have primarily focused on female factory workers and male artisans, two groups whose confrontation with industrial capitalism generated a vital labor politics and the presumptive origins of American class consciousness. The standard narrative traces the demise of proud artisans and republican daughters into beleaguered wage earners struggling to protect themselves against profit-driven manufacturers. In contrast, the lives of men who unloaded ships, cut shingles, or worked the mudmachine tell a more prosaic, but no less important, story. Career manual laborers possessed no link to an idyllic past. Their encounter with wage labor predated the decline of the artisan workshop and the arrival of factories on the American landscape. Their labor had never been shrouded in the "art and mystery" of a craft, but had always been more dirty than dignified. They used archaic technologies, worked alongside animals, and relied on their own physical strength above all else. Like the canal diggers who transformed the American interior with their blood and sweat, urban day laborers present a more representative account of wage labor's potentials and pitfalls for working people in the early republic.[5]

The mudmachinists made up a central stratum of Baltimore's laboring population. They were not the most vulnerable workers in a labor market that included slaves, free blacks, women, and children. They were, however, typical unskilled laborers: owning no tools, they exchanged brute strength for cash wages. No customary rights provided them recourse for grievances, and the casual nature of their work denied them job security. Because their work changed very little during the course of the market revolution, the mudmachinists experienced no traumatic encounter with technology or the work-time discipline of the factory. The workaday routine on the mudmachine generated sore backs and broken arms, but no strikes for better pay and shorter hours. However, it is precisely the day-in and day-out nature of work on the mudmachine that makes it possible to assess the long-term prospects of a wage-earning laborer in the early republic city.

The Health of Baltimore Harbor

"Happily situated at the Head of the finest Bay in the world, and commanding the resources of a very extensive and fruitful backcountry, Baltimore may reasonably calculate upon attaining a pre-eminence among the commercial Cities of the Union." So observed mayor Edward Johnson in 1813. Boosters like Johnson exuded confidence that the city would perpetually link Maryland and Pennsylvania farms to the Atlantic market. Merchants bragged of their connections to ports the world over, as well as of the excellence of the sailing vessels produced in Baltimore's shipyards. Farmers eagerly carted or floated their wheat surpluses to the city's mills and purchased ready-made goods in Baltimore's numerous shops. The only threat to commercial prosperity, warned Johnson, was an "interruption in our navigation." The mayor was not worried about a blockade by British ships or a wintertime freeze. Instead, Johnson referred to the perpetual erosion and silting that filled the harbor and impeded maritime traffic. Already, large ocean-faring ships could not dock at the heart of the commercial district, where depths rarely surpassed nine feet. Instead, they had to unload on the periphery of the city, or anchor in the harbor and transfer goods to smaller craft for delivery. Even more alarming was the prospect of shoaling at the mouth of the harbor. Unless the city remained vigilant, the harbor's ill health could spell the end of what Johnson called Baltimore's "great advantages."[6]

Baltimore's harbor posed several navigational challenges. Ships first had to travel four-fifths the length of the Chesapeake Bay. Roughly fifteen miles past Annapolis, captains veered northwest into the Patapsco River, which was less a river than a wide inlet. The first important maritime landmark on the Patapsco was the quarantine hospital at Hawkins Point, founded in 1795. Sailing onward, captains were on the lookout for a narrow opening ahead to the starboard side, leading into the northwest branch of the river. Two important structures marked the entrance to the strait. On one side stood Fort McHenry, made famous in the War of 1812 and the national anthem. On the other side was the lazaretto, the quarantine barracks where incoming ships, their crews, and their cargo had to pass a health inspection. Baltimore's officials feared that cargoes of hides and coffee might carry disease to the city. They also worried that the ballast water in the holds of ships produced the "noxious effluvia" believed to cause yellow fever. During summer months and when fears of contagion were high, ships sometimes had to deposit suspicious cargo at the lazaretto before proceeding to the city. At other times, ships were quarantined for several days at the lazaretto to ensure that no one aboard was infected.

From a ship's deck, one could see the outlines of the city ahead. Although a few piers extended into the water, most of the surrounding land was undeveloped. Passing what would become Canton and Highlandtown on one side and Locust Point on the other, ships soon came upon Fells Point. A narrow peninsula, Fells Point offered deep-water docking on its east side. Mayor Edward Johnson called this area "the boldest, deepest, and consequently most valuable part of our Harbor."[7] Numerous trading firms set up warehouses in the neighborhood, but the center of commerce lay farther upriver. To get there, ships had to clear the underwater mud bar between Fells Point and Federal Hill. Deepening this channel was a major concern of the city's merchants, who had located their counting houses and private docks ahead in the inner harbor, called the basin.

From an ecological standpoint, the basin was a perilous location for a mercantile empire. "There is not perhaps on the face of the earth so many excellent situations for a sea-port as in this vicinity," observed William Priest, an English visitor to the Chesapeake in 1794. But unfortunately, added Priest, Baltimore was "fixed on the very spot where the town should not be." The water in the basin was too shallow, too stagnant, and too foul. On the east side of the harbor, a large marsh stood between Fells Point and Jones Falls. Into this muddy flat ran whatever collected in the gutters of Fells Point and Old Town, as well as runoff from several small streams and runs. City planners had worked hard to grade neighborhood streets in order to promote drainage and prevent pools of stagnant water from accumulating in residential areas. "There is much to be done in Old Town to place it in a proper state," advised health commissioner Adam Fonerden in 1801, "such as digging down some streets and alleys & raising others and making them even so that the water may run off." Yet the drainage was often unseemly and included excrement, kitchen scraps, and spoiled produce and meat cast off from the market. Patrolling the cove in 1809, Fonerden discovered "a collection of filth and sometimes dead animals." Not surprisingly, the cove was a major public health concern. Scientific men of Fonerden's day blamed yellow fever on a toxic miasma emanating from putrefying organic material in the shallow water; modern epidemiologists blame the mosquitoes that bred there.[8]

West of the cove, Jones Falls emptied into the basin. Jones Falls was not particularly deep and "may be anywhere forded without reaching above a horse's knee." It ran through the city at a width of at least sixty feet, its course contained by stone walls, piles, houses, and wharves. Along its fourteen-mile journey through hilly Baltimore County and into the city, Jones Falls carried a tremendous amount of sediment into the harbor. It passed by some of the most tilled acreage in northern Maryland, as well as the sites of numerous flour mills. The city's woodlots had stood on both sides of the falls, but those stands were harvested and converted to farms at the end of the eighteenth century. Deforestation, intensive farming, and mill construction contributed to massive erosion. Local historian Thomas W. Griffith explained in 1824 that rapid economic development accounted for the harbor's sedimentation problem "as improvements increase and the soil is loosened."[9]

Draining the most built-up part of the city, Jones Falls carried an assortment of detritus into the harbor, and shoals frequently accumulated at its mouth. Moreover, Jones Falls intermittently flooded, sweeping away bridges, houses, and trees. During a horrible "freshet" in 1817, the water rose to twenty-four feet near the jail and to ten feet at its intersection with Baltimore Street. Hezekiah Niles reported a frightening scene as "houses, horses, cattle, with many swine—carts, drays, and other carriages with perhaps thousands of cords of wood . . . articles of household furniture and mechanical industry, hogsheads and barrels of whiskey, flour &c. &c." rushed toward the harbor. He added that "on two or three occasions, *human beings*, were seen mingled in tremendous confusion, dashing against each other, and impelled with irresistible force!"[10]

West of Jones Falls was the inner harbor, where the bulk of commercial activity transpired. Thomas W. Griffith recalled that the area was called the basin "because it is a pond open on one side only and surrounded by hills which preserve much stillness on the surface of the water." The basin appeared to be shrinking thanks to the erection of several lengthy piers far into the water. In the 1790s, merchants Cumberland Dugan and Thomas McElderry built two matching 1,600-foot docks, said to imitate those found in Liverpool and Bristol and lined with three-story brick warehouses. The names of private developers and mercantile clans festooned the city's other docks: Spear's, Smith's, Bowly's, and O'Donnell's, to name only a few.[11]

The young William Darlington commented on the waterfront development when he visited Baltimore in 1803: "There is 8 miles length of wharf—when there is but 3 miles length of water in the Basin on a straight line!" But Darlington was not impressed because "the water in those docks is always in a bad state owing to its stagnation and quantity of filth thrown in them." Predicting "they will prove an abundant source of pestilential fever," Darlington labeled the docks "truly Nasty." He concluded these comments in his journal with a screaming declaration that the docks were "offensive to the olfactories of 'The Author'!!!!"[12] Darlington's revulsion rivaled the sarcasm of "A Dutchman" a decade earlier in a letter to the *Maryland Journal*. The correspondent accused wharf owners of taking "special care to prevent their waters from being disturbed." He opined that the "beautiful and substantial scum with which they are generally adorned must prevent every species of vermin that may generate below from ever appearing above the surface to annoy our fellow citizens."[13]

There was a great annoyance, however, and it was commercial: silting rendered the docks incapable of receiving oceangoing vessels and threatened the fortunes of the city's merchants. The dock that had berthed the frigate *General Green* during the War of 1812 in nine feet of water was soon after "entirely filled up." As merchants and mayors had warned time and again, soon "the Basin will be filled up and the navigation entirely destroyed."[14] John Barron first noticed that his "highly productive wharf" in Fells Point was imperiled in 1815, just as a new scheme for grading the neighborhood's streets discharged runoff directly onto his waterfront property. Once the "water was rendered so shallow that it ceased to be useful for vessels," Barron hired one of Baltimore's most prominent lawyers, David Hoffman, a founder of the University of Maryland School of Law, to sue the city for damages. Barron won a $4,500 decision, despite the arguments on Baltimore's behalf by another Maryland legal luminary, Roger B. Taney, the attorney general of the United States. A higher court reversed the decision on appeal, and not long after, the silt in Baltimore's harbor piled all the way up to the United States Supreme Court. Chief Justice John Marshall delivered a surprising opinion that negated Barron's ability to claim Fifth Amendment protection from loss of property without due process. Legal scholars remember *Barron vs. Baltimore* for its limitations on the applicability of the Bill of Rights in the states, but the circuitous jurisprudence that ultimately led to the Fourteenth Amendment all began with the perilous silting of Baltimore's harbor. Lawyers aside, this was a case for the mudmachine.[15]

The Birth of the Mudmachine

A decade before Baltimore had its own mayor or city council, its public officials began to combat the silting of the harbor. The state assembly created the Board of Wardens for the Port of Baltimore in 1783, naming five men to oversee the erection of public wharves, collect tonnage duties on inbound ships, and maintain the harbor. The appointees were familiar with the latest dredging technology, some of which was already in use in Baltimore. Flour merchants John and Andrew Ellicott employed a prototypical mudmachine with a scoop and a horse-turned windlass when they built a wharf at Pratt and Light streets in 1783. Collecting a duty of a penny a ton from ships entering and leaving the port, the port wardens purchased their own mudmachines in 1791 for £209. Other expenditures that year included £22 for "wharfing across the Falls to prevent Dirt and Sand washing into the Basin" and £37 to laborers and carters for "raising mud out of the Basin." Labor costs remained low because the port wardens had access to local prisoners. Instead of incarcerating convicts, Maryland courts sentenced felons to "making, repairing, or cleaning the streets or Basin of the City of Baltimore." Such work constituted punishment in more places than just Baltimore: the rulers of the Barbary States of North Africa set captive American and European sailors to dredging their harbors in these same years.[16]

Like the problem of cleaning the seeds from short-staple cotton, the problem of silting attracted the attention of early republic inventors. In an age of invention, tinkers, engineers, and entrepreneurs attempted to sell improved mudmachines to cities like Baltimore. Virginian Peter Zacharie reported that "I saw when I was in Baltimore many machines to clean the harbour, all of which were very complicated and easily put out of order." In contrast, Zacharie praised the "simplicity" of his machine "as it will only get out of order by time and wearing." Its operation was indeed straightforward: "a single man by walking in a hollow Wheel will raise a Spoonful, containing a ton of mud, whilst another Spoon, by the same Operation goes down, to take in a like quantity." The machine also included a 32-foot scow with a trap door so that "a single man will empty it [of mud] in one minute." Zacharie received the first American patent for a dredging machine in 1791 and attempted to gain a monopoly on mud in Baltimore. Zacharie's demands were steep: he would direct the operations for $300 per year in salary plus revenue from selling the mud to property owners seeking landfill; the city would provide him a site for disposing any unsold mud and furnish "as many men shall be necessary" to work the machine. The port wardens did not offer Zacharie a contract, instead paying Christopher Cruse £163 in 1793 "for himself and labourers." They did, however, pursue Zacharie's advice for raising money through a lottery. In 1792, the Maryland General Assembly authorized a lottery to raise $5,350 for "deepening and cleaning the harbor and Basin." For a $5 investment, one lucky winner walked away with the $4,000 grand prize.[17]

The port wardens continued to search for effective dredging equipment. In 1793, they paid tobacco merchant Adrian Valck £123 for "procuring a complete model of the machine used in Amsterdam for clearing their harbour." Returning from Rotterdam and Dordrecht, Christian Meyer described to the wardens an impressive machine operated by two men and a horse. English traveler William Priest witnessed "two enormous machines . . . on the Dutch plan" at work in the harbor in 1794. He predicted that soon the channel "will be sufficiently deep to admit the largest merchantmen to come up to the wharfs of the town." However, efforts in Baltimore remained halting through the 1790s. Mud raised from the harbor floor became the landfill on which merchants erected waterfront warehouses, but in 1800, mayor James Calhoun reported that the machine was in such disrepair that the city council should not fund its use.[18]

Shortly thereafter, the port wardens hired Captain Stephen Colver to use a machine he had patented in 1798 to deepen the harbor. Able to bring up twenty-five cubic feet of mud in every scoop, Colver's machine "appears to answer very well, and to have rendered considerable service to the navigation," according to the mayor in 1802. It also brought Colver a substantial income. The city paid him one cent for every cubic foot of dirt he raised. William Darlington observed this "singular contrivance to clear the mud" during his 1803 visit to Baltimore. "It is wrought by 2 or 3 horses and fixed on a floating pile—so that it can be moved to any part," he reported, adding that each scoop required "about 10 minutes, but they have frequent intervals of greater duration in order to shift their situation." Darlington concluded that despite the delays, "it is a handsome fortune for the proprietor."[19]

Finally, in 1806, the mayor and city council decided to buy out Captain Colver and bring dredging under direct municipal control. Their primary concern was fiscal: they hoped to shave at least $1,000 from the $5,800 they were paying Colver each year. In the first year of public ownership, the mudmachine raised almost as much as it had under Colver's supervision, but at a savings of $3,141—no small feat considering that changes in Maryland's criminal code ended prisoner labor in the harbor and forced the city to compete with other employers for workers. Aware that dredging "will be required for a number of years to come," the city council appropriated funds for new scows and a new machine built according to Colver's design in 1808. When the city became the proprietor of the mudmachine, the diggers and scowmen became government employees, and their weekly payrolls entered the public record.[20]

Watching over it all was Alexander McDonald, superintendent of the mudmachine. McDonald recruited the workers, housed some of them, monitored their labor, and totaled the scowloads of mud they brought up and delivered to shore each week. He hired carpenters and blacksmiths to repair the machinery when necessary, and he purchased the rye and hay that powered the horses to turn the windlass. Residing at the intersection of Ann and Aliceanna in Fells Point, McDonald had an excellent vantage from which to watch the sedimentation of the harbor. Because the surrounding streets were graded to drain down Ann Street, McDonald could easily contemplate the Sisyphean nature of his task every time it rained.[21]

"Entered the Channel and Commenced Digging"

Superintendent McDonald was a meticulous recordkeeper. Every week he submitted a receipt to the city for the work he and his men had performed in the harbor. Although his spelling was erratic, his careful management of wages would have impressed the most miserly merchant.[22] In early 1808, McDonald had experimented with paying workers by the number of loads they could deliver to shore, but he soon converted to wages measured by the day. A man who spent only one day on the mudmachine received $1.12½, whereas a man who logged five and a quarter days walked away with $5.90⅝. From the appearance of the payrolls, the mudmachine operated on a straight wage and employees "found" shelter, food, and liquor for themselves (or perhaps negotiated off the books with McDonald). McDonald occasionally offered workers overtime or the chance to perform odd jobs for extra cash. For example, Alexander McQueen earned a few dollars in March 1811 for repainting the machines and the scows before dredging commenced the following week. James Flaugherty, James Wallace, and Joseph Rassee each spent one and a half days bailing water out of the scows in March 1814. Thomas Foley supplemented his income by $1 a week during fall 1818 by guarding the mudmachines at night.[23]

Work on the mudmachine paid slightly more than the going rate for unskilled male labor in Baltimore. Between 1808 and early 1815, the wage was $1.12½ per day, making a full six-day workweek worth $6.75. Hands working for contractors elsewhere in the city generally earned $1 per day, a rate that had been standard since the late 1790s.[24] Mudmachine employees earned a significantly higher wage than did men in the countryside. Farm hands and canal diggers made between 40¢ and 75¢ per day (usually through monthly or seasonal contracts), and take-home wages could be even lower after deductions for room and board.[25] In June 1815, the standard wage on the mudmachine increased to $1.25, as McDonald introduced a new graduated pay scale that made the top wage $1.37½ per day. The wage increase might have owed to a boom in the demand for maritime and construction labor during the summer of 1815. As jobs abounded in the wake of peace and the reopening of Atlantic commerce, McDonald needed higher wages to attract workers. The high rate of turnover on the mudmachine that summer suggests that laboring men found better opportunities elsewhere.[26]

When the number of available workers was abundant, however, McDonald could bring wages down or graduate his pay structure. In 1817, the city council gave McDonald the task of filling up the marshy land between Fells Point and Jones Falls, known as the cove. McDonald now directed a much larger operation than before, employing at least twenty men at a time, both on water and on land. The men who operated the mudmachine generally earned $1.18¾ per day, whereas those unloading dirt from the scows garnered $1.12½ per day, and those carting mud on land only $1 per day. When this project ended, McDonald returned the payroll to a standard wage of $1 per day, rising to $1.06¼ in July 1818, and then remaining at that level for the next year and a half. The economic contraction gripping Baltimore at the end of the decade allowed McDonald to lower wages without fearing the loss of employees. Men clung to their jobs in the panic year of 1819, with one-quarter of mudmachine employees staying six months or longer. In contrast, only one-ninth of workers remained put for that long during the 1815 boom.

For an unskilled male laborer, the difference of a few cents in wage rate was less important than the number of days he could string together. The primary virtue of a mudmachine job, then, was its constancy. Most other manual labor jobs ended with the completion of a given task. Men who unloaded ships rarely spent more than a few days in the employ of the same person. Unskilled laborers usually scrambled to piece together short-term jobs, but men tolerant of wet and dirty work could find a reliable source of income on the mudmachine. It dug week in and week out, because sedimentation paid little heed to market demand, credit contractions, and business cycles—all things that cut employment short in other sectors of the economy. The mudmachine did not produce a volatile market commodity, but performed labor that city officials deemed an essential public good. Annual budget appropriations in the tens of thousands of dollars kept the mudmachine working year in and year out.

Nonetheless, its employees were not guaranteed full weeks of work, nor could they assume year-round employment. The weather set the mudmachine's digging schedule, with ice, snow, and thunderstorms curtailing the number of annual workdays. Most significantly, the mudmachine sat idle each winter.[27] Operations ceased the week of Christmas and did not resume until at least March. The first week of digging did not arrive until April in 1813 and in 1814, and not until May 24th in 1809. During those winter months, Alexander McDonald received a daily stipend of $1 (half his usual pay) "for attending the mud machine scows and horses while not digging." As of 1814, McDonald began receiving a weekly salary of $12.50 for the entire year. His employees were not so lucky. They could not count on support during the winter months and were left to find other work (most of which disappeared each winter), solicit charity, or live upon meager savings. Mudmachine employees joined the ranks of numerous other laborers who required wintertime relief from public officials. Not until 1819 did the machinery become sophisticated enough to keep workers dry and therefore working throughout the winter.

Because of the winter furlough, mudmachine employees rarely found more than forty-one weeks of work each year. However, the weather eliminated workdays at other times in the year too. For example, the crew failed to log a full six days of labor during eight of the seventeen weeks between April 19 and August 21, 1814. The Fourth of July was an unpaid holiday. The sickly season in late summer also brought a halt to dredging in years when yellow fever appeared in Fells Point. The mudmachinists (again with the exception of superintendent McDonald) lost their jobs in August 1808 and August 1819. The latter outbreak was particularly deadly, killing some 350 Baltimore residents. Of the twenty-four mudmachinists employed before the epidemic arrived, fifteen did not return to work in October. They may have perished or found other work to sustain themselves in the interim. War could also interrupt the digging schedule, and the impending British attack on the city put a stop to the mudmachine's operations in August 1814. Work did not resume until March 1815, leaving employees to fend for themselves for six entire months. Half the men working just before the war did not return with the peace. Just as surprising in the wake of the nation's victory in a second war for independence, half the men did.

The vast majority of men who worked on the mudmachine did not last a month. The culture of transience in the early republic offers one explanation of the high rate of turnover. The first decades of the nineteenth century witnessed tremendous physical mobility, as young men left the countryside for new cities like Baltimore, and then set out for even greater possibilities in Frederick, Cincinnati, Lexington, Rochester, and countless other places that had barely been on the map a decade or two earlier. European immigrants were advised to land in Baltimore, work for a stretch, and then depart for inland destinations. "A person who comes to America is most likely to succeed by moving from the sea-ports, they being very full of people," advised Englishman John Woods. "Labourers in agriculture and many trades are sure of work in the Western country." Of course, pursuing new opportunities elsewhere required more money than most working men had in their pockets, but a general spirit of restlessness assured that most mudmachine employees would move frequently.[28]

Most workers left the mudmachine almost as soon as they arrived for a more specific reason: the work was disgusting and dangerous. "Who could endure the odours of the mud thrown out in warm weather upon the wharves?" asked a newspaper editorialist cursing the mudmachine's unsightly presence in the harbor. The payrolls offer some indication of what the labor entailed. For April 5, 1814: "Digging with handscoops at the End of Bowly wharf." For May 15, 1815: "Digging the bar with shovels in low water." For May 17, 1817: "collecting Logs and shoveling mud on the block." A complex system of pulleys, chains, and other moving parts, the mudmachine could consume people. A worker was killed in 1816, and a few years later, George Whitten "had the misfortune of having one of his hands

Annual days of employment on the Baltimore mudmachine, 1808–1819

Duration of labor (days)	Employees % (N=486)
One week or less (6 or fewer)	28 (135)
One week to one month (7 to 24)	24 (117)
One to two months (25 to 50)	12 (60)
Three to four months (51 to 100)	11 (54)
Five to six months (101 to 150)	7 (36)
Seven to eight months (151 to 200)	9 (46)
Nine to ten months (201 to 250)	5 (26)
Eleven to twelve months (251 or more)	2 (12)

Note: Percentages do not total 100 due to rounding of figures.

wounded by the machinery in the discharge of his duty." Countless other workers surely suffered from sunburn, heatstroke, and frostbite. Inventor Peter Zacharie lamented that the scowmen were "obliged to be in the mud up to their knees." He also proposed that the men "might have a little stove to warm their fingers now and then."[29]

McDonald does not appear to have provided the alcohol that kept most early American laborers warm. His meticulous payrolls recorded exactly how much feed his horses consumed but did not list expenses for liquor. Only once did a gallon of whiskey appear on McDonald's weekly bill to the city; that gallon could hardly have gone far among the fifteen laborers employed during the Jones Falls flood of August 9, 1817. When Captain Colver had directed the mudmachine in the early 1800s, he spent 62½¢ a day on liquor for his four men, or nearly the wages of a fifth worker. Daily rations of between a pint and a quart of whiskey came to an annual expense of $112.50. During the fortification of Baltimore in 1814, merchant Isaac Phillips advised public officials to provide "a reasonable quantity of grog" to the workers. At Ferry Point, military authorities served their hands 135 gallons of whiskey. The absence of this common perquisite and necessary anesthesia on the mudmachine may have contributed to the short tenures of most employees.[30]

Few workers had the stomach or the strength to come back day after day. Only 17 percent of employees (84 of 486) logged more than six months of work (151 days) in a given year. Despite holding jobs that minimized the perils of casual labor, the most dedicated mudmachinists still needed to locate additional employment for part of the year. When Hugh McKenzie and Robert McFarlan labored for McDonald on shore during the winter of 1817, they became the only employees to spend 300 days of a year on the mudmachine payroll. McKenzie and McFarlan were also part of a small cohort of workers who surpassed $150

Annual incomes on the Baltimore mudmachine, 1808–1819

Annual income	Employees % (N=486)
Below $10	32 (157)
Between $10 and $49	30 (146)
Between $50 and $99	12 (56)
Between $100 and $149	8 (38)
Between $150 and $199	7 (32)
Between $200 and $300	10 (47)
Above $300	2 (10)

Note: Percentages do not total 100 due to rounding of figures.

in annual income from the mudmachine. Men who earned $150 or more had several things working in their favor. First, they held their jobs during the peak wage year of 1815, when the standard rate was $1.25 per day. Second, they gained the higher wages of supervisory positions, making as much as $1.37½ per day. Third, they remained on the payrolls during the idle months, performing labor on land for below-normal wages. Finally, they worked during 1819, the first season without a wintertime layoff. Some workers managed to do all four things. Malcolm McPherson earned over $200 in seven of the eight years he was a mudmachine employee.

Men like Malcolm McPherson were a mudmachine elite. Indeed, the employees who logged the most days, garnered the higher wages, monopolized the winter work, and earned the most money tended to do so year after year. Between 1808 and 1819, superintendent McDonald paid out yearly wages above $150 on eighty-nine occasions; only fifty-two different men were lucky enough to be on the receiving end. Lachlin McLean, Mickel Gorman, and Alexander McQueen each earned over $150 in four separate years. James Flaugherty pulled in that much five times, topping $301 in 1815. All told, twenty-one workers distinguished themselves by working in multiple years and by earning above $200 in at least one of those years.

The surnames of the mudmachine elite point to the predominance of Scotch-Irish and Irish workers. The same held true among the casual workers who logged only a week or two on the job. Among the twenty-two men listed for the week of June 19, 1815, were Malcolm McPherson, Angus McDonald, Robert McFarlan, Hugh McKenzie, Lachlin McLean, James Flaugherty, Hugh Eggin, Hugh Cocklin, and two John Doughertys. Many of these surnames trace specifically to the northern counties of Ireland: Donegal, Antrim, Londonderry, Down, and Tyrone. To be sure, the majority of mudmachine employees bore less-distinctive surnames of English or Scottish origins: Anderson, Johnson, Smith, White, Williams, and

Baltimore mudmachine elite, 1808–1819

Employee	Payroll years	Years above $200	Highest income
John Calder	1810, 11	2	$238.21
Brian Dillon	1809–1811	2	$241.59
James Flaugherty	1809–1811, 1814, 1815, 1817, 1818	4	$301.34
Michael Gorman	1813, 1815, 1817–1819	1	$279.59
James Kerby	1815, 1817, 1818	1	$229.25
Duncan McBean	1818, 1819	1	$275.87
Angus McDonald	1810, 1811, 1815	3	$242.50
Robert McFarlan	1815, 1817, 1818	2	$362.56
Angus McIntosh	1810, 1811	2	$239.91
Hugh McKenzie	1815, 1817	1	$349.15
Alexander McLaughlin	1811, 1813	1	$230.60
Lachlin McLean	1815, 1817–1819	4	$349.31
John McPherson	1818, 1819	2	$252.75
Malcolm McPherson	1810, 1811, 1813–1815, 1817–1819	7	$345.87
Alexander McQueen	1808, 1809, 1811, 1814, 1818, 1819	3	$262.26
William Monroe	1817–1819	3	$325.16
John Otterson	1811, 1813–1815	1	$263.16
John Smith	1818, 1819	1	$289.87
James Stranoch	1818, 1819	1	$250.48
James Wallace	1809–1811, 1813, 1814	3	$238.77
John Woods	1813–1815	2	$225.25

Woods. Nonetheless, men with probable Irish and Scotch-Irish names far outnumbered those with names indicative of other ethnicities. Almost no distinctively German names appeared on the payrolls. In contrast, over 10 percent of the employees bore surnames beginning with "Mc," including the likes of Alexander McQueen, Duncan McBean, Angus McIntosh, and Archibald McCay. Another 20 percent featured ethnically Irish names, such as Mickel Barney, Patrick Connoly, John Fitzcharrel, and Hugh Murphy. When Englishman Joseph Pickering visited Baltimore in 1824, he observed "a number of Irish and Scotch clearing the bottom of the wharfs with horses and machines, and making new ones."[31]

As he watched the mudmachines at work, Joseph Pickering concluded that "Americans here do but little of the laborious work." This observation is more difficult to confirm, because surnames cannot reveal whether someone was native born or an immigrant. Certainly, many of the employees were immigrants, and in 1820, sixteen of the forty-one residents of superintendent Alexander McDonald's household were "foreigners not naturalized." Mudmachine employees did not appear on the militia muster lists during the War of 1812, which also suggests their status as recent immigrants. In fact, Owen Dougherty, David Dillon, and Michael Walsh (among others) helped build the fortifications for Baltimore's defense in 1814, a task charged to those exempt from militia service. Mudmachine workers who were institutionalized also left clues to their nativity. Archibald Smith's penitentiary record and Michael Gorman's almshouse admission both specify Irish birth. However, Richard (Dicky) and Zachariah Stallings's almshouse records indicate that father and son were both Maryland natives, and other mudmachinists were surely the American-born sons of immigrants.[32]

A more comprehensive social portrait of the mudmachinists is nearly impossible. Inconsistent spellings and nondescript names, coupled with the inherent marginality of unskilled manual laborers, make identifications more a matter of guesswork than certainty.[33] Only a handful of the mudmachinists ever appeared in the city directories, census rolls, or tax lists. In fact, fewer than ten employees of the mudmachine can be positively identified in any sources other than the payrolls.[34] To be sure, several John Smiths and John Woodses surfaced repeatedly, but none was ever described as a "labourer" or "scowman." Even men with distinctive names remained absent from the historical record. Malcolm McPherson surely earned enough to become a householder, but he appeared nowhere. Occasionally, there were lucky matches. For example, Owen Mullen had the descriptor "at mud machine" affixed to his name on the 1818 tax list. The troubling documentary absence of his co-workers, men who consistently garnered above-average wages, suggests that the standard sources of early republic social history lack comprehensiveness. Scholars who rely on such records to create occupational and wealth profiles risk excluding the bulk of a city's laboring population.

The lives of a few mudmachinists do tell longer stories. For example, the easily identified Owen Mullen had resided in Fells Point since at least 1814, when the directory listed him as a laborer on Bond Street. When the tax collector caught up with him in 1818, Mullen owned a small house on a lot that fronted only fifteen feet on Star Alley. His property amounted to $50, which made him prosperous enough to owe taxes but poor enough to fall into the bottom decile of wealth holders in his neighborhood. Mullen lived only a few blocks from mudmachine superintendent Alexander McDonald, and as a laborer he surely knew about jobs on the mudmachine. Mullen began working for McDonald in early 1817 (or potentially 1816, the year of the missing payrolls). Mullen earned $179 in 1817 shoveling out the scows, and another $84 for sixteen weeks of labor in 1818. The 1820 census found Mullen's household totaling six people, including three children under sixteen years old. Mullen himself was at least forty-five years old, as was a white female, presumably his wife. The final resident of the Mullen household was a free African American male between fourteen and twenty-six years old. This young man was likely a boarder, perhaps a relative of the neighboring African American families, the Sayers, Taylors, Caytons, and Browns. That the Mullens lived on

an alley surrounded by free black families suggests something of their own economic marginality.

Michael Gorman's life likewise testifies to the precarious existence of mudmachine workers. Gorman worked on the mudmachine in five separate years,
earning over $150 in four of them. He first appeared on the payroll in 1813, but
a Michael Gorman had surfaced in Baltimore twenty years earlier as a runaway
servant. Twenty-one when he ran away from his Philadelphia master Charles C.
Watson in 1793, the Irish-born Gorman fled to Baltimore alongside an Englishman named John Chapman. No sooner had they made it to Maryland than the
Baltimore sheriff apprehended and jailed them. A newspaper advertisement described the runaways, indicating that Gorman stood 5' 7", with dark brown hair,
and a thin visage "pitted with the smallpox." Gorman wore "a jean coat, black
satin waistcoat, nankeen breeches, cotton stockings, a pair of shoes with strings
and a high crowned hat."[35] It is not clear how Gorman escaped this predicament,
but he resurfaced in the 1810 directory as a scowman living on Aisquith Street
in Old Town. He was not a householder in that year's census, nor did he own
enough property to meet the city's $40 assessment minimum in 1813. In fact,
Gorman's $29 of property placed him on a list of householders specifically ex-
empted by virtue of poverty.[36]

In 1814, Gorman moved to Fells Point, taking up residence three blocks from
superintendent Alexander McDonald. Gorman purchased a tiny house on a sliver
of a lot on Wolfe Street. He had made his first appearance on the mudmachine
during the last few weeks of 1813 but found other work in the winter that prevented him from rejoining McDonald's crew later in 1814. When the British attacked Baltimore in September, Gorman worked on the city's fortifications at Fort
McHenry. Had Gorman been a native-born white, he would have served in the
militia. Instead, Gorman, along with other unnaturalized aliens and the city's black
male residents, fell under military compulsion to labor for Baltimore's protection.
Gorman's wartime service involved constructing defensive embankments out of
dirt—which undoubtedly prepared him for a successful return to the work of
dredging and creating landfill with the mudmachine in 1815. He was approximately
forty-two years old at that time.[37]

Gorman became one of the mudmachine's most diligent employees, logging
217 days in 1815; only two other men worked more. Missing only seven workdays
between June and December, Gorman gained access to a supervisory position
and the higher wages of $1.37½ per day. He tallied earnings of $279.59 that year.
Thereafter, however, Gorman's work on the mudmachine turned erratic. He missed
seven weeks of work in May and June 1817, sending him down to the lowest pay

rate of $1 per day when he returned later in the summer. He found work else-where for the first half of 1818 and remained the poorest (taxable) resident of his block of Wolfe Street. Unlike his neighbors, he owned no furniture or silver plate worth assessing; perhaps all his earnings went to support his family. When Gorman returned to the mudmachine later in 1818, he did so with newfound vigor. Between July 1818 and August 1819, Gorman labored for 326 of 354 possible workdays. After a yellow fever outbreak cut the 1819 season short, Gorman never reappeared on the payroll.

Gorman had not perished in the epidemic, but his demise was perhaps sad-der and certainly more prolonged. Gorman remained a resident of Wolfe Street, living there with his wife, Bridget. It is uncertain what work the Gormans per-formed in the early 1820s, but the value of their property declined back to $29 when the tax assessor returned in 1823. Later that year, some precipitous event sent Michael and Bridget to the almshouse. The institution's overseer character-ized Bridget as in "a state of mental derangement." Like Michael, she was Irish born and in her fifties. Bridget died after three months in the institution, and Michael never lived on his own again. He gained an unfortunate distinction as one of the longest-serving paupers in the almshouse. Described as a Catholic, a laborer, and a tobacco user in the official records, Michael Gorman died in Au-gust 1832 after 3,346 days in the almshouse, far longer than he had spent work-ing on the mudmachine.[38]

The mudmachine offered relatively steady wages, but they could disappear with alarming celerity and throw entire households into disarray. John and Jane Otter-son (often Auterson) were longtime residents of Baltimore. Their marriage likely dated to the 1780s, when both were in their early twenties. In the early 1800s, they resided near the waterfront on a block of Philpot Street that included six sea captains, six artisans, and two laborers (one of whom was John). The family's prospects for upward mobility seemed promising, especially once they appren-ticed their sixteen-year-old son, David, to a Fells Point shipbuilder. As his son pre-sumably learned craft skills, John Otterson worked as a day laborer. He gained a steady position on the mudmachine in summer 1814, but the work ceased with the outbreak of war. He, Jane, and the five other residents of the household (now situated on Happy Alley) needed to find another source of cash income until dredg-ing work resumed the following March. From then on, John brought home sub-stantial wages, totaling $263 in 1815. Nonetheless, they never accumulated enough property to appear on city tax lists. Perhaps they were headed in that direction, but that possibility ended when a chain on the mudmachine snapped and struck John dead in September 1816.[39]

After four months caring for four children "without any other means of support than her own industry," Jane Otterson petitioned the city council for a pension. She lamented that her wage-earning capacity was "far from procuring even for the necessary existence." With uncharacteristic generosity, the councilmen awarded her a one-time payment of $150 in light of the fact that John was killed "in the service of the city" and Jane was "now in a distressed situation." Shortly thereafter, Jane (now at least fifty-two years old) moved away from the waterfront to York Road on the city's northern boundary. But she and her children immediately fell out of the public record. Whether she remarried, resided with one of her married daughters, moved out of Maryland, or vanished into the city's impoverished population is unknowable. Regardless, the subsistent household the Ottersons established while John worked on the mudmachine disintegrated when he died.

Owen Mullen, Michael Gorman, and John Otterson were distinct because they established their own households. Most mudmachine employees did not. Some percentage of mudmachine workers lived in the households of their parents. Fathers and sons appeared together on the payrolls, such as Dicky Stallings and his son Zachariah in 1815.[40] The familial relationships among other workers with shared surnames are unknowable. Henry, Hugh, Lewis, and Thomas Griffin might have been strangers, or brothers, or three sons and a father. In general, most mudmachine workers were older, not teenagers on their way to better employment as they became adults. Hugh Coffee was in his thirties during his tenure on the mudmachine, whereas Michael Gorman, Owen Mullen, Dicky Stallings, and John Otterson were in their early forties. Wage labor appeared to work against adult white men establishing visible households of their own.[41]

Many mudmachine workers resided under McDonald's roof, which raises the possibility that he was an early republic padrone. Most of the thirty working-age men living in McDonald's Fells Point home in 1820 were immigrants. They may have arrived in Baltimore expressly to hook into McDonald's operation. In turn, McDonald may have supplemented his mudmachine income by charging his workers for lodging. He and his wife were the only residents of the household older than forty-five, while six girls and young women cooked and cleaned for everyone else. Charges for room and board did not appear on the weekly payrolls but were surely levied off the books. As with other bosses who oversaw employment on the waterfront, McDonald may have expected kickbacks. He was certainly no stranger to his workers. When former employee Archibald Smith faced a year in the penitentiary for stealing several blankets in 1814, McDonald came forward to vouch for his decency. "Archy" had once lived in McDonald's Ann Street house,

but he had not worked on the mudmachine since 1810. Still, McDonald could testify, "I can truly say I always found him an honest man."[42]

McDonald's influence over his men may have reached into electoral politics as
well. Once the franchise in Baltimore was expanded in 1818 to include nonprop-
ertied adult white men, the mudmachine became a political machine. Generous
funding for public improvements meant jobs for new voters, as the supporters of
mayor George Stiles were quick to tell "the Labouring Class of the Community of
Baltimore." In a rhyming electioneering broadsheet, they praised "our old mayor /
Who has done his full share / In cutting out work, for the carters and diggers /
The builders and riggers . . . / In fact the whole clan / Who can work to a man."
Stiles's opponents denounced the mayor for "filching money from the pockets of
the wealthy, to give employment to the indigent." Critics latched on to a proposed
$100,000 public expenditure to use the mudmachine to fill the marshy cove be-
tween Fells Point and Jones Falls. The true motive, they charged, was "to create
employment and preserve the health of an immense host of democratic tradesmen and laborers, who are so useful to [the mayor and his allies] at every returning election." Such accusations implicated McDonald in a system of political patronage, although the frequent change in mayoral administrations never seemed
to threaten McDonald's job. Nevertheless, enfranchised mudmachinists might
have had to think about their jobs before they cast ballots.[43]

McDonald's labor recruitment strategies are elusive, and only rarely did he advertise jobs. "Liberal wages will be given for a few more LABOURERS at the Mud
Machine," read an announcement in spring 1816. A few months later, McDonald
called for "a number of laborers . . . with whom contracts will be made either by
the job, day, week, or month." His second advertisement encouraged "owners of
stout, hearty *Slaves*" also to respond, but with the payrolls for 1816 missing, it is
impossible to know if he found any takers. One might imagine the hesitation of
slaveholding widows and merchants in renting their valuable property to labor
on the mudmachine. From the risk of injury from the machinery to the exposure
to disease, the mudmachine was a poor choice for a slaveholder trying to protect
the resale value of a working-age man.[44] Throughout the 1810s, the payrolls offer
little evidence of African American employment: no apostrophes as in "Goldsmith's Equillo"; no asterisks next to black people's names as in the city directories; none of the classical and diminutive names that typically marked slaves and
former slaves in the Chesapeake (Jem Lee, Nacy Oliver, Caesar Mayo, or Cato
Boyce); nor the assertive names of free people of color like Freeborn Rice.[45] Some
names on the payrolls matched African Americans listed in directories and tax
lists, but without enough information to be conclusive.[46]

McDonald's pay scales offer contradictory evidence about the presence of black workers. If one assumes that African American men were more likely to be shunted into the lowest-paying positions, then the five men who accepted a substandard wage of $1.12½ in 1815 deserve scrutiny: William Anderson, Henry Howard, George Washington, John Sebaston, and Sutton Boice. It was not likely their age accounted for the lower wage, because other payrolls show an occasional "boy" working for a mere 50¢ a day. They may have performed some lesser task, but the payrolls contain no notation. There were both black and white families with these surnames in Baltimore, leaving no conclusive way to establish the racial identity of these workers.[47]

On the other hand, if one supposes that African American men could never hold supervisory positions and earn higher wages than white co-workers, then Benjamin Enness presents a quandary. A Benjamin Enness earned a supervisor's wage of $1.37½ per day on the mudmachine in 1815. City directories show several white families with the surname Enniss, but also a free African American laborer named Benjamin Enness, who resided on Federal Hill. If this man worked on the mudmachine, then his supervisory position runs counter to the bulk of contemporary testimony as to how race organized labor in the nineteenth century. This question deserves further interrogation, but such a project requires more certainty than Benjamin Enness's identity will allow.[48]

Even if the mudmachine did have a handful of black workers, it remained an overwhelmingly Irish and Scotch-Irish endeavor. Indeed, the operation smacked of clannishness, especially considering the repetition of certain last names on the payrolls. Family relations may have been at the center of Alexander McDonald's recruitment strategy, which in turn reinforced Scotch-Irish dominance. During Malcolm McPherson's eight-year tenure on the mudmachine, seven other McPhersons—Alexander, Andrew, Angus, Duncan, Evan, John, and Philip—appeared on the payroll. James, Martin, Timothy, and John Craney worked together in late 1818. The Doughertys on the mudmachine in 1815 included Owen, Rodney, and two Johns.

In turn, families may have considered a spot on the mudmachine a valued possession. Kinsmen spelled one another during absences, lest the position fall into other hands. The Doughertys coordinated their labor to keep the job within their family. When mudmachine veteran John Dougherty missed the week of July 17, 1815, Owen substituted. The following week, John returned, and Owen fell off the payroll. But John made it up to Owen a few weeks later. John Dougherty left the mudmachine altogether, and his full-time replacement was Owen. Alexander Mikelhenny missed a week in April 1811 but could return the following week be-

cause John Mikelhenny substituted in the interim. Between fall 1818 and summer 1819, Alexander and John Watson virtually shared the position, alternating
six times.[49]

Employment for the Laboring Man

"The most important and valuable interests of the City—indeed its very existence—is involved in the preservation of the navigation of the Harbour," declared
mayor John Montgomery in 1825. The mudmachine was now more important
than ever, especially as "thousands of loads of sand and gravel" washed down Baltimore's streets and threatened to wash away the city's future. Baltimore had only
recently emerged from the Panic of 1819, and resuming commercial prosperity
depended on sustaining maritime traffic to the port. For the merchants of Baltimore's counting houses to get their shirts back, the mudmachinists would have
to take theirs off, get in the water, and dig.[50]

The great civic concern for the harbor did not extend to the circumstances of
the mudmachinists themselves. Calls for fiscal retrenchment in the aftermath of
the Panic of 1819 targeted the city's career manual laborers. Thomas W. Griffith
advocated replacing the mudmachinists with convict labor. Prisoners had been
common in the harbor only twenty years earlier, but the opening of the Maryland
Penitentiary in 1811 removed convicts from public view. Griffith saw this as a failure in penology. "The hulks and galleys of Europe" had once terrified all who saw
them, but the penitentiary failed to inspire fear in the hearts of would-be criminals. Griffith proposed for prisoners to work and sleep on the mudmachines in
plain view of all law-abiding citizens. Lest anyone believe this punishment too cruel,
Griffith pointed out that many "honest and worthy citizens" presently worked on
the mudmachine by choice. Under his plan, the state would profit by renting the
labor to the city, and the city would in turn save thousands of dollars in wages.
The only losers would be the mudmachine employees, but Griffith had "a word
to say" on their behalf. Should they be "deprived of work or obliged to take less
wages because the public have chosen to give trades to monsters or rogues," it
would constitute "an evil which cries aloud for redress." That was Griffith's last
word on the subject.[51]

Such a plan never came to fruition, but municipal savings arrived through a
drastic wage cut. The idea for a 75¢ daily wage originated in the office of mayor
John Montgomery, at least according to those who called him "the poor man's op-
pressor." Allegedly, the mayor wanted to lower the wage further. "Is there a man
who knows the toil and exposure of the city labourers, Mr. Montgomery excepted,

that would have the conscience to wish a poor fellow to labour all day upon the Mud Machine up to his middle in unhealthy mud and water . . . for the trifling pittance of sixty-two and a half cents?" asked one election-season polemic in 1822.[52] Over the next five years, wages fluctuated between 75¢ and 87½¢ per day. Although the mudmachine would soon have a stronger scoop and a steam engine, technological improvements did not guarantee more days of digging; an average year offered no more than 250 chances to earn a day's wage. Only the three workers who operated the steam dredge could claim the benefit of a guaranteed salary. For the other fifty mudmachinists, "the length of time that they can be worked in each year depends on the weather and the amount of appropriation placed under the control of the port warden."[53]

If the vagaries of weather made mudmachine work no different from other kinds of irregular labor, the mudmachinists no longer treated their work as casual. Payrolls from 1827 (the only other year offering a complete run) show that laboring men held onto their positions with tenacity. Nearly 40 percent of the 1827 workers remained for longer than six months, compared to only 25 percent of the workers during the panic year of 1819. The percentage of men who left the mudmachine in less than a month had fallen by half since the 1810s. The increased longevity of workers and the declining rate of turnover did not owe to better wages. In fact, the 75¢ daily pay constituted a significant drop in real wages over the course of the 1820s. The mudmachinists were not paid less than other manual laborers in these years, but they were no longer paid more, as had been the case in the 1810s. As always, the mudmachine's virtue was the relative constancy of its labor, and its allure of sustained employment discouraged an increasing number of men from trying their chances elsewhere. Spots on the mudmachine were actively sought: "If you have a vacancy in the mud machine," read one 1827 petition to the mayor, "you could give Imployment to Edward Castello, a man with a large family depending on him." As Castello's supporters explained, "he is a sober worthy man, but is a stranger in the city and can not get Imployment."[54]

Most remarkable about the 1827 payrolls were the familiar names. Alexander McDonald continued to direct the operations. Duncan McPherson, Walter Frasier, and Lachlin McLean—all holdovers from the 1810s—remained on the digging and discharging machines. Promoted to a supervisor, but only collecting $1 per day, McLean garnered nearly $100 less than he had in 1818. No employee's annual income in 1827 topped $250. George Whitten, whose mangled hand had earned him no sympathy from the city council in 1821, now worked on a discharging machine at the daily rate of 75¢.[55] Longtime Fells Point resident Owen Mullen also remained on the payrolls, albeit as one of the low-end "supernumeraries," whose titles betrayed the undifferentiated nature of their work. Career manual laborers figured prominently among the seventy-one men who labored on the mudmachine in 1827: twelve appeared as "laborers" in the city directory that year.[56]

As men stayed longer on the mudmachine and even became recognized in the city directories as householders, they nonetheless confronted the difficulty of supporting a family through manual labor. Thirty-two of the mudmachinists asked the city for a wage hike in 1834. "Considering they are constantly in an unhealthy atmosphere & employed only in weather working days," the petitioners sought a raise from 75¢ to 87½¢ per day. Eight of the signers had been laboring on the mudmachine since 1827, including John Whalen and Joseph Latte, who were neighbors on Slemmers Alley.[57]

Their plea for better wages was mild mannered in the context of 1830s labor unrest. Baltimore had seen some eight strikes in 1833, including one that involved seventeen different craft societies in the shipbuilding industry. Like New York, Philadelphia, and numerous other American cities, Baltimore had its own working men's political party and labor newspaper. When Baltimore's hatters waged a successful strike in 1834, they modeled exactly the rhetoric that might have served the career mudmachinists: low wages and seasonal unemployment made it almost impossible for a working man to support a family.[58]

But unlike craft unionists, the mudmachinists never went on strike to achieve their goals of manly independence. Instead they sent petitions to the mayor and city council that were as futile as the work of the mudmachine itself. No amount of effort could stop sediment filling up Baltimore's harbor, just as no amount of labor could guarantee a decent living to men on the mudmachine. Getting paid by the day was a recipe for hardship, as the mudmachinists pointed out to city officials again in 1838. This time the street scrapers joined their petition, because digging mud and picking up manure both were "a part of the scavenger work" that allowed the city to function. "They are necessarily much exposed to all kinds of weather, and receive for it a sum inadequate at the present time to the support of their families." Granted, the mudmachinists had seen their rate of pay return again to $1 per day, but "as there are many days in the year when it is from the state of the weather impossible to work, their wages is reduced to less than seventy-five cents per day, which is not enough to buy scarcely food, to say nothing of the raiment required for a family." Their hopes of becoming breadwinners no longer hinged on a higher daily rate of pay, but rather a salary paid rain or shine: $6 per week "throughout the whole year."[59]

The logic of the wage economy militated against such salaries for the mud-

machinists, street scrapers, or any of the free manual laborers at work in Baltimore. The virtue of wage labor was that it exempted employers from paying for
work they did not need or that they could not receive due to such circumstances
as a frozen harbor. This was precisely why Baltimore employers had come to rely
less on bound laborers, whether enslaved African Americans, indentured immigrants, or apprenticed teens. Casual labor had always been meant to serve the interests of employers rather than workers.

Precisely for that reason, any man who could avoid reliance on day labor presumably did so. As a result, it was widely assumed (and has remained so) that
backbreaking work fell primarily to the segments of society most vulnerable to
economic and physical coercion: slaves, free blacks, recent immigrants, and tran-
sients. Having lived in Baltimore for longer than the majority of the city's residents, Owen Mullen fit into none of these categories. His name was affixed to the
1838 petition seeking higher wages, indicating that Mullen had toiled on the mudmachine for upwards of twenty years. For Mullen and his co-workers, manual labor was not a life stage to be outgrown, but a career.

CHAPTER 4

A Job for a Working Woman

F our aggrieved Baltimore women petitioned the city council in 1816. These
hucksters—as both female and male street peddlers were known—had recently been fined several dollars for violating a new ordinance that made
hawking fruits and candles illegal outside the confines of the city's covered marketplaces. Although "poor, necessitous, and indigent," the four women had earned
enough from their petty marketing to support themselves and their children. But
under the new law, the almshouse loomed, a "final recourse" for women once
proudly reliant upon "their own personal industry." The petitioners predicted that
some cruel observers "taking human wants woes and difficulties into <u>only</u> a very
slight consideration, will say, 'why may not these women apply themselves to other
ways of getting a living?'" They replied with a catalog of the impediments they
faced in the early republic's urban economy: "To such it may be answered, that
these women have no mechanical trade, no manufacturing faculty, no stock, can
obtain no employment (for the present impeded state of business has caused large
Factories to cease their operations) whereby they cou'd obtain a scanty subsistence
for themselves and families."[1]

Although the 1816 ordinance against petty marketing applied to male peddlers
as well, it closed down one of the few avenues for a woman to earn a living by her
own labor. Except for a handful of successful "she-merchants" and dressmakers,
women were all but excluded from the trades and professions. The smartest
woman was unlikely to find a job in the counting houses that lined the city's waterfront, just as the most skilled woman would never bark commands to male journeymen in one of Baltimore's artisanal workshops. The strongest woman had little chance of finding work among the draymen and carters who unloaded the ships
at Fells Point. And before the 1820s, fewer than fifty of the most nimble women
found work in textile manufactories. Only through marriage or inheritance might
a woman gain access to a house and the potential income from sheltering and

feeding boarders. Otherwise, poor women could take in washing, finish shirts for piece rates, or hire themselves out as domestic servants. None of these endeavors offered a reliable subsistence, particularly during cold winters, summer epidemics, and contractions in the mercantile economy. No wonder the almshouse loomed large in the minds of the female hucksters and other women like them.

The narrow occupational choices and low wages available to working women were not new developments in Baltimore, nor in any of the growing urban centers of the early republic. Over several centuries in early modern Europe and colonial Anglo America, a set of social fictions had emerged to help assure that women's market labor would be, in the words of one scholar, "discontinuous, alternatively encouraged or suppressed, not linked to formal training, and generally badly paid." Even sympathetic observers attributed women's few opportunities to Nature, whose timeless laws had saddled women with children, and made them physically unsuited to strenuous manual labor and mentally incapable of the skilled handiwork of male artisans. "From necessity and the natural habits of their sex, it is well known that females cannot engage in those various occupations to which men can turn their attention, with so much ease as well as profit to themselves," explained an 1805 charity plea on behalf of impoverished women. Insofar as patriarchal culture had deemed female workers too busy with children or too delicate one moment and too clumsy the next, women's paid occupations were indeed few.[2]

Considering the centrality of female labor to American economic development, the scarcity of cash-earning jobs for women in boomtown Baltimore is surprising. The pattern of economic development now labeled as the "market revolution" owed much of its success to the harnessing of women's labor to an emerging national market: the rural Pennsylvania dairy women who buttered Philadelphians' bread, the New Hampshire farm wives who braided straw hats for New Yorkers' heads, or the Lowell mill girls who made the textiles that ended up on the backs of Ohio settlers and Georgia slaves alike. Alongside their peers who exchanged labor for wages in textile mills or whose cottage industry made the countryside a hotbed of early American manufacturing, urban women also found themselves in the midst of new market relations that converted their labor to a commodity.[3]

Instead of producing goods to be sold elsewhere, urban women performed the hidden labor of capitalist economies: the work of social reproduction. In addition to birthing and raising the next generation of workers, women did the washing, feeding, sheltering, and provisioning necessary for any port to function. Like the male manual labor that created the roads and docks necessary for commercial exchange, women's service labor built a crucial infrastructure for economic development. The labor of reproduction was long invisible because much of it was unpaid and took place within the confines of the household. It garnered little attention because women presumably fulfilled these roles by virtue of their nature, not because of a political economy that dictated who worked where and on what terms. The rise of what scholars have called the "Atlantic service economy" involved the commodification of reproductive labor. Labor that once fell primarily to one's own wife, mother, or daughter could increasingly be purchased from someone else's on terms that were casual, contractual, coercive, or some combination of all three.[4]

Baltimore's service economy brokered the labor of free and enslaved women to meet needs that were both timeless and new. Along the waterfront, a transient population of male sailors bought washing, sewing, and sex. On crowded streets, pedestrians purchased candles, fruit, and the other goods offered by female hucksters. In residential districts, middle-class families paid for labor that wives and daughters no longer deemed appropriate for themselves. Indeed, as the beneficiaries of the burgeoning urban economy adopted new standards for proper household management, they sought out poor women to perform the labor that "ladies" no longer would. In this way, domestic service became the largest sector of female employment in the early republic city.

As women workers entered the labor market in increasing numbers, the range of potential jobs for women did not grow accordingly. Great demand for women's labor never exerted an upward pull on wage levels, and if market forces had any impact on women's wages, it was to push them even further downward due to overcompetition in the few occupations where women clustered. Baltimore employers gained further advantage by treating diverse female workers—along lines of race, age, ethnicity, and legal status—as interchangeable. They simultaneously brought more free women into wage labor, while prolonging the enslavement of African American women. Able to purchase female labor by the day, week, month, year, or lifetime, employers reaped the benefits of a market economy that provided working women little in return.

An Employer's Bonanza

Nowhere was the unequal exchange more manifest than in the realm of domestic service, the largest sector of the female labor market. It was here that Baltimore employers exercised their greatest prerogatives in commodifying, accessing, and exploiting the free women who sought work and the unfree women who did not. For women whose labor was for hire, the goal was getting and keeping a job to maximize whatever meager returns were available. For women whose labor was

owned outright, the challenge was minimizing the work that one did to enrich
others and pursuing remuneration or dignity where neither was readily offered.

In choosing cooks, nurses, and maids, employers exercised a degree of discrimination unnecessary in hiring male ditch diggers. Domestic service was a totally different kind of employment, situating a stranger in the private spaces of
family life and giving her authority over employers' children, access to valuable
or cherished personal possessions, and the power to inflict harm or cause annoyance during the most routine aspects of daily life, such as getting dressed or
eating lunch. A wide range of tasks fell under the generic label *domestic service*,
and employers could seek highly specialized workers (ironers, cooks, wet nurses,
dry nurses, waiters, chambermaids, washers) or undifferentiated ones ("well acquainted with all kinds of housework" read an 1816 ad). But whether a domestic
servant was carting the contents of a chamber pot to the street, washing soiled
bedsheets, gutting a chicken, or nursing someone else's child, the city provided a
stifling environment for such labors.[5]

The close quarters of urban homes—upwards of seven people in living spaces
roughly one thousand square feet—placed domestic servants under constant
scrutiny, even as they navigated basements, attics, yards, back staircases, and the
outbuildings that dotted city lots. At the same time, the dense crowding of urban
neighborhoods—some 33,000 people crammed into Baltimore's one square mile
of development in 1800—could make fetching water just as suffocating as serving breakfast.[6]

In their nearly obsessive surveillance of domestic laborers and the predictable
disappointments that followed, householders regularly imagined that a better
worker—someone more diligent, more quick, more respectful—was out there
somewhere. The city's dizzying array of potential workers allowed would-be employers to imagine her with excruciating precision. Take, for example, four "help
wanted" ads that appeared in an issue of the *Baltimore Patriot* in fall 1834. The
first sought a woman "accustomed to doing house work," but said nothing about
the desired race, age, legal status, or skills. The second ad searched for an enslaved
African American woman to purchase or hire as a cook. The third asked for "a
middle aged white Woman for the purpose of cooking and washing." Finally the
fourth employer requested a "colored woman"—enslaved preferred but not
required—for chamber work.[7]

The demographic requirements of any given position usually disqualified the
majority of job seekers. However, householders additionally spelled out nebulous,
if unattainable, standards of character for the women and girls who would occupy
such sensitive positions in their homes. At minimum, they required "satisfactory

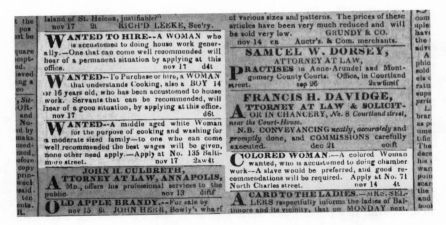

Domestic service advertisements, 1834. Employers of domestic servants articulated precise criteria for the workers they sought. These advertisements appeared in the *Baltimore Patriot,* November 18, 1834. Courtesy American Antiquarian Society.

recommendations," and at the extreme, "unquestionable testimonials of diligence, fidelity, and sobriety."[8] Reputation could trump both skill and demographic background as a qualification for hire. In an economy that presented women with few opportunities for paid labor, employers' expectations of their domestic workers further restricted any one woman's prospects for employment. While a large number of domestic servant positions were available in general, there may have been very few opportunities for a pregnant white teenager who had fled her unsympathetic family in rural Harford County for the anonymity of the city, for a recently manumitted black woman whose last work had been in the tobacco fields of southern Maryland, or for an Irish woman whose previous employer had sacked her over some missing handkerchiefs.

Assessing and reporting the character traits of would-be domestic servants had long been a concern of prosperous householders. Over several centuries in early modern England, employers had sought to rationalize the hiring of female domestic workers. The Elizabethan Statute of Artificers (1563), for example, had mandated the establishment of public offices to store character evaluations that employers would provide for their workers and which could be transported from place to place as laboring people sought jobs in new locales. By the mid-1700s, social commentators lamented that the earlier policy had never been implemented and called for a Universal Register Office to serve this purpose in the metropolis of London.[9]

Such institutions did not materialize in colonial British North America, largely because most domestic workers were not footloose and free, but were the daughters of neighboring (and thus, known) families or were indentured and enslaved girls and women whose unfree status gave their masters the legal power to coerce good behavior. Yet even the likeable Maine midwife Martha Ballard struggled with her hired "girls" and wished they would be more responsible and diligent in performing their duties.[10] When groups like the Society for the Encouragement of Faithful Domestic Servants finally emerged in 1820s New York and Philadelphia, they identified the fundamental problem of domestic service from the employers' perspective: "a hostile body has been found in the bosom of every family, mingling in all its concerns, but with a separate and opposite interest."[11] For employers, the result was the "servant problem" and the predictable complaints of the difficulties of finding "good help." For domestic servants themselves—and especially for those seeking hire—the result was a "master and mistress problem" and having to operate on the shifting terrain of employers' fickle preferences and summary judgments.[12]

Whether in the patriarchal households of the seventeenth century or the sentimental homes of the nineteenth, domestic service was never a straightforward exchange of labor for wages or sustenance. In the United States, anxiety and emotion set the contours of hiring in domestic service precisely because of the freighted meaning of servitude in a republican society. Laboring within another family had been a common experience for most unmarried females in early America, but such stints in domestic service presumably ended for free women when they married and began households of their own. But in places like Baltimore where demand for household help was high and where other opportunities for poor women to earn an income were few, the ranks of domestic servants came to include adult women, including those whose marriages and white skin could not protect them from such labor.

The direct subordination of household labor stood in glaring contrast to the personal independence celebrated in early republic political culture. Even without being enfranchised, white women shared the same republican fears of servility as their male peers, especially when the tasks they performed often fell to slaves. European visitors to the United States recounted their meetings with outraged American domestics who refused the label "servant," proclaimed themselves "helps," and denied their employers the title of "master" or "mistress." If Baltimore employers also worried about America's republican character, they did not show it. Rather than limiting domestic service to workers who were unfree, underage, or nonwhite, prosperous Baltimore families cast a wide net for female household workers and deemed the work appropriate for any woman who needed to support herself by her own labor.[13]

In the first decades of the nineteenth century, domestic service became the primary paid employment for adult Euro-American and African American women. At the same time, domestic service remained the standard toil for the city's enslaved women, as well as for teenaged girls, whether apprenticed or free. No census data or occupational surveys reveal the precise number of Baltimore households utilizing servants, but estimates from a comparably sized city, Boston, indicate that about one-third of households contained a nonfamily member performing domestic labor in 1830. In Baltimore, where such work could be both paid and coerced, that number was perhaps higher.[14] Individual employers had their own preferences but never reached a consensus that would limit domestic servants to a particular group. The only agreement was on the matter of character, a trait a domestic servant must possess in abundance. But because employers still differed on whether character was innately lacking in some workers (free blacks, for example), or could be inculcated in others ("wild" Irish girls), domestic labor could not become identified with a specific race, ethnicity, age, or legal status.

Where household workers might be black or white, native born or immigrant, slaves-for-life or term slaves, indentured or free, employers had great difficulty predicating their control on "natural" categories of fitness for servitude. In cities like Boston or Charleston, the relative homogeneity of domestic workers allowed employers to erect their class domination upon other categories of difference such as the presumed inferiority of Irish Catholics or the legal bondage of African Americans. But in border cities like Baltimore, the diversity of the female working population robbed employers of this key mechanism for rationalizing social dominance. At the same time, such a heterogeneous workforce provided employers the ability to move at will among entire categories of laboring people and to cast job-seeking women of every demographic description into a seemingly undifferentiated labor market.[15]

Even in the 1790s, when the bulk of domestic laborers had been indentured European servants, apprenticed Maryland children, and enslaved African Americans, employers enjoyed an unusual range of hiring choices. Baltimore householders weighed the costs and opportunities of, say, redeeming a German woman right off the boat from Hamburg; purchasing the remaining time of an Irish servant who had already toiled in Baltimore for four or five years and knew the ways of the city; spending nothing to acquire an apprenticed girl from the orphan's court, but then having to assume responsibility for raising another child; hiring someone else's slave for the year; or taking the capital risk to purchase an enslaved woman who might run away, die, or bear children who themselves could become valuable commodities. Baltimore householders occasionally made their choices in public view, such as when barrelmaker Robert Quail simultaneously posted a meager reward for his runaway indentured white servant girl, Margaret Alexander, and declared his intention to purchase "a young Negro Woman, of good temper and honesty" for his residence on Public Alley.[16]

Newspaper advertisements from the 1790s illuminated the range of options available to a man like Quail, who might be interested in buying the remaining term of an "indented Irish Servant Girl . . . a good Sempstress and House-Servant," or in owning "A very valuable Negro Woman . . . an excellent Washer, Ironer, and Cook," or in hiring "by the Day, A Black Woman . . . whose Honesty and Sobriety may be relied on."[17] In January 1793, readers of the *Maryland Journal* could consider purchasing one "strong, healthy Dutch servant woman" for two years, a second for three years, and yet a third touted as "an excellent spinner." Not long after, the *Hope* docked in Baltimore with a cargo of redemptioners and servants from Cork, just as in other years similar ships had arrived with bound laborers from the North Sea ports of Rotterdam and Hamburg, as well as from the Irish ports of Dublin and Waterford. Slaveowners advertised the black women they hoped to sell, as well as those they sought to recapture. For example, when twenty-year-old Mint fled her owner of fifteen months, Matthew Swan offered a $6 reward for her recapture and the trunk full of clothing she had taken with her. Reading about the similar escape of Irish-born indentured servant Mary Birmingham only a few weeks later might have disabused Baltimore householders of the notion that unfree domestic labor promoted a harmonious home. Nonetheless, urban employers continued to purchase or hire enslaved women and indentured servants, and to pursue those who had absconded.[18]

Child labor provided a common solution for Baltimore households seeking domestic help. Long-standing Anglo-American social welfare practices assured that children whose parents had died or proved incapable of providing for them would be reassigned to other households for the duration of their minority. In 1802, for example, Maryland's orphan's court bound sixty-eight girls and eight boys into Baltimore homes as domestic servants. These were not the craft apprenticeships that lent themselves to self-employment in adulthood; nor were these cases in which parents sought to improve their children's prospects for upward mobility. Instead, domestic service assignments were a long-standing mechanism for the state to unburden itself of dependent children. These arrangements provided urban householders with capable workers, as most domestic apprentices were teenagers not toddlers. Apprenticed girls also appealed to householders who preferred to see their relationship as more paternalistic than commercial. Such pretensions notwithstanding, teenaged white indentured servants fled their masters at least as frequently as enslaved African American domestics did—perhaps more often, since masters were less likely to advertise rewards for the return of less valuable property. Baltimore shoemaker James Fisher, however, thought it worthwhile to recover nineteen-year-old Mary Grady, an Irish servant with "tender eyes" and an inclination to head south toward Alexandria or Georgetown in Virginia.[19]

From the perspective of householders like Fisher, Baltimore could not provide an adequate supply of good domestic servants. Not even legal bondage could keep good domestic laborers ironing and folding. Worse, enslaved and indentured domestic servants were known to "practice their perfidy" right under the noses of their masters. "Even servants who are most tenderly used too often return evil for good," opined one newspaper writer in the aftermath of several suspicious fires in 1805.[20]

At that very moment, urban philanthropists were turning their attention toward increasing the labor pool with more tractable and better-trained servant girls. Prominent men and women in the cities of the new nation had noticed their streets overrun with children. In 1800, roughly 40 percent of the white populations of New York, Philadelphia, Boston, and Baltimore were younger than fourteen.[21] In the absence of compulsory public schools, children worked and played in the streets, behaving in "insolent, troublesome, and dangerous" ways. The Baltimore children who hit Mrs. Jerome Bonaparte with a snowball during an 1804 snowstorm were typical of the bad little boys whose fireworks and curses gained the attention of mayors and magistrates in every early republic city. Their sisters were no prizes either, according to the religiously devout. "We see a large number of this class of females growing up from generation to generation in a state not far removed from heathenism," explained the women of the Female Society of Philadelphia's Second Presbyterian Church in 1802. "Thus debased," these same girls "enter[ed] the middle and higher classes of life, in their capacities of servants, nurses, and housekeepers, mixing with and having the care of children at that period when the first and most lasting impressions are made." Only a careful regimen of religious education and job training could ensure "the happiness of hundreds of families."[22]

Wealthy Baltimore women were among the first in the nation to take the initiative, opening the Female Humane Association Charity School in 1800. A religiously diverse group of "Ladies" had bemoaned "the abandoned state of the rising generation, particularly the female part thereof, many of whom were literally raised in the streets in filthiness, rags, and vice." Their school hoped "to snatch the child from a fate similar to that of its mother." The girls would learn to read, write, cipher, and sew, before being "placed in reputable families, for the purpose of maintaining themselves by domestic labor and employment." Young women, thus trained, would gain "a fair prospect of obtaining for themselves an honest livelihood" as adults. Mrs. Chapelle, the schoolmistress, faced a difficult task because the children "were invariably taken from the lowest conditions in life; many, nay most of whom were, when taken into the school, not only destitute of common decency in their deportment, but wholly ignorant of the first principles of right and wrong; in truth some of them might have been called savages, whom it was necessary first to civilize, before they would be received into a reputable situation to obtain their living by domestic labor."[23]

Over the institution's first decade, 135 girls received training and were either bound out until their sixteenth birthdays or "returned to their indigent but reputable mothers, who wished to obtain the benefit of their children's labor." Twelve satisfied householders reported that their new bound domestic workers were "orderly, quiet, and industrious, and promise according to their conditions in life, to be useful members of society." Mary Hannah might have been happier had she gotten her apprenticed serving girl through the institution. Instead, she ended up with Ann Manning, "an artful piece" whose "tongue does not at all times speak the truth." When the girl ran away, Hannah volunteered a whopping 6¢ reward for her return. Although the Female Humane Association Charity School changed its name to the Orphaline Charity School in 1808, its project remained the same. The managers hoped to increase enrollment because "most persons who wish for female assistants in their families, prefer receiving them from an institution where they have been properly instructed for four or five years." The 1819 annual report praised the school for teaching the girls "such domestic duties as are calculated to give them habits of industry, as to render them equal to their future support."[24]

Although charity schools did not supply the bulk of household labor to urban employers, their influential directoresses helped make domestic service an appropriate occupation for free adult white women. By no means did Baltimore householders cease seeing enslaved black women as fundamentally suited for domestic service, but they made it clear that so too were poor adult white women. Their efforts assured that the pool of potential servants would never be limited to members of one racial or ethnic group, nor to workers of one particular legal status. As in male manual labor, the coding of domestic labor proved difficult so long as members of the free white majority might be labeled "savages" and relegated to the same rungs of the occupational hierarchy as members of legally unfree or subordinated minority populations. In theory, the enslavement of African Amer-

icans insulated free white people from the most servile forms of labor. As practiced in a city like Baltimore, however, slavery simply added an additional cohort
of workers into a larger labor market, expanded the choices available to urban employers, and perhaps made them more likely to see all labor as property they were
entitled to possess.

Had Baltimore householders desired to make domestic service the exclusive
domain of enslaved black women, they could have done so by competing with
buyers from Mississippi and Alabama for the thousands of female slaves who were
sold from rural Maryland during the early nineteenth century. It was no waver-
ing commitment to slavery—any more than it was a precocious color blindness
or belief in racial equality—that brought Baltimore employers to see domestic
service as suitable for free adult white women, even those who had become wives
and mothers themselves. Rather, urban employers had become more committed
to seeing labor in all its guises as a largely undifferentiated market commodity,
one for which the deserving men and women who were guiding Baltimore's boomtown growth should have the widest number of options. So many different women
toiled in domestic service not because of irresistible opportunity or the impartial
workings of an abstract market, but because urban householders closed off other
occupational opportunities, continued to rely on the legal servitude of slavery, indentures, and apprenticeships, and undertook institutional efforts to bring more
free girls and women into the labor force.

Baltimore employers showed their creativity in moving fluidly between different kinds of labor arrangements. Servants could become objects of middle-class
consumption, and householders like Ann Mackenzie Cushing could experiment
with different possibilities. Firing her free African American cook, Cushing declared her wish "to change for a white servant" in the late 1830s. Two months and
two Irish girls (Bridget Halpenny and Johanna Coughlin) later, Cushing began
paying wages to an enslaved woman named Rachel. When Rachel ran away, a succession of white women followed in her place. Between an employer's readiness
to fire workers and a laborer's willingness to quit, the high rate of turnover in the
Cushing home—seventeen women in seven years—comes as no surprise. But
clearly, the specific contours of Baltimore's labor market allowed Cushing to be
the type of employer who could whimsically fire a black woman for a white one,
then drive several workers to quit after a few weeks, dismiss others for any number of petty imperfections, and ultimately get the most dependable labor from
someone enslaved.[25]

Enslaved women like Rachel remained a key cohort of the city's domestic workers. Although slaves were declining as a percentage of Baltimore's overall popu-

lation, the absolute number of enslaved working-age women in the city grew during the 1810s and 1820s to reach nearly 2,000 by 1830. Of course, far more than 2,000 enslaved women worked in Baltimore during these years. Thanks to manumissions, sales, deaths, and escapes, the census taker would have seen an entirely different set of enslaved women's faces in 1830 than he had ten years earlier. For example, Christopher Chapman had owned twenty-five-year-old Ann in 1813, but fifteen-year-old Harriet and six-year-old Phoebe in 1823. Likewise, Matilda and Caroline labored as slaves for Captain John Carnes in 1823, but a decade later they were gone, and two other slaves now worked in their place. Bina and Eliza worked in Daniel Victory's tavern in 1823, but by 1836 they had been replaced by Lavinia. Because of a high rate of turnover, the number of enslaved women toiling in Baltimore was far higher than static census figures indicate.[26]

Baltimore employers came increasingly to see domestic service as the optimal use of enslaved labor. The bulk of domestic servants in Baltimore were not enslaved African Americans, but the majority of enslaved African Americans performed household labor. During the 1810s, 1820s, and 1830s, the typical Baltimore slave was not Frederick Douglass in a shipyard, but someone like Lyndia Holiday, a thirty-year-old woman who worked in a home on Gough Street. By 1830, over 60 percent of Baltimore slaves were female, and that percentage would grow in the following decades. Half of Baltimore slaveholders owned only a single person, most likely a girl or woman between ten and thirty-five years old. Such enslaved females resided primarily in Baltimore's residential wards, where demand for domestic service was highest. Although some enslaved women toiled in industrial settings like bakeries and tobacco manufactories, almost all advertisements seeking to buy or sell female slaves referred to housework. Similarly, runaway advertisements emphasized enslaved women's domestic labor. When Julia Dorsey escaped the Diffenderffer household in 1834, her owner described her as "well known in the city as my children's nurse." Enslaved women like Dorsey constituted a patrimony for generations of prosperous white boys and girls in Baltimore. Margaret Hanna went to court to demand the "servant girl" her father had willed to each of his four daughters. The tardiness of her late father's executor had left Margaret "deprived of the amoluments that might accrue from the services of such a servant."[27]

The majority of enslaved domestics did "the housework of a small family" (as many ads read), but others performed less intimate and more industrial forms of cooking and cleaning in hotels, inns, and taverns. At the Globe Inn, Fanny Fisher waited on guests and perhaps passed time by singing hymns in "a fine voice" before running away in 1809. By 1813, twelve tavern or innkeepers in the city held enough slaves to exceed the value of their real estate. Baltimore's largest slave-holder in 1813 was John Gadsby, whose thirty-six slaves waited on the guests of his Indian Queen Hotel. Two decades later, when British author Thomas Hamilton arrived at the Indian Queen, the staff was still almost entirely enslaved. Never having seen a slave before, Hamilton was surprised to note the "decent looking waiters and housemaids, observant of all external proprieties of demeanor, discharging their several duties with exactitude and distinguishable from European servants by nothing but color." This was quite contrary to his expectation of a slave as a man or woman "crushed by labour, degraded by ignorance, brutalized by the lash; in short a monster like that of Frankenstein."[28]

In far plainer settings, modest Baltimore householders gained access to enslaved domestic servants thanks to the prevalence of slave-hiring arrangements and the availability of term slaves who could be bought at discount for a finite period. In the first case, a market developed for slaves' time rather than for their bodies when slave rentiers—widows, doctors, merchants, and rural planters—leased workers by the day, week, or year to the city's middling families. Many novice slaveholders in Baltimore experienced mastery without incurring the risks, burdens, and obligations of outright ownership. A Baltimore householder named Eichelburger declined to purchase Eliza, the enslaved woman who worked for him, despite paying "a greater interest by way of hire than the sum which is asked for her." Eichelburger "prefers hiring her than holding slave property," reported a disappointed seller. At least one-sixth of advertisements seeking or offering enslaved workers in Baltimore referred to the possibility of hiring. "Wanted to purchase or hire, a colored Woman, or the time of one," read one advertisement in 1819. A similar ad promised either "a liberal price or wages" to the owner of an enslaved black woman to sell or rent. Advertisements promising wages for hired slaves did not reveal whether the worker or the owner would pocket the wage, but both possibilities were common. Eliza's wages from Eichelburger went directly into the bank account of her owner, Sophia Bland of Annapolis. But when Rebecca Garrett began working in Baltimore in 1832, she took her wages home to her husband, a free black man who in turn remitted an undisclosed amount to Rebecca's owner, Thomas Anderson of Anne Arundel County.[29]

Term slavery was a second adaptation that vastly increased the availability of enslaved domestic servants. When an owner legally recorded a manumission date in the future, the result was a term slave whose purchase price was significantly lower than a comparable slave-for-life. Maryland slaveholders had consented to these unusual agreements once it became clear that enslaved people had multiple possibilities for reappropriating their own labor, whether by escape to nearby

Pennsylvania or by disappearance into the crowded alleys of the Baltimore waterfront. Slaveholders saw delayed manumissions as a way to postpone the inevitable and squeeze additional profit from an unstable capital investment. By offering enslaved workers a long-term prospect of legal freedom, slaveholders gained a new mechanism for short-term exploitation.[30]

The market in term slaves coincided with the decline in the availability of other term-bound unfree workers, namely indentured servants and redemptioners from Europe. Although shipmasters continued to sell German girls "very fitting for housework or children's nurses" as late as 1819, and the orphan's court still apprenticed fifty to eighty children "to common housework" annually, these sources could hardly meet the demand for domestic service. Advertisements for female term slaves had begun appearing in the early 1800s: "Will be sold for a term of years, A likely, healthy Negro Girl" or "a Negro Girl, aged 14—has 13 years to serve."[31] A term slave remained a capital investment, but her price was typically 25 to 50 percent lower than a woman enslaved for life. Consider the 1818 sale of "a Negro Woman, about 23 or 24 years of age" with six years to serve. The new owner gained six years of labor for as little as $100—roughly the amount required to hire a free white domestic for only one year. Because the demand for term slaves was high, she might also be resold for a substantial portion of her original purchase price.[32]

A female term slave was a particularly appealing investment for middling Baltimore householders because her children held the legal status of slaves-for-life. To this extent, term slavery in no way liberated black women from what legal scholar Adrienne Davis has called slavery's "sexual political economy"—its appropriation of black women's biological capacities and its transformation of "sexual and reproductive relations [into] economic and market relations."[33] Like the enslaved woman for sale in 1818, most term slaves did not attain their freedom until their late twenties or early thirties, which almost guaranteed the arrival of children born into full legal slavery. Some owners used these children as leverage over their mothers, refusing to make youngsters into term slaves or to sell them into freedom until their mothers had faithfully served out their own terms. Only a decision by the woman's owner could transform her children into term slaves. Other owners envisioned generations of term slaves in succession—an endless supply of mothers and daughters laboring for finite periods "until the end of time," as one slaveowner stipulated in an 1820 manumission deed that applied to the unborn descendants of Negro Sarah. The enslaved woman for sale in Baltimore in 1818 already had an infant daughter and a toddler son entitled to manumission when they turned twenty-five and thirty, respectively. Their buyer gained a slew of economic advantages: six years of domestic service from a woman who could not quit at one-sixth the cost of hiring a free woman; a girl who would grow to replace her mother as a servant and who would labor with the same disincentive to run away, whose resale value would increase as she gained skills and approached child-bearing age, and whose children would be slaves-for-life; and a boy who, if given craft training, would gain a resale value far in excess of his mother or sister, or who could be hired out for wages that would easily cover the original purchase price of the entire family.[34]

Put simply, term slavery was a legal institution that served the interests of slaveholders more than it served the interests of unfree African American workers, even as it transformed enslavement into a life stage for a modest, but growing, percentage of Baltimore's black population. At least one-fifth of all slave sales in early republic Baltimore were for men, women, and children whose manumission dates had already been set. The lower price of these term slaves made slaveholding a possibility for a broad cross section of white Baltimore residents. In a city where only one-third of taxpayers owned slaves, middling white families were almost as likely as their wealthier neighbors to possess a slave. In 1813, among the bottom half of urban taxpayers, 23 percent of households owned slaves. A white family that owned a modest dwelling could, if it so chose, also own a black woman to clean it. Most white families who owned only one slave possessed a working-age woman.[35]

By the 1820s, however, the popularity of delayed manumission arrangements in Maryland had created a new cohort of workers in the domestic service market: free African American women. The dramatic rise of Baltimore's free black population—almost doubling in the 1810s alone to exceed 10,000 by 1820—owed largely to the in-migration of manumitted black women from throughout the state and to the prevalence of manumissions in the city itself. By 1820, there were twice as many Baltimore black women living in legal freedom as in slavery. Moreover, those free black women outnumbered their male counterparts by three to two.[36] Upwards of 60 percent of working-age free African Americans in Baltimore were women, many of whom had profiles like that of thirty-one-year-old Christiana Caw. Raised in Anne Arundel County, Caw received a promise of manumission in 1807 to take effect in 1815. Whether Caw had come to Baltimore to labor as a term slave or at precisely the moment her manumission took effect, she was typical of the free black women of Baltimore: born and raised in slavery and then liberated into free adulthood in the city. Many such women succeeded in establishing autonomous households in Baltimore. Nonetheless, more than one-third of black females between fourteen and forty-four years old resided in the households of their white employers; in the city's wards where demand for domestic service was greatest, over half of free black women resided in white households.[37]

Despite the large number of enslaved and free women of color working in the city, domestic service would become a primary occupation for Baltimore's white women as well. Household labor did not immediately connote racial degradation, which is why Baltimore editor Hezekiah Niles could profitably tell an anecdote regarding a Baltimore-raised white woman who got in trouble when she tried to fetch her own water in another Southern city. "It was business only fitting for negroes," her new neighbors told her. But nothing in this woman's experience in Baltimore would have suggested as much. By the 1820s, employment agencies in the city were advertising the availability of "white women [who] want situations as house-keepers, dry and wet Nurses, chamber maids, &c. all well recommended and of genteel appearance." Of course, urban employers had long sought white women for such labor, well beyond the alumnae of Baltimore's charity schools. Help-wanted advertisements in the newspapers specified a desire for a white woman, or perhaps more euphemistically, "a Woman accustomed to housework in Europe." Such ads could become even more precise, specifying not only a white woman but adding, "None but an American need apply." Employers in the 1830s sought white women as cooks, nurses, chambermaids, washers, and general house-keepers, which suggested that white skin offered no immunity from any particular aspect of domestic labor.[38]

Insofar as Baltimore employers advertised for white *women*—and not *girls*—domestic service had moved from a life stage for unmarried teens to a standard employment for grown adults. Advertisements even solicited middle-aged women. One employer sought "a middle aged white Woman accustomed to children," while another desired a "middle aged white Woman for the purpose of cooking and washing." Employers may have seen older women as more diligent servants whose job duties were less likely to be interrupted by a pregnancy or childcare responsibilities of their own. Although advocates of the poor like Philadelphia's Mathew Carey suspected that many unemployed females were too old to go out to service, some women proudly represented themselves as middle-aged when they sought housekeeping jobs.[39]

Early republic census records offer no way of estimating the prevalence of adult white women in domestic service, nor can we gain a more precise demographic portrait from the extant records of employment agencies or a Baltimore chapter of the Society for the Encouragement of Faithful Domestic Servants. Records from the almshouse, however, indicate that dozens of its "orphans" had mothers who relied on the institution to provide childcare while they worked in other women's homes. When Nancy Hignan sent her eight-year-old son into the almshouse in 1819, the admission warrant read, "being obliged to hire out in order to procure herself her own living, she can by no way provide for the poor child." Another noteworthy, if potentially unrepresentative, sample of adult white domestic servants comes from the Maryland Penitentiary, where twelve such women were incarcerated during the 1810s for property crimes. Thirty-one years old on average, these women followed varied paths into Baltimore: only two were foreign-born, while six had come from the north, including Ann Macklefish of Philadelphia and Catherine Jones from New Jersey. If New Englander Mary Miller had thought that she would find a better job in Baltimore because its domestic labor had been relegated to black workers, she was wrong.[40]

In fact, Baltimore employers were more inclined to see black and white women as interchangeable. While one trend in job advertisements saw demographic precision, another reflected indifference. Ads that obscured a demographic preference—"Wanted, for a small Family, A House-Keeper. She will receive good Wages, and will have very comfortable Accommodations"—were common from the 1790s onward. "A Woman is wanted to take care of a child in a genteel family," read an 1816 advertisement. But by the 1830s, advertisers made explicit their lack of preferences by including such phrases as "either White or Black" in the job description. "A Woman. (white or black.) to do the Washing and Cooking of a family is wanted," read a typical ad from 1833. Another employer sought "a Woman, (either white or colored,) to do the housework generally of a small family."[41]

Over the first several decades of the nineteenth century, the labor market for domestic service had become vastly more complicated. In advertisements, terms like "servant" did not imply legal bondage or blackness, just as descriptors like "colored" and "black" did not differentiate between free and enslaved African American workers. Employers subdivided domestic service into discrete tasks, and while advertisements specifying washing, ironing, and cooking often sought an African American worker, exceptions existed to every rule. The terrain could shift from neighborhood to neighborhood, and from idiosyncratic employer to employer. In the wealthy fifth and sixth wards of the city, for example, white householders bought enslaved women more frequently than they hired free black women as live-in servants. In the prominent Wirt household, two sisters debated whether to hire an enslaved or a free white nurse. "Mrs. A or any other white woman . . . might be apt to assume airs and be troublesome," advised Catherine to Elizabeth, recently delivered of a newborn in 1833. Despite a friend's offer to loan a reputable slave nurse, Elizabeth took her chances with Mrs. Armstrong. At establishments like the Globe Inn, owner J. W. Owings wanted a "White Girl" for a chambermaid and "two coloured Women, (slaves would be preferred)" for washing and ironing. The expansive, if unpredictable, market for domestic labor posed difficult challenges for job-seeking free women, for as domestic service became the largest sector of female employment, the number of positions suited to any one woman could be quite small. At the same time, the demand for domestic service weighed particularly heavily on the enslaved women of the city; black women's servitude outlasted that of their male peers, whose labor proved less valuable to Baltimore employers.[42]

Getting Hired

For the free white and black women who sought employment in domestic service, *character*—a nebulous qualification that revolved on middle-class standards of deportment—became a job seeker's most valuable asset or greatest liability. Working women often had an easier time mastering the latest techniques of napkin folding than protecting the traits of character desired of household servants. The emphasis on character put job-seeking women in a vulnerable position precisely because women's reputations were subject to constant surveillance and commentary in the patriarchal culture of the early nineteenth century. Employers had the advantage of defining character, whether as a matter of sexual and social behavior, of physical appearance and bodily carriage, or of manners and morals. More importantly, they monopolized the venues in which a working woman's character might be observed, discussed, and even converted into a discreet piece of information with its own market value.

Take, for example, the intelligence offices, or employment agencies whose gatekeeping helped to rationalize the labor market. Nathan Cobb opened one of Baltimore's first such establishments in 1810. In addition to offering a central location for city residents seeking lost animals or information on "rare and unusual articles of mechandize or traffic," Cobb's storefront promised "means of procuring places for servants, and servants for places." Working women and men would need to provide Cobb with a recommendation from a previous employer before he would refer them to a prospective employer (who presumably also paid Cobb's fee). By the 1830s, there were at least five intelligence offices in the city. "Domestics of all descriptions may find employment," announced the Register and Intelligence Office, which also advertised slaves, antiquarian books, and wallpaper for sale. At Lewis F. Scott's General Intelligence Office, "those having employment for deserving persons, male or female, in any capacity, can have their wants immediately supplied."[43]

As their names suggested, intelligence offices traded in information, much of which had circulated freely within city neighborhoods, but which now could be formalized and sold in an economy of paper. The transformation of surveillance into commodified information was a broader phenomenon in the early republic, and the buying and selling of character assessments shaped the prospects of enslaved African Americans and aspiring businessmen alike.[44] But the creation of knowledge around women was particularly problematic in a patriarchal culture that reduced female character to sexual chastity and condoned misogynistic violence against "disorderly" women.[45]

Testimony from criminal court proceedings, for example, illustrates that men could use violence with impunity against women whose sexual reputations were compromised. Benjamin Bowyer, a Baltimore mariner, avoided prosecution for theft in 1806 when his attorney labeled the accuser "a notorious and infamous prostitute." Thomas Potter's allies came to his defense in an 1814 rape case by calling his accuser "a wretch of the most abandoned character and unworthy of moral credit." When Ebenezer Lewis assaulted his wife, Mary, with a knife in 1826, David Richardson testified to Mary's behavior before marriage: "I can only state to you that previous to her marriage to Lewis that she lived immediately in my neighborhood—and bore the character of a loose woman and had two illegitimate children." Women's reputations were the subject of frequent speculation. In 1797, a Fells Point woman brought charges against her neighbor Hannah Duffy for adultery but later recanted the accusations as "false reports given me by malinquent and malicous people." A decade later, Henry Decoursey's wife came to the public market to find that a neighboring woman had posted handbills denouncing her as a prostitute—an outrage so great that Henry Decoursey horsewhipped his wife's detractor, Eugenia Gordon, "to check so vile a tongue." In 1818, a Baltimore jury conveyed the deepest misogyny in convicting Mary Davis as "a common scold"—the penalty for which was ducking in a pool of water. "So diabolical is her temper, so ungovernable her slanderous and infamous tongue, and so incorrigible her vicious propensities," declared her male accuser, that a ducking would be "far too mild for her outrageous outrages on society." When Maryland's governor intervened at the last minute to spare Davis her watery humiliation, countless Baltimore men were denied "the prospect of a most unusual scene."[46]

A woman's honesty and sobriety were no less subjects of public discussion than her chastity, although for female household workers—often physically vulnerable in age and size and presumed to be sexually available in the intimate settings of the household—these facets of "character" bled together. As the arbiters of reputation, employers gained a coercive power over their domestic workers. Without a good recommendation from a previous employer, a female servant would have difficulty securing future hire. A male construction laborer would not need a note from a building contractor to carry bricks at another job site up the street. In contrast, female domestics had to guard their reputations carefully, a fact that employers could wield over them to great advantage, even as employers were sometimes the greatest threat to a female servant's reputation. James Bryden, whose inn also housed the city coffeehouse, faced charges in 1805 for begetting a bastard child of "single woman" Elizabeth Butcher, perhaps one of the young women in his employ.[47]

A damaged reputation was hard to repair, although employers sometimes came to the rescue of their servants. When Judith Brady was found in the company of "bad women" in 1790 and prosecuted as a prostitute, her employer James Bowery reported that he had "never heard a dishonest thing Even Laid to her charge." Several former employers testified for Negro Nann, who had been accused of stealing in the public marketplace: "never in the whole course of our knowledge of her did we find any circumstances that would impeach her character as an Honest woman," they wrote. Robert Ballard had employed Nancy Walton for four years in his home and was shocked to hear that she had been charged with stealing goods from a burning building. "I never knew her to be guilty of a dishonest act," Ballard observed. "I did not at that time & nor do I now think she would steal a pin's worth." A preserved reputation meant the difference between future employment and a direct path from the jail to the almshouse. Elkin Solomon took back his servant of nineteen months, Catherine Potter, once it was proved that she was no prostitute but had merely been "inveigled away on that night by a neighbours Servant whom she did not suspect of keeping such company."[48]

At the same time, middle-class prescriptive literature—ostensibly directed to servants but more likely to be read by their employers—stressed the "duty" of candid character assessments regardless of the consequence to a working woman. Sarah Savage's 1823 *Advice to a Young Woman at Service* recounted the story of "Susan," who had been fired for drinking her mistress's coffee and eating her cranberry sauce. Other families in town had known Susan as "a smart capable girl," so she quickly had other opportunities for employment. But when a potential new employer visited Susan's previous mistress to "inquire about her character," the sad truth was revealed. "It was painful to this lady to be obliged to give the reason for which she had dismissed Susan, but she did not hesitate to do it, for she knew it was her duty." Meanwhile, Susan spent two unsuccessful months seeking a new job, pawned most of her clothing to cover rent, became sick, and hit rock bottom in the almshouse. Such was the cost of finding good help. As Catharine Beecher assured America's domestic servants, employers sincerely wished they could treat their household workers with more respect and higher wages. "Now if I only could find domestics who are intelligent, well-bred, neat in dress and person, and who so understand the proprieties of their station as to set a good example to my children," mused the stereotypical employer of Beecher's account. "But such domestics we cannot find."[49]

Often what stood between a working woman and employment were the unattainable standards and class condescension of urban householders. Even a leading spokeswoman of middle-class domesticity like Catharine Maria Sedgwick readily recognized "the failures" of elite women in "the contract between employers and employed." Prescriptive literature advised female employers to be more considerate and less hostile toward domestic servants. "Never think them mercenary, because they value money more than you do," advised Eliza Farrar in 1836 to the young ladies whose parents could afford household help. "Remember what a serious thing it is to have nothing but what you can earn by your own hands, and to be dependent in sickness upon your own scanty savings." Baltimore householders surely needed such reminders, insofar as their frequent complaints made it appear inconvenient to have a servant empty one's chamber pot.[50]

Polemical attacks on domestic servants were unsparing. One commentator— likely the curmudgeonly Thomas W. Griffith—declared that Baltimore householders suffered "under the insolence and depravity of hireling servants" and urgently needed to "place those scourges of society upon their proper footing." Another related an account of one Baltimore householder's attempt to hire a servant. The first woman to answer the advertisement could not bake, sew, nurse, or cook. The second "could do every thing but keep sober." The third had ten children of her own but was confident they would make fine companions for her employer's children. The fourth was an eighteen-year-old "with paint an inch thick" who insisted on two nights a week off to attend dancing school. And the final— and winning—applicant was a religious and moral mulatto woman, who waited a week before absconding with some silver spoons. This story illustrated that few Baltimore families "have servants that they are satisfied with, and many have none at all, preferring to be without them rather than put up with their ignorance, impudence, and idleness." When young Sophia May traveled from Boston to visit her Baltimore relatives in 1806, she was surprised to discover her hosts "much plagued" since "good servants are as difficult to procure here as in New England."[51]

Prominent householders called for strident gatekeeping to keep unsavory workers out of domestic labor. Proposed solutions in the early 1820s included coercing servants to work a probationary month at half wages or calling on Baltimore employers to form a pact to hire only servants bearing "a certificate, or certificates from persons of respectability, testifying their integrity, sobriety, industry, and capacity, according to the service for which they offer to perform." Employers would further pledge to give such certificates only to the most deserving and to help maintain a blacklist of "defaulting servants" deemed ineligible for hire. If employers acted in concert, they claimed, "in a very few weeks there will be a manifest change in the conduct of servants." Baltimore would become more like Europe, where there was "not so much difficulty on this score." Knowing better than to believe that there was no "servant problem" in Europe, Baltimore householders showed little enthusiasm for such collective policing.[52]

If working women in Baltimore were lucky to escape a formal system of character certificates and institutional surveillance—New York's Society for the Encouragement of Faithful Domestic Servants sent circulars to members to gather reports on household workers—they nonetheless had to prove their worthiness for hire. Proving the requisite qualities of character was essential, even for women who began their job search from the advantageous position of being able to advertise their services to potential employers. "Situation wanted" advertisements appeared regularly in the city's newspapers. "A YOUNG WOMAN, of respectable connections" promised "the most respectable reference" to a family desiring a seamstress willing "to make herself otherwise useful in the house." The two "middle aged" women who sought positions as housekeepers in 1809 advertised their ability to offer recommendations to interested parties. The only advertisements with no mention of character were those seeking the most intimate form of service, wet-nursing, where the more meaningful qualification was "a fine breast of milk." Employers who would never hire a maid fresh from the almshouse regularly sought out institutionalized women as wet nurses.[53]

Free black women were hardest pressed to market themselves to prospective employers. Many Baltimore white householders shared the hostile sentiments of Robert Goodloe Harper, a leading colonization advocate, that free blacks in general constituted an "idle, worthless, and thievish race." Thomas W. Griffith, who had served as an American diplomat in revolutionary France, explained that "it is not necessary to have been in Europe to see how much better people are served where they employ servants of their own colour." Griffith at least recognized that African American workers had no reason to trust the white employers who bore responsibility for the enslavement of their race. If Griffith understood free black servants and white employers in a state of perpetual warfare, acts of resistance should have come as little surprise. Nonetheless, routinely reported acts of theft and insolence fed white scorn for free black women as domestic servants; ex-

traordinary acts of arson or poisoning caused panic. The 1833 murder trial of Au-
rellia Chase caught the attention of white householders. Chase was convicted of
killing her Baltimore mistress, Elizabeth Durkee, with a bowl of arsenic-laced soup.
The city press reported that Chase received her death sentence with "either decided indifference or confirmed hardiness."[54]

White hostility was not the only obstacle facing a free black woman in search
of a domestic service job. Free black women may have faced a skill gap relative to
other working women. As easily as social commentators dismissed domestic labor as unskilled or as an innate aptitude of all women, such work was in fact skill
intensive, differentiated, and demanding. Catharine Beecher's contemporary
guide to female servants offered chapters of specific instructions for cooking meals,
setting and clearing tables, making beds, washing and folding garments, and maintaining oil lamps. The early republic's middle-class urban home remained a site
of production as well as consumption and required labor in processing food for
preservation and storage, as well as converting fabric into garments and linens.
The skills of domestic service were neither self-evident nor genetic, which is precisely why Baltimore women devoted so much attention to teaching young girls
the requisite skills to find gainful employment in domestic service. Free black girls,
however, lacked access to the charity school training of the Female Humane Association. More to the point, many adult free black women in Baltimore had spent
their childhoods in rural Maryland, where they were more prone to learn how to
hoe than how to sew. As a result, free black women may have possessed fewer of
the domestic skills sought by urban employers.[55]

Records from the Baltimore almshouse offer one glimpse into a skill gap between black and white working-class women. Between 1823 and 1826, a clerk
recorded information on the domestic skills of 370 of the 625 adult women who
entered the institution. Although the overseer left no statement of the criteria he
used in his evaluation, he credited new female inmates with such skills as knitting, carding, spinning, sewing, ironing, washing, scrubbing, and housework
(and usually in some combination). Such assessments are invariably problematic since the overseer's prejudices regarding nativity, age, and race may have predetermined the skills he recorded for each woman. At the same time, some of the
women may have seen advantages in listing certain abilities and not others, perhaps to gain a stint in the institution's kitchen or to avoid one in the turnip fields.
Created in the context of a difficult negotiation and mediated through the pen of
a partial interviewer, these data on women's skills are imperfect but nonetheless
suggestive that black women had less experience performing the mending and
sewing tasks that employers of household help often desired.[56]

The almshouse overseer placed over half of African American women at the bottom of the skill hierarchy, listing abilities in housework exclusively. When Annapolis-born Abigail Anderson entered the almshouse in 1823, the overseer recorded that she "can do nothing but housework." Similarly, thirty-year-old Rachel Wilson, one of the institution's few black Catholics, received "housework only" in her entry. Others included Kitty Davis, a recent arrival from the Eastern Shore, and the pregnant twenty-four-year-old Betsy Pepper. In contrast, only 15 percent of white women were listed as capable of only housework. Equally telling, white women were deemed capable of sewing, knitting, carding, and spinning twice as often as were black women (75 to 36 percent, respectively). In the higher needle skills of sewing and knitting, 54 percent of white women claimed (or were granted) competence, in contrast to only 9 percent of black women. Age seemed to have little bearing on these results. Among the larger group of 370, the average age of white women was thirty-three, and black women, thirty. Among women with housework skills only, the average age among white women was thirty-one; for black women, twenty-six. Although black women were younger, they were not primarily teens, whose abilities might prove narrower. Nativity made little difference in the skills of white women. European immigrants generally had skills beyond housework. In fact, three-fourths of Irish women showed experience in some combination of spinning, carding, sewing, and knitting.[57]

The birthplaces of African American women help explain the apparent gap in domestic skills. The majority of black women with only housework skills had been born in the tobacco-producing counties south of Baltimore. These women likely were born into slavery and spent their younger years learning to hoe and cure tobacco rather than to darn and mend stockings (although recent scholarship on quilting and cloth making on plantations calls attention to enslaved women as skilled artisans).[58] The transition to a grain economy on Maryland's Eastern Shore made such agricultural workers redundant and prompted the numerous manumissions that sent freed people to find work in Baltimore. Unlike other Southern cities where skilled, educated, mixed-race people (mulattoes, in nineteenth-century parlance) filled the ranks of the free, Baltimore's free black population comprised men and women only recently freed from enslavement, rural in origin, and surely less attuned to the mores of urban middle-class respectability. Such origins could disadvantage free black women seeking jobs or dissuade urban employers from seeking out black women.

At the same time, if free women of color had fewer domestic skills, it could also have been a function of white families' refusal to hire them. Job skills are learned experientially, and employers' preferences for enslaved black and free white domestics may have prevented free black women from gaining the skills desired by white householders. One employer in 1816 advertised for "two women to do all kinds of housework" but sought a very specific third domestic servant—"a white woman to sew." For those free black women who did have the requisite skills, a key strategy for hire was to place a "situation wanted" advertisement in the newspaper. Free black women placed such ads much more frequently than did white domestics and used the opportunity to inform prejudiced employers of skills in sewing, cooking, and washing. Still, direct competition from enslaved women— whose owners advertised them even more aggressively—pushed free black women further to the margins of the labor pool. One slaveholder offered to sell a twenty-year-old mixed-race woman "brought up to house work, handy with the needle, and of good character." Another advertised "a neat, cleanly servant woman, about 26 years of age, accustomed to plain cooking, doing the work of a chambermaid, washing, ironing, and sewing." By mentioning sewing skills, such sale ads implicitly dismissed free black women as suitable alternatives.[59]

Enslaved women were hardly conventional actors in the labor market. Seeking a job was rarely their prerogative. Such women could nonetheless play an active role in obtaining work as domestic servants in Baltimore. Take the provision attached to the 1809 advertisement for the "neat, cleanly servant woman" above: "She has a husband in the city, therefore, none need apply that don't want her services at, or near this place." Considering the willingness of Baltimore slaveholders to force enslaved women into the interstate slave trade, this ad attested to a remarkable, but unrecoverable, negotiation. Notarial records from New Orleans reveal that other enslaved Baltimore domestics, like Rebecca ("creole de Baltimore") or Fany ("native de Baltimore"), lacked such leverage. Enslaved women could extract other kinds of concessions from their owners, such as the ability to hire out their own time. Enslaved women found their way into the domestic service labor market by accepting responsibility for finding their employment and agreeing to remit their wages (or some percentage thereof) to their owners. In practical terms such enslaved workers might appear indistinct from free black domestics, but employers knew the difference, namely that legal bondage authorized violence as a method of labor discipline and made the slaveholder liable for the potential misbehavior of his or her human property.[60]

Runaway slaves also took coveted domestic service positions away from free black women. Hiring fugitive slaves was a fairly common practice in Baltimore, either because runaways would accept lower wages in exchange for cover or because employers could always collect the reward if the worker proved unsatisfactory. In 1805, the owner of a runaway named Chloe was sure that she had hired herself out in the city. Thomas Owen warned other Baltimore householders against employing his servant Ann, a twenty-three-year-old woman who had run away in 1816 and was reportedly "lurking about town."[61]

Making matters worse for free black domestics, the growth of Baltimore's free black population coincided with a feeble effort to celebrate the white domestic as ideal. "How are we served by our slaves and free blacks?" asked Thomas W. Griffith in an 1817 editorial. "Exactly as if we had just taken them by force of arms on the coast of Africa—obliged to watch them incessantly—and viewed by them as such masters should be, with fear and distrust." Such a situation was untenable but easily remedied by hiring white servants instead. In contrast to black workers, white domestics were "honest and faithful behind back as well as before faces." Already in Baltimore one could find "many native whites now in service, some for emigrants who have lately arrived among us, and others even in the service of native blacks," declared Griffith boldly. Although the latter cases must have been quite exceptional, Griffith contended that white servants working for black employers did not "produce on our minds any contempt of our colour." But white domestics working for white employers remained the best possible situation because "the servants identify their interests with their employers and feel no greater earthly pleasure than in meriting and receiving their confidence and protection through life." Griffith may have convinced some white households to exchange their black servants for white ones, but his cheery assessment of the relations between employers and white domestics was delusional.[62]

In spite of such idealized paternalism, domestic service became an increasingly confrontational site of class conflict in the nineteenth century. Hiring a white domestic hardly guaranteed a harmonious relationship, and court dockets and prison records reflected tension, subversion, and abuse. Domestic servants stole household goods, such as when sixteen-year-old Mary Crawford made off from Daniel Fowble's house with a dimity petticoat, several handkerchiefs, a comb, and pairs of gloves, shoes, and scissors. Ann Ray departed her employer's York Road home with several pieces of silver engraved with his initials (which were incidentally also her own), as well as "wearing apparel too numerous to mention."[63]

Misbehavior ran the other way as well, and domestic servants were regularly caught within the strife and pathologies of their employers' homes and forced to bear witness (often in silence) to extramarital sex, domestic violence, and disgusting scenes of filth. "I told them to get a black woman to clean out the room," testified Sarah Crawford in an 1804 murder trial. One unlucky domestic servant would have to confront the excrement-covered room containing the corpse of Phoebe Graham, who had died from either alcohol poisoning or a beating from her husband. In 1811, Eliza O'Donnell testified before the court that William S. Davis did not intentionally kill his wife when he pushed her off a chair. O'Donnell reported that she had witnessed alcoholic binges, knife-hurling fights, and enough verbal abuse to fear for her own safety. In the 1830s, Elizabeth Neilson witnessed her employer, John Lyons, seduce a "mulatto girl," with whom he "barefacedly and openly had connexion" while his wife was away.[64]

The forced intimacy of domestic service made it an unenviable way of making a living, and both black and white women resisted the excessive demands and moral condescension of their employers. One observer from Philadelphia even suggested that domestic servants should form a Society for the Encouragement of Faithful Employers: "Examine the details of the lives of many servants—the midnight parties, the watchings, the wakings, the card-playing, the gambling, the wine-drinking, the deception, the dissipation of various kinds they are called to witness—and yet they are expected to keep clear of all these things!"[65] Finding other ways of earning income would have been a constant goal for a woman reliant on her own labor for subsistence. Black and white women in Baltimore recognized that being hired as a domestic servant was difficult, but the greater challenge was in locating an alternative.

Opting Out

Baltimore provided working women with possibilities for earning an income, but the female petitioners who opened this chapter were correct: those possibilities were limited and low paying. Jobs that offered wages by the day or month were virtually nonexistent outside domestic service. A rare "Women Wanted" advertisement in 1809 would have brought little encouragement: "Five or Six women are wanted at the Franklin Paper Mills, to Pick and Sort Paper." The Powhatan Mills sought only three or four widowed women and fifteen young women when it hired in 1815. Before the 1830s, opportunities for women in textile manufactories were scarce, and those Baltimore women who did toil in industrial settings such as tobacco manufactories were usually enslaved. More common were opportunities for piecework performed in the streets or in a woman's own home rather than under the roof of an employer: rag picking, yarn spooling, and most importantly, finishing garments for merchant tailors. In 1834, clothier John Orem encouraged women workers to gather at his Market Street store, as he advertised both his extensive inventory in "ready made clothing" and his need for "a number of Seamstresses."[66]

Far more promising—but still precarious, as evidenced by the female hucksters—

was to become, in modern terms, a self-employed independent contractor. Whether hawking the products of their own handicraft, retailing prepared food and drink, or marketing their own sexual labor, working women were no less immersed in the market relations of early republic capitalism than their male peers who had begun to exchange their labor for wages. In the Harrison Street Bazaar, for example, "the stores in the second story are occupied almost exclusively by widows and other females, who are by this means making credible exertions to procure a livelihood for themselves and families."[67]

Working for oneself was hardly evidence of nascent entrepreneurism and could make a woman's livelihood even more precarious by subjecting income to minute fluctuations of the urban marketplace. At the same time, such self-employment offered the city's marginal workers, especially free women of color, their best income-earning opportunities. As laundresses, free black women removed a central task of domestic labor away from white oversight and relocated it to more autonomous spaces of black women's sociability and authority. Relative to free black men dependent on manual labor and white women reliant on piece rates for sewing slop, free women of color made Baltimore's racial organization of labor serve their interests.

For white women, petty marketing offered one viable means of earning cash, although the absence of hucksters, hawkers, and street vendors from city directories and tax lists betrayed their economic marginality. Neither petitions nor anecdotal sources identify female hucksters as African American. Black women did not dominate marketing in Baltimore (as they did in Charleston and other Southern locales) until later in the nineteenth century.[68] Although not legally banned from street peddling, African American hucksters were exceptional enough to require special permission for informal vending. Sarah Ross, whose failing health made it impossible for her to continue as a laundress, petitioned to sell "cooked victuals on the wharf" in 1838. Her former employer, Philip E. Thomas, president of the Baltimore & Ohio Railroad, testified to Ross's "good character for sobriety, industry, and quiet deportment."[69]

Most hucksters were white women who took special pains to identify themselves as widows when they made public appeals for looser marketing regulations. While some women may have worked on their own accounts, others labored as paid employees of rural farmers, of captains of Chesapeake Bay packets, or of city merchants. Poor women's petty marketing was common enough to justify an 1807 law licensing "poor persons" to vend from tables or baskets on public streets "fruit, cakes, nuts, and such other articles as have heretofore been customary for persons of that description to sell." Regardless, subsequent municipal ordinances—

usually passed at the instigation of more established and sedentary vendors who paid stall rents and license taxes at the covered marketplaces—constantly redefined what, when, and where women could peddle.[70]

Enforcing those regulations was, of course, another story, and female hucksters defended their livelihoods vigorously. The superintendent of the Centre Market warned of the "torrent of foul abuse and billingsgate language as the Hucksters always have in store against whomsoever dares to molest or disturb them."[71] Female hucksters showed no ignorance of market logic, and when accused of exorbitant pricing, replied "that a fixed and uniform maxim of Trade declares that according to the abundance of an article is the cheap [price] thereof." However much the hucksters raised the prices of a piece of fruit or a box of candles, the women reported, we "only increase them according to the necessity of profit, and in proportion to the expense and trouble incurred and endured, in order to supply that variety in your markets, which is always a desideratum with the People of your City."[72] Hucksters showed savvy in other ways too. When a municipal ordinance made it illegal for them to sell foreign fruit, the women were quick to declare that their limes, oranges, and lemons had been grown in the recently obtained Florida Territory.[73]

Clever legal arguments proved no more useful to hucksters than did attempts to play upon patriarchal assumptions of female dependency. "There are it is true among them some few poor indigent women, who are either widows, and much pinched with poverty, or have worthless drunken husbands with perhaps children to maintain," explained Centre Market clerk Robert Lawson, "and yet, no distinction can or ought to be made, which might license them to violate the ordinance with impunity."[74] In 1816, the city council did not remit the fines of the four "poor necessituous & indigent women" whose petition began this chapter.[75]

A larger group of female hucksters tried again in 1826 when a new licensing tax presumably made it impossible for them "to prosecute their humble but lawful Traffick, as the only means of their support and maintenance in Life." Eighteen widowed women, supporting themselves and seventy-seven children, contended that "in all probability, [we] will be thrown upon the charity of your city and forced to become the unfortunate Tenants of your Alms House."[76] An opponent of a similar state licensing law struck the same chord: "Its operation in our city will be most distressing; numerous widows and children who reside in miserable tenements and selling small articles to aid in support of themselves and family, and who can scarcely support nature or pay rent, will by this oppressive law be compelled to go to the Poor House for support."[77] The fact was, however, that hucksters were as likely to be seen as nuisances than as providing a public

service. "Let Hucksters make Shops of their Houses, or build or rent Shops elsewhere, and pay rent and taxes, as other people," implored gadfly Thomas W. Griffith
with little sympathy for female street peddlers.[78]

If selling goods like candles and limes proved untenable, women found the
opportunity to sell sexual access in a society with ample demand. Sex work could
bring a woman more income in the space of an evening than she might earn in
several weeks finishing shirts for a tailor. Prostitution was of course dangerous
labor, and beyond physical violence of clients, other dangers included extortion
by the city's watchmen. John Oldham lost his job on the city watch in 1833 for
"threatening some of the unfortunate females" at a brothel known as the Three
Gun Battery. Oldham demanded "connexion with them, or in case of refusal, to
carry them to the watch house." Surprisingly, city officials like the mayor and the
captains of the night watch acted to defend the women from such violence. "However degraded an individual may be," observed mayor Jesse Hunt in an 1832 di-
rective to the city's informal police force, "justice demands that they should not
be made the victims of cruelty." Hunt had personally seen to the firing of John
Langley, a Fells Point watchman who had entered a "House of ill fame" and beaten
one of the women, Elizabeth Burgis, with his "spear," or night stick. Langley had
been to the brothel only an hour earlier to collect "a small sum of money" from
the women. When he returned at 11:00 p.m., Langley dragged Burgis into the
street, beat her, and deposited her in the watch house. The mayor considered Burgis "an abandoned young woman and a disgrace to her sex," but thought it his
"duty to redress the wrong done to the most abandoned and destitute, with the
same promptness, as if done to the most respectable member of society."[79]

Commercial sex constituted a variegated sector of the economy, and the relationship of most working women to it remained nebulous. Poor women likely
used prostitution as a seasonal by-occupation or a stopgap measure to survive an
economic emergency. Entry in and out of the sex trade was not difficult, especially
because Baltimore's port brought a large number of transient males to town. Street-
walking dominated entire blocks of the city, and female proprietors rented out
cheap rooms by the hour in bawdy houses. Perhaps participation in commercial
sex attested to women's agency, but it typically indicated financial desperation.

Meandering through Fells Point in 1803, the twenty-one-year-old William Darlington stopped at "a noted place for those carnal lumps of flesh called en fran-
cais Filles de joie." Darlington, a congressman later in life, observed "a whole street
of them called 'oakum bay'—where many a Tar can, and doubtless does, dispose
of his rope yarn and old cables to advantage." Many women, not just prostitutes,
sold oakum, untangled strands of frayed ropes, to papermakers for converting into

pulp or to shipyards for caulk. Nonetheless, if Darlington was not offering a juvenile double entendre, he highlighted a convoluted relationship between prostitution and income. These women traded sex for raw materials that required additional labor before acquiring a cash value. It is conceivable that the presence of enslaved women in the city pushed Baltimore's prostitutes into such desperate deals. If the sexual coercion of enslaved women was as constant in Baltimore as in other locales of the early republic South—and there is no reason to suspect otherwise—then some proportion of potential customers gained sexual access through rape rather than hire.[80]

The commercialization of women's traditional household labor did have one key group of beneficiaries: free African American laundresses who could now support themselves on the labor that had previously been coerced within slavery. This was not true for all forms of domestic labor, insofar as most household service still required adult black women to sacrifice autonomy and labor under the watchful eyes of a white employer. But the commercialization of laundry—perhaps the most arduous facet of domestic labor—allowed free black women to work for themselves far from the supervision of their employers. As free black women began to outnumber enslaved women in Baltimore after 1800, so too did they come to dominate the city's laundry trade. In 1817, African American women accounted for 77 percent of laundresses listed in the city directory. As that niche expanded over the next several decades, laundry became the best route for a free black woman to acquire property of her own. Laundresses and washerwomen constituted 194 of the 231 African American female heads of households listed with occupations in the 1822 city directory; 250 of 289 in 1831; and 440 of 526 in 1840. Although the tax records are not as conclusive (due to missing occupational descriptors), some of the wealthiest free women of color made their livings as laundresses. Rachel Coale owned the most valuable house on Moore Alley, and her $250 of property in 1818 put her above the median wealth for both men and women, white and black, in the tenth ward.[81]

The physical labor of preindustrial laundry was astoundingly difficult, starting with carting numerous buckets of water—each weighing perhaps 25 pounds—from public springs or streams back to yards and kitchens for boiling. Washing itself took its toll on the body: aching backs from lifting water-logged clothing, burning hands from lye soaps and rough washboards. Such work might be comparable to the toil of male canal diggers. That most black women regarded laundry work as an improvement in their lives attested to the stifling intimacy and subordination of domestic service within a white employer's home.

Along the lines of labor patterns in present-day immigrant communities, black women saw entrepreneurial opportunity in laundry. Not only could laundresses put their own children to work on such tasks as gathering wood for fires to heat water or irons, they could also employ available men (husbands, brothers, relatives) in delivering finished laundry to customers around town. Such practices would insulate black laundresses from contact with white employers who had once owned them or supervised their domestic labor. The ability of laundresses to direct their own labor also promoted a female sociability, one that had its own distinctive cultural idioms. White observers along Harford Run complained to the city council in 1817 in regard to the "almost naked" style of a group of West Indian laundresses. In sum, laundry allowed free black women to remain at home, utilize family labor, work near friends, and avoid direct white supervision. Black women dominated the laundry business not merely because of racial proscription, but because they saw in the trade an opportunity for a better life.[82]

For a woman, getting a job was difficult because there were few jobs to get. "The number of employments which are accessible to females in this country . . . is very limited," explained an 1835 essayist in the *Southern Pioneer and Gospel Visitor*, a Universalist newspaper published in Baltimore. "Thousands are wasting their days in idleness, not because they cannot work, not because they will not work, but because custom does not warrant them engaging in certain pursuits for which they are just as well qualified by their intellectual and physical powers as men."[83]

More employment opportunities might have helped to alleviate female poverty, but the number of jobs could make little difference so long as *custom* placed other impediments in the way of women's economic self-sufficiency. The expansion of Baltimore's service economy brought an unprecedented amount of female labor to the marketplace. Yet it did so without transforming women into unfettered market actors whose aggregate bargaining would allow them to reap the benefits of increased demand for their labor. To the contrary, the legality of slavery meant that purchasers of domestic labor were frequently the purchasers of women's bodies. For many free women, confinement within male-headed households made it difficult to pursue better pay in other environs. The patriarchal presumption that women workers were never self-supporting, but always dependent on a husband, father, or son, kept wages below what a woman needed to support herself, let alone a family. The buying and selling of domestic work provided some women new opportunities to earn money but allowed very few of them to earn a living.

CHAPTER 5

The Living Wage

R esolved, That we the females of the city of Baltimore, who have for a series
of years been compelled to work at our needles for our maintenance, have
not received value for our labour, and that we believe the time has now come
when we should come forward in justification of our rights and privileges with
our sisters of other cities." So began the 1833 strike of Baltimore's seamstresses,
who sought economic justice as exploited laborers in a competitive market society. In return, they received public sympathy as females deprived of male support
in a persistently patriarchal society. The seamstresses asked whether a woman
could support a family through paid labor, but they did so in a culture that presumed a woman should do no such thing. Their situation raised fundamental questions about wage labor and dependence, as well as about the meaning of freedom
for women who, in the words of one supporter, "may literally be said to be bound
for life to the needle and thread."[1]

For several decades already, poor women in Baltimore lined up to get work
that paid too little. Second only to domestic service, sewing brought young and
old women into the ranks of wage earners. Their employers were entrepreneurial
tailors who reorganized clothing production around ready-made, ready-to-wear
garments destined for new markets near and far. Rather than building factories
or pursuing technological innovations, manufacturers simplified (or deskilled)
clothing construction to its most basic components. Doing so made it possible
to jettison the artisanal expertise of journeymen tailors and tailoresses and to
replace them with cheaper workers lacking expertise in design, fitting, or cutting.
Seamstresses—women whose expertise was limited to sewing seams—became
key clothing producers by performing what was dismissively known as slop
work: the stitching together of precut fabric, the sewing of buttons, and the affixing
of ribbons and other decorative flair to garments. From across the city, women
walked to the clothing shops to pick up materials, took them home to complete,

and then walked the finished garments back to the shops to exchange for pay. This "putting-out" or "outwork" system transformed the living quarters of thousands of Baltimore women into the city's workshops.[2]

Few workers, male or female, were more exposed to the vagaries of the market-place than seamstresses. Because they were paid by the finished piece, there was no ambiguity in the commodification of their labor. No other obligations or re-sponsibilities linked employers and employees: seamstresses did not reside un-der the roofs of their employers, nor did they promise allegiance in exchange for protection and moral guidance (the implicit social contract of dependent labor and the explicit legal contract of servitude). Laboring from home and therefore re-sponsible for the cost of heating and lighting their own workplaces, seamstresses assumed the overhead costs of production. Employers made no guarantee of fu-ture hire and held no legal ability to prevent seamstresses from quitting or seek-ing higher wages elsewhere. Seamstresses frequently lived outside the confines of male-headed households and were thereby exempt from the law of coverture that transferred ownership of wives' and daughters' wages to husbands and fa-thers. Liberated from the customary exchanges and legal bondage that structured colonial-era manufacturing, seamstresses were among the freest workers within early republic capitalism.[3]

At the same time, few workers were more insulated from the free play of the market than seamstresses, whose wages were fixed at sub-subsistence levels by women's presumed dependence on a male provider. Within the cultural logic of a patriarchal society, paid labor was at best a life stage for a woman, a prelude to marriage, childrearing, and reliance on a husband for subsistence. Since women were thought to be dependent by nature, there was no need to pay them the full wages (or "family wages") men demanded on behalf of their wives and children. In fact, women's sub-subsistence wages became a self-fulfilling prophecy: the pre-sumption of female dependence justified the secondary wages that in turn guar-anteed it. Because *female breadwinner* was a contradiction in terms, seamstresses received pay far below what most needed to support themselves and their families.[4]

Long before Baltimore's seamstresses organized, women "employed by the slop-shops" had garnered public attention for their impoverishment. Not even the most nimble-fingered women—ones free from the distractions of minding children or cooking supper—could complete enough shirts or coats in the space of a week to support themselves on piece rates. "The sum which they receive for their work, when done, is of so small account as scarcely to defray their necessary and im-mediate expenses," lamented one of the seamstresses' early defenders in 1805. Yet even as they entered the marketplace alone, their situation was invariably depicted in terms of their relationship to missing men, usually dead husbands whose absent wages thrust innocent women into paid labor. "A Widow's Friend" seemed a predictable pseudonym for one champion of "this numerous class of women [who] derive their daily support almost exclusively from such small pieces of work as can be had occasionally from the tailors, or on the very precarious employment to be procured from the shelves of the slopshop." It scarcely needed to be said that prostitution was the inevitable recourse of underpaid women lacking "men to work for them."[5]

Because their wages generated so much public discussion, seamstresses offer historians the best chance to assess whether a working woman could make a living. Philanthropic appeals and strike proclamations specified the number of shirts a woman might finish in a week or the weeks per year she might find employment from a slopshop. Although such sources were produced to sway public opinion, they nonetheless provide the most precise data of women's earnings absent the payrolls that survive for male manual labor. Tellingly, the newspaper columns, speeches, and broadsides that document the inability of a seamstress to earn a living by her own labor also convey few expectations that a woman should be self-supporting.

In their own time, seamstresses offered a vehicle to reckon with the moral consequences of capitalism. The work they performed raised general questions about the economic fairness of wages and gendered questions about the relationship of the sexes in a market society. The striking seamstresses in 1833 moved between these registers. Understanding themselves as exploited workers, they had little chance of gaining public support without representing themselves as women lacking male providers. The struggling mudmachinists had likewise moved between generic and gendered arguments as they petitioned for better pay as workers and fathers. But unlike the mudmachinists, the seamstresses provoked a sustained national conversation, engaged the energies of philanthropists, ministers, and political economists up and down the eastern seaboard, and became the beneficiaries of arguably the nation's first "living wage" campaign. Yet so long as independent seamstresses who waged strikes could be culturally reimagined as charity cases, women would have far more difficulty than their male peers in making work pay.

The Challenge of Self-Sufficiency

Independent adult women—*femmes sole*—constituted a discrete legal category in early America, but they were also a conceptual anomaly in a society that presumed female dependence on a male provider. For a single woman to support herself by working for wages might be understood as a temporary, if regrettable, expedient, but it certainly was not seen as a "choice," as it might be described today.[6] Nonetheless, the fact that a sizeable number of Baltimore women headed their own households suggests that economic independence was possible without a male breadwinner. In 1810, for example, women headed 318—or nearly 17 percent—of the 1,900 households in the working-class wards of Old Town and Fells Point.[7] Here and throughout the city, female householders with enough property to be recognized in city directories or on tax lists were often widows living off investment property in real estate or slaves. Other women inherited the stores and workshops of deceased husbands.[8] Self-sufficient women appeared in city directories as comb manufacturers, boardinghouse and tavern keepers, fishmongers, sausage dealers, nurses, midwives, school mistresses, shopkeepers, glovemakers, confectioners, cigarmakers, potters, and cordial distillers. Many of these women had access to productive property that would help convert their labor into income: a storefront, a market stall, a commodious house, or a workshop.[9]

Most laboring women, however, operated below the radar of the tax collector or directory compiler. While tax lists and directories are revealing of the number of successful women who attained property and a modicum of economic independence, they undercount female workers living within other households and obscure the number of women whose market labor facilitated existences too marginal to notice. In a city with perhaps 12,000 working-age women, the 1817 city directory identified only 95 seamstresses and only 426 women with occupations overall. Working women were more likely to appear in the records of the Maryland Penitentiary or the Baltimore almshouse than in the listings of the city directory. Among the 454 incarcerated Baltimore women during the 1810s and 1820s were 42 seamstresses, 35 washerwomen, 4 nurses, a weaver, and a sausage maker. In addition to nearly one hundred women with sewing skills, the Baltimore almshouse contained a milliner, a brushmaker, a tailoress, two shoebinders, several weavers, and a nurse. Twenty-eight-year-old Elizabeth O'Brion was typical of the working women who never appeared in tax records, city directories, or census returns. The Irish-born O'Brion had lived and labored in Baltimore since 1817, earning wages by binding shoes for merchant cordwainers. In 1826, however, she took refuge from her abusive husband in the almshouse. She also brought her two children, Ignatius and Oswin, to the institution. All three left after six days and disappeared into the city.[10]

Women reliant on their "own industry" were presumably unusual, but they were neither unanticipated nor invisible. Charity schools assumed that many poor girls would lack a male provider in adulthood and taught them skills to "gain a re-spectable maintenance for themselves in life." Women who petitioned the city gov-ernment or sought employment made explicit reference to themselves as primary earners. When female hucksters petitioned the city council in 1816, they reported having no other means to provide for their children, "save only their own personal industry." Likewise, the widowed umbrella maker Catherine Paul advertised in search of "patronage in supplying her with sufficient employment to enable her to live by her own industry and the strictest economy." In addition to repairing umbrellas, Paul declared herself "thankful for any kind of work in plain sewing, making children's clothes, &c."[11]

Self-supporting women composed a large enough segment of the laboring pop-ulation to warrant official concern whenever the city's economy slowed. As with male manual laborers, female workers in the needle trades were beset by seasonal unemployment. With "the sale of slops for the season being almost entirely over" in January 1805, "a very great many" women stood "idle." During almost every winter of the early 1800s, the city government orchestrated relief efforts to assist such displaced workers. As one observer noted, "The general and just complaint of these people are, that they can get no work, by which is understood that no la-bor presents itself which they can perform: from this circumstance, annual con-tributions must necessarily be made, or they be left to perish by cold and hunger." Although public attention fell largely upon male maritime workers, commenta-tors also recognized "women left with children, and without husbands to support them" among the seasonally displaced. In 1809, the mayor convened a commit-tee to consider "the numerous cases of industrious widows with families of or-phan children . . . who from want of the usual employment are rendered inca-pable of providing the common necessities of life."[12]

For the officials who oversaw Baltimore's wintertime poor relief efforts in the early 1800s, the limited number of working days—and not the rate of pay—explained the poverty of those unfortunate females forced to support themselves through labor. Accordingly, municipal leaders, clergymen, and philanthropists em-braced make-work schemes as an alternative to costly relief payments to unem-ployed workers during slack times. Government-sponsored work programs for poor women had a long history in North America. Boston leaders had envisioned a linen manufactory in the early 1750s, and soon thereafter employed the widows of the Seven Years' War spinning flax and wool. Philadelphia's Bettering House of the 1770s gathered materials for poor women to sew under the watchful eyes of Quaker stewards. During the 1780s and 1790s, Tench Coxe and Alexander Hamilton promoted state-sponsored, publicly subscribed manufacturing enterprises in Pennsylvania and New Jersey where poor women would find constant employment. Leaders in Baltimore found even greater inspiration from central Europe, as they studied Count Rumford's recent experiment with institutional-ized labor in Bavaria. Rumford's School of Industry served to discipline beggars but also to provide employment for the deserving poor who might otherwise be forced to rely on charity when work disappeared.[13]

In advocating a similar institution for Baltimore in 1804, a committee of the city's leading men touted the possibility of "permanent employment" by supply-ing cloth and other materials to the poor. Some needy workers would toil within the School of Industry, while others would be able to take the materials home for completion. Either way, the institution would pay "suitable recompense" (minus the cost of supplies) and locate merchants in the city "to receive at the market prices, the fruits of the labor of the poor." Other reformers in 1805 proposed a Baltimore Benevolent Society for the Benefit of Females to provide sewing work to "honest, industrious, deserving females" during wintertime slowdowns. Nei-ther the School of Industry nor the Benevolent Society was ever launched, but other philanthropic organizations found work for a handful of women each win-ter. By distributing flax, wool, and cotton to poor women in 1811, the ladies of the Aimwell Society "furnished employment to 58 indigent persons when they could not procure work elsewhere."[14]

The vast majority of paid sewing work for adult women came from Baltimore's merchant tailors, the entrepreneurs who helped to create and fill a new demand for inexpensive and standardized clothing. Clerks and other middling workers in the city required business dress and leisure attire for evenings out on the town. New roads helped make rural families into consumers of ready-made clothing, especially when the incentives for small-scale commercial agriculture reallocated the labor of wives and daughters away from making clothing. Finally, clothing man-ufacturers tapped distant purchasers on the expanding cotton frontier who sought cheap garments for enslaved workers. Whereas eighteenth-century plantations in the Chesapeake had dedicated some female labor to clothing manufacture, the new plantations of the cotton boom maximized enslaved women's field labor and turned to clothing manufacturers in urban centers to provide ready-made shirts, pants, and shoes.[15]

The reorganization of urban clothing production brought significant economic dislocation to male workers in the traditional craft workshop. In particular, jour-neymen tailors saw their prospects for prosperity disappear when their employ-ers sought to increase production by hiring "unskilled" seamstresses. As early as 1799, Baltimore's journeymen tailors lambasted the female "slop makers" and "plain needle women" who could find employment at such establishments as Mrs. Perry's "Ready made Linen Warehouse" on Market Street. Female slop workers would remain the imagined antagonists of downwardly mobile journeymen for the next several decades.[16]

Evidence of the growing number of seamstresses in a new clothing economy came not only from disgruntled competitors, but also from commentators concerned about the extent of female poverty in the city. The market for sewing work fluctuated seasonally, and with the ebb and flow of the international economy. "When any disappointment happens, or any interruption takes place in their business, every resource vanishes, as it were instantaneously, leaving them not infrequently reduced to the greatest poverty and distress," explained an advocate for seamstresses in 1805. But with few other opportunities, adult women—especially those who could not leave their own families for more lucrative employment as domestic servants in other households—literally lined up in front of the clothing shops to obtain piecework. "The clothing shops are over-run with persons seeking employment," observed Hezekiah Niles in an 1823 report on female labor in Baltimore. "Hundreds are willing to take in work that cannot obtain it," Niles added. When a group of clothing manufacturers petitioned the city council for preferential treatment that same year, they noted dutifully that "a great number of indigent females receive their daily support from [our] employ." Upwards of 3,000 Baltimore women toiled as seamstresses, according to an 1831 charity address on their behalf.[17]

Clothing manufacturers could be clever by depicting their newfound preferences for low-paid female workers in terms of public service. For example, when Ebenezer French advertised his "Ready made Linen Warehouse" in 1815, he appealed to the philanthropic instincts of would-be customers: by "patronizing such an institution, they do a positive, but indirect charity also, by giving employment and support to many respectable, but indigent females." French explained that his business had made little money over its first several months but nonetheless took "a consolation in reflecting that he has kept constantly employed, at satisfactory prices, from ten to twenty females, many of whom have families dependent on the labor of their hands for support." French hoped that Baltimore consumers would help him expand the "usefulness" of his operation. Describing the plight of one of his workers, a "female, the wife of a poor but respectable and honest man," French asked, "Who that is willing to labor, should be denied support?"[18]

The key role female seamstresses played in early republic debates about work and poverty owed to their distinguishing demographic characteristic: seamstresses were almost exclusively white. It is unclear whether clothing manufacturers conducted exclusionary hiring, or even whether the seamstresses gathering in front of clothing shops policed their own ranks and drove away women of color. Ownership of female slaves by clothing manufacturers was minimal, and low piece rates offered no incentive for slaveholders to send enslaved women to the slopshops. If free women of color participated in the needle trades, their numbers were negligible, at least compared with the sizable number of black laundresses.[19] Whatever the explanation, seamstresses' whiteness made them more eligible for sympathy but also raised anxieties about the social repercussions of their imperiled womanhood. Their ineligibility for enslavement made it all the more striking when reformers compared seamstresses to slaves or referred to them as living in bondage. Notably, however, white womanhood did not spare seamstresses from the expectation of having to trade their labor for wages in the absence of a male provider.

Whenever entrepreneurs touted new manufactories, they relied on what one historian has called "the tried and true mercantilistic argument that manufacturing was the best way of ensuring widespread employment for the industrious poor." Take the silkworm craze of the mid-1820s. When a display of "this interesting insect" came to Baltimore in 1826, supporters declared that silk cultivation "would give a more pleasing and profitable employment to thousands of widows and orphans, now dependent on the most precarious means of support." In broader discussions of American political economy, the poor women in slaveholding states like Maryland could be portrayed as the prime beneficiaries of new factories. "By the extensive introduction of the manufacturing system," Thomas Jones explained to Philadelphia's Franklin Institute in 1827, such women "would not only be redeemed from wretchedness, but become a mine of wealth to the country, instead of remaining a degraded cast, and a heavy burden." Factories would greatly relieve women from the "miserable and precarious subsistence" they earned from the merchant tailors.[20]

Surprisingly, it was Baltimore's leading advocate of manufacturing, the newspaper editor Hezekiah Niles, who reoriented the discussion away from the absence of jobs for women and toward the specific issue of women's pay. Although make-work programs would continue to have their advocates among the city's philanthropists, the viability of those efforts would now be evaluated by the rate of wages they paid rather than the regularity of the labor they offered. In one of his frequent endorsements of "domestic manufactures," Niles contended that poor women would find "far more profitable employment" in factories. How could it be otherwise when women received prices "so very low" for assembling clothing in their own residences? Inaugurating what would become a standard rhetorical tool in the debate over women's pay, Niles printed a price list: $2 per dozen vests, 12½¢ per summer roundabout (a kind of coat) or pair of pants. Niles did not comment on how many items a woman might assemble in a week, but cited a local report of one woman who took two days to finish a single roundabout. Earning 6¼¢ a day, no woman could pay rent and feed her own children.[21]

A woman's earnings as a seamstress compared very poorly not only with her potential income in a yet-unbuilt factory, but also to the prevailing wages in domestic service. Although domestic service was oppressive work that women strove to avoid, it offered pay that was far more constant and less likely to be interrupted by seasonal fluctuations in the economy. In addition to a monthly wage, domestic servants were compensated with the room and board that seamstresses had to purchase out of their wages. A housekeeper, cook, or chambermaid might garner a wage of $8 to $10 per month. While that amount comprised a paltry daily wage—one that paled in comparison to a male manual laborer's earnings of $1 per day—it was nonetheless several times greater than what a seamstress could earn through piecework. By most accounts, a domestic servant earned twice what a typical seamstress could earn in a year in wages alone. If room and board were calculated in, domestic servants would out-earn seamstresses by several more times.[22]

Stung by Niles's critique, the city's clothing manufacturers defended their piece rates and tried to return attention to the public good they provided in simply employing poor women in the first place. A group of twenty clothing-shop owners petitioned the city council in 1823 to limit competition from stall keepers in the public markets. With the impending winter and the seasonal downturn in demand, the clothiers "could with advantage dispense with the services of those females, but from motives of humanity they continued to employ them to save them from want." But, the clothiers warned, should the city council ignore their petition, "they will be compelled to abandon these poor females to seek support from some other source." The city was not forthcoming with new market regulations, which perhaps attested less to the clothiers' lack of political clout than to the obvious fact that even fully employed seamstresses would require public relief each January and February. Indeed, even charity appeals now focused on the rate of pay. "There are poor widow women, with half a dozen children dependent upon them for support, while the most they can possibly earn in a week would scarcely furnish delicacies for a single tea-table in a common family," revealed an 1828 plea for donations.[23]

Starvation or Pollution

The 1820s witnessed a national conversation about the legitimacy of wage labor in a republican society. Eighteenth-century political economists had conceived of wage labor as a degraded form of dependence and categorized male wage earners as unworthy of the franchise. But so long as wage labor was experienced and understood as a short-term expedient en route to propertied independence, questions of citizenship could be glossed over. By the third decade of the nineteenth century, however, enough men labored for wages in New York, Boston, Philadelphia, and Baltimore that questions resurfaced about the relationship of dependent labor and republican citizenship. The key voices here were no longer elite political economists, but working men and women who contended that the emerging capitalist economy blocked their access to the promises of the American Revolution. Politicized workers organized themselves into parties and trade unions, subscribed to such newspapers as the *Working Man's Advocate* in New York or the *Mechanic's Free Press* in Philadelphia, and thronged lectures by such radicals as Frances Wright and Thomas Skidmore. Public education, birth control, free thought, and the sanctity of private property were fair game for debate. So too was the question of whether workers were entitled to the full value of the labor they exerted to create a shirt, chair, or barrel for market.[24]

For the working-class critics of the emerging wage system, the fundamental issue hinged on the labor theory of value, or the notion that the fruits of economic exchange should accrue to those who did the work rather than to those who facilitated or financed the buying and selling of finished products. Workers condemned a system wherein a capitalist skimmed profit in the differential between the price of producing a good (in which the wage figured prominently) and the price received for the product (what the consumer paid). Because seamstresses were paid by piece rates, it was easy to compare the amount seamstresses earned for finishing a shirt with the sale price of the finished product. In principle, seamstresses could represent all workers harmed by the injustice of wage relations. In practice, they were troublesome figures through which to level a critique of capitalism because they were women.

If the disjuncture between a worker's income and expenses was universal, its consequences were precisely gendered. In the language of "artisan republicanism," struggling male craftsmen lamented that wages did not allow a man to provide for a dependent wife and children. Capitalist labor relations seemed to undermine patriarchal male prerogatives and to emasculate the working man who could not assume the role of sole breadwinner. This common refrain within early republic labor politics reflected the presumption that a woman's normative role was as a dependent wife rather than a self-sufficient economic actor. In the rhetoric of militant male artisans, the low wages paid to seamstresses were less a problem for the women earning them than for the male workers who were thus undercut and unable to satisfy their patriarchal obligations to dependent wives and children.[25]

Prosperous philanthropists and religious leaders put forward their own critique of early republic capitalism, and here seamstresses garnered greater sympathy. To many Americans, including those whose wealth was on the ascent in the first decades of the nineteenth century, the unfettering of market relations was neither an unambiguous good nor the fulfillment of human destiny. Elite commentators worried about the market as a solvent on the glue that held society together. Religious leaders feared new behaviors that seemed less inspired by Jesus than by the moneychangers he had cast out of the temple. Women's wages proved an excellent vehicle for such observations and earned seamstresses a cadre of prominent advocates and patrons. But even as the seamstress might represent all workers, her plight proved especially compelling for its gendered consequences. Pulling back from indicting the wage system outright and glossing over the patriarchal claims of male artisans, elite commentators drew a direct line from low wages to rampant prostitution. The danger of her sexual corruption usually trumped her claims to economic justice as a self-sufficient worker.[26]

Philadelphian Mathew Carey was at the forefront of the seamstresses' cause, and his reach as an editor and publisher made their plight a national issue. Known in his earlier career as a passionate defender of Irish liberation and then as a strident advocate of American industry, Carey had long expressed interest in "the low rate of female labour," which he pronounced "a grievance of the very first magnitude" in 1810. After retiring from bookselling in the 1820s, Carey devoted a great portion of his polemical talent to the problem of women's wages, especially what he considered the inexplicable illogic of paying women only a fraction of men's wages for comparable labor. "Where is the justice, where the propriety," he asked in an 1827 essay, "of paying five, six, seven dollars a week for male labour, and only a dollar, or a dollar and an eighth for labour similar, or nearly similar, performed by women?" As Carey researched the matter further over the next year, he learned that most working women actually earned less, what he termed "a sorry subsistence, at a miserable pittance."[27]

Carey took up the cause of women workers more aggressively in his 1828 *Essays on the Public Charities of Philadelphia*. The pamphlet's complete title indicated Carey's intent "to place in strong Relief, before an enlightened Public, the Sufferings and Oppression under which the greater part of the Females labour, who depend on their industry for a support for themselves and Children." Although Carey presumed that such wage-earning women were widowed or otherwise denied the support of a male breadwinner, his solution to women's poverty was not to relocate female workers into patriarchal households. Far more straightforward, Carey called for higher wages and chastised employers for "grinding the faces of the poor" in opposition to biblical precepts. "Ought not the labour of every individual in society to enable him or her to procure food, and raiment, and lodging?" Positing that even women workers—regardless of their relationship to a male provider— had an inherent claim to a decent living, Carey explained "that neither skill, talent, nor industry" provided urban seamstresses with the ability to support themselves or their children.[28]

Even as Carey cast the question of women's wages in terms of universal economic justice, he was quick to stress the gendered consequences of "the paltry, contemptible compensation for female labour." Low wages left women with five undesirable options: "to beg—to depend on the overseers of the poor, a species of begging—to steal—to starve—or to sell themselves to pollution." At bottom, however, women's choices narrowed to two: "STARVATION OR POLLUTION." Carey could not marshal specific data on prostitution as a subsistence strategy for poor women, but merely asserting this outcome gave moralists, philanthropists, and clergymen a stake in the wage issue and reintroduced a paternalistic concern for "those females who depend on their needles."[29]

In early 1829, Carey issued a "Report of Female Wages." In what would become Carey's standard mode of argument, the report offered tabular data contrasting a seamstress's maximum annual earnings from finishing shirts with her expenses for rent, clothing, and food. Taking unemployment, sickness, and childcare into account, the report was quick to remind readers of the "harrowing misery and distress that prevail among this class." By listing prevailing piece rates for women's labor and the costs of specific household goods like heating fuel, Carey and his allies dispelled the "great error" that the poor had only themselves to blame for their predicament. The report invoked the golden rule—"doing unto others as we would have others do unto us"—to chastise urban employers for paying starvation (or, implicitly, prostitution-inducing) wages. "Although the great and increasing competition in trade, renders it necessary to use rigid economy in the expense of producing articles for market," the report conceded, "it can never palliate, far less justify the oppression of the ill-fated people engaged in the production, by whose labours large fortunes are made, and the employers enabled to live in ease and opulence." Once they realized the "real state" of low wages, employers "will probably, as they certainly ought to, increase those wages," the report concluded.[30]

Not only did Carey collect data from charity officials in Philadelphia, but he corresponded with like-minded reformers in the other industrializing urban centers of the new nation. Ezra Stiles Ely, who had been ministering to New York's poor for nearly two decades, wrote to decry the condition of seamstresses in his city. Provocatively, Ely claimed that "a common slave" in the upper South was "better compensated for his labour, by his necessary food, clothing, lodging, and medicines, than many respectable mothers and daughters in this city." While such a comparison might sound preposterous in Baltimore, where the material deprivations of slavery were well known, it had a pronounced resonance for northern audiences and remained in Carey's arsenal in the coming years.[31]

Carey broadened the discussion further in July 1829, when he advertised a $100 gold medal for "the best essay (its merits to be decided on by competent and impartial judges,) on the inadequacy of the wages generally paid to seamstresses, spoolers, spinners, shoebinders, &c. to procure food, raiment, and lodging." Carey asked contestants to comment "on the probability that those low wages frequently force poor women to the choice between dishonour and absolute want of common necessaries." The winner, Joseph Tuckerman, Boston's "Minister to the City Poor," confirmed that seamstresses' low wages were a national problem with worrisome social consequences.[32]

Tuckerman's *Essay on the Wages Paid to Females for their Labour* reflected a broader ambivalence about the market in American society, as well as a particular anxiety about women's role in it. On the one hand, Tuckerman accepted "as general principles" that supply and demand determined wage levels. The oversupply of seamstresses, common laborers, and other menial workers in Boston explained why wages dropped faster than did the costs of food, housing, and shelter. Tuckerman absolved urban employers of purposefully exploiting the poor and instead ascribed low wages to inexorable market forces. On the other hand, Tuckerman proposed a remedy that would circumvent market logic: "to quicken the consciences of employers of the poor" so they might "sacrifice some of their own gains" on behalf of their employees. Tuckerman believed the Christian imperative to "do unto others . . ." would eliminate "oppression" and yield "a generous consideration of the hireling in his wages." Indeed, he argued, "the best charity which can be exercised towards those who are capable of labour, is to give them, as far as possible, the labour by which they may earn the means of their subsistence; and, whenever they are employed, amply to remunerate them for their services." The lives of the poor, then, would improve when individual employers adopted a Christian stewardship for "their suffering fellow creatures."[33]

Tuckerman was a peculiar choice for Carey's award, for the winning essay did not attribute the plight of poor women to their scant earnings. Following earlier moral reformers, Tuckerman located "other causes of the crimes and miseries of the poor, which lie far deeper than the question of the effects of high, or of low wages, upon their condition and character." The bulk of his essay described "the prevailing licentiousness of our cities" and spelled out a series of scenarios by which young women were brought to prostitution. "From the tavern bar, from the tippling shop, and the gambling house, the passage is short and always open, which leads to the deepest sinks of human infamy," he wrote. Such rhetoric had filled the publications of the Society for the Prevention of Pauperism in New York and Baltimore during the late 1810s and early 1820s, and one of Carey's great missions was to refute it, portraying poverty not as a matter of moral failing, but as a structural consequence of capitalist labor relations. In contrast to Carey's position that high wages precluded moral degeneracy, Tuckerman privileged Christian uplift over better pay. To improve the condition of the working people required not just raising their incomes, but *"improving their characters,"* Tuckerman wrote emphatically as he called on employers to take a personal interest in the spiritual development of their employees and poor neighbors.[34]

In Baltimore, philanthropic concern for working women surfaced in a May 1830 handbill. On face value, its origins were in a petition penned by twenty-two Baltimore "ladies of respectability and intelligence." These anonymous petitioners explained that seamstresses' wages were "entirely inadequate to their support" and that "the situation of this numerous and interesting class of society has a strong and powerful claim upon the benevolence and energies of the humane, to devise some means of remedy, or at least of mitigation of their sufferings." As Carey had in his earlier publications, the Baltimore women illustrated that prevailing piece rates of 12½¢, 10¢, and 6¢ for shirts and pants gave few seamstresses the opportunity to earn more than $1 per week. Presumably the women's petition found its way into the hands of men better situated to publicize the issue. Removing the women's names "from motives of decency," the men reprinted the petition as part of a short address, entitled "To the Public."[35]

Whatever artifice was involved in preparing the handbill, thirty-five Baltimore men affixed their names to it. Signatories include mayor Jacob Small; the president of the Baltimore & Ohio Railroad, Philip E. Thomas; the railroad's general counsel, John H. B. Latrobe, who was the son of the famous architect Benjamin Henry Latrobe; leading merchants Alexander Brown, Robert Oliver, and William Patterson, whose daughter Betsy had married Jerome Bonaparte in 1804; future Supreme Court justice Roger B. Taney; founder of the University of Maryland's law school, David Hoffman; the most prominent Irish immigrant to the city and president of the Hibernian Society, Luke Tiernan; and book publisher E. J. Coale, whose shop had distributed Tuckerman's essay in Baltimore a month before. As the powerful men who received this report confessed, "the state of things depicted in this exposé, makes a powerful appeal to the feeling of the humane."

Employing phrases that Carey and Tuckerman had publicized just weeks earlier, the Baltimore men moved back and forth between general principles of economic justice and the gendered consequences of women's low wages. While acknowledging that "competition of the employers" may have driven women's wages precariously low, the handbill invoked the golden rule to advocate a pay raise for seamstresses. Only better wages might "rescue this large and interesting class from the degradation and poverty in which so great a proportion of them are sunk." Of course, the risk of prostitution was never far behind, and the Baltimore petitioners reminded readers how easily underpaid seamstresses could "become a disgrace to the one sex, and a bane and a curse to the other."[36]

Borrowing phrases and data from one another, women and men in Baltimore, Philadelphia, New York, and Boston exchanged words and ideas in the late 1820s and early 1830s as they made seamstresses' wages a matter of both Christian morality and secular political economy. Baltimore's May 1830 handbill appeared in print a full month before a comparable piece appeared in Philadelphia, which suggests that information was flowing into Carey's Philadelphia offices from other cities as readily as it flowed out. In fact, Carey used figures on seamstresses' earnings provided by the Baltimore petitioners when he wrote to a group of New York philanthropists that same month.[37] Weeks later, in June 1830, twenty-five equally prestigious Philadelphia men reprinted a petition that they had also received from an unidentified group of women, whose "respectability, intelligence, and competence" gave them standing, but whose names would ultimately be "omitted from motives of delicacy."[38]

Baltimore attained a prominent place in the national conversation because of its Humane Impartial Society, a women-run charity organization that offered poor seamstresses piecework at a rate 50 percent above prevailing market rates. So unusual was their approach that Carey dedicated his major publication on women's wages—his 1831 *Address to the Wealthy of the Land*—to the organization. For nearly two decades, the group had watched other schemes for generating employment for Baltimore women come and go, especially those projects offering work at submarket piece rates so as not to encourage dependence. Charities in Philadelphia and Boston had also taken this miserly approach. At its founding in 1820, for example, Boston's Society for Employing the Poor promised needy women "considerably lower than the ordinary rate of wages." Fearing that "full wages" would cause seamstresses to "leave regular employment," Boston's benevolent women hoped to attract those "who prefer even low wages to idleness and beggary." Similarly, the founders of Philadelphia's Provident Society for the Employment of the Poor "purposefully fixed the wages at the lowest rates, to prevent applications from any who could find employment elsewhere." With great pride, its inaugural report of 1825 declared the institution's utility for "a worthy and industrious class of the community, who are not only willing to work hard and faithfully, but are also willing thus to work for extremely low wages."[39]

What distinguished Baltimore's Humane Impartial Society was its willingness to pay higher wages for clothing, thereby forcing market rates upwards. As one supporter explained, "the mode is to give work at a fair price, to poor women, and thus save them from misery, vice, or starvation, and by doing so to cause an advance to a reasonable rate in the wages which they receive from those who elsewhere employ them." With Carey as its most notable publicist, Baltimore's Humane Impartial Society gained national attention. The group's "fair prices" allowed women "to support themselves, without depending on the eleemosynary aid of charitable individuals, or benevolent societies, or on the overseers of the poor." In contrast, the submarket rates of other benevolent organizations had "perniciously and injuriously" harmed poor women by making it possible for merchant tailors to lower their own rates to the charity threshold. The only lamentable fact about the Humane Impartial Society was its shallow base of support in Baltimore. Carey considered it "deeply to be regretted that in such a wealthy and public-spirited city as Baltimore, this institution has but three hundred subscribers, although the subscription is but one dollar per annum." In fact, "for so glorious an object as rescuing such numbers of interesting females from penury and distress and all their demoralizing consequences," Carey contended, "had the annual subscription been five dollars, there ought to have been one thousand subscribers."[40]

Carey was right that wealthy Baltimore citizens thought themselves among the most civic minded in the nation. "In public spirit and patriotic feeling, she has no superior," declared local lawyer Ebenezer L. Finley in an 1829 speech on Baltimore's prospects as a commercial emporium. While Finley would give other rousing speeches in coming years, perhaps none expressed a greater concern for the future of his beloved city than his 1831 address on behalf of female seamstresses and the Humane Impartial Society. Finley contended that upwards of 3,000 Baltimore women were "willing to labor, but too proud to beg." In the face of low wages and scarce work, the poor or widowed woman "moistened her crust of bread with the tears of hopeless sorrow." As Finley explained, "after working all day, and many of the hours at night, when her heartless employer is enjoying the sweets of sleep, her wages are inadequate to the sustenance of nature."[41]

Like Carey, Finley offered very precise calculations of women's budgets: working a sixteen-hour day, "an expert seamstress" without children could earn no more than $52 per year, half of which would go directly to paying the rent. A less-skilled woman with children might earn far less and have "less than three cents a day" to purchase food, clothing, and fuel. That amount, Finley told his audience, was "so small, that any of you would be ashamed to give it to the most worthless beggar." Seeking contributions to the Humane Impartial Society, Finley differentiated the organization from other institutions that gave alms unconditionally (and thus encouraged abuse) or that offered jobs at submarket compensation. Baltimore's Humane Impartial Society succeeded "by dispensing, not charity, but work; and by requiting the poor widow for her labor, with *living* wages."[42]

The idea that wages should meet the costs of subsistence had a long history in the writings of eighteenth-century political economists, but Finley was apparently the first to employ the modern phrase of "living wages." More importantly, Finley invoked living wages as appropriate for women workers. When the concept had appeared earlier in Adam Smith and Thomas Malthus and later in the writings of John Stuart Mill and Francis Wayland, it referred to a wage sufficient to allow a working husband to support a dependent wife. Similarly, when 1820s and 1830s working men clamored for higher wages, they also defined a living wage as one that allowed them to function as a family's sole breadwinner. Finley acknowledged a different social reality, one in which women were often the primary earners in their households. As the Humane Impartial Society's own charter explained, the beneficiaries of the institution would be limited to "widows, women who have infirm, disabled, or sick husbands, and women with small children whose husbands are abandoned, or who have been deserted by their husbands." That such women had "no sufficient means of support, apart from their own exertions" attested to the absolute necessity of a living wage for female seamstresses.[43]

The Strike of 1833

Philanthropy alone could not guarantee economic competency to Baltimore's seamstresses. There were simply too many women in need: some 1,600 had applied to the Humane Impartial Society for sewing in 1830, but there was only enough work for 160. "The evil is but too apparent," noted the editor of the *Baltimore Patriot*, adding that he could not "say the same of a practicable remedy." A new remedy, however, was emerging for struggling workers at the end of the 1820s: a labor movement that would organize working men and women in turnouts (as strikes were often called) for better pay and shorter hours. By the end of summer 1833, Baltimore had its own labor newspaper (the *Workingmen's Advocate*), as well as dozens of new craft unions. Baltimore became the second American city (after New York) to establish a general trades organization, and it sent two mechanics to the Maryland legislature on a Workingmen's Party ticket. In July 1833, hatters staged a successful strike to resist the lowering of their wages. At the same time, seventeen different journeymen's societies involved in shipbuilding—including shipwrights, riggers, sailmakers, and even a union of black caulkers—went on strike to create a ten-hour workday in the shipyards. When Baltimore's seamstresses organized themselves into the Female Union Society in September, they declared "no method so likely to procure us relief, as that which has of late been successfully practiced by the mechanics of this city."[44]

The Baltimore seamstresses began their efforts at a propitious moment in fall 1833, just as the city's male artisans were celebrating the victory of their ten-hour system strike and marching in the anniversary celebration of the defense of Baltimore in the War of 1812. A "large meeting of the Workingwomen . . . engaged in obtaining a livelihood by the use of the needle" convened in Fells Point to protest the "insupportable oppression" of low wages. In hopes of establishing a standard bill of wages, the Fells Point assemblage called for "all those in the same avocation with ourselves" to meet for a citywide convention. Boldly, the women resolved to "enter into a positive agreement to take out no work from the shops until proper rates shall be established."[45]

This was risky business. Women acting collectively in the early republic had to carefully navigate the gender boundaries of American society. The prevailing gender ideology gave women powerful rhetorical tools to use in the name of reform but left them vulnerable to censure if they pushed issues too far.[46] Arguing from the position of motherhood enabled some women to make claims on government. Consider the rhetoric of the "distressed females" who petitioned Congress in 1816 to support the New Jersey textile factories that employed them. With "our helpless Infants crying for bread," the women reported that the cold winter had already "snatched" several children "to that world where they shall hunger no more and no more be witness to the miseries of their helpless families."[47]

In contrast, the American women who organized strikes in the 1820s and 1830s went well beyond sentimental motherhood to make claims on the public. When New York seamstresses orchestrated a turnout in 1831, they deployed arguments of abstract economic justice. Likewise, female strikers in Massachusetts spent less time appealing for sympathy than taking deliberate steps to increase their wages. In 1831, three hundred female shoe binders in Reading, Massachusetts, publicized the rates paid by different employers so that "no one may do good work for a less price than another." As they organized for a strike, members of the New England Association of Farmers, Mechanics, and Other Workingmen watched the Baltimore seamstresses closely. "Women are entitled to the same amount of wages as men, for the same quantum of services, and ought to receive it," declared Charles Douglass, editor of Rhode Island's *Artisan*.[48]

Around the country, working women made the same claim to a family wage as did men. "If it is unfashionable for the men to bear oppression in silence, why should it not also become unfashionable for the women?" asked a group of New York needlewomen in 1831. "When we complain to our employers and others, of the inequality of our wages with that of the men's, the excuse is, they have families to support, from which females are exempt," explained Louise Mitchell, secretary of New York's United Tailoresses Society. "Now this is either a sad mistake, or a wilful [sic] oversight; for how many females are there who have families to support, and how many single men who have none, and who, having no other use for the fruits of their employers' generosity, they child like, waste it."[49]

As the Baltimore women were strategizing in 1833, they received a huge shot in the arm from the editor of the *Baltimore American*. The paper republished the eight Mathew Carey essays that had been printed in Philadelphia two years earlier as the *Address to the Wealthy of the Land*. A week before the Fells Point seamstresses resolved to strike, Carey's emphatic "LOW RATE OF WAGES IS THE ROOT OF THE MISCHIEF" jumped off the page and, in the words of the newspaper's editors, served to "strengthen the general abhorrence for this system and impress more deeply the necessity of some change." Introducing Carey's text, the *American* decried "that honest industry, faithfully executed by a female, with perseverance and patience beyond that which is asked of the severest male occupation, should be repaid with so niggard a hand, and such cold-blooded carelessness of the physical wants and consequent moral disposition of many a sufferer."[50]

While Baltimore newspaper readers digested Carey's critique of the moral sentiments of the wealthy in September 1833, the city's working women moved ahead with their plan for a strike. "We feel it a duty due to ourselves, and to those who are dependent upon us for support, to seek some remedy for the wretched and deplorable condition under which we now labor" began the published announcement of a September 20 meeting. If a single woman could not subsist on piece rates, the seamstresses asked, "how will the poor helpless widow fare with five or six small children entirely dependent on her feeble efforts with her needle for a support?"[51]

Like their learned male advocates, Baltimore seamstresses mixed a calculated economic analysis with gendered appeals for sympathy and a religiously sanctioned charity. While not above invoking the "disgrace and ruin" of prostitution and the image of shivering widows, the seamstresses nonetheless preferred the language of universal economic justice. Like working men and women elsewhere, the Baltimore seamstresses adhered to a labor theory of value that presumed fair exchange between worker and employer. Capitalists were entitled to reasonable profit from the differential between the cost of the labor they purchased and the price of the commodities they sold, but they could not maximize that gap by driving wages below the subsistence needs of their workers. If moral exhortations would not stop merchant tailors from such "face-grinding" practices, then Baltimore women would set their own wages and refuse to work for any employer who failed to meet them. The phrase "until we obtain value for our labour" appeared in many of their published announcements and attested to their commitment to producerist mores.[52]

By the end of September 1833, Fells Point and Baltimore women had coordinated a price list and named a committee of women "to call on every gentleman keeping a clothing store" to determine "who are and who are not willing to pay the prices." Knowing that a strike would imperil those seamstresses most desperate for income, the strike organizers sought to provide for the neediest women "until the prices can be obtained for our work." Interestingly, they expected male artisans and workers to provide that support and proposed ward meetings to raise a strike fund from their male counterparts. Jacob Daley, an Old Town chairmaker, served as treasurer of the strike fund "for the benefit of the poor and destitute who are not able to do without assistance during their struggle for better prices."[53]

The strike began on October 1, 1833, with the women vowing to work only for employers "willing to give an equivalent for their labour." That same day, the *American* reprinted the segment of Carey's *Address* that praised Baltimore's Humane Impartial Society for paying reasonable wages to seamstresses. If an underfunded charity organization could pay 18¾¢ for muslin shirts and duck pantaloons, surely the prosperous merchant tailors of the city could do likewise.

The strike elicited an immediate response from the city's clothing manufacturers, who convened at a coffeehouse on Calvert Street. According to one merchant tailor, Samuel Armor, the meeting attendees voted to make the striking women a counteroffer of a 25 percent rate increase. But Armor reported that a small minority of the clothiers soon undermined that agreement. Intending "to quiet in order to deceive," these renegade clothiers happily signed the official price list of the Female Union Society but secretly vowed to abandon the commitment as soon as it was convenient. Thinking themselves victorious, the seamstresses then published their price list on October 23. Playing to the broader public's fixation on prostitution as the inevitable result of poverty, the women headed their price list with the adage, *"Give to Industry its* DUE REWARD, *and Society will preserve Morality."* As importantly, they included the names of the twenty-five clothiers who had agreed to the new prices and the names of the nine who had not. At risk of being added to the latter list, Armor blew the whistle on his colleagues rather than facing public opprobrium as a face-grinder.[54]

The Female Union Society was virtually silent after publishing its price list in late October. Only a small newspaper entry announced its monthly meeting in November, this time held in the Methodist church in Old Town rather than in the more secular settings of the earlier assemblages in the Harrison Street Bazaar or Holiday Street "Assembly Rooms." A cryptic, if discouraging, inscription ran at the bottom of the advertisement: "This Female Union Society is not dead, but according to the poet 'still liveth.'"[55] Even though he had not met the seamstresses' demands, Samuel Armor reported that the "large number of females in my employ" were "perfectly satisfied" with his more modest rate increase. Moreover, "numbers are calling on me daily for work," Armor noted, suggesting that the Female Union Society had failed to mobilize all of the city's seamstresses in solidarity.[56] A survey of piece rates taken in 1835 revealed that seamstresses were earning far below the levels set during the strike two years earlier, and in some cases lower than the shocking figures Mathew Carey had cited in his spirited defenses of female laborers.[57] Perhaps the clearest assessment of the strike's outcome was the persistence of female poverty and the elevation of the seamstress as an object of charity in the subsequent years.

Women Workers as Charity Cases

The ensuing spring witnessed not the resurgence of organized women workers striking for fair wages, but a sustained campaign by male workers on behalf of seamstresses recast as passive recipients of charity. "If any class of the community actually need and deserve a change for the better in their condition, it is unquestionably helpless, oppressed woman," read a column in the *Mechanic's Banner and Workingmen's Shield*, a Baltimore labor weekly. The working men's paper was quick to naturalize women's labor itself and declare all adults responsible for their own support, even women. "We do not think that they were designed merely as automaton ornaments, about a house," the editors observed. Instead of fuelling an egalitarian labor radicalism, however, "the woful [sic] depreciation of female labor" should mobilize "the patriot, the philanthropist, and the Christian" to act in defense of women. That a seamstress "should be accustomed to toil with far greater diligence than the veriest slave, and still be unable in many cases to procure even the absolute necessaries of life," the paper asserted, "is a burning disgrace upon any community, and a scandal upon any people." More to the point, "How will the vices of society be checked, while labor is thus degraded?"[58]

Heeding the call was John F. Weishampel, a Fells Point newspaper printer and entrepreneur. In the next several years, Weishampel would supply a rhetorical critique of seamstresses' wages rivaling that of Mathew Carey, while at the same time orchestrating an institutional solution to female poverty—a trading society to provide an outlet for women to market their wares and presumably receive full value for their labor. If the clothiers could not be trusted to deal fairly with their female employees, then the United Workingmen's and Women's Trading Society of Baltimore would simply eliminate them from the equation. Known as the Seamstresses' Society, Weishampel's enterprise would parallel the Ladies' Depository Associations founded in New York and Philadelphia in 1833.

Baltimore's Seamstresses' Society opened its storefront by July 1834 and marketed the goods of one hundred female members. But the men and women who ran the operation saw it as much more than a cooperative. "This society will unquestionably be of more essential benefit to the community than all the Relief funds and all the Savings Institutions combined," boasted advocates, who thought they had finally founded Baltimore's elusive School of Industry. Clergymen like Stephen Williams of the Seaman's Bethel and Robert J. Breckinridge, the orthodox Presbyterian editor of the *Baltimore Literary and Religious Magazine*, rallied behind the enterprise. So too did many of the city's leading men who had signed the 1830 broadside decrying seamstresses' low wages and who now formed the institution's standing committee. Weishampel made sure that each of them received a complimentary copy of Carey's *Address to the Wealthy of the Land*, lest any of the prominent doctors, lawyers, merchants, and ministers misunderstand their responsibilities.[59]

Although at least one female veteran of the 1833 strike, Eleanor Whearett, participated in the new Seamstresses' Society, the enterprise was fundamentally a form of poor relief, not a sustained critique of capitalist labor relations. Like the Humane Impartial Society's clothing store, the cooperative was less an alternative economy than simply a mechanism "to relieve their indigent members, by giving them employment." The virtue was that "the widow, the orphan and the aged" could "support themselves by honest industry," while the society would pay them "*fair* and *just* prices." The latter was not inconsequential, for charity societies in other cities continued to provide sewing to needy women at submarket rates. Nonetheless, a charitable impulse drove the men and women who spearheaded the Seamstresses' Society. "Hoping that something may be done to ameliorate the present condition of those females who are forced to work for support," one concerned citizen celebrated the "pious clergy and professional gentlemen, and other philanthropists" who had undertaken this "work of benevolence." Indeed, by the start of 1835, Weishampel "and a lady" were soliciting donations door-to-door "to aid the oppressed and depressed women." Considering the "great privations" of wintertime and a paralyzed urban economy, "the distress existing cannot be described." Weishampel reminded potential donors, "what you give to the poor, you lend to the Lord."[60]

Despite being "the best operation for the poor that was ever proposed to a people," the promises of the Seamstresses' Society proved difficult to deliver. Fundraising was slow, and the institution devoted much of 1835 to planning a theatrical benefit starring Junius Brutus Booth, Maryland's most famous resident Shakespearean actor (and the father of the man who would be Maryland's most famous presidential assassin). The event raised only $69. The Fells Point Reading Room on Shakespeare Street was not much more successful. For 3¢ a visit or 12¢ a week, interested gentlemen could peruse the seventy-five different newspapers to which Weishampel subscribed.[61]

The Seamstresses' Society also faced internal dissention over the role of female officials in the institution's governance. Weishampel and the present board of directors stood firm that the society's work was "too laborious, and of too great importance for ladies to attend thereto—and therefore [we] do not wish to have ladies in the Board."[62] Women in leadership positions posed a nuisance for Weishampel and his allies who wanted to proceed "in this good work." Dispelling other public misconceptions—that the enterprise would "support the indolent and lazy," or that the cooperative clothing store constituted a monopoly, for example—the Seamstresses' Society proclaimed itself "founded upon fair republican principles." Offering assistance to needy seamstresses would not sap their industry, but the prospect of annual dividends would "encourage them to work for their bread."[63]

And therein was the problem: women were desperate not because they lacked diligence and industry, but because their wages were "too low to live by."[64] A series of riots convulsing the city in August 1835 contributed to the realization that working people were at the mercy of much larger economic forces in a capitalist society. Several hundred families had lost all their savings in the collapse of the Bank of Maryland in 1834 due to the irresponsible speculation of its directors.

Revelations of malfeasance emerged through 1835, although the blameworthy financiers remained unrepentant and refused to release their records to public scrutiny. After one too many delays, rioters took to the streets for several days, destroying property and taking revenge on those who would so callously destroy the savings of "women and orphans." Ironically, some of the victims of the public violence had been among the leading defenders of the seamstresses in earlier years. E. L. Finley, the advocate of living wages, led a brigade of militia against the riots before having his arm broken in a shower of rocks and brickbats.[65]

The injury to "widows and orphans" galvanized the philanthropic impulses of the Seamstresses' Society one last time. Still attempting to get the cooperative off the ground, Weishampel called for a meeting to collect information on women's wages. Armed with data, the society would enlist the city's churches in the cause. "We feel assured that the Clergy will, when they know what low prices are given for work, open their churches and take up a collection to aid the funds of the Society now waiting to receive assistance at their hands," declared Weishampel. Almost two hundred women—"being principally poor women and some of us indigent widows"—stood ready to participate in the cooperative, but the enterprise lacked the capital it needed to open for business. Most of the women members could ill-afford the 25¢ monthly fee to participate. "If this society be suffered to die away for the want of a few hundred dollars, we shall never again have any prospects of being redeemed from our present state of oppression and poverty," declared the women dejectedly. They noted an earlier attempt "to raise prices by a stand out," but declared that 1833 effort a failure "as we had no proper persons to carry our object into effect." The women believed a cooperative clothing society was their best hope, but only if the city's clergy could fundraise on their behalf. Calling it "the duty of the Ministers of the Gospel of Christ (friend of the poor)" to take up collections in their congregations, the women made a final plea.[66]

Without question, the city's clothiers still paid inadequate wages that made women reliant on charity to avoid "an untimely grave." Prevailing piece rates were too low for single women, let alone for mothers with "helpless children to provide for." As Weishampel would contend, "the rich and lordly Clothiers" had received the benefit of the doubt when they said they gave "the women *good prices.*" Twenty-five seamstresses provided evidence to the contrary, which Weishampel published to demonstrate "that women who have no more than such an income to support them, are in the most abject poverty." Anyone who recalled the Female Union Society's price list from the 1833 strike would notice the large number of items—flannel drawers, men's overalls, coarse muslin shirts—now paying less than a dime per piece. On the strike list, no garment had earned below 12½¢, which had been the same low rate that caused Mathew Carey such alarm in the late 1820s. Nor was it the case that Baltimore seamstresses could make more of these low-paying garments in the space of a week. One dollar per week was at the high end of what a woman with children or with "sickly or worthless husbands" could earn.[67]

Although Hezekiah Niles brought Weishampel's findings before the national readership of his *Register*, the Seamstresses' Society and its clothing cooperative remained moribund and $1,000 short of the necessary start-up capital. Its directors voted to halt their work in December 1835, noting that "the board sympathizes with the sufferings of the thousands of poor women in the city during the winter season particularly caused by the trifling prices paid them for their work and regret that it was not in their power to benefit them this winter."[68]

For four decades, seamstresses' low wages had been an issue worthy of public discussion in Baltimore. Neither the ardent support of social commentators, nor the militant outpouring of women's activism, nor the heartfelt attention of religious benevolence managed to increase women's earning power. That working women could not support themselves on their wages was an incontrovertible fact of early republic life. But then again, in a patriarchal culture that could explain the existence of female laborers only through men's failings, it was widely presumed that no woman should have to support herself by her own earnings.

The proliferation of wage-earning women in the first decades of the nineteenth century did little to change the presumption of women's dependence, let alone to legitimate women as workers entitled to subsistence wages. Such a conclusion runs counter to the narrative of female emancipation that celebrates women's emergence as autonomous market actors and concurrent liberation from the fathers and husbands who held legal claims to their labor and earnings. But for women who were already liberated from patriarchal dependence on a male provider, the market was no friend. The presumption of female dependence fell particularly hard on the large population of women with no men on whom to rely: widows, women abandoned by husbands, and women married to men whose wages were inadequate to support a family, including the disabled or injured, the enslaved, and those who worked at sea or far from home. Whereas low wages typically deepened a woman's dependence on a man, the absence of a male provider then accelerated women's dependence on the state and its public welfare apparatus.

Even as seamstresses' poverty could indict the morality of their prosperous employers, the issues of women's imperiled "virtue" and working-class immorality were never far behind. What might have been an explosive political issue—the exploitative nature of wage labor in a republican society—became, in one historian's words, "a far more manageable sexual scandal."[69] Situated in the realm of charity rather than in the realm of politics, the paradoxical condition of market freedom for women "bound for life to the needle and thread" could be converted into something more tidy. The consequences for seamstresses were continued low wages and increased reliance on charity.

CHAPTER 6

The Hard Work of Being Poor

I n Atlantic seaports from Boston to Baltimore, the cost of living far outstripped what a single worker could earn through the most diligent labor. For male manual laborers and female seamstresses alike, the "constant employ and high wages" promised in job advertisements proved illusory. Instead, the seasonal rhythms of the maritime economy kept ditchdiggers and dockworkers idle during several months of the year, while low wages prevented women from covering the costs of food, fuel, and shelter. The difficulty of transforming paid labor into subsistence compelled working men and women to pursue other sources of income and to develop creative techniques for stretching dollars and minimizing expenses.

Historians have given these strategies telling labels—"economies of make-shift" or "cultures of expediency"—to capture the combination of scavenging, scrimping, sharing, pawning, panhandling, fencing, gambling, hustling, cooperating, and competing necessary to feed hungry children, fend off evictions, and avoid the almshouse. Staying afloat required the utmost economic prudence and involved strategic decisions regarding work opportunities near and far, the careful management of resources, cleverly adaptive living arrangements, and perhaps the two cardinal virtues of the early republic's capitalist culture—delayed gratification and a willingness to work oneself harder in order to better the circumstances of family members.[1]

The struggle of Baltimore's laboring households to stay afloat was not difficult to see. The pursuit of subsistence took men, women, and children into public spaces and precipitated numerous encounters with the law. Children gathering wood chips in tattered coats and families waiting for free bread gained public attention every winter. Yet for many observers, such scenes reflected not the shortfall between wages and living expenses but rather the poor management, dubious morals, and limited ambitions of working-class families. The fact that a laboring man could earn $1 per day—"This may seem incredible with you, but it is a fact," Dr. Joseph Brevitt wrote to his father back in England—made it impossible to imagine anything other than unlimited prosperity. Advice manuals presented America as easy street for newly arrived immigrant laborers, who "cannot be too grateful to Providence for the blessings they enjoy." As John Melish described in his 1819 guide, "The wages in America are better than in any other country, and the living is reasonable, so that labourers can live very comfortably and save a little." Officials at Baltimore's almshouse were equally incredulous that there could be poverty "where the means of obtaining a comfortable subsistence are so abundant as in this community, and where labour is at the same time so amply rewarded."[2]

The scenes of suffering at the almshouse or in Fells Point when a financial panic and a yellow fever epidemic coincided in 1819 told a very different story, but those with the power to identify the structural causes of poverty rapidly shifted the responsibility for poverty onto the poor themselves. With the exception of the labor radicals of the 1820s and 1830s, or men like Mathew Carey and John Weishampel, who advocated for impoverished seamstresses, early republic commentators explained poverty as a function of idleness, intemperance, and improvidence. In the process, they all overlooked the dedicated labor, self-restraint, and careful planning involved in scraping by.[3]

"i am a pore man and have a family and have to worke weary hard to make boath ends meet," declared Baltimore dockworker Axim Johnson in 1825. He was in prison at the time, but even when Johnson was earning regular wages on the waterfront, he and his family had struggled for material survival.[4] Trying to live on the wages of a day laborer or of a seamstress required constant efforts to locate additional income and to cut the inevitable expenses of daily living. Finding a job did not secure men, women, and children from the pangs of hunger or the shivers of winter, though it might postpone the threat of real privation for a time. The challenge of balancing income and expenditures necessitated a range of survival strategies common to all working-class households: scavenging discarded produce at the market, pawning clothing to meet the rent, applying for assistance from charitable agencies during Christmastime. Informal, illegal, and underground exchanges also proved critical. Working-class households operated very close to the edge, and a workplace injury, an unintended pregnancy, or an arrest could precipitate the fall. New adversities generated new survival strategies, but as Baltimore's seamstresses, sailors, and slaves discovered time and again, the rules of the game had been set up to make being poor incredibly expensive and labor intensive.

Households

How did someone earning at best $1 a day—but not every day—get by? It was certainly not by going it alone. Even as the labor market in Baltimore reduced workers to atomized units for purchase or hire, subsistence was not an individual pursuit. The centerpiece of working-class survival was the creation of collective economic enterprises, otherwise known as households. These collectivities—rife with their own internal inequalities and by no means egalitarian—sometimes took the form of patriarchal marriage-based family units, but they could also involve people cohabitating outside of marriage or of any affective or kin relationship whatsoever. Households were often multigenerational, multifamily, and in Baltimore, multiracial. Households typically combined the labor of adults and children, with the wages of some members converted into meals and medicines by others. As one member of a household hawked candles for a penny apiece, another might remit wages from a Virginia fishery during shad season, or raise a few dollars each month in cloth and flour from a charity society. Yet another might walk the docks each morning looking for wood chips to build a cooking fire. Because the earnings of any one of these individuals would prove inadequate to paying for "the necessities of life," pooling resources was essential.[5]

In the context of early America, a household typically referred to a unit of economic production that brought together kin and unrelated laborers under one roof and subsumed their identities under a white adult male. Such households were the building blocks of colonial British North America and remained fundamental to the social organization of the early republic United States. One need look no further than the decennial federal censuses of the early 1800s that grouped large numbers of people (adult men and women, children, tenants, servants, slaves) anonymously under the one name of the "head of household." The legal dependence that a woman assumed under marriage, that an apprentice assumed under indentures, that a child assumed by virtue of his or her minority, or that a slave assumed in bondage were components of the same system of patriarchal authority, one predicated on adult white men's property ownership, political enfranchisement, and putative monopoly on coercive violence.[6]

The patriarchal household constructed one man's nominal independence on the dependence of numerous others on him. Dependence was a fraught label, but it scarcely described the material relationships within working-class households. For seamstresses, mudmachinists, and mariners, the combination of irregular employment and low wages guaranteed that heads of households would find themselves dependent on others rather than in the position of providers. Even when a household comprised a single nuclear family of husband, wife, and children, mutual dependence characterized their struggle to procure food and stay warm. Moreover, the living arrangements of so many urban workers defied patriarchal norms by creating households that were ad hoc or predicated on necessity rather than on kinship. For these reasons, the kinds of households at the center of working-class subsistence were rarely the patriarchal households typical of early America more generally.

For working-class men, patriarchal prerogatives were much to be desired, but usually just out of reach. The broader culture of early America presumed adult white male independence and female dependence, and laws restricting married women's rights to property and political participation promoted that outcome. So too did wages so low that they made self-sufficiency unattainable for most laboring women. Still, laboring men made poor providers. Whenever male laborers complained about their wages or sought work on the municipal payroll, aspirations to patriarchal responsibility were never far behind. "I am entirely out of work and have a poor and helpless family and being deprived of work for at least two months past they are actually in want of the necessarys of life," pleaded George Bayly, a carter in search of a city contract in 1827. Stephen Stimson had "a helpless family entirely dependent on him for a subsistence," which is why he hoped the mayor would appoint him a night watchman in 1830. When Fells Point watchman John Langley was fired in 1832 for beating a prostitute, his supporters reported that "if he is deprived of this situation now as winter is approaching, we are afraid his family will either suffer or will have to go to the Alms House." Langley had "no trade" and his "large and helpless family" needed the $30 monthly salary paid to city watchmen.[7]

The ideal of the patriarch also figured in the petitions of criminals seeking early release from prison or relief from fines. Facing jail time for beating two women in 1811, William King told the court that his wife and seven children were "entirely dependent on his daily labour as a brick layer for their sustenance." Were King "dragged from his family at this time and immure[d] in a dungeon, his wife and little children would most indubitably fall upon the humanity of the citizens of Baltimore and doubtless suffer extremely by the inclemency of the approaching season deprived of the common necessaries of life." The aforementioned Axim Johnson, who had attacked a constable "when i was in liquor on the warfe at my worke," was able to finagle a pardon in 1825, after telling the court about the "distress" of his family.[8]

Such formulaic pleas were often deceptive, for working-class households rarely subsisted on a man's wages alone. The typical laborer's daily dollar was insufficient for "a man with a wife and family, to lay by a sufficiency to pay rent, buy fire wood, and eatables, through a long, severe winter," explained an 1804 appeal for public charity. Although assistance from charitable organizations helped many Baltimore families make it through a long winter, the real trick to household viability was a gendered division of labor that adapted to the broader configuration of the urban market economy. A working woman needed a man's wages because she could not earn sufficient cash on her own to purchase food, clothing, fuel, or housing. A working man needed a woman's unpaid labor to transform his wages into sustenance. If a laboring man were forced to cook his own meals, do his own laundry, and mend his own clothing, he could scarcely log enough hours at the city's brick-yards or shipyards to earn a wage. Moreover, purchasing those services at market rates would cost several times his yearly wages. As the historian Jeanne Boydston calculated, the market value of a woman's unpaid domestic labor outstripped the total amount of wages earned by most laboring men, making the acquisition of a wife one of the savviest things a poor man could do. A wife's contribution to the family economy in unpaid labor alone was twice the cost of her maintenance. As a Baltimore literary magazine advised "young men" in 1800, "Get married: a wife is cheaper than a house-keeper, her industry will assist you many ways, and your children will soon share and lighten your labor."[9]

Conjugal units of husband and wife stood at the center of many working-class households. In the waterfront neighborhood of Fells Point, over half of white households in 1820 contained a sole adult man cohabitating with an adult woman. But in a maritime economy, such demography belied the mutual dependence—and the precariousness—of the working-class household. According to Baltimore officials, Fells Point was the neighborhood where "most of the hardy mariners reside, by whose efforts, and at whose hazard those enterprises are conducted, upon which the prosperity of this metropolis, as a sea-port, mainly depends." But that prosperity came with a cost: "The father is necessarily separated from his family for great portions of the year, and the duties of domestic life, devolve wholly upon the wife."[10]

This was certainly true for Charles and Biddy Pasture, who lived apart from one another for the long spells whenever Charles went to sea. During those times, their physical household vanished and Biddy, a five-foot Irish woman with brown hair and fair skin, took up residence as a domestic servant in a wealthier family's household. Departing on a privateering voyage in 1813, Charles gave power of attorney to his "loving friend and wife," so that she might collect his share of prize money or military pension if he perished. Charles made it back to Baltimore alive but without a newfound fortune that might allow the Pastures to maintain a home of their own year-round. Biddy was still living and laboring in other people's homes in 1817, when she was convicted of stealing from her employer. Her stint in the penitentiary proved the undoing of the Pasture household: Charles abandoned her, and Biddy ended up in the almshouse.[11]

The dangers of seafaring also accounted for the precariousness of Fells Point households. "The casualties incident to a seaman's life leave many widows, with children depending only upon them for their support," reported advocates of a new public school in the neighborhood. Elizabeth White thought she had lost her mariner husband of four years in a naval skirmish with a French ship in the East Indies in 1798. She promptly formed a new household with a new man. For better or worse, her old husband, Benoni White, was not dead. Returning to Baltimore three years later, he discovered Elizabeth had married a ship carpenter and was carrying her new husband's child. Benoni took these developments in stride. When Elizabeth faced indictment as a bigamist, he came to her aid and petitioned the court for clemency, signing himself "Benoni White, the first husband."[12]

As a working-class woman, Elizabeth White acted wisely in seeking access to another man's wages once Benoni disappeared. Conjugal households disintegrated whenever men's wages were removed from the equation, as the wives of law-breaking husbands reported time and again. "I have in both single and married life until of late enjoyed a competency and saw good days," declared Lydia Grace in 1814, "but a sad succession of disastrous events has ruined our hopes and reduced us to poverty." She and her six children could not withstand her husband's indictment for stealing an iron ship's anchor. When the thirty-eight-year-old distiller Martin Overfield fled Baltimore in 1818 with some stolen watches, he "left his wife and three children without any hope of support but through the beneficence of the public, or private humanity." Likewise, when William Woolen was sent to jail for assaulting another man in 1807, his household disintegrated. His wife entered the almshouse, where she gave birth to their third child. But with one parent in jail and another in the almshouse, the other children were "at the mercy of [their] neighbours, either to be supported by their generosity or turn'd away without the care of Father or Mother."[13]

Desertion terminated many women's access to male wages. German-born Hester Halloway lived and worked in Baltimore for twenty years, until her husband deserted her in 1825. "Wanting employment," she and her two-year-old son, John Francis Halloway, spent that spring in the almshouse. Mary Thompson and her three children had to take refuge at the almshouse "when she was deserted by her husband (who ought to have protected her) in actual poverty—far away from parents and in a land of strangers." The Thompsons had immigrated to the United

States from England in the 1820s, living first in Philadelphia and then arriving in Baltimore. Mary was pregnant with the couple's fourth child at the time of her husband's departure in 1830.[14]

Of the many personal failings that could dissolve working-class households, none ranked higher than men's drunkenness. The useless and inebriated husband became a standard image in the fundraising appeals of Baltimore's fledgling temperance movement. "Now all the time that he is drunk, his labour, or the price of it, is lost to himself and his family, who are effectually deprived of it, and suffer for the want of it," warned the Maryland State Temperance Society in 1836. With an incapacitated father, "Who supports his family?" The responsibility first fell to relatives and friends, and then to the "charitable and benevolent." But more likely, "his poor miserable wife and worse than fatherless children, must go to the alms-house." As insufferable as these moral reformers struck many Baltimore residents, they were correct that the lost wages of a drunken husband imperiled household survival.[15]

While men's wages were essential to the survival of most households, a wife's disappearance could prove just as disastrous. Jane McCormick escaped her abusive husband, Robert, by fleeing to the almshouse in July 1825. But without Jane to cook, clean, and perform childcare, Robert and their four-year-old son, John, were unable to survive on their own; they were soon reunited with Jane in the almshouse. James and Mary Alexander found themselves in a similar predicament. Married, they had three children, and in Mary's words, "behaved ourselves justly and honestly." That is, until January 1791, when Mary earned a year in prison for stealing a brass candlestick, three pewter plates, and a pair of cotton hose. Regardless of whether Mary stole the items for her family's use or to exchange for supplies needed for family subsistence, her imprisonment threw the household into turmoil. As some prominent gentlemen who knew the family explained, James Alexander was "an Industrious Honest man and very poor, [and] His wife's misconduct made him miserable indeed." With Mary gone, he had to spend two months as a housekeeper. In her petition to the governor for an early release, Mary observed that while she was in jail, James was "deprived of doing anything for his small family by his daily labour, being oblig'd to stay home and take care of them[,] they being small." James eventually asked the almshouse trustees to take his children: "he has the care of three helpless children and the only means to support both him and them is what he can earn by his labour." He added (with perhaps a delusional boastfulness), "If his wife could be set at Liberty they might be all supported by his earnings." Mary framed her pardon plea in similar terms: she asked to be set "at Liberty that she might be able to support her poor distressed family."[16]

Both James and Mary claimed that their own work "supported" the household. James envisioned his role as breadwinner and cash earner, whereas Mary imagined herself as the structural underpinning of the household. The reality—one perhaps they recognized once Mary was pardoned in March—was that working-class women and men were bound together in mutual dependence.

Whether because of a spouse's untimely death, a personal failing, financial need, or a shortage of suitable partners, Baltimore's laboring men and women resided in nonconjugal households as both a short-term expediency and as a permanent subsistence strategy. Depending on the neighborhood, women headed between 10 and 20 percent of Baltimore households. Along the waterfront in Fells Point, women headed 14 percent of households in 1810. Propertied widows headed one-third of these, but working-class women (widowed or otherwise) headed the remaining two-thirds. The patterns of residence in these households were telling. Nearly half contained children younger than ten, indicative of women's responsibility for children who could not yet make sizeable contributions to the household economy. One-fourth contained an adult man between twenty-six and forty-four years old—perhaps a sibling or boarder who could contribute cash wages to the household budget. Another fourth housed a younger man in his teens or early twenties, probably a son with cash-earning potential who had returned home after completing an apprenticeship. More than a third of female-headed households contained a second adult woman in residence. Dorothy Colehouse and another woman older than forty-five lived together with two young children and a teenaged boy. Mary Grice headed a household with two other women, a teenaged girl, and a young man in his late teens or early twenties. Jane Carwell's household included another adult white woman and a free person of color (whose sex and age were not recorded by the census taker). Polly Raven was not yet twenty-six years old when she created a household with another woman similarly aged.[17]

By 1820, nearly 20 percent of households in Fells Point and the adjacent working-class district of Old Town were female headed, but the growth of such arrangements in no way attested to their economic security. Half of these households were too poor to owe city taxes. In comparison, only one-third of male-headed households fell below the assessment minimum. Even the women who did gain the notice of the tax collector were of meager means, collectively owning less than 7 percent of the wealth in these wards. Women like Margaret Procter and Priscilla Morrison lived in modest circumstances. Both were widowed seamstresses whose miniscule property should have exempted them from paying taxes at all. Procter's house on Friendship Alley was valued at $15, as was Morrison's tiny house on Liberty Street. The furnishings in each of the houses were valued at $2.[18]

Women headed a higher percentage of black households than white ones, but the disparity was not nearly as great as in other slaveholding cities. In 1810, women headed 30 percent of black households in Baltimore, compared with upwards of 50 percent in Richmond and Petersburg. On face value, free people of color in Baltimore were remarkably successful in creating male-headed households, doing so at the same rate as their peers in New York and Philadelphia— places where slavery had ebbed earlier and the interstate slave trade posed far less a threat to the integrity of black families. When black men and women in Baltimore escaped the sales and sexual violence endemic to slavery, they were quick to make autonomous nuclear families a centerpiece of their newfound freedom. Such efforts often required great patience, especially if a husband or wife was waiting for a manumission date to arrive or for one spouse to accumulate the cash to purchase freedom for the other. Robert and Ruth Guy could finally start a conjugal household to raise their young son, Moses, in 1807, but it had required Robert first to attain his own manumission and then to negotiate the purchase of his wife and child through a white intermediary. In 1811, Cornelius Cole paid $200 to attain the freedom of his wife Debbie and their children, Robert and Maria. Perry Blake, a free black man, fought on an American ship during the War of 1812, while his wife Charlotte remained an enslaved servant to the family of Jesse Levering. As the fighting reached Baltimore, Charlotte's support to American soldiers inspired Levering to free her at war's end. Perry and Charlotte Blake could then begin life anew.[19]

Such success stories mask the additional challenges facing black men and women in forming conjugal households. Although common poverty meant a hand-to-mouth existence for all working-class Baltimore residents, slavery and its attendant legal regime subjected African American households to a host of additional burdens. The inability to offer legal testimony against whites, for example, left African Americans vulnerable to abuse and fraud. Theodore B. Denny learned this firsthand when his white landlord's adult son, Frederick Tensfield, barged into his home in 1830 and demanded rent that had already been paid. Denny and Tensfield came to blows, and Tensfield filed assault charges. The entire affair took place in front of Denny's aged mother, his wife, and their six children, but because all were African American, none could testify in court to counter Tensfield's version of events. With Denny sentenced to an eight-month prison term and slapped with $55 in fines and court costs, his family could scarcely stay intact. "From the unfortunate difference in testimony established by law," explained Denny from prison, "is the injured party made to suffer . . . Your Petitioner had no chance of even originating a doubt on the minds of the jury."[20]

Slavery posed a far larger problem for African American households in Baltimore, for it meant that black parents had to fear the kidnapping of their free children or that enslaved relatives could disappear into the hands of slave traders on any given day. Especially precarious were households that included enslaved members, something not uncommon in a city where many slaves were living far from their owners. Slaves sent by rural owners to hire out in the city were quick to form households with free spouses or relatives, but those arrangements could be shattered at the whim of those with legal title to black bodies. Whenever a slaveholder died, the disposition of the estate threatened to rip apart the living arrangements hired slaves had made for themselves.

Black families that included free and enslaved members did everything in their power to purchase the liberty of loved ones. In doing so, they added further costs to already strained budgets and faced expenditures unknown to working-class white households. Devoting hundreds of dollars to liberate a father, wife, or child, black households had little money left over for better housing or more nutritious food, let alone for such productive property as a cart or horse that might generate additional income. Such burdens made it almost impossible for black families to escape poverty.

Another obstacle to the formation of black households was Maryland's pattern of slaveholding and manumissions, which created a substantial sex imbalance. In Baltimore, there were three black women in their teens, twenties, and thirties for every two black men. The lack of suitable marriage partners increased the chances that a black woman would either head her own household or live under the roof of another family's household. Even if marriage partners had been available, black women's labor as domestic servants frequently confined them to employers' households. Indeed, more than one-third of marriage-aged black women in Baltimore lived in white households. These circumstances did not necessarily prevent marriage or having children but made cohabitation with a spouse difficult.[21]

The occupational opportunities of free black men also worked against cohabitation, especially so long as seafaring and domestic service remained prominent employments. During the months that her husband went to sea, Charlotte Blake might have had to follow her white counterpart Biddy Pasture back into domestic service under someone else's roof. The persistence of slavery further imperiled conjugal integrity. When Rebecca Garrett's free husband left Anne Arundel County for Baltimore in the 1820s, she was left behind. Her husband, William, had to pay her owner a yearly fee for them to be reunited in the city. Likewise, when free black women took enslaved men for husbands, the possibility of cohabitation depended on acquiescence from a white owner. As enslaved men were hired out to a new employer, called to the countryside to labor during the harvest, or worst of all, sold away, many free black wives found themselves in "abroad" marriages.[22]

Under such circumstances, it is remarkable that nearly 80 percent of Baltimore's free people of color managed to reside in African American households during the early republic period. This was possible because black households typically expanded beyond a single conjugal family into multifamily or multigenerational living arrangements. According to historian Barbara Wallace, most African American households were male headed but "augmented" to include additional adults or even a second family. Although some of these arrangements entailed one family taking in boarders to earn extra income, others reflected cooperative arrangements. Rebecca Hill, for example, resided with her fiancé, her mother, her stepfather, and her siblings. The two men of the household had gotten berths on a voyage and would presumably return home with cash needed to restock the cupboards. But because sailors' wages were never enough to support an entire family, Rebecca and her mother did laundry and picked oakum for additional income. When Hill was mistakenly jailed as a prostitute in 1796, neighbors reported, "the mother being thus deprived of her daughter's aid cannot subsist herself and children, this inclement season." Only Rebecca Hill's early release allowed the household to survive until the two husbands returned from sea.[23]

Children could be found in almost every working-class household, black and white. Early republic Baltimore was awash in kids, and when the census taker came around in 1820, 41 percent of Baltimore's population was under fifteen and too young to remember Jefferson's presidency firsthand, let alone recall the eighteenth century. These children did not go unnoticed by the adults who saw them as overrunning the city. Civic leaders complained regularly of misbehaving boys who lit fireworks, carried knives, flew kites, threw stones and snowballs, and swam naked in the river after puberty had made it indecent to do so.[24]

Children presented adults (sometimes natal parents, sometimes not) with both opportunities and obligations. For working-class parents, feeding hungry mouths proved the more pressing issue. "Hear their children crying for food," implored a wintertime charity appeal to assist the working poor in 1804. Relief efforts consistently invoked hungry children, like the ones seen in Fells Point in 1837 with "starvation staring them in the face." In terms of numbers, the pressures may have been greater for white households, which typically contained more children than did black households. The city's demography gave white men and women a better chance of finding a suitable partner and of experiencing a higher birthrate.

African American households may also have contained fewer children because many black children remained enslaved in other households awaiting the date of a delayed manumission to arrive. In response, many free parents devoted their scarce earnings to redeeming their children, and the huge sums required to purchase freedom left little money to feed those already free.[25]

Although costly to support or to liberate, children nonetheless served a household's economic viability. In addition to performing unpaid domestic labor or scavenging woodchips for fuel, children could contribute cash to the household economy through paid labor. Starting at age twelve, boys and girls found hire as domestic servants, where they collected wages and perhaps gained access to the castoff clothing and table scraps of their employers. Baltimore manufacturers were also eager to mobilize the young outside the home (and outside the traditional master-apprentice relationship). Christian Slemmer offered "constant employment" to "three or four steady boys and girls, in the winding of yarn" in 1809, while Samuel Sower promised a dozen boys under fifteen "liberal wages, for performing very light work at the Baltimore Type Foundry." The city's burgeoning textile industry eyed teenaged girls as workers, with the Baltimore Manufacturing Company seeking ten or fifteen "to attend the Water Looms" in 1815. "By industry they would earn a handsome competency," a promise that must have appealed to many working-class households. The Union Manufacturing Company transformed its labor force over the 1810s, switching from apprenticed boys to some one hundred wage-earning girls by 1820. The overall number of children earning wages in urban manufacturing was small, but their earnings could prove indispensable to working-class households.[26]

Households without other access to male wages—especially female-headed households that contained boys—were banking on the future earning power of those children as they grew older. For widowed women, sons promised to deliver the crucial wages that ceased with a husband's death. The widowed Mary Wells lost her son Daniel during the War of 1812 and was thereby "deprived of that assistance and support which had he survived he would have been able to have afforded her." Describing herself as "old and infirm and altogether unable to gain a support by labour," Wells hoped that Baltimore's government might provide her a pension. Before teenaged John Cunningham got tangled with the law in 1826, he worked to support his mother and eleven siblings, even though he had already gotten married and fathered a child of his own. Johanna Williamson suffered a blow when her son was arrested for stealing a parcel of clothing. Neighbors and patrons worried less about the son than about the mother's well-being. "She is poor, but honest and industrious and lives reputably," testified Williamson's landlord in an effort to get the boy bound out to a ship's captain. "He may yet become a good man if pardoned."[27]

Through the 1820s, apprenticeships remained a promising avenue for white households to augment the earning power of their sons. At any given moment in 1810s and 1820s Baltimore, roughly 2,000 apprentices resided in the households of coopers, shoemakers, and other tradesmen. Most of these indentures were entered voluntarily by parents and began when a son was fourteen or fifteen. For poor households, indenturing a son meant one less mouth to feed in the short run and better wages in the long run. However, apprenticeships in Baltimore were hardly the idyllic melding of craft training and surrogate parenting that some imagined. Because they had an alternative supply of enslaved children, employers were able to reduce the benefits they offered to white apprentices. Upon reaching majority age, an apprentice shoemaker or tailor might not be able to envision a clear trajectory to becoming an independent proprietor with his own shop, but he could certainly begin to earn journeyman wages that would help support the household of his parents. African American parents, however, hesitated before assigning legal responsibility of a child over to a master craftsman, especially a white man who might be indifferent to the growing threat slave-trading kidnappers posed to black boys in Baltimore.[28]

In both black and white households, the presence or absence of children reflected the countless individual choices that men and women made regarding if and when to marry, to begin childbearing, and how far apart to space births. Existing data does not reveal whether Baltimore men and women postponed marriage or childbearing in response to economic circumstances, nor does it allow historians to calculate working-class fertility rates. But in all likelihood, working people in Baltimore were similar to their peers in Philadelphia in forming reproductive relationships both inside and outside of legal marriage, and in relying upon birth control methods to limit family size.[29] Although Maryland law required the fathers of children born out of wedlock to indemnify the state against future welfare costs, city courts were not aggressive in pursuing bastardy cases and collected from fewer than twenty men per year in the early 1800s. Blacksmith Andrew Miller posted a $30 bond in 1806 for impregnating "single woman" Biddy Cane, while Tony Jackson, a free man of color, paid twice as much in 1811 for fathering two children with Rachel Matthews. Unmarried mothers did not have to fear being denied public charity in Baltimore, but they could not count on the government to make fathers support their children nor to protect women from the sexual coercion that initiated many pregnancies.[30]

A high rate of infant mortality befell working-class households. When Baltimore's Board of Health began tallying mortality data in the late 1810s, they found that children under ten accounted for half of all deaths in a given year. The majority of those children had not survived to see their first birthdays. The same term used today to describe malnourished and protein-deficient children—marasmus—appeared on 1810s mortality schedules as a cause of children's death. Officials also recorded upwards of one hundred stillborn babies annually, although it seems likely that many more went unreported. But for an accident, the city would never have discovered newborn twins buried in candle boxes behind a house in 1823. "The inability of the father to pay for coffins and other funeral expenses was the cause assigned for the mode and place of interment," explained the coroner's jury. As one scholar has recently argued, the circumstances of the urban poor were more Malthusian than Americans (then and now) have been willing to admit.[31]

Such alarming "statisticks of destitution" shocked Reverend Stephen Williams during his tenure as a missionary to the poor of Fells Point and Old Town. During 1836 and early 1837, Williams counted an average of 3 children in the 900 white households he visited, and 2.3 children in the 650 African American households he called upon. He found noticeably few children more than six years old and calculated that one in three black families and one in four white ones sent at least one member to live as a domestic servant in another household. Presbyterian minister Robert J. Breckinridge publicized Williams's findings in his *Baltimore Literary and Religious Magazine*. "[A]mongst the poor of this city the average of life is short; their increase is very slow;—and the mortality amongst young children very great," he wrote. Although Breckinridge would use such findings to argue for improved public education and religious instruction, he recognized structural poverty as the key undoing of working-class households: "causes are at work, in this city, which are so sensibly felt by the poorer classes, as materially to shorten life, prevent the natural increase of the population—and force households to separate, that they may obtain a livelihood." Those causes, he added, "operate upon the *blacks*, with nearly double the force, that they do upon the *whites*."[32]

The infectious diseases that regularly ravaged the city redoubled the insecurities of working-class households. Although boosters liked to proclaim Baltimore's salubriousness—and it was a healthy place relative to Charleston, New Orleans, or even Philadelphia—the city was susceptible to regular outbreaks of yellow fever, smallpox, and by the 1830s, cholera. Epidemics fell especially hard on Fells Point, with yellow fever decimating the neighborhood in 1800 by killing 850 people in the waterfront district and neighboring Old Town. Casualties were lower in 1819, largely because municipal authorities evacuated Fells Point residents to a camp on the city's northern outskirts at the first sign of the epidemic. Nonetheless, many laboring men and women were either "reduced to beggary by not having their usual labour and wages" or else fell deeper into "poverty by the deaths that occurred in their families."[33]

Epidemics usually encouraged elite Baltimore residents to condemn the city's poor for immoral and unhealthy living, but long-time resident John Weatherburn reasonably concluded that yellow fever flourished "in those parts inhabited by the lower order of the people, where cleanliness is not duly attended to, and where their diet and drink is not of the most wholesome kind." In any given year, hundreds of men and women in their twenties, thirties, and forties fell to diseases that are familiar to modern eyes (consumption, typhus, dysentery) and those that are not (catarrh, St. Anthony's fire, and mortification). As a group of Fells Point doctors explained, "the proportion of the poor is vastly greater" in their neighborhood, "and when sickness prevails, either in the usual, or in the epidemic, or malignant forms, their helplessness is in proportion to their poverty." Dr. Henry Diffinderffer's case records from a free clinic show just how frequently laboring men and women in their twenties, thirties, and forties were sidelined with sicknesses and injuries. Fells Point's Happy Alley seemed nothing of the sort in fall 1827 as its working-age inhabitants sought treatment for bilious fever, colic, pleurisy, phlegmon, constipation, and mania a potu (madness from drinking or *delirium tremens*), as well as such maladies as an inflamed leg, a sore foot, a burn, and a bruised face.[34]

In what one scholar has called a "climate of calamities," working households teetered on the brink of disaster when one prolonged illness, one spell of unemployment, one brush with the law, one encounter with a slave trader, one particularly cold week, one accidental fire could mean the difference between staying afloat and dissolution. There was little margin for error, and no matter how hard some families tried to plan ahead, the other shoe always threatened to drop. Consider Thomas Cardiffe, a Revolutionary War veteran, who left his wife Elizabeth and their three children behind in Baltimore when he went to work in an Eastern Shore fishery for a few months in 1793. Having "procure[d] the necessary support for himself and Family," Cardiffe returned home and was "much surprised and beyond measure distressed to find his poor children destitute of a mother's care." Because Elizabeth had no visible means of support during Thomas's absence, she had been arrested as a vagrant. Like other poor women, Elizabeth's need to feed her family took her into the streets, and a watchman might have apprehended her scavenging discarded fruit behind the market or collecting rags to sell for an extra income. Without a house to call her own and without Thomas to attest to her honesty, Elizabeth Cardiffe stood before the law no different from the prostitutes, fortune-tellers, and vagabonds whom the vagrancy statute targeted.[35]

Four similar stories of working-class life from early 1834 illustrate the fine line that separated getting by from utter privation. Simon Kemp, "one of our most sober and industrious mechanics," was hanging a bell on the roof of a hotel in 1834 when he slipped and fell. As doctors amputated his broken leg, the possibilities for Kemp, his wife, and their six children changed radically. That same month, a fire destroyed the Warren Factory, one of Baltimore's largest textile producers. "By far the most distressing circumstance connected with this event," reported the newspaper, "is the fact that between seven and eight hundred persons derived, directly or indirectly, their support from this establishment, and are thus suddenly deprived of employment at this very inclement season." Not far away on Aliceanna Street in Fells Point, a poorer family coped with its latest adversity: the father too sick to work, the oldest of the three children sick as well, the youngest "almost burnt to death" when its clothes caught on fire "whilst the mother was out gathering chips." Across the city on Howard Street, a fifty-year-old enslaved woman named Rachel lived with her teenaged son, John, far away from the Annapolis woman who owned them. In lives that approximated freedom, Rachel was an active member of the Baptist Church, while John knew how to read and write and cut a distinctive figure for himself as "something of a dandy." But once their owner Sophia Bland decided that she had "indulged them too much," Rachel and John's household was threatened with extinction.[36]

Baltimore provides limitless examples of the instability of working-class households. Imperiled as they were by forces far beyond their control, it was no surprise that laboring men and women struggled so hard to manage the aspects of daily survival involved in paying rent, heating an apartment, or purchasing food. As useful as the household was as a survival strategy, it still left little room to maneuver between what could be earned through labor and what needed to be purchased at market.

Basic Expenses

"A poor person who lives in poverty and misery, and merely from hand to mouth, has not the power of availing himself of any of those economical arrangements in procuring the necessaries of life which others in more affluent circumstances may employ," explained Robert Mills, the architect who designed Baltimore's Washington Monument and a keen reader of Count Rumford's treatises on the poor of Munich. Perhaps Mills was thinking of those households forced to purchase wintertime wood a few logs at a time. Wood was cheaper in bulk, but only for those with an available $5 to buy a cord and a yard in which to store it. For households that could not devote an entire week's wages to a single purchase, the alternative was to buy in smaller units—10¢ or 15¢ at a time—at a substantial markup over the bulk price. Mills might equally have had in mind those households that bought flour by the peck rather than the barrel, or those that had to buy bread because they lacked the proper stoves to bake it themselves. Renting their apartments rather than owning their own homes, many working-class households transferred their earnings to a landlord and gained no equity as houses in the developed parts of Baltimore became more valuable each year. Perhaps Mills even considered the African American families that had to include the purchase of loved ones in their monthly budgets. Without question, being poor was expensive.[37]

Money posed the initial challenge to working families—not merely the lack of it, but rather the variety of currencies circulating with fluctuating values and redeemability. Workers had no assurance of being paid in metallic coins of recognized value, nor any guarantee of receiving paper money that was current or redeemable at face value. Dozens of Baltimore banks, hotels, and merchants issued paper currency in amounts as small as 3¢. According to working-class critics, many employers went to "money markets" every Saturday to purchase bills below face value in order to pay laborers at the end of the week. A stevedore due $5 might be lucky enough to receive a $5 note issued by the venerable Bank of Maryland; he might also receive a handful of dubious notes from a vanished bank in Harford County or redeemable only at a particular store. Working people had to decide when and where to use their "good" bills or coins and otherwise negotiated the value of questionable notes with landlords and storekeepers. During the national banking collapse in 1837, Baltimore's city council issued some of the only currency to carry the backing of the government itself. Even then, a 6¼¢ note might buy a 6¼¢ loaf of bread, but it might not.[38]

Extant family budgets from the early republic are difficult to locate. Trade unions sometimes published the expenses of a typical family in order to argue for better wages. In 1809, for example, striking New York City journeymen carpenters reported that rent, wood, clothing, and food cost their households in excess of $10 each week. Mathew Carey printed the living expenses of laboring families to substantiate his claim that "their wages are inadequate to their support, even when fully employed." Such budgets may have been rhetorical, but they document the expenses facing working-class households. Incidentals like candles (for lighting), soap, medicines, needles and thread, blankets, shoes, and cooking utensils placed additional demands on household budgets beyond food, fuel, rent, and clothing. Charity appeals encapsulated these costs as the "necessities of life," a phrase potentially vague insofar as one person's necessities might be another's luxuries. Judg-

Baltimore 6¼¢ currency, 1837. Small change was a big problem in early republic Baltimore. The circulation of small bills worth less than their face value intensified the challenge of converting wages into food, fuel, and shelter. At a moment of particular economic instability in 1837, the City of Baltimore issued currency that would presumably hold its value longer than the bills of private banks. Courtesy Maryland Historical Society.

ing from what Baltimore's civic leaders distributed to the poor during the cold winters of the 1810s, no household could do without sugar, tea, and coffee. But those same relief efforts revealed that poor families also lacked money for flour, butter, coats, and shoes.[39]

Obtaining the necessities of life presented working-class households with a series of cash obligations that their wages could not consistently cover. Much depended on variables within a household: a woman in the last months of a pregnancy was unlikely to supplement a husband's earnings by doing laundry. Other variables were external, such as a spike in wood prices during a cold February, the disappearance of construction jobs when yellow fever appeared in September, or sustained periods of inflation (as was the case between 1802 and 1814) that resulted in falling real wages.[40] Such constantly changing circumstances make it impossible to pinpoint a working-class standard of living but highlight the range of possibilities and challenges facing laboring households as they struggled to meet their expenses.

Throughout much of the early republic period, working-class households counted on what historians (since E. P. Thompson) have called a "moral economy" to keep necessities like bread affordable. Anglo-American culture frowned on the notion that a "just price" was whatever the market would bear. Certain commodities like flour should be sold at prices that allowed a miller or merchant a fair return on his investment but that neither gouged consumers nor threatened the ability of the poor to obtain necessities. If vendors artificially drove up prices by withholding goods from the market or inflated the prices of items like bread or flour beyond the reach of common people, municipal governments had the obligation to set the price or the people had the right to seize what they needed and pay what they deemed fair. Similar logic explained why early republic cities so carefully regulated their food markets, establishing precise hours of operations, setting rules as to what commodities could or could not be sold, and empowering inspectors to levy fines or condemn outlawed products.[41]

Baltimore's municipal ordinances spelled out where the city's consumers could shop, what they could purchase, and in some cases, exactly what they would pay. Calls for new regulations invariably invoked the needs of Baltimore's working-class households. When storekeepers called for a crackdown on the hucksters who sold inferior candles on city streets, they argued, "the poor, who are the principal purchasers of them, are very much injured and defrauded, without remedy, as the sellers are unsettled and unknown." The grocers who wanted the right to sell meat outside the market insisted that current regulations were "an oppression to the Poor, who are only able to buy the Small Cut pieces." Although butchers, bakers, and even candlestick makers (early republic tinsmiths) complained from time to time about being denied the profits of unregulated exchange, a broader social consensus sought to protect common people's basic consumer needs from the vagaries of market forces—at least for the first few decades of the nineteenth century.[42]

Baltimore's bread assize illustrates the career of the "moral economy" and its impact on working-class consumers. Mayor James Calhoun called for the assize in 1802 "so that the purchaser may know how much he gets for his money." The resulting law stipulated that loaves could be sold in two—and only two—sizes: $1\frac{1}{2}$ pounds and 3 pounds. Public inspectors regularly visited bakeries to weigh bread, and private citizens could reap a 5¢ reward by reporting bakers who were light in their loaves. Bakers were ostensibly free to sell the loaves for whatever they pleased, but custom kept prices fixed at $6\frac{1}{4}$¢ and $12\frac{1}{2}$¢. As baker Daniel Evans complained to the city council in 1809, "our loaves have been for many years sold at the sixteenth or eighth of a Dollar and we consider it out of our power to alter the price of the loaf as often as the price of flour varey." Accordingly, while wages and other prices fluctuated, the retail cost of bread stayed constant for more than a quarter-century.[43]

Rather than an unmitigated boon to working-class consumers, however, the bread assize posed a problem for households with less than $6\frac{1}{4}$¢ to spend. Some bakers argued that working people needed smaller loaves at lower prices. "Among the vast population of our growing city, there are a great number who cannot at all times make it convenient to divide their pittance in such manner as to procure the actual necessaries of life," contended twenty-five bakers in a petition to the city council in 1827. Forced to sell their loaves on credit or risk the fine for baking smaller loaves, these bakers lamented that their kindheartedness—never refusing "to a fellow creature of that portion of bread which he is only able"—threatened their own livelihoods. Other bakers saw this as a disingenuous claim, accusing the petitioners of seeking "the <u>trade totally unrestricted</u>: should this ever be the case, then the public may look out!!" But it was not only disgruntled bakers who saw the assize as anachronistic in a "free and liberal" society. "A free competition," claimed the *Baltimore Patriot*, "will always insure a larger loaf and better bread from the baker, than municipal regulations can do." A revised assize in 1828 loosened the enforcement mechanisms. Moreover, a growing number of bakers sought loopholes in the law and sold loaves to retailers and hucksters who then resold smaller portions of bread to consumers. The good news for working-class households was that they could now purchase bread for less than a nickel; the bad news was that they got less bread for their money, and as one observer complained, retailers took "a profit of from 30 to 40 per cent, paid by the poor."[44]

Urban households had few opportunities to supply their own larders. Although the periphery of the city was undeveloped, it was not a commons where city residents might forage or hunt. When urbanites shot game and fished on the outskirts of town, landholders prosecuted them as poachers.[45] Nor could Baltimore's poor easily raise livestock within the city. Between 1797 and 1820, public ordinances kept the urban range closed, making it illegal to graze swine freely on city streets. The prohibition made it "lawful for all persons to kill or cause to be killed all Swine running at large in any of the Streets, lanes or alleys in said city." In 1807, two clever hog catchers, Jesse Hicks and Nicholas Martin, captured fifteen loose pigs, sold them in the market, and kept half the proceeds for themselves. But if urban grazing was illegal, nuisance laws also made it difficult to keep pigs in a sty. Health officials feared that slop could produce the miasma believed to cause yellow fever. Citizens regularly brought complaints against their neighbors whose pens generated intolerable levels of "stench and filth."[46]

After the 1819 yellow fever epidemic, city leaders began to frown on hog sties and reconsidered their opposition to open grazing in city streets. Dr. Joseph Brevitt suggested combining prophylaxis with poor relief. "Hogs perambulate the most secluded holes and corners, gorge with voraciousness and rapidity every kind of garbage, vegetable and animal, and remove them with the celerity of legerdemain," Brevitt observed. Indeed, "a hog running at large is friend to everyone he visits, whilst a hog confined is the most intolerable nuisance we can possible conceive." Brevitt's pork-relief plan encouraged the poor to expend a mere dollar on "a pair of rabbit-sized pigs" each spring. As the pigs spent the summer eating "what would be a nuisance and cause of disease," Brevitt continued, "they grow to the delight and provision of the poor man and [his] hungry offspring." Instead of depending on public charity during the winter months, "a helpless family" could now subsist on three hundred pounds of pork. The city council found this logic compelling enough to allow swine free range between May and November. Although it is unknown if any poor families pursued Brevitt's plan, public officials were quite pleased to use pigs as street sweepers. The Board of Health reported in 1826 that the grazing swine consumed "a vast quantity of offal, which is daily thrown out upon the streets, & which would become offensive and unwholesome in a few hours." As for the friendliness of urban pigs, Brevitt may have overstated his case. The *Baltimore Patriot* urged "CAUTION" to its readers who might visit the site of the city's Washington Monument. "One of the numerous hogs which hold undisturbed possession of Washington Square," the paper reported in 1822, nearly killed a child whose life was saved only by a passing adult. As another boy stood on the corner eating a piece of bread and butter, a hog snatched his lunch, as well as his hand, dragging him across the street. Yet another child with an apple had her wrist "dangerously wounded" in the same way.[47]

Because Baltimore's ordinances allowed street grazing only during half the year, careless pig owners frequently saw their animals taken up by municipal officials each November and December. "They could not save their bacon," quipped a newspaper account of mayor Jacob Small's success in clearing the streets of "the swinish multitude" in 1826. Seized pigs were sold at public auction, where their former owners—"frequently females," reported the mayor—typically repurchased them for as little as 5¢. "From the clamour they create," said Small of these poor women, "no person will bid against them." The women's collaboration assured that it would be cheaper to repurchase one's wayward pig several times over than to confine and feed it until the streets reopened in May. Still, periodic sweeps of the streets could be "cruelly hard on the poor." Mayor Samuel Smith relayed the "truly distressing and afflicting" story of several "poor distressed women" who "lost the meat with which they expected to feed their children" under this law.[48]

Bread and meat were the two largest components of a spartan and nutritionally deficient working-class diet. Small wonder that constipation was among the most frequent ailment of the Fells Point poor who sought medical attention. Urban workers generally ate far less nutritiously than did rural workers, who had greater access to fruits, vegetables, and dairy products. Even almshouse inmates had a better diet, dining on a weekly menu that included four days of meat soup, two days of salt meat, and one day of fish, as well as the fresh vegetables grown on the institution's farm. In contrast, the urban poor received the vast majority of their sustenance from carbohydrates and stimulants, chiefly bread, tea, coffee, and sugar, as well as alcohol. Market regulations made it difficult to obtain inexpensive New England cheeses and salt cod as alternative sources of protein, much to the regret of market clerk Robert Lawson, who touted salt fish as an "excellent substitute for beef." While working-class households could not afford the coconuts and pineapples that sometimes appeared in the market, their food budgets did include an occasional vegetable (2¢ for a head of cabbage), butter (25¢ per pound), milk (6½¢ per quart), as well as coffee (25¢ per pound), tea ($1 per pound), and sugar (10¢ per pound). Food peddlers offered warm meals to those with coins in their pockets, although supper at the stand of an oysterman or a pepper-pot soup vendor may have been more convenient than economical.[49]

Procuring food required cash. Even a meager food budget could consume more than half of a man's weekly earnings. Hezekiah Niles asserted in 1815 that a working-class family of six could eat heartily for 30¢ per day, but that figure underestimated per capita bread consumption, presumed that families would bake bread rather than purchase loaves, and included no vegetables, fruit, milk, or beer. Not even the most rigorously run penal institution could cut daily food costs below 8¢ per person. More likely, a household of six faced food expenditures in excess of 50¢ per day, or above $3.50 per week. Recall that a male manual laborer earned $6 in a good week, and far less during seasonal slowdowns. The inability of households to cover their food expenses became obvious every winter when the city organized the distribution of supplies to the needy. During winter 1805, the city distributed 25,000 quarts of soup and 18,000 loaves of bread to upwards of 1,000 households. Eleven hundred households took relief during the cold winter of 1810. Between 5,000 and 7,000 Baltimore residents received food aid in the winter months of 1817. A municipal soup society served 31,725 quarts of soup and 22,646 loaves of bread in 1820.[50]

As with food, the need to purchase wood for heating and cooking placed a burdensome cash demand on household budgets. Winters in early republic Baltimore were far colder than today, as evidenced by the regular freezing of the harbor. The same cold weather that put mariners and dockworkers out of work ratcheted up their need for wood for heating at precisely the moment it was most expensive. A household with some small savings could make a deposit on wood in the summertime to lock in a reasonable price, and proposals for "wood banks" circulated in the early republic. But for families living hand-to-mouth, such economical measures were out of reach. Instead, working-class households purchased small quantities of wood at retail prices, spending by some accounts upwards of $50 per winter, or roughly $2 per week until their money ran out. Poor households then suffered miserably in the cold or depended on charity to obtain fuel. "*Hundreds* of families are almost perishing for want of wood," reported one alarmed observer in early 1815. The word "perish" appeared regularly in descriptions of poor families lacking firewood. After distributing wood to nearly 1,400 households in 1822, civic leaders warned that "there still remains something to be done to save a great number of poor from perishing." A group of charitable women visited poor households in 1827 and observed "suffering children around their bed crying for fire to warm themselves."[51]

Barney O'Connell recalled the freezing winter of 1805 when "the rich men of the town had to send out wagons to haul in wood from the country to distribute among the poor, to prevent them from perishing with cold." An early Irish Catholic immigrant to Baltimore, O'Connell found himself "poor, and not only poor, but unable to work" that winter. Moreover, his wife, Judy, and their sons, Dennis and Patrick, were all stricken with typhus. "The weather grew colder every hour—but there was no increase to our scanty supply of blankets—the fire on the hearth went out—for we had not a stick of wood to keep up the flame—the barrel of meal was exhausted, and there was not even a potatoe in the house," O'Connell recounted. Only the benevolent intervention of a wealthy Irish merchant saved the family from the almshouse. Households without such patrons relied on municipal assistance for wintertime wood, but such aid was rarely enough. During the winter of the O'Connells' distress, the managers of the city's emergency relief program identified "many persons in a state of wretchedness and want so deplorable, that unless timely relief is afforded, they must perish."[52]

Rent posed the next challenge to the limited budgets of working-class households in Baltimore. Very little evidence exists to pinpoint the monthly expense of renting a small apartment or house in the city. One advocate of the female seamstresses contended, "The rent of a room, even the most indifferent, is never less than fifty cents per week." Regardless of price, paying rent was the common experience of working-class households in Baltimore, especially in neighborhoods like Fells Point, where absentee landlords and a handful of wealthy families owned most of the housing stock.[53]

The history of the city's famous rowhouses attests to the symbiotic interests of large Maryland landowning families (like the Howards, Catons, and Fells) and capitalist builders who developed blocks of new rental housing on speculation. A ground-rent system allowed landed proprietors to parcel out lots to builders who gained inexpensive access to land for development. The landholders attained a modest return on 99-year leases and saw the value of their own property rise as the developed parts of the city extended farther outward with each year. Builders lined newly opened streets—and in Fells Point that included any number of narrow alleys—with wooden and brick (after a 1799 fire-prevention ordinance) rowhouses, usually two-and-a-half stories tall, two bays wide, one or two rooms deep, and with a kitchen located in the basement or in an outbuilding on the back half of the lot. The Federal Assessment of 1798 found more than one hundred houses in Fells Point that were only one story tall and with as little as 192 square feet of living space.[54]

While some laborers and laundresses became the owners of such miniscule houses on streets like Happy Alley, most Fells Point rowhouses were sold to more prosperous artisans, purchased as dowers for widows, or bought as investments by shopkeepers, lawyers, and merchants. Property-owning widows and artisans often lived adjacent to their tenants, but records of formal leases do not survive. The process of renting living space was certainly more informal than in Manhattan, where all leases expired on a single day, and May 1st brought chaos to city streets as everyone moved at once. In contrast to New York's pandemonium, there was little for observers to see in the experiences of Baltimore renters. Court-ordered evictions were not common for renters in arrears, and if landlords sent their overdue tenants to debtor's prison, police records did not speak to the frequency. Suffice it to say, rents as low as 50¢ per week would challenge working-class households, especially those whose primary wage earners were seamstresses earning far less on their best days of sewing. For those households with access to a laboring man's dollar wage, rent was not oppressive when work was available. But should a man lose a week's employment to an injury, to the slowing of maritime traffic, or to bad weather that put construction projects on hold, only a landlord's leniency prevented eviction.[55]

Medical care was another regular expense of working-class households—a disproportionate need given poor diets, debilitating labor, and cramped housing in fetid, low-lying neighborhoods. "The honest poor are dreadfully afraid of a Doctor's bill," reported one public health advocate in 1822. Because no doctor's assistance could be had for less than $1, laboring men and women who were sick either suffered in silence or left their homes to seek medical care in the almshouse. The deadly 1800 yellow fever epidemic galvanized efforts to improve public health in Baltimore, and the city's philanthropists and physicians founded a free clinic to provide medical assistance to those who could not otherwise afford it. By 1804, the Baltimore General Dispensary was assisting over one thousand patients each year. Funding came from private benefactors, who recognized their dependence on a healthy workforce. "The poor are numerous—many of them must be sick, and when sick, they cannot perform those offices for the rich, or the easy, without which they cannot experience the enjoyments of life," explained a donor in 1805. Patients came to the institution with acute symptoms like emesis (nausea), chronic ailments like rheumatism, and specific injuries like hernias (common among workers doing heavy lifting), dislocated limbs, and infected wounds. When Mary Newton of Primrose Alley arrived at the dispensary in December 1804, she exhibited "severe chills, succeeded by pain in all her limbs." But when she refused to take an emetic, the consulting physician scribbled in the casebook, "Mary Newton's disease seems to consist in wretched poverty more than anything else."[56]

What really ailed the sick of Fells Point was the lack of doctors serving the neighborhood after 1810, once the dispensary stopped serving the area because so few of its prosperous residents had made donations to support free healthcare. Even after a new, second dispensary had been founded to serve the eastern parts of the city in 1817, over 90 percent of Baltimore's physicians practiced elsewhere. The campaign to raise funds for the second dispensary highlighted the impact of illness and medical care on working-class budgets. Advocates contended that Fells Point was "most in need of medical aid, from the number and condition of its poor, but the least able to procure it." For example, the wives and children of Baltimore sailors did not have access to the hospital operated by the United States government for the men of the navy and merchant marine. The cost of medicine or a doctor's visit would prove disastrous to a household struggling to survive until a man returned from sea with wages. After laborer George Whitten caught his hand in the mudmachine's gears in 1820, the ensuing injury put him out of work for eight weeks and subjected him to a weighty doctor's bill. Without wages and facing this new expense, Whitten had become "indebted for the necessities of life." It was exactly men like Whitten that the founders of the second dispensary had in mind when they chided the institution's unforthcoming donors: "These poor people have been useful to you when prosperity attended our commerce, and they have on this record a strong claim to your attention."[57]

Clothing and shoes constituted yet another major expense for Baltimore's working-class households. Although clothing was increasingly inexpensive to produce—recall the seamstresses' low wages—it remained costly enough for many laboring people to lack enough of the warmer varieties to survive Baltimore's winters. In 1805, almost three hundred women and children were "temporarily clad by the bounty of their fellow-citizens," but many more "still remain almost naked and in the utmost distress, from the want of raiment to protect them from the keen and piercing blasts of a rigorous winter." Calls for "old and superfluous cloth-ing" regularly appeared in public charity appeals, and merchants were encour-aged to provide "coarse woolen wrapping and remnants they may have little or no use for." During the winter of 1810, the city provided Mrs. Kane a pair of shoes, while Mrs. Peacock received three yards of flannel, four yards of muslin, three yards of calico, one and a half yards of blue coating, and two blankets. Even if shoes and clothing added only $10 or $15 a year to a household's budget, these were crucial expenditures, especially for those who worked outside in strenuous conditions. Male manual laborers could easily work through several pairs of shoes and pants in a year. It was no coincidence that when servants and slaves ran away, they took as much clothing with them as possible. The extensive catalog of cloth-ing in most runaway advertisements attests to the challenges working people an-ticipated in obtaining additional clothing in the future (as well as to clothing's ex-changeability for cash in the pawnshops where many poor people had to purchase their clothing secondhand). Likewise, coats and jackets figured in enough crimi-nal prosecutions for theft to suggest that these items often stood beyond what do-mestic servants, sailors, and day laborers could afford.[58]

Virtually every working-class household struggled to meet the costs of clothing, medical care, rent, fuel, and food. Now imagine the additional burden of having to budget several dollars each week for the freedom of oneself or a loved one. The opportunity to escape slavery through purchase dictated the allocation of cash in many of Baltimore's African American households. As one scholar of manumis-sion has noted, "Baltimore masters not only bought slaves but also sold freedom."[59]

African Americans seized the opportunity, but not without enduring tremen-dous hardship and privation. A term slave at the Maryland Chemical Works, Sci-pio Freeman worked nightshifts for an extra 25¢ and took on additional labor in order to purchase himself two years ahead of his 1835 manumission date. Whereas the manager of the factory had been paying a free black woman to house the com-pany's slaves, Freeman negotiated responsibility for his own room and board and pocketed an extra $1.50 each week for himself. Working far harder than any white or black employee at the factory and living on rations far more meager, Freeman could scarcely have had time to eat or sleep in pursuit of his freedom.[60]

In another telling story of industriousness, Beverly Dowling negotiated a $200 purchase price with his owner in August 1833 and was able to deliver the first $100 within a month of striking the deal—probably savings from his previous employment as the manservant of Jerome Bonaparte (Napoleon's nephew, born to Baltimore's Elizabeth Patterson in 1805). As part of the deal, Dowling "had his owner's consent to go at large to make up the price he was to pay for his freedom." In pursuit of that money, Dowling kept an oysterhouse, ran a bootblack shop, and even served as a waiter on a steamship that ran between Baltimore and New York City. With the ebbs and flows of his employment, Dowling paid another $23 toward his freedom in October 1834, $50 in June 1835, and the last $27 the following October. Dowling was a fast-moving character, and the agent of his owner could rarely track down the man he sarcastically called "his lordship." Yet even a man as energetic as Dowling still had trouble raising the cash for his purchase, and because he was nearly two years overdue on the second $100 he owed, his owner had him arrested as a runaway and sold to the notorious slave-trader Austin Woolfolk. A contentious freedom suit followed, culminating in Dowling's liberation in 1837.[61]

Purchasing freedom placed a tremendous burden on African American households that had to balance immediate subsistence needs against payments to the owner of a relative or loved one. At least one Baltimore couple sold themselves into indentured servitude for seven years in order to raise the funds necessary to purchase their son. In other households, parents purchased the freedom of a daughter and then immediately bound her to a white employer as a servant in return for the money the family needed to purchase the freedom of a second child. Such purchases often involved white intermediaries, perhaps a benevolent Quaker patron, but perhaps a callous broker who might hold on to the deed of sale until fully repaid with interest.[62]

Not all free black parents who purchased their children from white slaveholders immediately manumitted them. Under Maryland law, "indigent" African American men and women could have their free children removed from their homes and bound out as indentured servants. But because no one who owned a slave— property of significant value—could ever be ruled indigent, free black parents could actually protect the integrity of their families by maintaining children as slaves. Enslaved children could also serve as collateral for loans that free black parents could use to purchase their remaining children still in the hands of white slaveholders. The vast majority of the several hundred black slaveholders in Baltimore were parents who owned their children as an expediency.

The necessity of purchasing freedom impeded the economic advancement of many African American households. In scraping together enormous sums to liberate family members from slavery, black households diverted capital that might have otherwise purchased real estate, a storefront, or a cart—productive property that would raise household fortunes over several generations. Because black families were forced to channel all savings toward buying basic human rights for themselves, they had nothing left to invest. The wages they earned flowed back into the pockets of the city's slaveholders, amplifying the already enormous economic inequality. Without the added expense of purchasing freedom, black households in Baltimore might have moved out of poverty more rapidly. Even as the majority of black Baltimore residents lived in freedom, slavery accounted for the persistence of their poverty.

Strategies of Makeshift

To meet the costs of living, working-class households engaged in scavenging, bartering, and a host of informal exchanges. The underground economy that sustained these efforts regularly skirted the boundaries of legality. Enforcement of the law, however erratic, thus presented additional challenges to household survival.

One common strategy was to enter the world of short-term credit and pawning. At a time when much of daily commerce was conducted on the books rather than in coins, grocers, landlords, and storekeepers extended credit to customers whose best prospects of paying were in the future. Credit might constitute a short-term expediency for both buyer and seller until a husband returned from sea with several months' wages or until warm weather revived the construction sector. Recording a debt in a ledger book was standard practice throughout the early republic, but in a fast-growing city like Baltimore, vendors were probably leery of offering credit to recent arrivals. The city's bakers claimed to lose much money by providing bread on credit to people they "may never see again." Laboring men and women who could marshal a recommendation from an employer or who could claim some shared ethnic or religious connection had a better chance of attaining credit from Baltimore storekeepers. But insofar as prevailing racist ideology denigrated African Americans as untrustworthy, it is doubtful that black households could access credit with the same ease as working-class whites.[63]

Attaining food and firewood on credit was necessary for working-class households, but it also entailed substantial risk—namely the possibility of imprisonment for failing to repay a debt. Debtors' prison remained a powerful tool in the hands of early republic creditors, even as a growing chorus of critics decried the practice as a "relic of a barbarous age." It was a creditor's prerogative to order the arrest of a defaulting debtor, whose jail term would last until the debt was repaid, the debtor sought the protection of insolvency laws, or the creditor relented. While celebrated cases of debt imprisonment involved merchants and financiers fallen on hard times, the practice in 1820s and 1830s Baltimore involved poorer individuals who owed far smaller sums. At the height of the practice in 1831, 959 Baltimore residents served jail time for debt, with 53 prisoners owing less than $1, and half of all incarcerated debtors owing less than $10. Even after legal reforms sought to spare those whose debts were small, more than half of the six hundred prisoners in 1834 owed less than $10. African Americans constituted one-third of these small debtors.[64]

Noticeably absent from debtors' prisons were women. The legal practice of coverture sent husbands to jail for debts their wives had incurred, but adult women living outside of marriage could assume debts seemingly without the risk of imprisonment. Women's immunity from imprisonment may have given cohabitating couples an incentive to eschew marriage in order to lower the risk that using credit would result in a wage-earning man's imprisonment. Likewise, credit may have figured more prominently in the survival strategies of female-headed households able to borrow with relative impunity.

Pawnage offered another route to obtaining needed cash. As in New York and Philadelphia, laboring men and women in Baltimore could convert a spoon, a quilt, or a hammer into 50¢ or $1. Critics of the practice drew attention to the serial pawning that allowed a seamstress or mariner to convert a ring into rent on the thirtieth of one month and to redeem the item only a few days later. Legal pawnbrokers had to purchase a license and post a bond with the municipal government, which regulated rates and fees. Unredeemed goods could not be sold for at least six months, and then only by auction.[65]

At least five licensed pawnbrokers were in business in 1832. Sarah Millem, who operated a store near the bazaar on Harrison Street, offered "very liberal advances in CASH on all deposits of Jewelry, Silver Plate, Dry Goods, Furniture, Beds and Bedding, Clothing, and Goods of every description." Cognizant of how working-class households used pawning, Millem advertised herself to customers "such as require TEMPORARY RELIEF." Other brokers were less subtle: "*Money! Money!! Money!!!*" announced Solomon Eytinge. An observant Jew, Eytinge warned customers, "No business will be transacted on Saturdays." When Eytinge sold his inventory in September 1834, the staggering assortment of pawned goods included teaspoons, creamers, sugar tongs, ladles, umbrellas, handkerchiefs, bonnets, shawls, linens, and carpentry tools. Even the most marginal households usually possessed one item that might have once belonged to a genteel family or that attested to the wider availability of "respectable" domestic goods in the early republic.[66]

Pawnbrokers stood on the legitimate end of a much wider spectrum of petty entrepreneurs who traded goods between their rightful owners, their current possessors, and buyers seeking low prices. Baltimore officials knew that an underground economy in clothing, household goods, and even foodstuffs provided every incentive for needy people to engage in theft. When a widowed woman like Elizabeth Cruse—"cast on the wide world without friends and without money to buy bread for herself and her family"—stole twenty yards of linen from a neighbor in 1810, it was likely that she would exchange the cloth for cash. Cruse might have sold the linen to a huckster, who in turn sold it to a middling family across town. Invited to wait in the foyer, the huckster might avail herself of a set of forks kept in a sideboard or a tea tray resting on a table. Those stolen goods might then end up in an unlicensed pawnshop, where a needy woman like Elizabeth Cruse might hope to purchase them cheaply and regain some of the genteel trappings she lost when her husband died.[67]

Women played a key role in Baltimore's underground economy of goods—as domestic servants with access to the possessions of wealthier families, as hucksters who sold their wares outside the official marketplace, and as illegal shopkeepers who fenced stolen goods. Take for example Ellen Barnett, an Irish woman who took a wet-nursing job when she arrived in Baltimore. As Barnett would later explain, "she (like many others in Baltimore, but unfortunately for herself), undertook to advance money on deposits, or, in other words, to keep, as is very common in the country she came from, a pawnbroker's shop." Goods began coming in: a silver-plated teakettle stand and fruit basket, fourteen knives and sixteen forks, a set of sheets and pillowcases, a quilt, and a looking glass. Almost immediately, Barnett was arrested for receiving stolen goods—an offense common enough by the mid-1820s that Baltimore's municipal authorities had preprinted indictment forms with blanks left for the relevant information. Ignorance that such goods had been stolen constituted no legal excuse, but Barnett's woeful story helped her get a reduced prison term. "She is a poor simple woman, who has not good sense," reported the constable who searched her house, adding that Barnett "had been taken in by the persons who stole what I found in her house."[68]

African Americans occupied a peculiar place within Baltimore's underground economy. On the one hand, prevailing racist hostility cast suspicion on black men and women who had goods to pawn or sell. One pawnbroker offering cash for clothing, books, and furniture was careful to include "none will be purchased from people of color" in his 1809 advertisement. The ordinance regulating pawnbrokers in Baltimore banned dealings with slaves who lacked written permission from their owners. On the other hand, Baltimore storekeepers regularly purchased what black men and women had to offer with few questions asked. The enslaved carters who brought rural produce to city markets and wharves presumably shepherded pilfered goods into the hands of free black men and women to resell or trade. Baskets of apples and bags of grain fell mysteriously off the backs of carts, prompting irritated whites to demand more vigorous policing of the disorderly "crowds of people of color" gathered outside the markets.[69]

Pilfered goods readily found a place in the shops of white storekeepers. Daniel Crowl purchased two boxes of raisins and a drum of figs from William Grant, an African American man who reportedly received dried fruit from an employer in lieu of wages. If Crowl suspected the goods were stolen, he rationalized the purchase "owing to the extreme severity of the season, and the great stagnation of business of every kind." Some years earlier in 1803, the prosperous shopkeepers Thomas and Margaret Tate allowed Caleb Dougherty to make numerous small purchases on credit. A slave to a rural Maryland owner, Dougherty represented himself as free and periodically settled his account by providing the Tates with cloth, blankets, suspenders, coffee, sugar, and even a barrel of flour. Dougherty had purportedly received the goods from his father in the country and one day even brought along "an elderly looking mulatto man" as if to convince the Tates of the story. Eventually other customers noticed that the Tates' entire inventory comprised stolen goods, and soon thereafter Thomas Tate and Caleb Dougherty were both arrested. In such circumstances, African Americans stood far more exposed before the law due both to their inability to testify against white accomplices and to the higher punishments stipulated by law for people of African descent.[70]

The city's watchmen were another key node in the underground economy. As likely to commit crimes as to prevent them, city watchmen confiscated a range of "stolen goods" that ended up in secondhand stores, unlicensed pawnshops, or the homes of watchmen themselves. The conviction of a watchman like David Holmes in 1827 perhaps spoke less to a culture of corruption than to the fact that watchmen's wages required their households to enter the underground economy to survive. When prospective watchmen applied to the municipal government to be hired, their petitions invariably discussed the dire financial circumstances of their households. So too did their frequent petitions for higher wages. Watchmen's households were little different from other working-class households, and the stolen child's frock and petticoat that Holmes received may have helped dress his household at a time when his wages could not.[71]

One of the most lucrative underground trades was in alcohol, which provided a particular opportunity for female-headed households to transform the small apartments where they finished shirts and cared for children into makeshift taverns. Baltimore's licensing system made entry into tavern keeping relatively easy, but the $16 annual fee stood beyond the incomes of most women. Ann Johnson had purchased a license in 1807, but when it expired a year later, she "was straining every nerve to raise a sum of money sufficient for the purchase of a new one."

She continued to serve customers under her old license, only to accumulate $100 in fines for selling several pints of gin and whiskey. A widow with five children, Johnson could neither pay the fine nor "expiate her offense in jail" because "her children must in the meantime be thrown upon the world without a friend or protection and be left to rely upon indiscriminate charity for a miserable subsistence." Her vivid plea convinced the city court to waive her fines, but many other women were not so lucky. "Aunt Juno" Clarke was one of three African American women (and nine women in total) who faced fines and jail time for operating illegal taverns in 1816. Prosecutions for illegal alcohol vending—or keeping a disorderly house—would increase in the 1820s and 1830s, leading to the conviction of women like Susan Bryan, a mother of six whose "husband has absconded and left his family in the most indigent circumstances." The household of watchman Richard Good served alcohol during the hours he was patrolling city streets. "The fact is that his wife was the cause of this trouble," claimed one of Good's patrons, but such an observation obscured the need for working-class households to combine a man's wages with other sources of income.[72]

Scavenging also figured prominently in working-class survival strategies. Among the refuse on Fells Point streets, the assiduous (and desperate) could locate rags to sell to papermakers, coal to burn for heat, scrap metal that might be recycled for cash, and fruit and vegetables past their prime but still edible. During the months when municipal ordinances required pigs to be kept in sties, according to one observer, "the poor people in this place . . . make it their business to go from house to house and collect all the offal of kitchens and convey home for the purpose of feeding their hogs." Scavenging required keeping a mental map of which houses offered the best scraps, which grocers offered end-of-the-day discounts, which butchers gave away bones for stew, and which wharves were piled with discarded barrel staves. Women and children paid close attention to the yards of carpentry and coopering shops, for these were prime places to locate wood chips for making fires—although not always with the approval of the men laboring there. Thirteen-year-old Mary Ann Zwigler surveyed an Old Town lumberyard for chips in 1829 before she was chased off by Joshua Johnson, who was cutting shingles. "I will settle Johnson's knitting for him," the teenager was heard to say, and indeed she did by accusing him of starting a suspicious fire in the neighborhood.[73]

The line separating scavenging from stealing was often in the eye of the beholder. Ann Harnett was convicted of stealing a cartload of wood in 1791, but protested, "The wood for which your petitioner is sentenced was nothing more than carpenters chips hewn from logs to square them on the wharf." Occasionally the courts recognized the dire circumstances that blurred scavenging and stealing. Once William Nevit was sentenced to jail for stealing 41 pounds of copper (presumably to resell to a scrap dealer), the judges who convicted him called for a pardon. "The prisoner had endeavored to obtain employment and offered to work even for his victuals only—but could not get it," reported Judge Nicholas Brice, adding that Nevit "committed the theft in question under the pressure of <u>extreme necessity</u>."[74]

Although the underground and illegal economies helped working-class households attain the necessities of life, survival generally required partaking of private charity. Assistance from private benevolent organizations and out-relief payments from the municipal government were never enough to provide total support, but they nonetheless played a crucial role in household budgets. Mathew Carey declared it an "erroneous opinion" that "the poor, by industry, prudence, and economy, may at all times support themselves comfortably on eleemosynary aid," and Baltimore taxpayers supported fewer than 100 pensioners annually with meager payments of $40 or less. Private organizations offered even less in the way of cash and on average provided needy households with less than $5 in relief each winter. Despite the chorus of critics who depicted the poor as slackers who preferred handouts to hard work, charity merely supplemented household budgets with a few dollars in cash or a few yards of fabric. The large numbers of Baltimore residents lining up in winter for soup, wood, or coats attested to the indispensability of such relief. Some aid required substantial labor before it could be made useful. For example, the Aimwell Society offered relief in the form of unfinished cloth for women to stitch and then sell back to the society's agents. The emergency aid offered to Biddy Matthews and Ann McGuilen in 1810 included flannel and muslin to sew into linens and clothing for their families. Typical of those receiving wintertime relief from the city, these two women garnered between $6 and $9 in wood, cloth, shoes, blankets, tea, coffee, and sugar over the space of four weeks while the harbor was frozen. In the mixed economy of poor households, charity was not qualitatively different from a cash wage, a salvaged coat, or a pilfered melon.[75]

Lotteries and gambling provided one last opportunity for poor men and women to meet their expenses. As the funding mechanisms of churches, orphanages, and schools throughout the country, lotteries were regularly drawn. Baltimore was home to one of the nation's most prominent ticket brokers, Jacob Cohen, who published an entire newspaper devoted to lottery news. Critics worried that this "species of Gambling" was "more extensively ruinous than any other species of gambling, on the account of the facilities it affords for great numbers to indulge without public exposure." "Its deluded victims," continued an 1834 petition asking the legislature to ban lotteries, "are chiefly of the labouring and poorer classes." Other forms of betting—faro tables and wheels of fortune—figured prominently in grand jury reports, and gamblers were commonly thought to be "the cause of many a poor family suffering."[76]

The appeal of gambling, of course, was that a stroke of fortune could reverse one's humble circumstances, provide the funds to buy one's freedom, or dissolve the anxiety about how to pay the bills. Baltimore's lottery vendors fed these fantasies in vivid advertisements featuring humble men and women catching money-laden fish off the good ship *Fortune* or collecting gold coins falling freely from the back of a carriage. "WAKE UP OLD TOWN," screamed an 1834 advertisement that told of a working-class woman from the neighborhood who had won $1,200 in a recent drawing. "She had four small children to scuffle for and never did money come in a better time for her," the ticket vendor reported at the start of another cold Baltimore winter. Similarly, gambling on faro promised an easier way of making ends meet for both white and African American laboring men (whose indiscriminate mixing was a frequent cause for complaint). Gambling's appeal seemed all the more reasonable relative to the high danger and low rewards of digging a canal for $1 a day. Middling and elite men could gamble with relative impunity, so long as they were not "gambling for a subsistence." But for working-class families, subsistence was a gamble, and in that light, there was little difference between waiting on a dock for a ship to arrive and ponying up a few dollars on a lucky number.[77]

Improvidence and Industriousness

Most prosperous residents of Baltimore could not fathom the labor that went into working-class survival. Public officials, policymakers, and social commentators rarely acknowledged the labor that kept households afloat, but instead attributed poverty to the failure of laboring people to embrace the new logic of the competitive marketplace. In what appeared to be an open society where individuals rose and fell on their own merits, hard work and careful planning were the guarantors of prosperity. In turn, failure betokened laziness and improvidence. Because the wintertime disappearance of work was predictable, working-class households should have planned better during the summer months. "Whilst they have full employment for nine months in the year, they should look forward by weekly or monthly savings, to provide for the three months of winter," chided a newspaper correspondent in 1817. "They should seriously think of providing for old age, for sickness, and for the other accidental contingencies of human life," the writer concluded while the port was still frozen shut.[78]

The belief that thrift would elevate poor families galvanized the founders of the Savings Bank of Baltimore. "The Mechanick, the Labourer, the Sea-faring Man, the Apprentice, Male and Female Domestick, and the industrious poor of every description" could now gain interest on their savings. A surplus dollar deposited each week for a year would generate a $54 nest egg to guard "against a time of need." Promotional literature depicted the bank as a ship coming "From the port of Economy" and bound "To the harbor of Independence."[79]

The bank's records, however, suggest that savings accounts were of little use to a laboring population whose wages rarely extended beyond the immediate costs of living. Depositors were primarily artisans, widows, or drawn from the ranks of such new white-collar occupations as clerks and teachers. Of the deposits made in May 1820, only one in five came from a laborer or seamstress. Very few account holders withdrew money in January, February, and March, suggesting that most depositors were not in fact putting away money for the winter. Attesting to the paternalistic uses of the institution, many accounts were opened in the names of minors, elderly parents, or servants whose employers deposited their wages directly into the bank each month. Withdrawals required a written request ten days in advance. For most working people in Baltimore living hand-to-mouth, a bank account was an unaffordable luxury.[80]

Believing that every dollar deposited was a dollar "saved from luxury and dress," the bank's directors echoed a growing consensus among Baltimore elites that poverty owed to bad decision making and to a general lack of economic rationality on the part of working people. Such sentiments could be heard every winter, even as Baltimore's charitable citizens dutifully raised money for the needy. The poor "will not look beyond the day that is passing over them," argued one newspaper correspondent in 1805, who then struck a philosophical note by observing, "it is owing to this circumstance that we have them at all" to perform "the meaner offices of labor." When poor people were not wasting their money on lotteries, critics claimed, their savings instead purchased alcohol. Free wintertime soup, complained one observer, transformed wages into "a surplus capital to be invested in whiskey." Not founded until 1829, the Baltimore Temperance Society was several decades behind city officials and other moral reformers in lamenting the extent of alcohol use in working-class households.[81]

Elite commentators were quick to assert that the poor could and should work harder. Drawing a comparison to the industrious habits of the city's entrepreneurs, writers in the city's newspapers ascribed laziness and lack of foresight to working people. In this discourse, *idleness* was not a condition that befell working people when the port closed but a state of mind that accounted for their poverty. Baltimore's free people of color faced particular attack for lacking "ambition." Their detractors reimagined men like Scipio Freeman or Beverly Dowling—Baltimore slaves who had bought themselves into freedom with an unrivaled industriousness—as lazy and unable to compete in the urban economy.[82]

It was one thing to fault domestic servants, mariners, seamstresses, and mud-machinists, whether black or white, for not performing menial labor with grander ambitions, but quite another to denounce them as lacking industry. The process of finding a job, keeping a job, and transforming wages into subsistence was work in and of itself. Yet, Baltimore's merchants, manufacturers, bankers, lawyers, clergymen, and elected officials proved unduly worried that men and women with no choice but to labor for a living might somehow sustain themselves in idleness. That anxiety would reveal itself in a regime of institutions and penal practices to instill industriousness in those purportedly lacking it and to compel labor from those withholding it.

CHAPTER 7

The Consequence of Failure

As career manual laborers, Dicky and Zachariah Stallings spent their days looking for enough work to meet the cost of living. Dicky had moved to Baltimore around 1800 from Calvert County, the center of Maryland's plantation economy and the place where his son Zachariah had been born only a few years earlier. Growing up in Baltimore, Zachariah and his six brothers depended on their father's earnings and the resourcefulness of their mother, Nelly, to keep the family afloat. By a stroke of good fortune in 1813, Dicky (then in his early forties) found a place on the mudmachine and garnered consistent wages digging muck out of Baltimore's harbor. Twenty-year-old Zachariah assumed his father's spot on the mudmachine in 1815 and began adulthood as a wage laborer. Within five years, Zachariah headed his own household in Fells Point, where he lived with his wife, their two young daughters, and an older man and woman, perhaps his parents. Their neighbors were free African American carters whose families held enough property to pay taxes in the early 1820s. In contrast, the Stallings family never earned a sufficient amount to gain the taxman's attention, and their household teetered close to the edge. The fall came in June 1825, when a venereal disease made it impossible for Zachariah to work. Thirty years old and without other options, Zachariah did what impoverished Baltimore residents had been doing for a half-century when times were desperate: he went to the almshouse.[1]

Located on the outskirts of the city, the almshouse was a public resource for those who could not support themselves through labor. This single institution functioned as a hospital for the sick, an asylum for the mentally ill, a prison for convicted vagrants, a workhouse for the unemployed, and a shelter for the homeless. Although the name "almshouse" connoted the Christian duty of quietly giving charity to the poor, this publicly funded secular institution was embedded in the visible politics of legislative budgets, tax assessments, and patronage appointments. American almshouses emerged alongside other eighteenth-century public wel-

Baltimore almshouse, 1832. In the early 1820s, Baltimore spent $100,000 to build a new almshouse on the outskirts of the city. Calverton had been a Baltimore gentleman's country estate before becoming a destination for the city's poor. Fielding Lucas, Jr., *Picture of Baltimore, Containing a Description of all Objects of Interest in the City . . .* (Baltimore: Fielding Lucas, Jr., 1832). Courtesy American Antiquarian Society.

fare practices such as paying to board the indigent with neighbors or issuing cash pensions to the disabled. The Maryland Assembly had first funded Baltimore's almshouse in 1773 and frequently legislated new policies for the institution's governance. Just a few years before Zachariah Stallings became sick, the legislature authorized construction of a new facility, whose cost would exceed $100,000. Since before the American Revolution, and with greater certainty in the decades that immediately followed, impoverished people like Stallings could count on the government as the provider of last resort.[2]

To access the almshouse, Zachariah Stallings first needed an admission warrant from his "ward manager of the poor," a prominent neighborhood resident appointed to assist the indigent while simultaneously guarding the city budget from imposition. Stallings might have come to the door of John Robb's Bond Street home or sought the prosperous shipbuilder along the waterfront. Either way, Robb found Stallings sufficiently "in distress" to authorize his admission. "I cannot judge of his feelings," lamented Robb, whose expectation of such knowledge reflected the intimate relations of a neighborhood where the wealthy and the poor lived side by side, enmeshed in a web of mutual obligation.[3] However, Stallings's inscrutability allowed him to maneuver past the city's gatekeeper. If reticence had proved fruitless, Stallings had other scripts at his disposal: behaving erratically, acting the supplicant, or simply knocking on Robb's door day after day. A compelling narrative of need—whether crafted by a needy person or imagined by a kindly neighbor—was the ticket to a bed, a new set of underclothes, and three meals a day at the almshouse. As one administrator sarcastically noted, Baltimore's poor may have been too lazy to work but were "not wanting in industry and ingenuity in coming [up with] a 'good story' for the street passenger, the benevolent housekeeper, or the Ward Manager."[4]

Armed with an admission warrant, Stallings could now enter the almshouse. The institution's rural setting was no accident, but a way to insulate the downtrodden from the corrupting influence of the city, and vice versa. Indigent people hobbled along the macadamized road leading toward the almshouse, and entrepreneurial carters sometimes picked them up in hopes of being reimbursed by the city. At the institution's gates, the overseer met new arrivals, supervised their bathing and shaving, replaced their clothing, and recorded their names, ages, occupations, birthplaces, and ailments in an enormous leatherbound volume. While some came to the Almshouse "too low to speak," others—propertyless in most regards—claimed ownership of their own elaborate life stories. But by virtue of holding the pen and paper, the overseer distilled entire lives into only a few words: *labourer, venereal, no religion, tobacco*, in the case of Zachariah Stallings. This data would help the almshouse trustees determine the causes of poverty and develop more aggressive means of curing it, such as solitary confinement for those who refused to work the almshouse farm. Well ahead of their peers in other American cities, Baltimore officials had made it virtually impossible to receive public relief except by performing compulsory labor at the almshouse. By making public assistance a worse choice than toughing it out on one's own, Baltimore anticipated the "less-eligibility" standard of Britain's New Poor Law by a decade.[5]

Yet Stallings had not been deterred, perhaps because it was so easy to skirt the almshouse's labor requirements. The institution charged paupers 30¢ for each day spent in residence, a debt that a sick person could repay through labor after recuperating. But once Stallings had regained his strength, he "eloped," as did nearly a quarter of all those who left the almshouse in 1825, and forced the city to swallow the costs of his upkeep. Despite its goal of becoming self-supporting, the almshouse's rising expenditures levied what its own trustees called a "heavy tax . . . upon the sober and industrious portion of the community for the support of the idle and intemperate." In truth, the poor tax weighed less on the pocketbooks than upon the benevolent spirit of Baltimore's leading citizens, who called for an ever-more rigorous program of institutional discipline. The almshouse's overseer vowed that absconders like Stallings would not gain readmission when they next needed it. But even as public discourse increasingly demonized the poor, Stallings could remain confident in public relief as a right that no administrator could contravene and no politician would challenge. Using the almshouse on his own terms, Stallings made a mockery of the less-eligibility concept.[6]

The experiences of Zachariah Stallings at the Baltimore almshouse support several competing interpretations of the early American public welfare system: that poor relief reflected a civic culture of benevolence, that almshouses disciplined workers in the service of capitalism, or that poor people used the system just as much as it used them.[7] Historians have typically advanced these interpretations as mutually exclusive by pulling one strand or another from the indivisible fabric of a public welfare regime that served, surveilled, *and* suited people like Zachariah Stallings. A richer interpretative model emerges at the intersection of elite benevolence, social discipline, and pauper agency. How else to understand Stallings's next brush with the social welfare system, as the weather turned frigid in January 1826?

Only six months after eloping from the almshouse, Stallings sought readmission with another warrant from the manager of the poor in Fells Point, John Robb. But waiting at the almshouse door was overseer John Morton, determined to turn him away. In the ensuing confrontation, Stallings asserted that the overseer could not legally exclude anyone in dire circumstances. In a brilliant appeal to Morton's presumed investment in the early republic's culture of sensibility, Stallings posed a question straight from *Charlotte Temple*: would Morton be the man who turned the poor Zachariah out to perish in the street? It did not work. Morton shrugged. But when word of this exchange reached the more susceptible Robb, he resigned his office in protest. Morton was unapologetic as he recalled his reply to Stallings's question: "I might have replied in the affirmative to the hypothetical query," especially if it had been posed by a "sturdy vagrant, or one labouring under no disability but what a few hours of abstinence from liquor would remove."[8] The standoff pitted Stallings (an impoverished laborer intent on using the public allowances made for his support) against Morton (an administrator engaged in the project of disciplining those who refused to earn their living by the sweat of their brows) against Robb (a wealthy neighbor concerned that no resident of Baltimore should freeze to death on a cold night).

This showdown revealed the multiple instrumentalities of public poor relief in the early republic, while exposing the inadequacy of the almshouse as a mechanism of capitalist discipline, an expression of philanthropy, and a resource for the poor.[9] Zachariah Stallings ultimately succeeded by going above Morton and Robb to solicit an admission order from the almshouse's trustees, the seven appointed governors of the institution. Among the most prominent men in Baltimore, the trustees firmly held that a community's most prosperous residents were obliged to protect its most vulnerable ones. In an exchange that benefited the privileged and the poor alike, the performance of Christian duty, civic benevolence, and noblesse oblige propelled Stallings through the almshouse gates.[10] Once inside, Stallings encountered the state's disciplinary apparatus for isolating, punishing, and rehabilitating workers who could not—or would not—sell their labor for wages.[11] But the regime of institutional control neither fazed nor reformed Stallings, who had compelled the city to spend more money to provide more aid to more people than the municipal budget allowed or elected officials desired.[12] The open arms that welcomed Zachariah Stallings back to the almshouse did not belong to Baltimore's civic leaders, benevolent residents, and employers; nor did they belong to the institution's overseer and trustees. They belonged to Zachariah's parents, Dicky and Nelly, and his nine-year-old daughter, Elizabeth, all of whom were already in the almshouse. No one could claim this as a victory.

The Uses of the Almshouse

From the time of its founding in 1773, the almshouse belonged not to the city's elites, but to Baltimore's poor, who incorporated it into their strategies of subsistence and familial integrity. The ranks of the institutionalized poor included orphans at the start of life, elderly men and women nearing the end, the mentally and physically disabled, new mothers, and people of all ages recuperating from diseases and injuries. When the almshouse trustees visited the institution in 1784, they discovered "the insane, the ulcerous, the weak & sick, the Labourers, males and females all together." Although the trustees were appalled to find the inmates "promiscuously huddled into two rooms," they touted the usefulness of this single institution to a diverse clientele. Not all needy Baltimore residents used the almshouse in the same way—white parents were more willing than black parents to institutionalize their own children, for example—but almost all used the almshouse in one way or another. Visitors to the institution in 1804 might meet centenarian Negro Joseph, who had frostbitten feet; John Doyle, who was recovering from a gunshot wound; and Mary Foley, whose ulcerated hands made it impossible to support herself by sewing. James Campble, Daniel Murphy, and Mary Blake were there on account of a generic "sore leg," a nebulous affliction that some relief administrators came to see as a ploy to gain access to public support. Two decades later, even as the almshouse had become a larger and more regimented operation, its clientele remained unchanged. When Zachariah Stallings entered the institution during the first week of January 1826, so too did twelve-year-old Mary Cain, who had been orphaned; Sarah Sharp, a young African American Catholic woman with a sore hand; and James Trefant, a fifty-seven-year-old intemperate Massachusetts cobbler who had been in Baltimore for less than a week. Zachariah's admission marked not the dissolution, but rather the reconstitution of his own family under the institution's roof.[13]

When work disappeared or some other circumstance made it impossible to stay afloat, impoverished people exercised their claim to public relief by entering the almshouse. Fluctuations in annual admissions attested to both the irregularity of the urban economy and the agile usage of the institution by Baltimore's working poor. At the start of 1800, forty-four men, fifty-two women, and seventeen children resided in the institution. While many departed as soon as the weather warmed in March, others arrived in the summer months to take their places. Over the space of the year, nearly three hundred men, women, and children sought admission. Through the 1800s and 1810s, the number of Baltimore residents seeking admission to the almshouse stayed relatively flat, especially in light of the city's rapid population growth. However, the Panic of 1819, an economic collapse that lasted well into the 1820s, tripled the demand for refuge at the almshouse, even as it sent the city's overall population into decline. "The growth of pauperism amongst us, has been so rapid within the last two years, as to transcend all our calculations," reported the almshouse trustees, besieged by more than 1,000 admissions in 1823. "There is more misery and suffering, and a greater amount of privation in Baltimore in one month now, than there used to be in a whole year," lamented editor Hezekiah Niles.[14] The decline in admissions by 1824 owed less to the return of economic prosperity than to the enforcement of a compulsory labor policy at a new almshouse facility. Even as the new institution encouraged those teetering on the edge of failure to consider other options, over 770 people entered the almshouse with Zachariah, Dicky, Nelly, and Elizabeth Stallings in 1826. Annual admissions topped 1,100 in 1829, a spike attributable to the needs of impoverished European immigrants and laborers constructing railroads and canals in the vicinity. Admissions again jumped in 1834, the year of a local banking collapse, and in 1839, when the panic that began two years earlier reverberated locally. Regardless of fluctuating applications for admissions, the almshouse had between 400 and 600 residents at any given moment in the 1820s and 1830s.[15]

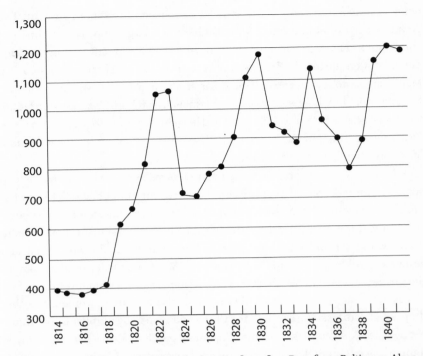

Annual admissions to the Baltimore almshouse, 1814–1841. Data from Baltimore Alms-house Admissions Book and almshouse trustees' annual reports; see chap. 7, note 15.

Because entering the almshouse entailed a forfeiture of numerous personal freedoms, going there was never a decision made lightly. What the trustees had called a "dreary abode" in 1784 remained an unwelcoming destination. By the 1810s, the facility had become overcrowded, with the disabled, elderly, and sick mingling with petty criminals and the insane inside its walls. A visitor in 1811 was repulsed to find the "victim of misfortune and disease stretched out on a dirty sack half-filled with oak leaves, with no other covering than a filthy rug." Inmates— a telling early republic term equating those who resided in the almshouse with prisoners—endured numerous indignities, like sometimes being forced to wear large crimson patches with the initials "B.P." (for Baltimore Poorhouse) on their clothing. The published regulations of the almshouse spelled out a long list of forbidden activities: lying, cursing, swearing, lewd talk, acting obscenely, gambling, reading immoral books, playing unlawful games, drinking, smoking in bed, and making fun of administrators and maniacs. Plus, it was lights out at 9:00 every night. Violators could be removed to solitary confinement or be placed on a diet of bread and water. The work requirement—predicated on the notion that poor people needed to be taught to appreciate the value of work—forced inmates to perform field labor or such other tasks as building coffins (much in demand) and untangling strands of old rope.[16]

But no matter how hard public officials tried to make the almshouse unappealing, desperate people still saw the institution as a better alternative than extreme privation in a Fells Point alley. Committed to hygiene, order, and efficiency, administrators created an institution where the material conditions were oftentimes an improvement for the truly indigent, where meals were warm and regular, and where state-of-the-art (put less generously, experimental) medical care came at the hands of doctors and students from the University of Maryland School of Medicine. The new facility that opened in 1823 was especially prized for its rigorous systematization of relief. As mayor John Montgomery observed, "the establishment is extensive and splendid, and the comfort of the paupers and cleanliness appear to be particularly regarded and attended to, and excellent discipline to pervade every department of the Institution." From the perspective of public officials, institutional regimentation promoted health, instilled traits of responsibility, and achieved a kind of Enlightenment beauty through the regularity of its operation. From the perspective of needy people, however, the same institutional regimentation held a different attractiveness, one based on the certainty of relief from hunger, care for an injury, and shelter from the cold.[17]

The guarantee of a warm meal and a warm bed compared favorably with the perilous experience of living hand-to-mouth while the harbor remained frozen and the price of firewood skyrocketed. Built to hold between 800 and 900 residents, the new almshouse alleviated overcrowding and made it possible for every adult to have his or her own wooden bedstead—a noteworthy amenity at a time when many men and women were used to sharing beds with fellow lodgers in boardinghouses or with kin in their own homes. Regulations called for every inmate to receive a plate, knife, fork, mug, clean clothing, a comb, a pillow, sheets, and three blankets during winter. The menu guaranteed meat six nights each week.[18]

Although it was intended to serve the permanently incapacitated and dependent, the almshouse played as great a role in the experiences of the broader working-class population whose need for relief was seasonal or temporary. Indeed, the almshouse trustees were surprised that so many functional adults were "choosing" to institutionalize themselves or family members for short stints to recover from an injury or a drunken spree. Forgetting that destitution was the presumptive condition of an almshouse resident, some inmates willingly paid the 30¢ daily fee for room and board, or thought themselves as getting the better deal in exchanging their daily labor for institutional lodging. Relative to the physical and psychological expense of scrounging for rent, food, and fuel on the outside, life on the inside delivered "greater cheapness, even when [residents were] compelled to make the legal compensation in money or labor." The trustees were well aware that the almshouse offered "comforts and indulgencies, which the honest, sober labouring man, with the most unremitting application and frugal management, can seldom provide for his family."[19]

In the most urgent cases, the almshouse provided temporary shelter to those otherwise homeless. Escaping from the cold was one of the reasons that Zachariah Stallings had sought to return there in January 1826. The night before his rebuff from overseer Morton, Stallings had kept from freezing by lodging in the Fells Point watch house, the equivalent of a holding pen at a police precinct. But once Stallings gained his admission to the almshouse in January, he did not just stay for a few nights, but made the decision to spend the winter, leaving only once the weather warmed in March. Stallings was not alone in using the almshouse to compensate for the wintertime failures of Baltimore's wage-labor economy. December typically saw the highest number of admissions of any month of the year, and the almshouse usually reached its greatest occupancy during January. Very few departed in the midst of winter, but once March came, upwards of one-fifth of the residents walked through the gates and back toward the city. Dicky, Zachariah, and Elizabeth Stallings exited the almshouse one after the other in March 1826.

The snowbirds who wintered in the almshouse were primarily men like Stallings, whose need for relief was a function of the seasonal disappearance of wage labor. In contrast, women's use of the almshouse did not vary with the seasons, because low wages made dependence chronic. Consider the fluctuation of the almshouse population over the course of a year. As 1830 started, for example, the institution housed 255 adult men and 252 adult women. In April, when maritime and construction jobs were most available, the number of men in the almshouse fell to 178, while the number of women remained almost unchanged at 241. But as the wage-earning season ended, men flooded back into the almshouse, bringing December's population to 309 men and 255 women. And by the following April, the number of men had once again fallen to 170 while the number of women remained virtually the same. Outside of a few exceptional years, this pattern of seasonal usage was typical.[20]

Men's wintertime use of the almshouse brought rebuke from moral reformers, who retold Aesop's fable of the diligent ant and the improvident grasshopper in hopes of inspiring Baltimore's workers to save their summer wages for win-

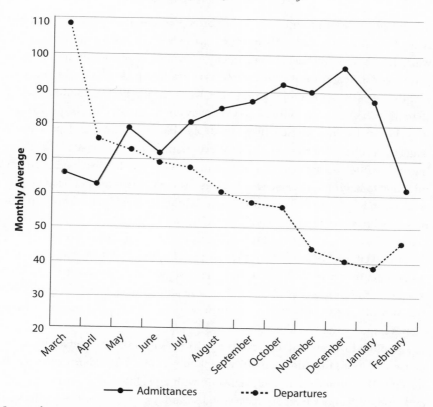

Seasonal usage patterns at the Baltimore almshouse, 1824–1841. Based on 17,083 admission records and 13,082 departure records. Departures include inmates who received an official discharge or who eloped, but not those who died in the almshouse (3,990) or were bound out as apprentices (477) over the eighteen-year period. Data from Baltimore Almshouse Admissions Book and almshouse trustees' annual reports; see chap. 7, note 15.

tertime necessities. With a modest proposal in 1828, a local satirist made light of so many Baltimore workers going into storage for the winter: "*Be it enacted*, that on the twenty-fifth day of December in the year above named, and ever after that, on the day of the month aforesaid, that all poor people be carried out of the city; then and there to be frozen as stiff as possible, there to be piled up as lumber till the summer season; and moreover that the state provide public refrigerators for the benefit of all such as are not easily congealed." The fake legislation made it the responsibility of public officials to oversee the defrosting of laborers once the weather warmed.[21]

Although this Swiftian proposal was disturbingly close to reality, the almshouse had a year-round utility to Baltimore's poor. Monthly admissions began rising from June onwards, with the difference between average summertime and wintertime admissions usually being only ten or fifteen people per month. Dangerous construction labor sent injured workers to the almshouse in summer months, especially men toiling on public works in the nearby countryside. In 1829, the Chesapeake & Ohio Canal Company employed upwards of 3,000 men in arduous digging, housed them in deplorable conditions, and paid them largely in alcohol. Broken men trickled into the almshouse at a constant clip. Summer also witnessed the arrival of impoverished German, English, and Irish immigrants to Baltimore, people who became "a charge upon the public almost as soon as landing." The end of summer typically brought epidemic disease to Baltimore, with yellow fever and cholera sending not only sickly people to the almshouse, but also those whose livelihoods were interrupted when their employers fled the humid city. A fire at a factory, the collapse of a bank, and a host of other particular circumstances could send admissions skyrocketing. Some of the busiest months at the almshouse were July 1823 (102 admissions), October 1829 (140), and May 1834 (105), illustrating the institution's year-round importance to Baltimore's impoverished residents.[22]

Although institutional food rarely merits rave reviews, the diet at the almshouse was more nutritious and diverse than was usual for laboring people in the city. The dinner menu included soup with an eight-ounce portion of beef on Mondays, Wednesdays, Thursdays, and Saturdays; salt pork and vegetables on Sundays; mush and molasses on Tuesdays; and herring with hominy or rice on Fridays, in deference to Catholic residents. Inmates received at least one pound of bread each day and drank a molasses-sweetened beverage of coffee and rye for breakfast. In 1814, the trustees called on the overseer "to be more circumspect in his purchase of provision for the poor taking care not to have so large a proportion of bone in their meat, to have their bread attended to and well baked (particularly the indian) and to have vegetables mixed with their soup." A group of visitors from Philadelphia were surprised to find that the almshouse did not serve its inmates "shins, necks, heads, or other rough meats." The almshouse farm yielded an abundance of produce to further supplement the inmates' diet. The 1825 harvest included 16,000 heads of cabbage, 2,400 tomatoes, 1,245 bushels of turnips, ample carrots, string beans, and onions, as well as 4,000 gallons of milk from the almshouse cows and enough cream to make 1,735 pounds of butter.[23]

Equally impressive was the amount of free clothing distributed at the almshouse. Like the food, institutional garb was far less objectionable than might have been expected. Whereas most penal institutions outfitted inmates in recognizable stripes, the almshouse provided apparel that was virtually indistinguishable from the attire of impoverished people at large—except newer. Public officials suspected that needy people entered the almshouse for the explicit purpose of being outfitted, or worse, of obtaining clothing that could be sold for alcohol. The fungible nature of clothing irked almshouse overseer John Morton, who reported, "it had been a practice with many of the Paupers to runaway from the House, and sell the cloathing which they had obtained there at the first tippling shop." Even the administrators of Baltimore's jail believed that institutional clothing could "afford an additional inducement to the commission of breaches of the peace and other offenses." New inmates at the almshouse received a set of body linen (underclothing) and a range of wearing apparel. January 1834, for example, saw the distribution of 58 pairs of shoes, 123 shirts, 42 shifts, 38 frocks, 12 petticoats, 44 pairs of pants, 34 roundabouts (short coats), 18 vests, 34 handkerchiefs, 38 pairs of socks, and 16 caps. New clothing came in handy for someone like Zachariah Stallings, who arrived at the almshouse in garments that the overseer described emphatically as "All Old."[24]

The almshouse also functioned as an early republic emergency room, and its hospital proved especially important to residents of Fells Point and Old Town, two working-class neighborhoods underserved by doctors. Hernias, sprains, and fractures brought dockworkers and brickmakers to the almshouse, as did the fevers that canal and railroad workers contracted in the swampy Maryland countryside. Respiratory diseases like pneumonia and consumption, as well as intestinal ailments like dysentery and diarrhea, were common among those seeking treatment. Some of Baltimore's finest doctors practiced at the almshouse, and students from Baltimore's two medical colleges were eager for residencies where they would see a wide range of cases and have frequent opportunities to perform autopsies. Dr. James Smith, a tireless public health crusader, initiated Baltimore's first smallpox vaccinations at the almshouse in 1801. Smith's successors continued to pursue innovative treatments and boasted of patients' high rate of recovery—a feat considering the desperate circumstances of so many of the patients they treated. More advanced medical care was, of course, a mixed blessing for inmates, and the number of sore leg complaints declined once doctors grew more interested in practicing surgery. It was too late for Samuel Every, a twenty-one-year-old African American hostler, who fled the almshouse after his sore leg was amputated in 1825.[25]

Pregnant women—especially those who needed to publicize the fathers of their newborns in order to gain child support—sought out the almshouse's lying-in hospital. Most years saw fewer than two dozen infants delivered at the almshouse, but doctors were careful to record their paternity. A woman's testimony given at delivery was understood to be unimpeachable, and a new mother could later use almshouse records in paternity claims. When twenty-one-year-old Mary Ann Reland gave birth to daughter Elizabeth in June 1825, she told doctors that the father was Frederick Hess, a Federal Hill butcher. Reland had arrived at the almshouse in her seventh month of pregnancy, brought the child to term in the institution, received medical services at the public expense, had Hess's paternity entered into the public record, and was given permission to leave the almshouse two weeks later with her daughter. Susan Jonqua, a thirty-three-year-old widow whose parents had brought her to Baltimore as a young girl when they fled Saint Domingue, delivered baby Priscilla at the almshouse in 1823. Jonqua named tailor John Bayou as the father, recuperated, and left with her child a few weeks later. Other women used the almshouse to deliver babies who might prove disruptive to their households or communities. In 1825, nineteen-year-old Hester Ann Myers came to deliver a baby conceived with William Sergant, who was likely an employee in her father's brass foundry. Several Euro-American women who had become pregnant with African American partners delivered in the almshouse, a choice made visible in the way that officials affixed labels like "coloured," "black," or "Negro" to babies born to nominally "white" women.[26]

For parents who could not or did not want to keep their children, the almshouse became a repository for abandoned infants and toddlers. Three-year-old George Carson spent a week in the almshouse in 1826 because "the man with whom the mother cohabits compelled her, as she says, to bring the child here." When four-year-old Julia Tight arrived in the almshouse, the overseer recorded that the girl's disappeared mother, Lucy, was "said to be a Drunken Worthless person." Yet women like Lucy who left children on the doorstep of a neighbor or in a public setting could count on the almshouse to provide care, as it did for Mary Monday (so named for the day of the week she was found in the cart of a bacon merchant), Alexander Hogg (left outside the French Street home of sign painter John Gardner), and Mary Jane Fields (discovered by a shoemaker in an abandoned house on Whetstone Point). Public officials regretted that the almshouse might abet the practice, seeing "little difference between voluntary abandonment of an infant by the mother and direct infanticide." Expressed in the least charitable terms, the trustees suspected that "if women of loose character and habits are permitted to leave the fruits of their illicit intercourse at the Alms House, to suit their own concealment, it is much to be feared that profligacy will increase." Fells Point brothel keeper Ann Wilson gave officials no satisfaction when she brought six-month-old Ann Choherty to the almshouse in April 1826 and claimed "to know nothing of the parents." Despite a policy that accepted children into the almshouse only with a parent, abandoned boys and girls continued to enter the institution, even as its gallingly high rate of infant mortality supported the trustees' stark comparison to infanticide.[27]

Parents of older children also relied on the almshouse to care for children they could not support. In early 1819, for example, Nancy Hignan began looking to place her son, an eight-year-old boy described as "quite lame," into the almshouse. After seeking assistance from the manager of the poor in her neighborhood, Hignan eventually secured a letter to almshouse trustee Robert Walsh. The letter explained that because Hignan was "obliged to hire out in order to procure herself her own living, she can by no way provide for her poor child." If Nancy Hignan sought long-term care for a disabled child, other parents used the almshouse as a temporary shelter and intended to reclaim their children in the near future. The parents of Benjamin, Martha, Mary Ann, and Ann Rebecca Collins—ranging in age from three to eight years old—sent their four children to the almshouse in January 1825 and retrieved the younger two siblings in August. In the intervening time, the older two siblings were bound out as apprentices, a known risk (or benefit) of using the almshouse for childcare. Eleanor Haskins, who had moved to Baltimore from Massachusetts a decade earlier, brought her two children to the almshouse in September 1825 while she recuperated from a venereal infection. When she departed after the winter had passed, her children, John and Mary Elizabeth, stayed behind for three more years.[28]

For the able-bodied children of poor families, the almshouse was a potential passport to a new household. Maryland law permitted the almshouse trustees to enter the children of indigent parents into agreements of indenture, regardless of the parents' wishes. The institution bound out nearly one hundred children between 1806 and 1818, and then accelerated placements in the 1820s, even as apprentice labor was on the decline in Baltimore's economy. Almost fifty children were bound out in 1825 alone. "Their connexion with their worthless relatives is thus generally broken off," the trustees explained, "and bound out at an early age to good places, they learn better habits and may become useful members of society." Children such as twelve-year-old Margaret Tagert were not orphans in the sense of having two deceased parents, but were legal orphans defined by the indigence of their parents. Born in Ireland, Tagert had lived in Baltimore since she was seven. When she arrived at the almshouse in late 1825, the overseer recorded that Tagert "has a father and mother in Town whose character is very bad." An ideal candidate for an apprenticeship, Tagert was bound out within a month.[29]

Zachariah Stallings surely anticipated his daughter Elizabeth's fate when he eloped from the almshouse and left her behind. For young Elizabeth Stallings, however, being bound out in March 1826 might raise her fortunes, even if she were apprenticed only to learn housework at the residence of an urban merchant or a Baltimore County farmer. "To be found in sufficient meat drink washing lodging and apparel and at the expiration of her time to have customary freedom dues," read a typical almshouse indenture that stipulated far more material comfort than Elizabeth would have known in the Stallings household. Indentures prescribed a rudimentary training in reading, writing, and arithmetic to the rule of three, which was presumably more education than Elizabeth would have received in her family. To be sure, almshouse apprentices were typically placed in low-end industries such as shoemaking, ropemaking, and snuff manufacturing, where the trajectory from apprentice to master was unlikely. Many indenture agreements simply put boys to work in farming and girls in housework and "plain sewing," suggesting that such apprenticeships provided basic household labor rather than an induction to the "art and mystery" of a craft. A number of Pennsylvania farmers took apprentices from the Baltimore almshouse, as did urban employers like Dr. Joseph Brevitt, who would famously suggest giving pigs to the poor in 1819. Tobacconist Balthusard Nicholas indentured three boys in little more than a year to work in cigar making. The Spanish-born tobacconist Marcelino Gonet took four boys in 1812 and 1813 for his snuff manufactory. Perhaps Gonet became too familiar with what the almshouse had to offer; having gone bankrupt when he expanded his business into wine importation and now sixty-six years old, Gonet became a resident in 1824.[30]

With notable resourcefulness, Baltimore residents intent on entering the almshouse found a way to do so. Public officials had attempted to erect a solid line of defense by forcing needy people to obtain an admission warrant from a ward manager of the poor. "The discretion of intelligent men is the best known protection against abuses of charity," proclaimed Thomas W. Griffith, one of the almshouse trustees and a firm believer in expertise. While the amateurs who administered private charity "were liable to be imposed upon by pretend paupers," public officials could presumably discern the deserving from the undeserving. Every case was different, explained Griffith, and the lack of a fixed eligibility standard was useful because "any certain condition or contingency, which should be universally known, to secure a public maintenance would infallibly encourage idleness and extravagance in the poor." But contrary to Griffith's hopes, Baltimore's poor turned the lack of explicit standards to their own advantage.[31]

Each ward manager had his own threshold of need, and some were known to be more softhearted than others. The trustees complained in 1829 of the "too great ease" by which able-bodied adults were getting into the almshouse, but they tried not "to cast any imputations upon the conduct of the gentlemen, who, with the most benevolent intentions perform the duties of ward managers." Nonetheless, it was clear that the ward managers were "liable to imposition." That was what alms-house overseer John Morton had said about John Robb, the ward manager who had assisted Zachariah Stallings. Morton found Robb to be utterly indiscriminate and had previously sent a letter instructing him to reject those who had eloped from the institution. Yet Robb continued to issue the warrants. One can hear Morton's exasperation when another Fells Point lollygagger—Zachariah's father, Dicky—appeared at the almshouse in January 1826. While the records of most other inmates contained descriptions of specific maladies like rheumatism or frost-bite, the entry for Dicky Stallings read, "Nothing the Matter."[32]

But even when ward managers held the line, needy people knew how to work the system. Turned away in 1831 by the ward manager in her neighborhood, an elderly Baltimore woman went immediately to find the ward manager in the ad-jacent district. When he explained that the case was outside his jurisdiction, the woman proceeded to Lambert Thomas, a prominent cabinetmaker and former city councilman, whom she convinced to pen a letter on her behalf. "My opinion is from the statement of the old woman & daughter that she should be permit-ted to go to the almshouse," wrote Thomas to the mayor. Knowledgeable in the overlapping authority of ward managers, trustees, the almshouse overseer, and elected officials, impoverished Baltimore residents were not easily deterred. In-deed, Zachariah Stallings's return to the almshouse owed specifically to his suc-cess in pitting a trustee and a ward manager against the overseer.[33]

Public officials greatly feared imposters and convinced themselves that the in-stitution was rapidly becoming a destination for "strangers who come to our city, often from a great distance for the express purpose of entering our Alms House." An 1829 report claimed that some Pennsylvania laborers had walked "upwards of One Hundred Miles" in order to enjoy the superior comforts of Baltimore's almshouse. The trustees may have misinterpreted seasonal patterns of mid-Atlantic labor migration, but they credited the region's poor with tremendous in-genuity in "throwing themselves into Baltimore just as the winter sets in, exhibiting all the appearances of poverty and disease, with the obvious intention of getting themselves provided with comfortable quarters during the inclemency of the sea-son in our Poor House." In law, admission was contingent on having lived in Bal-timore for twelve months, and as late as 1826, the city paid to send a handful of nonresidents back to their original communities. However, residency requirements were seldom enforced, and the almshouse's practice was to turn almost no one away. An official tally showed that one-fifth of those admitted to the almshouse in 1833 had been in Baltimore for less than a year, but that figure did not account for the "great efforts" that the needy "made to deceive the Managers of the Poor, and the Overseer, on this point." The trustees assumed the number of "strangers" was much higher and lamented having to admit upwards of one hundred people annually who had been in Baltimore for less than a week. Some were European immigrants who arrived on American shores penniless, but others were allegedly career vagrants who traveled from institution to institution in search of the best food or most comfortable beds. It surely brought the almshouse trustees little consolation to learn that their institution stacked up nicely against those in neighboring cities. "I must say for Baltimore that its poor-house accommodations are not to be sneered at," reported a pauper who had spent time in almshouses in Boston, New York, Richmond, and Norfolk. "I should have made out right well there, hadn't it been that the company was entirely too promiscuous for a New York anti-nigger man."[34]

The presence of African Americans in Baltimore's almshouse was noteworthy. African Americans appeared in the almshouse at the same rate as they resided in the city itself, comprising 20 to 25 percent of both populations. In light of the obstacles placed in the way of their economic advancement, African Americans should have been overrepresented in their need for public relief. Legally, free people of color had the same rights to use the almshouse as any other Baltimore residents, a surprising situation considering that the city's black population was denied access to such other institutions of civil society as public schools, the jury room, and the ballot box. Unsurprisingly, however, discriminatory practices resulted in the underrepresentation of free people of color in the almshouse relative to their actual need. None of the ward managers of the poor were African American, which added a complicating racial dynamic to the already tricky process of negotiating for an admission warrant. Once in the almshouse, black inmates were segregated to the least desirable sections of the building, often forced to share the dank basement with lunatics and incorrigibles. Leery of kidnapping and reenslavement, African American parents feared the involuntary indenturing of their children to white employers. Almshouse officials took the threat seriously enough to require a $500 bond from anyone receiving a black apprentice from the institution, but the number of African American children in the institution remained disproportionately low; white children outnumbered black ones at a rate of seven to one in the mid-1820s. While the almshouse was a resource for all of Baltimore's poor, it was clear that not all poor people could use public relief to the same advantage.[35]

Those African Americans who came to the almshouse were among the most desperate, often arriving with conditions that made it unlikely they would eventually return to the city. Some were castoff slaves, such as seventy-year-old Joseph Bristo, whose owner, Mrs. Muccubbin, had abandoned him. A "deranged" woman named Lucy came to the almshouse in 1816 when owner John S. Horn refused to support her any longer. Others were nonagenarians and centenarians like Monday Lane, who had been born a slave in Virginia in the 1730s, came to Baltimore in the 1780s, did not get his freedom until 1804, and died in the almshouse in 1825. Effa Hutchins had been born in Africa in the 1730s, arrived in Baltimore in 1805, and died in the almshouse in 1826. Cases of blindness, insanity, missing limbs, consumption, and old age were frequent, and during the mid-1820s African Americans left the almshouse in coffins nearly as often as on foot. The mortality rate for institutionalized African Americans was twice that of white inmates. Yet those who survived sought to make the institution serve their interests, whether by staying just long enough to deliver a baby or to survive a cold winter. A Maryland-born Methodist, Hariet Sacks spent the winter of 1825 in the almshouse, although (according to the overseer) "nothing ails her." Eighteen-year-old Jacob Webster got frostbite while piloting a boat on the Chesapeake and chose to spend the rest of the winter in the almshouse. Rhode Island sailor Adam Hazard disembarked in Baltimore in September 1825, proceeded directly to the almshouse to recover from a venereal condition, and eloped when he had recovered a month later. Harriet Johnson, a twenty-three-year-old woman born in Baltimore County, came to the almshouse in early 1825 to deliver a baby, and then left with her infant daughter, Sarah, the following fall.[36]

Although the almshouse population might be distinguished by its "promiscuous" assortment of abandoned children, elderly ex-slaves, and the mentally and physically disabled, the institution's largest cohort comprised white men and women of working age. By the mid-1820s, white men and women in their twenties, thirties, and forties were two-fifths of those seeking admission. By 1830, that figure had reached three-fifths. The trustees were especially perplexed because such people "should be in the vigor of life." Unlike children (who were frequently bound out into more prosperous households) or the elderly (who often died in the institution), working-age men and women were particularly agile in coming and going as it suited their convenience. Zachariah Stallings's mother, Nelly, for example, left the almshouse in April 1823, returned in July for a nine-month stay until April 1824, left for six months, returned in October for the upcoming winter, left again in June 1825, but came right back in August for a ten-month stay that overlapped with the stays of her husband, son, and granddaughter. Jane Evans

may have set the record with fifteen entries in a six-year period. She "can do nothing as she says," wrote the incensed overseer in the admissions book. "Many are
admitted several times in the same year," explained the trustees, "taking their discharge as soon as they are cured, and returning to the same excesses and vices,
which first reduced them to the necessity of seeking public charity."[37]

Most notorious were people like Zachariah Stallings, those who had every advantage and whose poverty could easily be ascribed to personal failings. These
were white men who had been born in the United States or who had immigrated
in childhood, who had resided in Baltimore for at least five years, who had been
in the almshouse multiple times, and who typically left the institution by eloping.
Adult white men appeared in the almshouse at a greater rate than they did in the
city itself, and outnumbered adult white women and all people of color in the institution. Admissions records provide detailed data on over five hundred men like
Zachariah Stallings, who entered the almshouse in the mid-1820s. The men were
almost evenly divided between native born (primarily in Maryland, but with some
hailing from as far north as Maine and as far south as Georgia) and European
immigrants (primarily Irish, English, and German, but with an occasional Italian,
Swede, or Pole). Among native-born and immigrant men alike, half had lived
in Baltimore since before 1819, and even a quarter of the immigrants had been in
the city for longer than a decade. With "labourer" listed as their typical occupation, such men did dangerous work that made them prone to injuries and illnesses.
They eloped from the almshouse three times as frequently as did women inmates,
and a quarter of them would return to the almshouse again in the next two or
three years.[38]

On occasion, the overseer acknowledged that the irregularities of the urban
economy—rather than irregularities in living—made failure common among
adult white men: "Elpeled Loring, 54, born in Massachusetts, sailor, Methodist,
resided in Baltimore 16 years, poverty" or "Jonathan McIntire, 56, born in Ireland,
distiller, Presbyterian, no tobacco, resided in Baltimore 23 years, want of employment." Charles Volk had come to Baltimore from Germany as a teenager in the
1790s. Over the next two decades, he obtained a tavern license, purchased property, testified in several criminal court cases, and became an innkeeper. Yet between 1824 and 1827, Volk—now listed as a "tavern keeper and sausage maker"—
spent three stints in the almshouse, including a five-month stretch attributable
to "want of employment."[39]

More frequently, the overseer blamed the poverty of working-age men on alcohol. John Drummond was "dead drunk when admitted" on Christmas Eve 1825,
and Baltimore-born shoemaker William Kinman arrived "very drunk" to the

almshouse the following year. "Intemperance" appeared in the admissions book as the primary reason that men like Zachariah Stallings entered the almshouse in the mid-1820s. When the trustees compiled their annual report in 1826, they determined that almost all maladies that brought people to the almshouse—venereal diseases, ulcers, insanity, wounds, and fractures—were ultimately "traced to drunkenness." The following year, the trustees declared, "that but for this fruitful source of human misery, an Alms House would scarcely be needed in our community." That was the position of overseer John Morton, who repudiated Zachariah Stallings as representative of an entire class of drunken opportunists. The almshouse's willingness to allow people like Stallings to cycle in and out, contended Morton, "looked so much like furnishing these persons with the means of gratifying their vicious propensities, at the expense of the fund, which had been destined, by the sober and industrious part of the community, for the relief of the sick, the infirm, and the aged."[40] Of course, one man's imposition was another man's ingenuity. Knowing that they would be relieved before they would be left to perish, Stallings and other impoverished Baltimore residents were neither too drunk nor too debauched to claim public relief on their own terms.

The Uses of Benevolence

The ability of the poor to claim the almshouse as a resource owed to the anxieties and ambitions of Baltimore's prosperous citizens. After all, Zachariah Stallings could use the almshouse as he desired only because John Robb, the manager of the poor in Fells Point, could not fathom a needy person dying in the streets. Baltimore's leading citizens, through their relationships with needy neighbors, articulated personal aspirations for salvation and standing, as well as their civic aspirations for Baltimore's national preeminence. If public relief assisted not just the deserving, but also an occasional shirker, this was the price of sustaining what mayor Edward Johnson called "that benevolence for which our city has hitherto been distinguished." The benevolent ideal served Baltimore's elected officials, civic leaders, and wealthy citizens, just as it served the city's poor with emergency wintertime relief, pension payments, and institutionalized shelter. Newspaper editors boasted of the "well-known liberality of the good people of the city," who cared for the poor as a sincere expression of Christian duty and as a social performance that broadcast what was inside a man's heart to his neighbors, co-religionists, and business associates. Such behavior was perhaps as much self-interested as selfless but nonetheless explained why three generations of Stallingses had a safety net.[41]

Public poor relief stood on shaky intellectual ground in the first decades of the nineteenth century, as educated Americans encountered the European political economists who implicated public poor relief in the expansion of human misery. Scholars like Thomas Malthus, Count Rumford, Jeremy Bentham, Thomas Chalmers, and Patrick Colquhoun contended that public welfare rendered laboring people unfit to succeed in a competitive market society. Puzzled by the inexplicable growth of poverty in a nation liberated from the artificial inequalities of Europe, American civic leaders in the 1810s and 1820s formed voluntary associations to study the social costs of public relief. Most notably, the Pennsylvania Society for the Encouragement of Public Economy and New York's Society for the Prevention of Pauperism posited indiscriminate charity as a leading cause of urban poverty. "The poor begin to consider it as a right," explained Boston mayor Josiah Quincy in 1821. "Next, they calculate upon it as an income," which struck Quincy and others as an unjust transfer of wealth from hard-working taxpayers to degenerate idlers. "The stimulus to industry and economy is annihilated, or weakened," Quincy continued. Worst of all, "the just pride of independence so honorable to man, in every condition, is thus corrupted by the certainty of public provision."[42]

Hostility to public relief had been gaining momentum in Baltimore since the 1790s, usually prompted by the annual solicitation of "emergency" donations to see the poor through wintertime. Citizens had raised £300 in 1792 to provide firewood to the needy, but when none of the recipients volunteered to cut timber and "thereby earn a Part of the Help afforded them," one angry observer proposed to cut off this "useless Part" of the community. Wintertime fundraising could generate civic pride and even a reelection issue for mayor Thorowgood Smith, who asked voters in 1808 to "Recollect his conduct during the hard winter three years since." Increasingly, however, the predictable appeals for donations every January and February irritated voters, as well as the man who defeated Smith for mayor that year, Edward Johnson. "In severe weather, it is easy to excite the sympathetic feelings of the benevolent Citizens of Baltimore and raise by way of contributions such sums of money as the necessities of the moment call for," explained Johnson, but this method was "partial, oppressive, and inadequate to the extent of our wishes." Johnson attacked poverty by arresting vagrants and closing tippling shops, but come 1817, his successor in office, George Stiles, could still complain that "The Public are every winter much harrassed with the wants of the Indigent." While grudgingly chairing the distribution of food, clothing, and fuel that February, Stiles heaped contempt on those requiring assistance: "there can be no doubt, but in nine cases out of ten they are the consequence of improper conduct on the part of the sufferers themselves." Not long after, as the

Panic of 1819 reverberated in Baltimore, a local branch of the Society for the Prevention of Pauperism carried the message to its logical conclusion and called for the outright abolition of public relief.[43]

With public relief—and its recipients—increasingly suspect, Baltimore's almshouse became an easy target. "Let us have a workhouse under proper regulations, and the management of an active Magistracy, and separate the sheep from the goats, the idler, the drunkard, and the spend-thrift from those who Providence afflicts with sickness and poverty, and unavoidable distress," urged the editors of the *Baltimore American* in support of the "due punishment of those men, who spend their time and their money in tippling houses, and neglect their families, relying on the generosity of the inhabitants to support them in winter." As almshouse expenses soared in the early 1820s, even the trustees were disgusted. "Pauperism has always kept pace with the utmost efforts of philanthropy to relieve and cure it," they lamented in a scathing 1823 address to the Maryland legislature. "Wherever a refuge has been provided for indigence," they observed, "idleness and vice have never failed to crowd it with inhabitants." After complaining of the number of drunkards and prostitutes who cycled through the almshouse only to be "refitted and prepared for new scenes of reveling and debauchery," the trustees judged the institution little more than a gift "to the idle, the profligate and the licentious." Indeed, "a cool and calculating philosophy"—that is, the Malthusian political economy contending that poor relief worked against the interests of the broader society—required subjecting "those who spend the vigor of early life in intemperance and sensual indulgences, [to] the good old rule, that 'he who will not work, neither shall he eat.'" The "dread of starvation" would force the Zachariah Stallingses of the city into self-reliance.[44]

The trustees of the Baltimore almshouse stood on the brink of renouncing over two centuries of Anglo-American public policy. Yet, "in defiance of all the dictates of Philosophy" (again referring to the ascendant school of what we now call "classical economics"), the trustees could not take that next step. "Our sympathies and feelings will govern us," they insisted, as they proclaimed the imperative "to stretch out the hand of charity to human suffering, whatever may have produced it." Public relief was no mere matter of public policy, but was a moral obligation grounded in a benevolent human instinct. Their inability to renounce relief was "the result of those natural affinities which binds man to his fellow, and which are seen to operate strongly even in savage life." Legislation "may direct, but cannot subdue or destroy them," declared the trustees in support of benevolent sentiments whose "most unlimited indulgence is authorised and enforced by divine authority."[45]

By grounding public poor relief in religious obligation and an innate human instinct, the trustees of the almshouse, like other philanthropists in the late eighteenth and early nineteenth centuries, constructed benevolence through Christian charity and a culture of sensibility.[46] The boundary between the two was unstable, if nonexistent, but Christian charity had a much longer history and a particular intensity in a city that one scholar has called "the religious capital of the young republic." From the imposing edifice of the nation's first cathedral to the makeshift sanctuaries of dozens of revivalist churches, the obligation to assist the poor was unavoidable for Baltimore's Catholic, Methodist, Episcopalian, Baptist, Swedenborgian, Dutch Reformed, and Unitarian residents (to name only a few of the vibrant sects in the city). "To part with a portion of what Providence has blessed us, for the relief of suffering humanity, is a Christian duty incumbent on us all, and one for which we shall be rewarded," explained one Baltimore resident in 1817. "The shivering mother, the starving infant, whose naked limbs you have clothed, and whose table you have covered with plenty . . . will eloquently plead at the *Throne of Mercy* for rich and ceaseless blessings on your heads," read another plea for wintertime relief. Across denominations, Christian duty required men of means to relieve the wants of their impoverished (if sinful) neighbors. The leading men of Baltimore did so through an institution that Maryland law tellingly referred to only as the "poorhouse." Yet "almshouse"—with its evocation of the religious charity of a distant past—became the standard appellation in Baltimore.[47]

To recognize the suffering of others was not only a religious imperative, but also a requirement for claiming a place within an expanding culture of sensibility that made the ability to feel the pain of strangers a proxy for one's creditworthiness, respectability, honor, and attainment of a class-specific masculinity and femininity. The poor were necessary for sustaining the social economy of sensibility, for their presence in the urban milieu provided the frequent opportunity for affective experience. "I have heard many citizens, of feeling hearts, lament over the extreme sufferings of the poor," began a typical wintertime appeal that situated public relief within a script for performative benevolence. Baltimore's "humane" citizens constituted themselves as men and women "of feeling" through direct interaction with the poor, but as importantly through exchanges with one another as newspaper readers and correspondents. "The scenes which I have witnessed would melt the most obdurate heart," reported Richardson Stuart, an Episcopalian nail manufacturer and visitor to the poor who was worried about his name being left off a published list of those involved in the 1805 relief effort. The culture of sensibility bled into a precocious sentimentalism as charity appeals brought readers into private domestic spaces to reveal the disordering effects of poverty. In a gratuitous 1807 account, an unemployed man returned home and "look[ed] upon the wife of his bosom and the children of his affection with torpid eye, and whilst they demand something to satisfy the calls of nature, answers with the bitterest tears—*I have nothing.*" When newspaper accounts splashed the headline "HUMAN MISERY" or reported on families "not having clothing enough to cover their nakedness," the cultural imperative to feel the suffering of the poor slid into voyeurism and what Karen Halttunen has called the "pornography of pain."[48]

No matter how exasperated some had grown with supporting the city's poor, benevolence remained a celebrated virtue and an important component of Baltimore's self-image. Even the almshouse could generate civic pride and attest to enlightened philanthropy. City guidebooks and maps depicted the almshouse to praise Baltimore's rising fortunes, not to showcase the impoverishment of its workers. In that same spirit, Baltimore's leaders gladly hosted Alexis de Tocqueville's 1831 visit to the almshouse.[49]

The ongoing effort to rationalize the public relief system and stem abuses resulting from "indiscriminate charity" generated more of the face-to-face encounters—and the print representations of those encounters—so essential to the performance of benevolence. In 1809, a committee of prominent men "visited the families applying for relief and extended the hand of charity to them in proportion to their several necessities and the sums collected." Women's voluntary associations administered private charity in a similar fashion. A committee of six members of the Female Humane Association undertook "to visit the sick and relieve the distressed deserving poor who come under their notice; endeavouring to discriminate, and to apportion their charity as they find them more or less worthy." The 1818 law creating ward managers of the poor to issue almshouse admission warrants placed the direct interaction of the wealthy and the needy at the center of public poor relief in Baltimore.[50]

That same year, Baltimore resident Thomas W. Griffith offered the broadest elaboration of public benevolence in his history of the Baltimore almshouse. A Baltimore native born in 1767 and emissary of the Washington administration in 1790s France, Griffith was a gadfly who commented publicly on such diverse issues as putting prisoners to work on the mudmachine, hiring white women as domestic servants, and ridding the streets of female hucksters. He wrote unsolicited letters to the mayor and city council offering free advice on regulating the city's markets and curbing illegal taverns. As an administrator of Baltimore's almshouse, Griffith defended public poor relief at precisely the moment when it was under the greatest attack.

Griffith saw in the almshouse "an asylum for distress which has been raised and maintained on principles of the broadest liberality." Griffith pointed to the "united contributions of the whole society—merchant, farmer, and artisan— and since the Revolution at least, according to their property or fortunes, making everyone a joint and separate benefactor; and by the equal admission or relief of the poor inhabitants, sick or afflicted, of every sect, age, or color, interesting all in its immediate welfare and future existence." Simply put, public relief functioned as the glue that bound together the diverse citizens of a republic. "In such a state of society as this," he concluded, "the only difference of opinion which can be tolerated among enlightened men relate[s] merely to the manner of relief." Policymakers could calibrate specific pension programs or institutional regimes, but "provision of some kind must be made for the sons and daughters of affliction." Failure to do so "might render doubtful the disadvantages of the savage state or the benefits of civilization."[51]

In contrast to other celebrants of Christian charity, Griffith was unusually frank in connecting benevolence to self-interest. That members of society should tax themselves to provide for the needy was essential "not only because [charity] is commended by heaven and imposed on our feelings by nature, but because the title to superior wealth, when most legally acquired, might be shaken, if a state of suffering was permitted to arise." To be sure, the elite of Baltimore rarely worried about a revolt of the dispossessed masses, and perhaps they did not need to, based on their monopoly on state violence.[52] Yet men like Griffith were nonetheless invested in maintaining the social stability that facilitated their prosperity and rightfully anxious that market forces could undermine the equality among adult white men essential to republican governance. Griffith was a Federalist and a Unitarian, but such sentiments could be found among Baltimore's Jeffersonians, National Republicans, Democrats, and Whigs, as well as its Catholics, Quakers, Presbyterians, and Jews.

The intertwining of civic leadership, philanthropy, and elite self-interest becomes evident in the prominence of those men leading poor relief efforts. The annual committees to distribute emergency wintertime relief in 1804 and 1805 comprised men familiar to anyone who had ever strolled the waterfront, visited a church, or voted in a municipal election: Thomas McElderry owned the city's longest wharf, founded the Union Bank, served as vice president of the Baltimore Hibernian Society, and managed the fund-raising lottery of the Second Presbyterian Church; Jeffersonian merchant Andrew Buchanan had helped coordinate Baltimore's response to the 1793 yellow fever outbreak, and later sat on the city council; Jesse Hollingsworth was a slaveholding Federalist flour merchant who had served in the Maryland Assembly in the 1780s and acted as a trustee of the Female Humane Association; Revolutionary War veteran Joseph Sterett was an Episcopalian, director of the Baltimore Insurance Company, and manager of the Baltimore Dancing Assembly; tea merchant Emanuel Kent belonged to the Methodist Church, the Mechanical Fire Company, and the city council. Likewise, the almshouse trustees spun a web of interlocking leadership that blurred public and private interest. Even as they divided on party and religion, they formed a cadre of civic leaders invested in Baltimore's liberal reputation.[53]

Lower on the social ladder but immersed in the same cultural logic stood John Robb, the ward manager of the poor in Fells Point who refused to allow Zachariah Stallings to die in the streets. The job of ward manager was more workaday than suited the city's wealthiest residents or most prominent gentlemen but nonetheless involved making choices based on "the dictates of humanity," as one 1827 report observed. Ward managers tended to come from the ranks of the moderately prosperous: entrepreneurial and self-employed men whose careers in public service were only beginning. By the time he had become a ward manager, Robb had already joined with other Fells Point men to found the Washington Benevolent Society and the Marine Bible Society.[54]

When the upwardly mobile Robb met the downwardly mobile Stallings, each stood to gain; in effect, each had a story to tell, a performance to enact. Historians cannot know what motivated Robb to take the stand he did, although modern observers are usually skeptical of nineteenth-century do-gooders whose Christian philanthropy presumably served as a front for class domination. Indeed, no matter how vocally elected officials, relief administrators, and middle-class volunteers situated their activities in a religiously sanctioned charitable impulse or a universal human sympathy, "helping" other people invariably involved value-laden judgments that reflected and amplified inequalities of power between the giver and recipient of charity. John Robb surely could not escape that dynamic in his responsibility to sign admission warrants to the almshouse. But it was precisely that exchange that invested men like Robb in public relief, just as it was that exchange that made it possible for Zachariah Stallings to spend his winters on the public's dime.[55]

The Uses of Discipline

Critics could not dislodge the presumption of public responsibility for the poor, but their bitter denunciations of "downright and detestable imposters" and "an ignorant, idle, profligate, and abandoned population amongst us" resonated among policymakers and private citizens. Impoverished men and women might readily deny the hostile rhetoric that conceptualized poverty as an individual moral failing, but they faced its consequences when a middling housewife instructed her servants to turn away begging children from the kitchen door. The accumulation of testimony—whether a grand jury report declaring the city "infested" with vagrants, a newspaper item about a fraudulent beggar posing as an epileptic, or a medical report blaming the poor for a yellow fever outbreak—prompted far greater scrutiny of the impoverished. As one Baltimore resident concluded in 1816, "The great object of Charity is, not an indiscriminate distribution of alms to importunate strolling beggars in the streets, who have brought themselves to poverty by idleness and drunkenness, and who ought to be put down by an active police." The same writer succinctly explained that true benevolence was not feeding the hungry and clothing the naked, but rather making the needy "useful to themselves and society." This was a project of an entirely different order.[56]

Its local origins were in the 1804 effort to build a School of Industry. In the midst of raising over $2,500 to sustain those displaced by a freezing winter, numerous newspaper contributors invoked the success of Count Rumford's workhouse in Bavaria. Rumford was once Benjamin Thompson, a New England schoolteacher turned British loyalist during the American Revolution. Having served in the British army and been knighted by George III, Thompson entered the employ of the elector of Bavaria. After reorganizing the elector's troops, Thompson became a count of the Holy Roman Empire, choosing the name Rumford (the former name of Concord, New Hampshire) in deference to his American roots. A physicist and an expert on the properties of boiling liquids, Rumford became an apostle of hot soup and designed innovative stoves to aid in its efficient preparation. Rumford turned his organizational talents and experimental kitchens toward poor relief. His coup de grace was the workhouse in Munich, a city of 60,000 law-abiding citizens and, as Rumford recalled, several thousand beggars who strolled about "levying contributions from the industrious inhabitants, stealing and robbing and leading a life of indolence and the most shameless debauchery." Deploying the elector's army on January 1, 1790, Rumford cleared the streets of vagrants, conscripted poor families at their residences, and brought them all to a sparkling new facility on the edge of town, called the School of Industry. There, the poor received housing, job training, and hearty (yet economical) servings of potato and barley soup. Over the entrance gate was Rumford's motto: "No Alms Will Be Received Here."[57]

By the time public clamoring for "a permanent establishment" in Baltimore reached its zenith in February 1804, Count Rumford had become a household name. Advocates boasted that the Bavarian experiment paid for itself, bettered public morals, and diminished crime. Support for these claims came from Rumford himself, in such tracts as "Of the Fundamental Principles on which General Establishments for the Relief of the Poor May Be Formed in All Countries." Circulation records from the Baltimore Library Company show that *Rumford's Works* had collected little dust since its acquisition in 1798. The volume spent the spring of 1804 in the hands of Reverend Elijah Rattoone, associate rector of St. Paul's Episcopal Church and a member of the committee appointed to study the wintertime needs of Baltimore's poor. The count had become required reading among the city's policymakers, who would borrow liberally from him in the coming months. Rumford had warned that "to prevent the bad impressions which are sometimes made by names which have become odious, instead of calling it a workhouse, it might be called 'A School of Industry.'" Not only did they adopt Rumford's gentler name, the founders of Baltimore's School of Industry followed Rumford's suggestions to place upright religious leaders at the head of the project, to manage the institution under a centralized committee of unpaid civic leaders, and to rely on voluntary subscriptions for funding. Rumford had also noted that establishments for the poor hinged on community support and advised their promoters to issue a convincing public proposal before commencing a project. In August 1804, the city papers carried a lengthy manifesto outlining "A Plan for Establishing a School of Industry, with a view of bettering the condition of the poor and affording them permanent employment."[58]

The philanthropic agenda of the School of Industry centered on providing the poor with the ability to help themselves. Donors would "adopt the only effectual means of putting an end to the sufferings of the poor by introducing a spirit of industry among them." The institution was to function just as its name suggested, as a place where the impoverished would study, learn, and internalize the ethos of a competitive, commercial society. Presumably, the needy would appreciate such reeducation far more than any handout. "By putting it into his power to maintain himself," the school would provide a poor person with "infinitely more delight . . . than by supporting him in idleness and laying him under a load of favors, which he can never in the smallest degree requite." Having already criticized the poor for their sense of entitlement, the school's advocates now implied that the poor resented the burdens of receiving charity.[59]

As they imagined a worker's utopia, the school's founders envisioned a sophisticated program of surveillance and socialization. Rumford had contended that such a project hinged on gentleness and patience and advised, "nothing will tend so powerfully to reform [the poor] as kind usage from the hands of persons they must learn to love and to respect at the same time." Apparently forgetting about the help of the Bavarian army, Rumford declared that "force will not do it." Instead, Rumford and his Baltimore imitators advocated a regime of coercive kindness. Although a proposed legal ban on almsgiving might anger the poor by leaving them nowhere else to turn, the institution's many amenities would numb them to the freedoms they had sacrificed to become orderly and "useful" citizens. Once inmates became dependent on the comfortable facilities of the School of Industry, the mere threat of expulsion would bring the recalcitrant into line. In Baltimore, "incorrigibly idle or lazy workers" would lose access to hot soup, while the workers "most conspicuous for their order, sobriety, and tractable behavior" would win rewards.[60]

The institution had special designs on poor children, who would be trained "in good habits." The plan enjoined the directors to "use all proper means to induce the parents of poor children to send them to the institution, as soon as they may be capable of earning anything by their labor." Even children too young to work had a place. In Munich, Rumford immobilized toddlers in high chairs on the shopfloor and forced them to watch older children spin hemp and flax. Made "jealous of those who were permitted to be more active," these children "cried" for the opportunity to work. "How sweet these tears were to me," recalled Rumford, as he liberated these children to join in the production activities. Harnessing the labor of Baltimore's poor children would constitute "a real addition to the wealth of the community."[61]

Wealthy Baltimore residents quickly subscribed several thousand dollars to the project, but the urgent needs of the subsequent winter consumed the money that had been raised. The School of Industry remained in the imaginations of civic leaders as pleas for emergency wintertime charity appeared year after year. When Edward Johnson became mayor in 1809, he redoubled efforts to create Rumford's workhouse in Baltimore.

Only forty-two when he became mayor in 1809, Edward Johnson began his public career in close contact with the city's poor. Having served as an almshouse physician and a justice of the orphan's court, Johnson recognized that the disappearance of work caused poor people to suffer each winter. "Many who solicit our charity are in the full enjoyment of health and strength and plead as their only excuse <u>want</u> of employment," he reported to the city council in 1810. But despite his awareness of seasonal unemployment, Johnson also lamented "the great Increase in Idle and wandering Poor who have of late infested our City." The city council did likewise, blaming indiscriminate poor relief for making Baltimore into a magnet for vagrants "from other counties of this state and also from other states of the Union." Pursuing the strict enforcement of liquor laws, a tough vagrancy statute from Annapolis, and funding for a revivified *House* of Industry, Johnson and his allies on the city council made distinguishing between the deserving and undeserving poor the centerpiece of public policy in 1810s Baltimore.[62]

Vagrancy laws were old tools for controlling disorderly populations, with seventeenth-century English laws pertaining to "masterless men" surviving the American Revolution nearly intact. Baltimore's 1804 vagrancy law conveyed an archaic flavor in its prohibition on jugglers and fortune-tellers (in addition to those who had no visible means of employment, who lodged in open air, and any woman "reputed to be a prostitute"). The law stipulated a two-month term in the almshouse for those found guilty of vagrancy, but lax constables and the almshouse's permeable walls rendered the law ineffective. At Mayor Johnson's request in 1812, the legislature put teeth into the statute by sentencing vagrants to a year of hard labor in the dreaded Maryland State Penitentiary. Built in 1809 on the outskirts of Baltimore, the penitentiary housed notorious criminals behind its castlelike walls. Mayor Johnson called the statute "very efficient" and promised that with "due vigilance we shall probably be able to get rid of the many Pick-Pockets and other Vagabonds, who have for some time past infested our city."[63]

Johnson's pursuit of the House of Industry also sent him to Annapolis, where the state legislature granted incorporated status to the institution's trustees and permitted them to raise the necessary $30,000 by selling lottery tickets. The effort was beset by chronic delays, as well as criticism of state-sponsored gambling; after all, lotteries, like indiscriminate almsgiving, offered the poor something for nothing. The cold winter of 1817, however, silenced critics as the wintertime needs of the poor reached new heights. Whereas the winter of 1805 had sunk the School of Industry, the trials of February 1817 brought the seasonal suffering of the poor back into the public eye. The new mayor, George Stiles, organized an emergency relief program, and generous citizens donated over $6,500. But with winter showing no signs of abating and many remaining without food or fuel, Stiles feared that "little visible or permanent good" had come from his work. Worse, "the most profligate, abandoned, and unworthy objects" had imposed on the public's benevolence, as they always did when the city offered indiscriminate aid "on the spur and moment of the occasion." Only a House of Industry "would relieve the citizens from the continued calls and importunities of the street beggar."[64]

The visionary workhouse garnered unprecedented support in the city's newspapers, and sales of the lottery tickets skyrocketed. Except this time, supporters touted the House of Industry not as a worker's sanctuary, but as a penal institution. As Stiles said threateningly, "it would be only necessary for many that now ask alms, to know that such provisions was made for them and they would take care of themselves."[65]

Following the costly winter of 1817, public sentiment toward the poor grew colder. As not to encourage begging, charity organizations instituted new safeguards to insure that only the "necessitous and deserving" received aid. Each week, the Fells Point Humane Society deployed investigators to the homes of its clients. When interviews with neighbors yielded evidence of "gross immorality or attempts to impose," the visitors could immediately delete the offender from the relief list. Other reformers dismissed all charity as counterproductive. By one critical account, free wintertime soup promoted drunkenness "by leaving [working] peoples' earnings as a surplus capital to be invested in whiskey." The emphasis on moral failure pushed the problem of seasonal unemployment into the background and brought intemperance to the foreground. If alcohol accounted for the misery of the poor, then cold weather did not warrant special programs. Commentators imagined typical wintertime sufferers as those "who after the idleness and dissipation of summer, imagine that they have only to complain and cast themselves on the honest earnings of the sober, industrious and economical portion of our citizens." The wintertime disappearance of work presumably made no difference in their debauched lives.[66]

Like its predecessor, the House of Industry was delayed by the immediate needs of the poor. This time, the economic dislocations of the Panic of 1819, which coincided with a yellow fever outbreak in Baltimore, stalled fund-raising and, perhaps more importantly, the will to civic improvement. The almshouse—the implicit target of so much of the criticism of indiscriminate charity—would have to suffice. Nonetheless, the men running the almshouse had not been oblivious to the conversations taking place in the city, and several of the trustees served on the board for the House of Industry. More importantly, in 1816 the state legislature had given them the opportunity to build a new almshouse for Baltimore. Securing a parcel of farmland several miles removed from the city, the trustees designed a facility intended to deter needy people from using it. When the almshouse opened at Calverton in 1823, its penal approach to poor relief enshrined social discipline as the highest form of civic benevolence.

Although all the almshouse trustees were distinguished, none would become more famous (or wealthy) than Philip E. Thomas, who served as the first president of the Baltimore & Ohio Railroad in 1828. But before dedicating his organizational skills to the nation's transportation system, Thomas left his mark on Baltimore's poor relief system.

In 1822, Thomas, the son of a Quaker minister, assumed the presidency of

Baltimore's Society for the Prevention of Pauperism (SPP), an organization founded on the belief "that pauperism grew with the enlargements of charity; that funds appropriated for the relief of the needy and the destitute, increased the numbers of paupers, in proportion to the extent of those funds; that the cries were more importunate as such bounty was expanded; that charity in fact so far from alleviating distress, seemed to create objects for its own consumption." Intending for the poor "to maintain themselves by their own industry," Thomas and the SPP considered public works programs as much a "gratuity" as monetary handouts. "It is first necessary to fit the poor for employment," read one SPP pamphlet. "They cannot, but by their own folly and vices, long remain indigent . . . *Those who wish will find employment.*"[67]

Baltimore's SPP disappeared in 1822, but Thomas translated the defunct organization's agenda into public policy as a trustee of the new almshouse opening in 1823. If Thomas had once declared that charity allowed the poor "to supply their wants without the pain and trouble of labour," the Calverton facility would foreclose that possibility through surveillance, physical punishment, and a compulsory work requirement. By the time Thomas had turned his attention to building a railroad, Baltimore's almshouse had become the envy of relief administrators throughout the nation. As a committee of Philadelphia officials noted with admiration, Baltimore was able to "derive an income from that class who are always the greatest burthen." Boston's Artemas Simonds concluded that "a rigid, uniform system toward paupers, like that of Baltimore, doubtless has the effect either of driving the idle, dissolute, vagrant class to other places, or of compelling them to reform their course of life."[68]

The first step was to eliminate the possibility of getting relief outside the almshouse. Already, Baltimore was very stingy in its use of pensions or out-relief. Most pensions were pegged at $30 per year, paid in quarterly installments of $7.50—hardly enough money to support someone in idle luxury and substantially less than even a seamstress could earn on her own. Applicants for pensions in Baltimore were carefully screened and often denied. In 1817, trustee Robert Walsh received a plea to support Hetty Peirce, who was "<u>very infirm</u> and at the advanced age of 78. Not able to procure the necessaries of life," according to her advocate, Maria L. Johnson. "She is <u>deserving</u> and I shall be gratified if you can place her on the '<u>pension</u>' list," wrote Johnson. The best that the trustees could do was to offer a single payment of $10 to help Peirce along. In other cases, annual pensions were paid to those providing care rather than to the indigent person. Elizabeth Pessener received $30 in 1816 for boarding Thomas St. John, a small child whose father was in the army and whose mother was in the penitentiary. William

Schultze went from being a pensioner himself to becoming the caregiver to the three-year-old orphan George Keighler—and thus the recipient of the child's $30 pension. With the opening of the new almshouse, the trustees cancelled all existing pensions and required reapplication with a testimonial from a prominent taxpaying citizen. Almost all of those originally on the list were returned to the relief rolls once it was found they had "the same disability or circumstances" and "have produced satisfactory certificates." Yet the average pension was under $20, and only 137 of Baltimore's 70,000 residents could claim this meager assistance in 1826. In contrast, Philadelphia supported ten times as many pensioners among a population not quite twice as large.[69]

The second step was to study, catalog, and classify the inmates. The SPP had long advocated such methods of surveillance, and the new almshouse opened with vastly improved recordkeeping. Beginning in 1823, each entry in the admissions book listed birthplace, length of residence in Baltimore, religion, malady, and other information that might prove useful in assessing the pauper's situation. The almshouse was not a venue where such data might be used to exclude, but as the trustees explained, such methods would reveal "the causes which have led, and are still leading, to this melancholy exhibit of human suffering and demoralization." Each year's annual report deployed the data in tabular form to support an argument; for example, that intemperance was the "grand cause of pauperism amongst us," that the city should build a House of Refuge for juvenile delinquents whose "vicious habits" made it impossible to bind them as apprentices, or that Baltimore's citizens were paying "a heavy tax to maintain a population entirely alien to the city and county." The presentation of "these degrading facts" rarely resulted in changes in public policy but did mark the increasing rationalization of institutional relief.[70]

The third innovation was the use of penal technologies. One ambition had been to construct a stepping mill, a circular contraption that forced men "to earn their bread by the sweat of their brows." These treadmills had captured the imaginations of American penologists in the early 1820s. Noting the device's "salutary effect on vagrants and rogues," Hezekiah Niles could not "apprehend any thing more irksome than this kind of labor—disgusting from its sameness, excessively fatiguing, and seemingly without object or end." In what may be the largest woodcut image to appear on the pages of the *Baltimore Patriot*, the newspaper depicted this "great and important invention" in 1822. "It will be a terror to all 'evil doers' in Maryland, and will rarely be visited a *second* time by those who have *once* tasted this wholesome discipline." Baltimore's mayor John Montgomery was especially concerned once Maryland legislators altered the city's vagrancy statutes and be-

Proposed almshouse treadmill, 1824. At a time when daily newspapers published
few images, this large woodcut filled the width of two columns of the *Baltimore Patriot*,
November 15, 1822. Penal reformers hoped that treadmills would force vagrants to "earn
their bread by the sweat of their brows." Advocates of a treadmill in Baltimore borrowed
this image from Stephen Allen, *Reports on the Stepping or Discipline Mill, at the New York
Penitentiary . . .* (New York: Van Pelt and Spear, 1823). This item is reproduced by permission of The Huntington Library, San Marino, California.

gan sending those "who are able but unwilling to work" to the almshouse. He
hoped that the assembly might compensate the city by funding a treadmill "for
the punishment of persons of the above description."[71]

The funds for a treadmill never arrived, but the almshouse overseer had an
even more stunning piece of penal technology at his disposal: the shower bath, a
veritable water-torture chamber reserved for vagrants who had eloped from the
almshouse. As described by an admiring committee of Philadelphia relief officials,
"The Shower bath is a small apartment or case, to the back of which slats are nailed
in such a manner as to form nearly a semi-circle, and a corresponding semi-
circular frame is attached to the inside of the door; so, as when shut, to completely
inclose the sufferer, and keep him in a perpendicular position. Above, a barrel is
fixed, with small holes in the bottom of it, and is so managed, that either the whole

quantity of water may descend at once, or drip very slowly. This last is considered the most effectual mode of punishing, and is quite severe." Such bodily punishments revealed the state-sanctioned violence at the heart of Enlightenment penology, and collapsed the boundary between prisoner and pauper.[72]

The final component of the almshouse regime was compulsory labor, a part of what the trustees referred to as "wholesome discipline." Whereas the School of Industry had been conceptualized as a venue for learning job skills and earning wages when the city's economy slowed, labor at the almshouse was meant to make the institution self-supporting while deterring the city's poor from going there in the first place. Boasting of the Baltimore almshouse's efficiency and economy, its trustees credited coerced labor: "the requirition [sic] of some sort of labour from all such paupers as are able to work serves to reduce the expense of their support while it tends in great measure to prevent an increase in the House of idlers who are able to maintain themselves." Over twelve months in 1825 and 1826, inmates wove 3,710 square yards of fabric, manufactured 666 pairs of shoes, sawed 1,566 feet of fencing, harvested 16,020 heads of cabbage, and performed other labor valued at over $7,000. In some years, the farm marketed its surplus in the city and recouped several hundred dollars. By some accounts, the most desperate city residents committed "breaches of the peace and other offenses" to earn jail time rather than have to take refuge in the almshouse. For would-be inmates, jail looked better than the almshouse "simply because they are made to work in the one, while in the other they spend their time in idleness."[73]

Even as most inmates eloped before working off their debt to the almshouse, the compulsory labor regime brought Baltimore substantial cost savings. Compared to the largest industrializing cities of the Northeast, Baltimore spent far less to support its poor. For every man, woman, and child living in Baltimore in 1827, the municipal budget allocated 26¢ for poor relief. Per capita, Boston expended twice that amount, and Philadelphia nearly three times as much. By 1834, Philadelphia's poor tax burden had climbed to $138,000. In those same seven years, Baltimore's annual expenditures on the poor fell from $18,000 to under $16,000. The expense of maintaining a pauper in the almshouse fell from $44 per year in 1822 (before the farm started) to $26 per year in 1831.[74]

By minimizing outdoor relief and designing an almshouse to either deter or exploit the needy, Baltimore attempted to implement the system envisioned by the Society for the Prevention of Pauperism. This enterprise was not a betrayal of the benevolent ideal, merely a redeployment predicated on the notion that charity tended "to injure rather than benefit" its recipients "by inducing them to relax their own exertion for their support." To assist the poor was "foremost in the catalogue of Christian virtues, but the same inspired volume which inculcates its practice has also declared (and we cannot revoke its decree) that man shall earn his bread by the sweat of his brow—that is, by his own labour," explained an apostle of a benevolence grounded in discipline. What greater gift could be given to an impoverished person than the opportunity to strive for success?[75]

The Incomprehensibility of Poverty

The almshouse imposed labor on those who refused to sell their time for wages in the marketplace, as well as on those who could find no buyers, and those whose poverty attested to their unrelenting familiarity with backbreaking toil at job sites throughout the city. Yet, a penal almshouse did not prevent Baltimore's poor from using the institution to their own ends, any more than it transformed them into docile workers who had internalized the self-disciplined logic of the market. But when the needy showed too much entitlement and too little responsibility, they risked alienating their prosperous neighbors who had enshrined public relief as a hallmark of civil society. As the city's leading citizens came to see the poor as deviant, they began advocating measures that were neither liberal nor benevolent. Pauper agency, elite benevolence, and capitalist discipline had distinct yet simultaneous agendas, and they often functioned at cross-purposes. The almshouse served all these ends, but whereas Baltimore's employers, civic leaders, and elected officials found other vehicles for compelling labor, fulfilling religious duties, and displaying their public spiritedness, Zachariah Stallings and his family possessed fewer and fewer resources to stay afloat on their own.

Zachariah, Dicky, Nelly, and Elizabeth each had to navigate through sympathetic officials, hostile administrators, and a set of policies at once charitable and punitive. Their experiences were unexceptional, insofar as moral condemnation and compulsory institutional labor had become fastened to the civic guarantee of public relief during the previous three centuries of European and Anglo-American social welfare practice.[76] As in other cities, Baltimore's public welfare system devoted much of its energy to imposing work requirements on seamstresses, laundresses, and mariners who needed no reminding that their livelihoods—and those of their entire households—hinged on physical labor. In fact, just as economic stability became less likely for those whose labor was for sale in early republic Baltimore, civic leaders and policymakers increasingly represented poverty as inconceivable, to quote the almshouse trustees, "where the means of obtaining a comfortable subsistence are so abundant as in this community." Indifferent to the structural causes of economic hardship, Baltimore's relief officials attributed poverty to individual moral failing and sought to effect personal rehabilitation through institutional discipline. The benevolent ideal found its highest expression in what one scholar has called the "tough love" approach of compelling the poor to fend for themselves.[77]

While the Stallings family was presumably caught between an erratic urban economy and a coercive relief regime, there was still plenty of room for them to maneuver. The consensus sustaining public relief was too great for a "work or starve" alternative to gain traction. So long as the claims of charity, benevolence, and civic pride were negotiated in the face-to-face encounters of a Zachariah Stallings and a John Robb, then the almshouse would remain as much the property of those using it as those running it. The more serious problem facing laboring families was their "work *and* starve" reality. Baltimore's public relief system successfully prevented people from dying in the streets but gave the poor far less support than they needed in an economy defined by its seasonality and inadequate wages. The families of men who earned wages digging mud out of the harbor had always been poor, but the culture of the early republic now denied the legitimacy of their poverty. Under such circumstances, Zachariah Stallings's ability to maneuver into the almshouse for the winter—only to find most of his family already there—was small consolation indeed.

CHAPTER 8

The Market's Grasp

A thriving port in a languishing slave state, Baltimore perplexed early republic travelers, who were unsure how to situate the city in the emerging American taxonomy of North and South. When New York jurist James Kent visited in 1793, he compared Baltimore favorably to Manhattan and Boston "as a great Mart of Commerce." The city's "hot Bed growth" was "owing to enterprizing Capitalists," abundant in Baltimore and absent from the sleepy tobacco port of Annapolis just thirty miles away. English astronomer Francis Baily drew a similar conclusion when he arrived from Norfolk in 1796: "Instead of that apparent decay of trade, that want of emulation, and propensity for gaming, we beheld everywhere [in Baltimore] that spirit of improvement so congenial to a free and flourishing people."[1]

Visitors who began their journeys above the Mason-Dixon line, however, often focused on Baltimore's affinity with points farther south. "One of the first things that attracts the attention of the stranger is the greatly increased number of blacks that he meets in the streets," observed the self-described English gentleman William Blane upon arriving from Philadelphia in 1828. To those unfamiliar with American geography, Blane offered a simple explanation, namely, "Maryland, in which the city is built is a slave State." Readers of New York's *Freedom's Journal* heard similarly from an African American traveler who needed little time to determine, "Baltimore was never designed to be the abode of your humble servant. A man of colour, educated at the north, can never feel himself at home in Baltimore." In 1830, William Lloyd Garrison drew an even starker conclusion near the end of his nine-month residence in Baltimore. "There is nothing which the curse of slavery has not tainted. It rests on every herb, and every tree, and every field, and on the people, and on the morals," he explained to his worried friends in Massachusetts. "Of southern habits, southern doctrines, and southern practices, I am heartily sick," the twenty-four-year-old Garrison lamented from the jail cell to which he had been sentenced for libeling participants in Baltimore's thriving slave trade.[2]

It is no surprise that the northernmost city in the South and the southernmost city in the North elicited such varied reactions from visitors. The architects of Baltimore's rise hitched their wagon to the free economies of the North and West, but as employers and propertyholders, they availed themselves of Southern social relations to build capital in human property, to compel labor through physical coercion, to saddle a sizable portion of the free population with a subordinate legal status, and to discipline the Euro-American workers who formed the majority of the city's laborers. The coexistence of transient wage workers and lifelong slaves in the same occupations puzzled many observers, as did the racial coding of labor in a slaveholding city where the majority of low-end workers were white. Term slavery, alongside indentured servitude and apprenticed labor, often made bondage a life stage, rather than an absolute category that distinguished free whites from enslaved blacks. Equally confounding were the enslaved workers who managed their own time, arranged their own hire, and lived outside the direct supervision of their legal owners. The sawhorse equality of enslaved, free black, and white workers at mixed-race job sites made Baltimore, in the words of one observer, "a kind of mongrel, neither one thing nor the other."[3]

A quarter-century before Abraham Lincoln proclaimed the perils of a "house divided," a chorus of Baltimore commentators, jurists, elected officials, and social reformers began warning that the city was reaching a crisis moment. Baltimore could fully embrace free labor or more aggressively defend slavery, they argued, but could not sustain both free labor *and* slavery. Once seen as an engine of prosperity, the hybrid economy now provoked anxiety about race wars, social anarchy, and economic ruin. Eliciting such alarmist forecasts were a series of local events, such as the militia's suppression of Baltimore & Ohio Railroad workers in 1829, a cholera outbreak in 1832, a banking collapse in 1834, and the riots that left a dozen Baltimore residents dead the following summer. National political developments like Nat Turner's 1831 slave insurrection in Virginia, the formation of the American Anti-Slavery Society, the emergence of the second party system, and the Panic of 1837 reverberated in Baltimore to the extent that they highlighted the instability of the city's mixed labor regime.

Jurists, newspapermen, and treatise writers attempted to resolve Baltimore's presumptive crisis by positing seemingly incontrovertible rules for who should work where, on what terms, and what would happen if they did not. The prevalence of delayed manumissions, self-hiring arrangements, and out-of-state sales galvanized those invested in further entrenching slavery as well as those pursuing its abolition. The nominally free but legally disadvantaged status of free people of color elicited polemics from white colonizationists and from the advocates of black civic equality. The legitimacy of the wage system—the presumption that workers and their employers bargained as legal equals in the marketplace—inflamed the passions of those touting the virtues of a society held together through self-interest as well as those on the losing end of unfettered market relations. In all cases, the consequences of delay were dire: impending warfare between slaves and masters, whites and blacks, the propertied and the propertyless, and workers and their employers.

The tension of being "neither one thing nor the other" had been present for the entire course of Baltimore's development, although always more a problem for the people performing labor than for those purchasing it. An outpouring of new arguments in the 1820s and 1830s made urgent the resolution of Baltimore's hybrid status, but the decisions of Baltimore's employers attested to the durability of the status quo. If the ability to choose among and combine different kinds of workers had not suited their needs, employers would have paid more attention to the abolitionists, colonizationists, proslavery politicians, black clergymen, union leaders, political economists, and others calling for the city to commit itself decisively to the free-labor future of the North or the slaveholding future of the South. New conceptualizations of "how work worked"—some existing only in the realm of print and public discourse, others gaining traction in law and social policy—brought few positive changes to the workaday world of Baltimore's laundresses, mariners, and street pavers. Working men and women reevaluated their survival strategies in response to shifting expectations, opportunities, restrictions, and vulnerabilities, but the difficulties of making work pay persisted for all those whose labor was for sale.

If anything, the challenges of scraping by became greater as Baltimore became more committed to slavery *and* more committed to free labor over the course of the early republic. Advocates of a new liberal political economy valorized the market as the best vehicle for matching those who needed labor with those who needed to work, even as the much-vaunted invisible hand sounded the slave auctioneer's gavel with the same dexterity it orchestrated the bargaining of employers and employees over wages and hours. In continuing to function simultaneously, contractual freedom and legal slavery did not bring about the apocalyptic denouement anticipated in the printed commentaries of the 1820s and 1830s. Rather, their potent interaction ensured that labor and those performing it would be understood interchangeably as commodities, while leaving all working people increasingly exposed to the vagaries of the market.

The Chattel Principle

At first glance, Baltimore appeared to wash its hands of slavery by the end of the 1820s. Over the previous decade, as the city's white population grew by 25 percent and its free population of color by 40 percent, Baltimore's enslaved population declined by a small fraction. That trend continued over the 1830s, with nearly 1,000 fewer slaves appearing in the 1840 census than had appeared a decade earlier. At the end of the 1830s, slaves constituted only 3 percent of the city's population, down from a high of 11 percent in 1800. Historians have generally followed the lead of an 1835 visitor who observed, "In this city there appears no strong attachment to slavery, and no wish to perpetuate it." By most accounts, the decline in the absolute and relative number of enslaved people in Baltimore confirmed the general rule of slavery's incompatibility with urban growth, whether because of owners' inability to exercise the required supervision over slaves in complex and crowded spaces or their increased access to cheaper and more productive wage workers. By such logic, Baltimore was no "slave city" and was easily the weakest link in Maryland's slaveholding regime.[4]

However, slavery was far more crucial to Baltimore's economy than census data can convey, or than historians see if they only consider slavery as a labor system. The number of people who experienced slavery in Baltimore greatly exceeded those present for each decade's enumeration. Between the snapshots offered in decennial returns, rural slaves moved in and out of the city for spells of work; and as term slaves attained their manumission dates, daring men and women escaped, and the unfortunate were sold away, others were sent to take their places. Census figures mask this mobility and underrepresent the continued importance of slaves in manufacturing, commercial, and service jobs.[5]

But at the same time, these slaves were far more than mere workers whose numbers fluctuated with demand in particular industries. Slaves' bodies did not just perform labor, but also stored capital as a highly fungible form of property. The governing logic of slavery was what Walter Johnson has described as the "chattel principle," or the ready convertibility of a human being into cash. The mere possibility of such a conversion created wealth on paper with substantial consequences both for slaveholders and for the economy at large.[6]

Simply by creating a balance in a ledger book, slave ownership boosted an individual's net worth, opened access to credit (without slaves needing to be listed explicitly as collateral for bank loans), and facilitated the intergenerational transfer of wealth. Maryland subsidized property in slaves, assessing them far below market value, usually at a discount of 60 to 70 percent. A Baltimore slaveholder whose ten slaves were worth $3,000 paid taxes as though his property amounted to only $1,000. Yet any one of those ten slaves could easily be transformed into $300 cash far more rapidly than could real estate or other types of property. In the aggregate, the thousands of slaves who passed through Baltimore in a given decade functioned as several million dollars in circulating capital, with a further multiplier effect as additional capital followed in the form of credit loaned against the book value of slaves. To tap the wealth stored in enslaved bodies did not require Baltimore to house a huge open-air slave market where hundreds of people were bought and sold every day. Rather, it was the *prospect* of convertibility that defined the "chattel principle." Slaves created paper value for the people who owned them, a paper value that could easily surpass the value of labor an enslaved person performed in a Baltimore shipyard or bakery.[7]

That Baltimore slaves embodied liquid wealth owed to the interregional slave trade. Less crucial as urban workers than as plantation hands, slaves were valuable in Baltimore because they were valuable elsewhere. Demand in cotton-producing regions reverberated in Baltimore, as local merchant Robert Gilmor recognized firsthand when he traveled south in 1807. "The discovery of the cotton crop is but a new thing in Carolina & Georgia," he recorded in his journal after touring a "noble plantation" that utilized Eli Whitney's gin to prepare short-staple cotton for market. The new technology "renders negroes valuable," he added upon learning that adult slaves were selling for upwards of $350 in Charleston.[8]

With the Atlantic slave trade closed in 1808, Baltimore became a prime locale for cotton planters to acquire laborers. "Wanted to Purchase, Thirty or Forty Negroes of all sorts and sizes," read an increasingly common variety of advertisement after 1815. Hotels and taverns served as common sites of speculation. Buyers interested in fifteen to fifty slaves could be found at Matthew Walker's Eagle & Plough on North Howard Street, Marriot's Cross-Keys on Lombard Street, or William Fowler's tavern at the sign of the sunflower. By the 1830s, potential field hands were selling for as much as $650, a figure conveying the economic ambitions of the "Gentleman from the Territory of Arkansas" who offered to "pay the highest prices" for thirty Baltimore slaves in 1834.[9]

Such large-scale transactions typically fell to professional dealers who used sophisticated networks of information, purchasing, and transportation to link the Chesapeake and the cotton frontier in a single market. The pioneering figure in the trade was Austin Woolfolk, an Augusta, Georgia, businessman whose "Cash for Negroes" ads first appeared in Baltimore newspapers in 1815. Relocating to the city in 1819, Woolfolk planted his agents (often relatives) in the countryside, frequented estate and bankruptcy sales, and placed advertisements calling for one hundred slaves at a time. Woolfolk's most significant innovation, however, was the use of water transport to ship Maryland slaves to New Orleans. Transportation costs were slightly higher by sea, but boats delivered slaves to market in a fraction of the time it took to march chained slaves across five states and minimized avenues of escape. "The number transported by sea from the single port of Baltimore by a noted trader of that place is believed to exceed several hundreds per annum," reported a national antislavery meeting in 1828. With other members of the Woolfolk clan handling the New Orleans side of the business, Austin and his white house on Pratt Street became fixtures of the Baltimore landscape. By the account of a modern historian, Woolfolk shipped nearly 2,300 men, women, and children from Baltimore to Louisiana between 1819 and 1832.[10]

The scale of Woolfolk's operation made Hezekiah Niles and other Baltimore boosters profoundly uncomfortable. Their enthusiasm for commerce did not extend to the rampant buying and selling of human beings. "Cash for Negroes" advertisements made Niles "blush for the honor of the art of printing," and the editor of the *Baltimore American* sought to exclude such ads from his pages. Broaching "a subject shocking to humanity," mayor John Montgomery asked the city council to outlaw private jails where traders held "slaves of both sexes in irons, until sufficient numbers are collected, to be exported."[11]

Although the advertising ban lasted no more than a year, and the city council refused to regulate facilities associated with interstate commerce, large-scale slave-trading moved into the shadows. "The trade is not a clandestine one, but being offensive to the feelings of a large portion of the community, it is in a great measure withdrawn from public observation," reported the Latin lexicographer E. A. Andrews when he visited the city in 1835. Woolfolk, for example, regularly conveyed his human cargo to the docks under the cover of night. To critics, this practice was designed "so as to avoid the public gaze, and prevent examination." In both the popular and abolitionist press, Baltimore's slave trade took on the attributes of gothic horror: dungeons, chains, gags, dark carriage rides in the dead of night, and scenes of terror along the foggy waterfront, all orchestrated by a cabal of stealthy predators.[12]

The domestic slave trade was terrifying, and the psychic costs to enslaved people great. Although most Baltimore slaves were not themselves survivors of the Middle Passage, the lore of that trauma must have made the prospect of being loaded onto a New Orleans–bound boat especially horrific. On their visit to the Baltimore almshouse in 1831, Alexis de Tocqueville and Gustave de Beaumont encountered an African American man made insane from fear of Austin Woolfolk. "The Negro of whom I speak imagines that this man sticks close to him day and night and snatches away bits of his flesh," observed Tocqueville in a literal description of man stealing. In a novelistic retelling of his American travels, Beaumont used this "furiously demented Negro" to denounce the cruelties of the slave trade. "His madness presented a horrifying spectacle and made a painful impression upon me," recalled Beaumont's narrator as he explained the man's fear that Woolfolk "was constantly at his side, awaiting the moment when he could cut out from his body strips of flesh." Readers of *Marie* learned that Woolfolk "was, perhaps, the foremost dealer in human flesh in the United States; all the colored population knew and abhorred him; it seemed that all the vileness of slavery was personified in him." Descriptions of Woolfolk's "dungeons" appeared regularly in antislavery writings, as did the tragic suicides of men and women about to be shipped from Maryland to the Deep South.[13]

The rising value of Baltimore slaves assured not only that more of them would be sold to the cotton frontier, but also that those left behind would have less leverage in securing freedom. In the 1810s and 1820s, many slaveholders had refused to sell slaves out of state. Of the *Baltimore Patriot* advertisements offering life slaves for sale in 1816, one-third excluded purchasers who would transport slaves beyond Maryland's borders. When the General Register Office opened in 1821 as a rendezvous for buyers and sellers, it too banned speculators and offered slaves "for this State only." But by the 1830s, comparable restrictions on purchasers had largely disappeared, suggesting that Baltimore slaves had less capacity for influencing the outcome of sales.[14]

Rising prices in the national market were likely passed along to Baltimore slaves seeking to negotiate self-purchases. Term slaves also labored under greater vulnerabilities, as owners found new excuses to renege on promises of freedom, and traders carried them illegally into states where delayed manumissions had no legal standing. While the domestic trade encouraged Baltimore slaves to run away, it raised the stakes for those who attempted to escape. As the market value of slaves rose, so too did the rewards for capturing runaways. Only a handful of slaves in the 1810s warranted $100 rewards, but by the 1830s, rewards of $200 and $300 were more frequent. Forty-year-old Pompey rated such a reward as someone "generally known about the markets in Baltimore, having been employed for a considerable time in the capacity of market-man." Likewise for twenty-five-year-old Moses Bennett, a skilled sailor whose St. Mary's County owner had been sending him to Baltimore for more than a decade.[15]

Larger rewards and an awareness of the market value of slaves proved enticing to some of the city's poor white residents, including Johnston Karney and Samuel Quay, who found themselves in possession of the runaway Rachel in June

1819. Fetching beer from his basement, Quay had discovered Rachel hiding behind a barrel. He and his wife, Isabella, listened to Rachel's account of running
away from an abusive master and agreed to allow her to stay the night. The beer
had a different effect on Quay's friend Karney, who hatched a plan to cash Rachel
in. But rather than wait for an advertisement to appear in the newspaper in hopes
of garnering a reward, Karney sought higher returns by selling the girl to Austin
Woolfolk. The ruse ultimately collapsed, and both Quay and Karney went to prison,
but theirs was hardly the cleverest attempt to convert a captured runaway into a
tidy profit. In 1827, one Baltimore man posed as the famed antislavery Quaker
Elisha Tyson (deceased for several years) in order to lure a South Carolina runaway
into custody. The renown of the Tyson family for filing freedom suits on behalf
of enslaved men and women made the trap irresistible. Baltimore's crowded alleys
still shrouded runaways, but larger rewards gave escaped slaves greater reason to
be leery of neighbors. The dangerous dash for the Pennsylvania line became a
risk worth taking.[16]

"The state and condition of the slaves in Maryland, is not to be considered so
deplorable, perhaps, (in one sense of the word) as in some other parts of the United
States," observed the Maryland Anti-slavery Society in 1826. After all, enslaved
men and women in Baltimore had used what power they possessed to gain concessions from their owners. Forced to protect bondage in the short term by granting freedom in the long term, Baltimore slaveholders codified delayed manumissions and offered the resulting term slaves protection from being sold out of
state. Other slaveholders acceded to self-purchasing agreements, fundamentally
exploitative but with tremendous benefit to the person able to purchase his or her
liberty. Many enslaved adults resided outside of the direct surveillance of their
owners, hired their own time, and organized their lives in ways that approximated
freedom. Such practices seemingly made Baltimore slavery "mild, in comparison
with that experienced by those in more southern latitudes." But the intensification of the domestic slave trade indicated otherwise, for "in no state in this con-
federacy" were slaves "more subject to the painful and distressing evils of family
separation, and the grievous consequences resulting from it." Recall, for example, the fate of Equillo and his relatives once Sarah Goldsmith's executor sold them
apart in the late 1820s.[17]

The ramifications of the domestic slave trade were also substantial for African
American families living in freedom. "While the southern market holds out in-
ducements for the slaveholder to sell, it also urges him to kidnap, smuggle, and
purchase again to meet the demand," observed William Lloyd Garrison. He might
have had in mind the story of twenty-five-year-old Fortune Lewis, who was

knocked unconscious on Baltimore's Pratt Street and conveyed to the District of Columbia for sale in 1822. Although his captors picked his pockets of money, they missed his freedom certificate, and only by that stroke of luck did Lewis have his freedom restored.[18]

Kidnapping schemes took many forms. Hack driver Reuben Shipley lured Henry Adams into his coach and proceeded to a nearby boardinghouse to sell the free black man to a waiting purchaser. Another free Baltimore man traveled to Norfolk with an employer, who promptly tried to sell him there as a slave. The 1822 kidnapping of Bill Johnson, a thirteen-year-old indentured boy, revealed the cooperation of two criminals, one black and one white. James Callahan and John Bauseman pretended to take Johnson to see his mother, but instead delivered the boy to a man "who purchased negroes for the *southern market*." Only the fortuitous interference of Baltimore's Protection Society thwarted "the infamous plan of the *white* and *black* kidnappers." Founded in 1816, the Protection Society was one of several short-lived benevolent organizations that fought the illegal enslavement of Baltimore residents. Their efforts saved James Johnson, a free barber, from being carried to New Orleans as a slave in 1821. Johnson made a poor target, as "a resident of the neighborhood for the last ten years, who always acted as an honest upright person, sued and was sued, and in every respect was known as a free man." Nonetheless, his close scrape with kidnappers suggests the vulnerability of even the most successful free people of color. African American men and women with the skills, aspirations, and resources to move out of poverty could be taken as slaves with near impunity.[19]

Black families making the transition from slavery to freedom found themselves regularly imperiled by seemingly ancient titles to the bodies of one or more members. At the start of 1827, Joshua and Margaret Fennell assumed their family's firm footing in freedom. Margaret and their three daughters had exited slavery in 1820, a process that had begun three years earlier when their owner converted them into term slaves. But before their manumission dates arrived, the owner died. Such deaths often triggered sales to settle the deceased's estate and imperiled earlier promises of manumission, but in this case, the owner's executor accelerated the process by granting Margaret and the girls to Joshua (who was already free) as "a free gift." Reunited in freedom, Joshua and Margaret built new lives for themselves and saw the arrival of two new grandchildren. However, in 1827, a newly surfaced claim on the estate of the original owner sent the executor, Amos Ogden, Jr., scrambling for $800 and back into the lives of the Fennells.[20]

Ogden went to court to challenge his own "gift," claiming that the estate still owned Margaret, her daughters, and their daughters too. He contended that the two granddaughters had no claim on freedom because Maryland law established the children of term slaves as slaves-for-life unless otherwise specified. Ogden ultimately succeeded in imprisoning four members of the Fennell family before the case was litigated. Surviving records do not reveal whether the Fennells fended off this attack on their integrity, but cases of this nature drew the attention of Baltimore reformers. "There have been instances where two or three generations of children have been seized and reduced to slavery, by the posterity of the original master, who, no doubt, never intended to reclaim them," explained the Anti-slavery Society of Maryland in 1827, perhaps in direct reference to the plight of the Fennell family. The organization's efforts to prevent the seizure of de facto free people (that is, enslaved people living "at large") through a statute of limitations met no legislative success.[21]

The Fennell case offers a telling example of how the chattel principle gave slavery in Baltimore such longevity in the lives of African American families and in the urban economy as a whole. Ogden did not need the Fennells to toil in a cigar manufactory or to staff a boarding house as maids and cooks. He sought them because they could be readily transformed into the $800 for which he was liable. Historians have long thought the market a solvent on the bonds of slavery in a place like Baltimore, where a large cadre of free workers competing for wages provided employers with a cheaper form of labor. The relative productivity of enslaved and free workers in an urban setting, however, offers only part of the story. Situating Baltimore in the regional economy of the American South reveals that the market could serve to entrench slavery as readily as to undermine it. Distant purchasers on the cotton frontier gave Baltimore slaveholders a powerful incentive to hold firmly to slavery even after it had been supplanted by other sources of labor in the city. To be sure, Baltimore slaveholders were not outspoken proslavery ideologues and were slower than their peers to the south in proclaiming slavery a positive good. Baltimore slaveholders were more likely to envision a slave-free (and African American–free) Maryland, achieved through African colonization or the sale of most slaves to the lower South. But until that day arrived, they reaped the benefits of a political economy that converted their ownership of human beings into liquid capital.

The fruits of that transmutation could be seen in the beautiful homes of wealthy families, the increasingly refined architecture of the urban landscape, and the cultivated displays of elite sociability. As importantly, the artifacts of that transmutation—a broadside announcing a reward for a runaway, a "Negroes Wanted" ad in the newspaper, a blank slave-sale form available from a local printer—offered an object lesson in human commodification. The chattel principle made it easier to conceptualize workers as commodities, a development with consequences for the city's free laborers as well.

Labor Is Good to Eat

"Labor is a commodity," declared Baltimore newspaperman Hezekiah Niles in 1835, "and persons may dispose of, or purchase it, at discretion the same as bread and meat." The antislavery Niles was not defending Baltimore's prominence in the national slave market, even as his words evoked the buying and selling of human beings just a few blocks from his office, and indeed, without much difference from vending a barrel of flour or a side of beef.[22] Niles championed a different model for buying and selling the brawn of a stevedore or the stamina of a laundress: a marketplace of "free labor" in which employer and employee met as legal equals to exchange work for wages. Such deals were struck thousands of times a day in Baltimore, but the wage system was hardly recognized as the self-evident way to organize an entire economy. Wage earning itself was a suspect activity associated with unmanly dependence, rather than a hallmark of self-owned freedom. For that to change, it was necessary for people like Niles to promulgate several social fictions: that buyers and sellers of labor met in a metaphorical marketplace; that they did so as legal equals; that impartial forces of supply and demand set the rate of wages; and that the market distributed its rewards fairly to those who earned them through diligence and industry.[23]

Historians have described "free labor" as an ideological project whose success as a shorthand for the social relations of the wage system owed much to crafty wordsmiths, clever lawmakers, and those far more likely to hire labor than to perform it. Baltimore certainly possessed the necessary resources for an ideological recasting of wages as normative. Niles had the most prominent platform as the editor of the national newspaper of record. A relentless celebrant of the American "home market," Niles foresaw prosperity in the national integration of manufacturing, commerce, and agriculture. Of the three, manufacturing was the weakest link, and the protariff Niles rarely missed the chance to celebrate the opening of a new factory or the possibilities of a new invention.[24] As Niles gathered news to propel his developmental agenda forward, Baltimore lawyer Daniel Raymond provided intellectual support in his two-volume *Elements of Political Economy* (1823). One of the first writers in the United States to engage Adam Smith and David Ricardo in substantive dialogue, the New England–born Raymond predicated his findings on what one historian has called "the divine law of labor," or the notion that human beings must earn their wealth through the sweat of their brows. Like other political economists, Raymond saw market forces as the basic determinant of whether labor would be remunerated sufficiently to purchase bread.[25]

Elite cultural production advanced the free-labor ideal, but not in a vacuum. As legal scholars have argued, jurists played a key role in collapsing labor to two basic categories, enslaved and free. State court cases from around the nation created (in theory) a stark division between the bound condition of enslaved workers and the status of all other workers who could presumably claim ownership of their own bodies, the right to choose their own employers, the privilege to work free from physical violence, the ability to quit, and the capacity to defend their earnings and property in court. In practice, that dichotomy made little sense so long as married women could not own their own wages, free people of color could not testify against whites in court, and free white men forfeited wages they had already earned if they left a job prematurely. But as a legal fiction, the notion of only two categories of labor seemed unproblematic to a growing segment of the population, including many working people themselves. Large enterprises (like the Baltimore & Ohio Railroad), local juries, and trade unionists alike found an advantage in casting labor as a form of property whose value was subject to market forces. But whether they reified workers as "hands," gave workers more leeway to sell their time to the highest bidder, or demanded the right to bargain for better wages, the common denominator was an understanding of labor as a commodity.[26]

Consider the telling example of the five hundred indentured servants brought to Maryland in the summer of 1829 to work on the Chesapeake & Ohio Canal. Already employing 3,000 men in the Maryland countryside, the C&O sought to augment its workforce with bound labor imported from Britain. In exchange for ocean passage, these workers owed the company three months' labor, after which they could expect $10 per month in wages, plus food, shelter, and liquor. After a debilitating voyage, several hundred of these men found the conditions on the canals intolerable and they absconded; some fled upon stepping foot on American soil. Two recaptured men filed a habeas corpus petition in federal court and purportedly declared "they could not make themselves slaves." Initially, in a decision tinged with regret, the court upheld Maryland's 1715 law compelling their performance. However, when the C&O began legal proceedings against other absconded laborers in the Baltimore city court, the results were different. The C&O had the right to sue runaway workers in civil trials, but it was clear that juries had far more sympathy for the workers' right to pursue better wages in the city or along its pet project, the B&O Railroad. These workers could not be compelled to work, and the failed use of indentured labor along the C&O suggests a broader consensus around the idea that employers must compete with one an-other in the market to recruit and retain workers, while laboring people could le-gitimately use their mobility to seek better opportunities.[27]

In the aftermath of the C&O debacle, employers did not stop trying to compel labor through legal bonds, any more than workers suddenly began reaping living wages through their market freedom. But as Baltimore witnessed the massive ex-pansion of its wage-earning population in the 1820s and early 1830s, the ques-tion of how labor would be brought to the market—and understood once there—became more pressing. The city's poor relief regime, for example, sought to discourage impoverished people from relying on the almshouse for support. The less-eligibility policy presumably made it more desirable to continue to search for work in the city than to sacrifice one's freedom in the almshouse.

New institutions like public schools and moral reform associations also oper-ated from the premise that labor was self-owned property that individual work-ers must be prepared to vend in the marketplace. Advocating nondenominational schools akin to those operating in Boston, Baltimore's city council contended that public schools offered "the best corrective to pauperism" by instilling in the chil-dren of working parents the moral values essential to upward mobility. After a series of ward meetings, petitions, elections, state laws, and local ordinances, Bal-timore opened three public schools for white children in the fall of 1829. A pro-posal circulated the following year to open a House of Refuge to "send [juvenile delinquents] forth to usefulness, as honest and industrious members of society." The larger thrust of moral reform—especially in the context of a vibrant evangel-ical culture—was toward individual self-possession and the ability to compete in the marketplace.[28]

Of all the voluntary associations contributing to the notion of labor as a com-modity, none played a larger role than the trade unions of skilled artisans. Rela-tively quiet during the 1810s and early 1820s, Baltimore trade unions reemerged at the end of the decade to protect the declining economic prospects of skilled workers. Their first obligation was to establish their right to organize and engage in collective action, for strikes were of questionable legality, and the organizers of earlier efforts faced jail time for conspiracy. To gain standing, artisan leaders embraced the fiction that workers and employers met as equals in the market-place. If employers could combine their resources as capital, then workers could combine *their* resources and constitute themselves as unions. In the bargaining that followed, the only issue was how much work would be exchanged for how much money. Indeed, when Niles declared labor a commodity like bread and meat, he added that the only reasonable limitation on its sale was the length of the workday. The fundamental assumptions of capitalist labor relations were not up for negotiation, and after the ten-hour day was established with minimal controversy in Baltimore (relative to Boston and Philadelphia, where the issue was far more contentious), pay was all that remained to haggle over.[29]

Surprisingly, Niles's desire to bring an increasing amount of labor to the marketplace did not antagonize skilled workers invested in the prerogatives of the older craft workshop. Instead, when Hezekiah Niles sought election to state office in 1831, he was transformed from an elite printer into "the Working-Man." As one broadside implored, "let us elect our old faithful friend and MECHANIC, the man that has been working for us for 30 years, and endeavoring to raise up our character, and get us good wages for our labor." The fact that Niles ran as a National Republican posed a small problem, but as his working-class supporters argued, "Jacksonism should not prevent us from voting for Hezekiah Niles."[30]

As the mudmachinists and street scrapers watched the colorful artisan parades from the sidewalks (not having been invited to march with them in various civic celebrations), their prospects were deeply affected by the concessions that skilled laborers made to the wage system. Common wage laborers had little leverage as they attempted to negotiate the terms of their employment in the 1830s. Their periodic, and noticeably unmilitant, petitions for $12\frac{1}{2}$¢ or 25¢ raises suggest that the game was over before it was begun.

Low-end workers also had to cope with a more crowded labor pool as impoverished European immigrants began coming to Baltimore in great numbers at the end of the 1820s. Although Baltimore in no way rivaled New York as a point of entry, it did surpass Boston, Philadelphia, and New Orleans in welcoming immigrants during the early 1830s. Nearly 41,000 "foreigners" disembarked in Baltimore between 1827 and 1834. Over 11,000 had fled Europe's 1832 cholera epidemic. Health administrator Samuel Martin successfully defended the city from similar epidemics, but feared future "difficulties and embarrassments while the tide of emigration sets so rapidly in upon us, nay almost to overflowing."[31]

The arrival of tens of thousands of European immigrants massively expanded the pool of workers in search of hire, but their travails made crime, disease, and poverty increasingly visible and undermined Baltimore's promise of opportunity to all comers. It is impossible to know how many of these immigrants remained in the city, but almshouse records reveal that Irish and German inmates came to outnumber native-born paupers by the early 1830s. Almshouse administrators believed that European nations were shipping the inhabitants of their own poorhouses to the United States as a cost-saving measure. Attempting to pull up the welcome mat, Baltimore civic leaders asked the Maryland legislature to help combat "the annoyance we experience from a swarm of foreign beggars of both sexes and all ages, who infest our streets and who we have every reason to believe constitute the very refuge population of foreign cities." Penalties on ship captains and head taxes on immigrants did little to slow the arrival of those who had nothing but their own labor power to sell.[32]

Baltimore was ready to deploy the labor of the most desperate immigrants on the internal improvement projects emanating from the city. The Baltimore & Ohio Railroad functioned as the test case for the large-scale mobilization of wage labor. By the time ground was broken on the B&O in 1828, its president, Philip E. Thomas, had spent nearly a decade making sure that Baltimore workers would sustain themselves through labor and labor alone. First as a leader of the city's Society for the Prevention of Pauperism and then as a trustee of the almshouse, Thomas contended that virtually all forms of charity—including such make-work enterprises as the House of Industry—discouraged workers from fending for themselves. But as the rising number of almshouse admissions and labor strife on railroad construction sites made clear, institutionalization was not always a worse choice than selling one's labor on the open market.[33]

In 1834, Baltimore militias intervened in Prince George's County, where factions of Irish B&O employees were harassing local residents and battling one another. A group of alarmed property owners decried the laborers as "a gang of ruffians and murderers, combined together under the most solemn ties to carry into effect such hellish designs as their passions or prejudices may prompt them to commit." Three hundred laborers were arrested and marched to the Baltimore city jail. Those workers who had avoided arrest then made their way back to Baltimore to regroup. The *Baltimore Republican*, the city's Jacksonian newspaper, spoke in their defense. Had the contractors exploited the workers less, "we would be spared the disagreeableness of seeing three hundred persons marched through our city, whose patched and tattered garments, whose long and squalid beards, and emaciated countenance, plainly indicated that they had suffered the greatest privations."[34]

The marked bodies of the B&O workers made urban spectators as uncomfortable as did Austin Woolfolk's nocturnal slave marches to the docks. A Quaker, Philip Thomas had surely hoped the two kinds of commodified labor would never be confused for one another. In fact, what distinguished the B&O from numerous other Chesapeake internal improvements was the exclusion of enslaved workers. Just as the subcontractors responsible for segments of the track were banned from compensating workers in alcohol, so too were they prohibited from using slave labor. In organizing railroad construction in this manner, Thomas contributed to the perception that Baltimore must cast its lot with either slavery or free labor. Replacing one model of commodified labor with another, however, did not automatically alleviate human suffering, as the ragged workers on the B&O made clear.[35]

Certainly Thomas was not alone in envisioning all labor as belonging to self-owned individuals who bargained with employers over the rate of pay. It made no difference, presumably, whether the employer was an individual or one of the nation's most highly capitalized corporations. Such an uneven contest was not necessarily alarming. "We are disposed, for the sake of argument, to admit that capital has an advantage over labor," explained the editor of the *Baltimore Daily Transcript* in 1836. Yet, it could not be otherwise so long as "talent gives its possessor a power to push his fortunes beyond the man of plodding industry."[36] Celebrating the capacity of an impartial market to dole out material rewards, the advocates of American economic development rarely paused to explore the consequences of transforming labor into an undifferentiated commodity "like bread and meat." In the ensuing scramble, those selling their labor like bread and meat would find it increasingly difficult to afford either, while their spent bodies revealed the voraciousness with which the market could consume them.

"The Negro Is Always a Negro"

As a Baltimore worker eligible to be sold like bread and meat, the twenty-year-old enslaved caulker Frederick Bailey recognized the perils of commodified labor for working people in the city. The declining fortunes of Maryland's tobacco economy meant that Eastern Shore slaves were increasingly sent to Baltimore to earn wages (as was the case for Bailey) or to be sold to the cotton frontier (as was the case for some fifteen of his close relatives, many by Austin Woolfolk no less). Bailey was one of the lucky ones, a point he emphasized once he escaped slavery and took the surname Douglass in 1838. Frederick Douglass's several years of labor in Baltimore attested to the reinforcing logic of the chattel principle and the free-labor ideal. The former sanctioned violence against all black workers regardless of their legal status and invested Maryland owners like Thomas Auld in preventing their slaves from escaping. The latter assured that Douglass would circulate from employer to employer in search of a day's wages, albeit at a rate that would not guarantee subsistence to a man with aspirations to a family. Wage labor and slavery converged as Douglass hired out his own time and then promptly handed over his wages each week. The slaveholder "received all the benefits of slaveholding without its evils," while Douglass "endured all the evils of a slave, and suffered all the care and anxiety of a freeman."[37]

Douglass was rightfully indignant about the outright theft of his labor but unduly optimistic about what wages could buy in Baltimore. As a skilled caulker, he earned $1.50 a day, at least 50 percent more than the street scrapers did and more than twice what domestic servants and seamstresses could earn. His future wife, a freeborn woman named Anna Murray, scraped by on the "economy of makeshift" typical of menial laborers in the city. When Murray pawned a feather bed to purchase Douglass a railroad ticket to make his escape, this was not likely the first time she had put her belongings into hock, if only to meet the more mundane expenses of paying rent or purchasing firewood. At the same time, the "hungry little urchins" who had once helped Douglass learn to read attested to the material privation facing white families reliant on wages. Their access to bread—a product whose own price was now pegged to the market with the termination of Baltimore's bread assize—depended upon whether their fathers could find work for more than nine months a year and whether their mothers were agile in stretching low wages into sustenance. Contrary to the narrative arc of Douglass's own life story, working for wages did not guarantee an escape from material privation.[38]

The constrained livelihoods of most people of color in Baltimore highlighted the limitations of market freedom for those lacking a commensurate legal freedom. Those most invested in the social fictions of a market society had two choices. Douglass took the first: to attack the legal inequalities that disadvantaged blacks. Even while still enslaved in Baltimore, Douglass joined a secret debating society, challenged the accommodationist leaders of black churches, and socialized informally with free men of color, all the while developing arguments in favor of abolition and civic equality.[39]

Hezekiah Niles and the majority of white commentators in Baltimore took the second: to attack black people for giving lie to the notion that an impartial market distributed rewards according to merit. While recognizing the force of legal discrimination, Niles nonetheless thought it easier to eliminate black people from Maryland than to alter the white prejudices that created inequalities before the law. Niles was not an active colonizationist but looked forward to a day when slaves and free people of color no longer lived in Maryland. White workers were not inherently better, only made so in the context of a legal system that precluded black upward mobility. "[T]hat which leads white persons to acquire knowledge, merit, distinction, and gain wealth, has but a small influence over the poor negro, because he cannot enjoy such things, if obtained," Niles explained. To be sure, Niles admitted his acquaintance with "several persons of color who are more worthy of confidence than whites of their class generally are" and who but "for the color of their skins, would rise to eminence." And yet, nothing could be done: "the negro is always a negro—in a class of his own; not for crimes by himself committed, but by the repulsive feelings of the whites."[40]

Other prominent whites in Baltimore were less generous. The chief justice of the city's criminal court, Nicholas Brice, denounced all free people of color as "a sort of middle class, neither slave nor free" and thereby "exempted from many of the motives for obedience which influence slaves, and possessed of some rights in common with free men which encourage them in acts of insubordination." Brice hoped that Maryland could enact a program of gradual emancipation coupled with forced colonization.[41]

For Douglass, Niles, Brice, and an increasing number of observers, Baltimore's position between slavery and freedom was untenable. No event raised the stakes higher than Nat Turner's 1831 slave revolt in Southampton County, Virginia. In the wake of rumors of a regional race war, panicked whites in Baltimore transformed the ambiguous status of the city's self-employed slaves and free people of color into an alarming social problem. The resolution brought intensified racial domination but neither a Baltimore free of slavery nor one where earning wages held the promise of making a living.

In August 1831, a handful of enslaved Virginians planned to execute slaveholders in the countryside, gather additional arms and men, and march on the small town of Jerusalem. The uprising fell apart quickly, but not before more than sixty whites and several hundred blacks met violent deaths. Whereas many of the slave rebels were immediately captured, the putative leader, Nat Turner, disappeared into the woods. Several months elapsed before he was caught.[42] From the outset, rumors swirled about the extent of the uprising, the whereabouts of Turner, and the outbreak of similar revolts throughout the South. Baltimore newspaper readers, for instance, learned that rebellious slaves in North Carolina had burned Wilmington and were on their way to Raleigh. Rumors of uprisings continued through the fall, with several mysterious missives arriving at Baltimore's city hall to provide word of impending violence. A confiscated letter to a black resident of Fells Point told of "eight hundred people in town that were going to help murder the damd white people." With Turner still at large (as far as people in Baltimore knew), the plan for "the overthrow of the whites" seemed plausible, even its proposal to kill everyone except Quakers, whom "we can make work for us when we get possession of the country." Elevating fears through the fall months was intermittent news of "the rising of the Blacks" on Maryland's Eastern Shore, in Baltimore County, and even along Saratoga Street, where black men in military uniforms reportedly performed drills under the cover of night.[43]

Meanwhile, at James Lucas and Emanuel Deaver's print shop on Calvert Street, artisans furiously set the type of the explosive *Confessions of Nat Turner*. Baltimore readers were the nation's first to confront the purported words of the leader of the Southampton insurrection and Thomas R. Gray's reflections on the potential of enslaved people to commit horrific violence. "Each particular community should look to its own safety," warned Gray. The next Nat Turner—a slave with a lenient master and whose calm exterior masked murderous rage—could live and work in Baltimore as surreptitiously as anywhere else.[44]

The repercussions of Nat Turner's insurrection were immediate in Baltimore, but white fears focused less on the city's slaves than on the free population of color. "The diabolical butcheries recently committed by the blacks in Virginia, have produced, naturally, great excitement," reported one Baltimore newspaper, and "left the public mind favourably disposed to any practical plan to get rid of the Free Blacks."[45] Events in Southampton provided ammunition to advocates of exiling black Americans to West Africa. In 1832, the state of Maryland pledged $200,000 to create Maryland-in-Liberia as an enterprise completely distinct from the project of the American Colonization Society. The colony at Cape Palmas received its first Maryland settlers the following year. Nat Turner remained a potent symbol for the project's advocates. "Maryland had been taught a lesson, written in characters of blood, in the scenes which had been witnessed, almost within sight of her borders, and her people determined to profit by the instruction," explained the *Address of the Young Men's Colonization Society, to the Young Men of Maryland* in 1835.[46]

The defamation of free people of color was a staple of colonizationist rhetoric. After all, the best argument for the huge expenditure of transporting tens of thousands of people across the ocean was the greater cost in not doing so. "It is unnecessary to explain to the citizens of Maryland the evils of a colored population; they see and feel them daily," noted a committee of Maryland legislators assigned to study the viability of colonization in 1832.[47] Advocates of removal cited crime statistics to prove that free people of color were dangerous, church statistics to show they were hopelessly immoral, and health statistics to suggest they would die en masse under the burdens of freedom.[48]

For some whites in Baltimore (as was the case in Virginia as well), Nat Turner's insurrection prompted calls for the abolition of slavery. But the more common response was to declare black people unsuited for freedom, while at the same time curtailing freedom significantly. The colonizationists "design to make us miserable here, that we may emigrate to Africa with our own consent," observed William Watkins, a contributor to Garrison's *Liberator* under the penname "A Colored Baltimorean." As the Turner panic gripped Baltimore in October 1831, Alexis de Tocqueville heard nearly the same thing from a local informant. "People want to make living in Maryland unbearable for them," reported John H. B. Latrobe, the future president of the Maryland State Colonization Society.[49]

The attack on free people of color invariably compromised African Americans still living in slavery. Proclaiming the hopeless prospects of free blacks but lacking the infrastructure to remove them from the United States in any substantial number, colonizationists discouraged slaveholders from granting freedom to Baltimore slaves. Asked about manumission by Tocqueville, Latrobe noted it was possible, "but we often notice that freeing them produces great troubles, and that the freed negro finds himself more unhappy, and more stripped of resources than when a slave." When colonizationists were not masking their arguments in philanthropy, they cut right to the chase: "You may manumit the slave, but you cannot make him a white man," argued Robert Goodloe Harper. Even the most virulently antislavery white writers adopted a fatalist tone that absolved them of responsibility for discrimination against free people of color. "If our slaves could be delivered from a state of bondage at once, and compelled still to dwell among us, it would not better their condition, or cause them to be more respected, happy, or independent," explained John Hersey, one of the leading religious figures in early republic Baltimore. "In this country, the black man must ever remain a degraded, insulted, and oppressed character."[50]

There is no way to determine how many Baltimore slaveholders ceased to offer manumissions as a way to avoid adding another free person of color to the city's population. The rise of the free black population during the 1830s suggests that manumissions continued apace, but it is certainly easy to imagine that some individual slaves had greater difficulty negotiating self-purchase with owners whose ears were bombarded with screeds against the supposed free black menace. In the aftermath of Nat Turner's rebellion, Maryland adopted a law requiring newly manumitted slaves to leave the state, and although the law was almost never enforced in Baltimore, the legal threat of exile may also have deterred enslaved men and women from pursuing formal manumissions.[51]

If colonizationists lamented that free blacks in Baltimore had too much freedom, free people of color suffered from a legal code with too much slavery. Passed in response to Nat Turner, the 1832 Act Relating to Free Negroes and Slaves privileged racial status over legal status and subjected free people to many of the same prohibitions and penalties that operated upon slaves. Maryland law raised the specter of reenslavement for free people of color convicted of certain crimes, with the additional possibility of being sold out of state. The law also banned free people of color from moving to Maryland and stipulated fines for employers hiring these illegal workers. There is no evidence that this facet of the law was ever enforced

Minstrel sheet music cover, 1833. The caricatured images on the cover page of this 1830s minstrel song belie the seriousness of the lyrics inside. "Broder let us leave, Bucra lan for Hettee," read the first verse of "Ching a Ring Chaw" (Baltimore: Geo. Willig, Jr. [ca. 1833]). By leaving the United States for Haiti, free people of color would presumably find lives free of exploitative labor and social degradation. Courtesy Brown University Library.

in Baltimore, and white employers had little to fear from the new Black Code. Its power, even when unenforced, hung far more heavily over free black migrants. The fine for settling in Maryland was an enormous $50 a week, and anyone unable to pay could be sold into temporary slavery to cover the costs. By virtue of subsequent legislation, Maryland-born blacks faced new constraints on their rights to market goods in public spaces, to hire out on steamboats plying the Chesapeake, or even to work at jobs that would keep them out past a curfew.[52]

The legal system so disadvantaged free people of color in the urban economy that some observers contended that free blacks were actually worse off than slaves. "These facts cannot probably be questioned," opined E. A. Andrews when he visited Baltimore in 1835, "but in explanation of them it ought not to be forgotten, that a very prominent cause of the degradation of the free blacks, is not their own freedom, but the slavery of others." Slaveholders were "interested in making it appear that freedom is no blessing, and they have, to some extent, the power to prevent its becoming so."[53]

Even under such oppression, free people of color rarely concluded that conditions warranted leaving Baltimore. Several decades earlier, Baltimore's Daniel Coker led a small group of black émigrés to new, if painfully short, lives in Sierra Leone. During the 1820s, however, free blacks in Baltimore argued vociferously against forced colonization on the premise that their pasts and futures were in the United States. The free African American population continued to grow in Baltimore during the 1830s, a migration encouraged by the comparably worse treatment of free blacks in the Maryland countryside. If free people of color did not actively pursue emigration, the premise of a better life elsewhere nonetheless gained traction in popular culture. The minstrel song "Ching a Ring Chaw," whether sung by blacks or about blacks, envisioned their liberation from menial labor and enhanced personal dignity in Haiti. Even as it set its lyrics in caricatured dialect, the words told of the work that would *not* have to be done in Haiti: no hod carrying, oyster opening, sod digging, shop scrubbing, rag picking, wheelbarrow running, or food vending. Just as important were the opportunities for black men to protect daughters from indignities at the hands of whites, and to imagine sons might "rise in glorious splender/And be like Washington, [their] country's defender."[54]

Feeling the Invisible Hand

White supremacy confined people of color in Baltimore, but the flip side was not abundant opportunity for the city's growing population of Euro-American laborers. Consider two sets of petitions arriving at city hall in the 1830s. The first came from free people of color facing legal discrimination in trying to earn a living. To work past an evening curfew, hack driver Alexander Henson needed a white patron to testify he was "a sober, Honest man and worthy of the privilege he asks for." David Roberts worked in the daytime as a porter and at night as an oyster shucker in a restaurant, but walking home late at night, he was "molested by the watch." A white patron also had to petition on his behalf for a passport. Similar requests arrived for waiter Benjamin Ford and beer bottler Perry Boudley, whose brewery shift ran from 10 p.m. until 2 a.m. Black women were less likely to need to travel in search of labor, but their opportunities to earn cash through their labor were also constrained by the presumption that gatherings of black people were inherently disorderly, if not dangerous. When Mary Downs, a former slave, sought to have a dancing party "to raise some money for her own benefit," she needed three white men to petition the city council to grant her permission. Their request identified Downs's previous owner, called her "an Honest, Respectable Woman of Color," and noted that she needed funds "as her Husband is at present absent from Baltimore." Louize Randall had her landlord petition the mayor so that she might have "the liberty of making a super once a weeke as she has a large family of children."[55]

These petitions rang with desperation, but it is instructive to read them alongside those arriving from free white men at the same time. The tenor of the petitions that arrived at city hall from white men seeking one of sixty night watchman positions, for example, highlight the difficulties facing even the most privileged of self-owned workers. John H. Becker applied because "employment at a price adequate to the support of a family cannot be had." Martin Peterson complained, "business is so very dull that he can get no employ and has no other means of supporting himself and family." Bennett Gill sought to become a watchman because he "has never learned aney trade and Depends on Labouring for the support of his family." Joel W. Alcott had a trade but lost a hand in the machinery of the Spring Factory. The accident, he reported, "has greatly incapacitated me for manual Labour." Dennis McGlenn was similarly downwardly mobile, insofar as the death of his horse ended his career as a carter and sent him scrambling for other employment. James Trego was "a man of large family—who is anxious to settle down with them instead of going to sea." A veteran of the War of 1812, Stephen Stimson had "served as a soldier and took part in the toils and dangers of that period," but now found himself unemployed and burdened with "a helpless family." Thomas Donahue "has been unfortunate for some time back, at times without work." Thomas Bennett wanted an appointment because "his occupation as a rigger will not afford a living for his family particularly during the winter." Richard Herrington had lived in Fells Point for many years but now said he was "in very indigent circumstances, having a wife and four children to support, having the prospects of a sad winter before me, and nothing to do." "All I want is to be constantly employed," he added plaintively.[56]

These petitions testified to the struggles of all working men to find steady work and decent wages. Black men had no prospect of being appointed to the growing number of patronage positions on the municipal payroll, but this form of affirmative action for white workers had limited utility. Jobs on the city payroll ultimately promised little in the way of economic security. Watchmen earned a $25 monthly salary that even mayor Jacob Small thought "but a scanty pittance for the arduous duties required of them." A thirty-two-foot-long petition with 1,200 signatures arrived at city hall in 1834 calling for a modest raise to $1 per night. Mud-machinists, street scrapers, and other manual laborers fared no better.[57]

Difficulties intensified for career wage earners like James Gardner, who worked as an oarsman in the boat that conveyed Baltimore's health inspector around the harbor to inspect incoming ships and to visit quarantined patients at the lazaretto. A "laborer" living on Star Alley in Fells Point, Gardner began rowing for the Health Department in 1806, and despite the position lasting only six months each year, he returned every summer through at least 1838. As of 1834, Gardner and his three fellow oarsmen earned $30 each month, which was $5 more than the city watchmen, but in a capacity that brought them only a half-year of steady income. They had to fend for themselves through the winter, when other employment opportunities virtually disappeared. The oarsmen—each "a common ordinary labourour" beset by "the great rise in provisions"—sought raises in 1836, but with no success. In 1838, the city physician Samuel Martin appealed to the mayor on their behalf, noting that during winter months "they have much difficulty in getting even small jobs of work to aid them in support of themselves and families." Martin hoped in particular that Gardner—a thirty-two-year veteran of the boat and known fondly as "Old Jemmy"—could be appointed as a city watchman until his rowing skills were next needed.[58]

City jobs became available at a propitious political moment for white men. The expansion of the franchise to include unpropertied adult white men—a change in Maryland that took place in 1818, well before the typical chronology of "Jacksonian Democracy"—served to further normalize wage labor and those who performed it. If the street scrapers had once been persona non grata in the republican ideology that equated wage labor with degraded dependence, they now became a desirable constituency for candidates seeking office.[59] The politicization of public work left laborers vulnerable to changing administrations but also provided an opening for job seekers. James Polk had served on the city watch, but because he had supported "the Jackson Candidate" in a mayoral election, he was "considered unholy and dismissed forthwith." As a "strenuous supporter" of Jackson, "our present venerable Chief Magistrate," Elijah Threlkeld was also fired. The election of Jesse Hunt, a Democrat, to the mayoralty gave hope to Polk and Threlkeld, just as the 1838 election of Sheppard C. Leakin emboldened another job seeker whose "interests have always been identified with the Great Whig Party."[60]

More significantly, the new patronage economy of public labor combined race, ethnicity, and party affiliation in a volatile mix. Broadsides declared candidates to be the working man's friend, while candidates attacked one another for cutting the wages of city laborers or being unfriendly to the Irish. A month before he was elected mayor in 1826, Jacob Small needed his supporters to reassure the "Irishmen of Baltimore" of his "kindness to Foreigners and Emigrants."[61]

Race emerged as the more salient feature of Baltimore politics, as white day laborers identified themselves with the mainstream camps of the Democrats (Jacksonians) or Whigs (National Republicans). The presumed "threat" posed by free blacks to the livelihoods of white workers figured prominently in Baltimore electioneering. Contrary to developments elsewhere, those identified as Democrats were not the first to exploit the racial resentments of downwardly mobile whites. Seeking election to the state assembly on an anti-Jackson ticket in 1828, Luke Tiernan's supporters asked Baltimore's Irish voters to reject "the Southern policy, which is to employ the negro and not the poor white man to do the work." In the 1836 presidential campaign, Baltimore's white laboring men were once again told that the Democratic Party's nominee preferred black people to whites. Martin Van Buren's election would mean "the control of our institutions may pass into the hands of 'colored people,' as they are called." On one broadside, a caricatured black Van Burenite on the way to voting declares "Stan bak, you poor white trash; you got no property . . . So you poor white bog-trotters and clod-hoppers stan back." By 1840, Van Buren's supporters in Baltimore had turned the tables, celebrating the Democrat's opposition to debt imprisonment and servitude, while claiming that his Whig opponent, William Henry Harrison, "voted to sell a White man into slavery more abhorrent even than negro slavery."[62]

Politicians found a powerful weapon in the notion that blacks and whites were trapped in a zero-sum game. Its impact on elections unclear, such rhetoric nevertheless cast a menacing shadow on Baltimore's future. "We mustn't deceive ourselves; the white and black population are in a state of war. Never will they mingle," explained Benjamin H. B. Latrobe to his guest Alexis de Tocqueville in October

Whig campaign broadside, 1836. Both the Democrats and Whigs used race-baiting strategies in their political campaigns. This Whig broadside lambasted Martin Van Buren, the Democratic nominee for president. Fifteen years earlier during a New York Constitutional Convention, Van Buren had supported property requirements that disfranchised some poor white men while allowing a handful of propertied African American men the right to vote. Now Baltimore voters were told that Van Buren preferred black voters to white ones, even as no African Americans could legally vote in Maryland. Courtesy Library of Congress Printed Ephemera Collection.

1831. "One of them will have to yield place to the other." Tocqueville developed these insights in "The Future Condition of the Three Races in America," a chilling section of *Democracy in America* critical of white racism but ultimately resigned to eventual extinction of those of non-European ancestry. Antiabolitionists in Baltimore threatened to hasten the process: "One hostile movement on the part of the negroes and their comrades, the abolitionists," anticipated the editors of a Fells Point newspaper, "would probably do more toward thinning the colored population than ten years' labor of all the colonization societies put together."[63]

On occasion, inflammatory rhetoric exploded into violence, never more famously than when white journeymen beat Frederick Douglass in a Baltimore shipyard. Workplace violence of this sort was not so exceptional as to warrant public comment at the time, but neither was it typical. Sporadic outbursts of violence failed to create racially exclusive job sites, and in some cases, black victims of white violence attained the legal recourse that Douglass was denied. For example, a white watchman named Armacost lost his job in 1833 for "abusing an innocent coloured man and dragging him away from his own door without any provocation." The following year, another black victim of the watch received justice after surviving a beating at the hands of an officer named Howard. Municipal records reveal "a mutual arrangement has taken place between Howard and the coloured man by which five dollars per month is to be retained in the hands of the officers of the night watch out of Howard's monthly pay until the sum amounts to thirty dollars which is to be paid over to the coloured man for the purpose of paying his Doctor's bill and indemnifying him for the time which he has been and may continue to be unable to work in consequence of the injury which he has sustained."[64]

Such an unusual outcome should not obscure the vulnerabilities of free people of color to violence, but it does suggest the limitations of racial exclusion as a strategy of upward mobility for impoverished whites. Time and again, employers and elected officials proved uninterested in allowing one segment of the working population to restrict another. Even when efforts moved through legal channels, the owners of brickyards, tanneries, and other productive enterprises in Baltimore offered no support to white workers seeking to eliminate black rivals. Likewise, Baltimore employers paid little heed to the advocates of colonization, who offered convoluted, if remarkably assured, analysis of the relationship of race and labor. "The employment of slaves tends to make labour disreputable, and thus to produce indolence, and consequently poverty and vice, among the free; and as all slaves are colored, the employment of colored labourers, even where free, creates or sustains the same prejudice against honest industry," contended the leaders of the Maryland State Colonization Society. "Colored labourers exclude an equal number of whites, who would gladly be industrious and sober, if they could find employment." Baltimore employers remained unconvinced, as evidenced by their frequent advertisements for "A good HAND, either black or white" or "A Woman. (white or black)" to hire.[65]

———

Despite alarming pronouncements, Baltimore's hybrid economy changed little over the course of the early republic period. In the lives of day laborers, domestic servants, and other low-end workers, the color line operated erratically, plunging white and black workers into shared circumstances of economic privation. The violence that befell working people was less explosive and episodic than made mundane and persistent through legalized slavery and the ascendant ideology of market competition.

If Baltimore found no resolution, lucky individuals did. Frederick Douglass's famous escape in 1838 reveals much about labor at the intersection of slavery and freedom. His flight hinged on his risk of being sold to the cotton frontier (a threat levied by Captain Auld), the promise of self-owned labor in the North (his New England destination), Baltimore's thriving port (Douglass escaped dressed as a sailor), its position as a hub of the newest transportation technology (he left via railroad), the close ties between free people of color and slaves (his future wife, Anna Murray, purchased his ticket), the city's vibrant underground economy (he had purchased identification papers from a retired sailor), and the mobility of black and white labor throughout the Chesapeake (he encountered black and white workers he recognized from Baltimore in Havre de Grace and in Wilmington, Delaware).[66]

Douglass would become emblematic of the market's capacity to lift the humblest American to a position of respect, or at least emblematic of the capacity of an individual to transcend the market. His time in Baltimore, however, suggests the vulnerabilities of all working people whose labor constituted a commodity. For Douglass—like Hezekiah Niles and virtually all other celebrants of the free-labor ideal—*choice* was the highest good, tantamount to freedom itself. But law, economic necessity, and the superior power of employers constrained the choices of all workers, even those already free. Dealt a bad hand, they embraced market relations as legitimate when it served their interests, tried to turn market logic back on their employers when viable, resisted it to the best of their ability when it imperiled their families, and in most cases simply coped with it by scrimping and scheming to stay afloat with wages that failed to cover the cost of living.

Douglass once quipped that an advertisement announcing a vacancy for a Maryland slave (presumably to replace him) would turn up no takers, and he was right to insist on the vast gulf separating the lives of slaves from free people. But while the material conditions of those he left behind in Baltimore offered no brief for slavery, neither did they sound a ringing endorsement of the market's power as a force of human liberation.

Conclusion

To tell the story of American opportunity and freedom also requires telling the story of brute labor, severe material privation, and desperately constrained choices. American commercial success has always depended on more than the entrepreneurial energy of merchants and financiers. It has also depended on men digging mud out of harbors and women stitching cheap shirts by candlelight. To focus historical attention on impoverished workers does not obviate the reality of prosperity for a growing percentage of Americans in the early republic period. Quite the contrary, it is only by considering the ways in which human labor was assembled, deployed, and exploited that we can fathom how an increasing number of families were able to partake of a new world of consumer goods, to reside in new kinds of refined houses and neighborhoods, and to attain new standards of respectability.

Whenever human labor is bought and sold as a market commodity, prosperity and privation serve to create and reinforce one another. American civic culture, however, has left little possibility for recognizing the contingencies through which opportunity for some has had its basis in the foreclosing of opportunity for others. Instead, we have articulated as our foundational ideology that material (and perhaps spiritual) rewards follow hard work. This is what makes the United States exceptional, we are told: Americans jettisoned the artificial hierarchies that had long limited human ambition and created a new world of upward mobility for anyone mustering the requisite luck, pluck, and effort. This mythology's genealogy can be traced from Captain John Smith's description of North America as a haven for people of "small means" in 1614, through Benjamin Franklin's artful *Autobiography* and Alexis de Tocqueville's celebration of social mobility, to the rags-to-riches stories that remain a staple of American popular culture. This mythology undergirded Cold War liberalism and can be seen today in the conservative repudiation of the Welfare State. When the current U.S. naturalization exam asks prospective citizens to describe the country's economy, it requires them to answer "capitalist" or "market"; it does not ask them to contemplate the contingent social relations marked by these labels.[1]

Would-be citizens must also know the name of the national anthem, "The Star-Spangled Banner," as well as facts about the flag that shares the same name. To learn this rudimentary history of the War of 1812 is to be invited into America's national story, a story that at first glance has nothing to do with the day laborers, slaves, and seamstresses whose struggles are retold in this book.[2] Yet on closer consideration, these stories are precisely the same—but only if we grasp the centrality of casual and coerced labor to the broader history of American progress.

The most famous flag in America flew over Baltimore's Fort McHenry on September 14, 1814, the morning after the British bombardment. There would not have been a need for a Fort McHenry to protect Baltimore's port had it not been for the labor invested in keeping the harbor open and free of sedimentation. In a war fought largely over issues of commercial navigation, the vitality of Baltimore's harbor explains its importance to British military designs but also situates the lives and livelihoods of the city's mariners, boardinghouse keepers, laundresses, and prostitutes in America's "Second War of Independence."[3]

Well before hostilities broke out in the Chesapeake, Captain George Armistead desired an enormous flag to fly over Fort McHenry—one "so large that the British will have no trouble seeing it from a distance." In 1813, he contracted the job to Mary Pickersgill, a Fells Point widow who supported her mother and her daughter by sewing flags and insignia for ships passing in and out of port. Born in 1776, Pickersgill was not the typical widowed seamstress of the charity appeals, but rather a second-generation flag maker and a businesswoman who relocated her operations from Philadelphia to Baltimore in 1807. The U.S. government paid Pickersgill $406 for a thirty-by-forty-two-foot flag with fifteen broad bars of red and white, and fifteen bright stars affixed to a field of blue.

In some ways, Pickersgill shared common survival strategies with other poor women in Fells Point: she and her mother pooled labor and resources in a multigenerational household lacking a male breadwinner; they took in boarders in a house they rented but did not own; and they depended on sewing work for income. Pickersgill's economic success offers a compelling testament to "female self-sufficiency" in the early republic, as the museum devoted to her memory explains. Of course, Mary Pickersgill was not self-sufficient. No one who worked for a living could be. She was reliant on family labor, including that of her daughter Caroline, but also the work of Grace Wisher, "a free African American apprentice," and another black woman who resided under her roof. Sewing the Fort McHenry flag was such an undertaking that Pickersgill took on additional labor for the summer it took to complete the task. Her neighborhood had no lack of adult white women desperate for sewing work and teenaged girls available for hire.[4]

Without disputing Pickersgill's own diligence and self-denial, her economic viability makes sense only in light of her ability to access other people's labor. In fact, so successful was Pickersgill that by the 1830s, she had become the president of the Humane Impartial Society, the Baltimore charity organization famed for distributing work to needy seamstresses and paying them above market piece rates in return. Just as Christian Baum (the contractor who built the bridge over Jones Falls) makes little sense without the enslaved Equillo, and just as John Robb (the Fells Point warden of the poor) requires Zachariah Stallings as his foil, so too does Mary Pickersgill need another seamstress—one more exposed and dependent than herself—to become an icon of female independence to generations of Baltimore schoolchildren.[5]

The flag that Captain Armistead ordered for Fort McHenry accomplished its mission of attracting the British to Baltimore, and after an entire night of bombing, the flag was raised so that Americans at a great distance would know that the nation had survived the onslaught. The most famous person to see the flag was Maryland lawyer Francis Scott Key, who spied it from the deck of a British ship moored in the Chesapeake. Equally unmistakable from that vantage were defensive fortifications that had been thrown up around Baltimore during the previous weeks. Key wrote a poem about the evening and morning of September 14, 1814: "O'er the ramparts," American citizens glimpsed their flag and rejoiced that the star-spangled banner yet waved.

The building of the ramparts was an extraordinary event in Baltimore's history. Writing to associates in New York, merchant George Douglass observed, "at least a mile of entrenchments with suitable batteries were raised, if by magic." For Douglass, this was a great testament to Baltimore's civic virtue, especially the collective effort of "all sorts of people, old and young, white and black." Mixed-race labor did in fact construct the ramparts, just as groups of white and black men had worked side by side to lay out Baltimore's roads, build its bridges, and sink its piers. The mobilization of manual labor for Baltimore's defense in 1814 conscripted all able-bodied men exempt from militia service or, in other words, noncitizens. That included David Dillon, a thirty-six-year-old Irish Catholic just arrived in Baltimore, whose future held a stint on the mudmachine in 1815 and a stay in the almshouse in 1825. Career manual laborer James Flaugherty also worked on Baltimore's defenses, perhaps aided by his experience as one of the longest employed mudmachinists. "Laborer" Solomon Jackson had been a householder on Camden Street since 1802, and he worked on the Jones Falls bridge under Christian Baum in 1809 before taking up a shovel in defense of country in 1814. Vincent Blake had an equally long residency in Baltimore, while Jesse Bunch had also labored at the New Bridge in 1809. Abraham Benson, Cato Hughes, Nicholas Kinnard, and Uriah Smith were among the free men of color compelled to labor on Baltimore's fortifications. Enslaved men were also ordered to work for the public, although their legal owners were paid for their time. At least one slaveholder was dissatisfied by the loss of income accompanying the city's use of his four slaves. "I think it is too hard for a poor man like me who has six sons to raise and who has no property only them four negroes to support my family," explained Peter Zacharie in search of 50¢ per day per man.[6]

Francis Scott Key was a slaveholder and a colonizationist who hoped that the United States would be liberated not only from British oppression, but also from the presence of African Americans in its midst. Like so many of his generation, Key imagined his nation comprising free white men pursuing manly independence, and he wrote this motif into his famous song. The British had clearly abandoned these republican values, as evidenced in the way they fought the war. In contrast to the United States, where citizens took up arms to defend their rights, the British hired mercenaries and even deployed regiments of enslaved soldiers to fight their battles. Key upbraided the British for bringing "their foul footsteps' pollution" to America's shores. Here, in the now-forgotten third verse of the song that became our national anthem, Key made an explicit contrast between freedom and oppression: *"No refuge could save the hireling and the slave/From the terror of flight, or the gloom of the grave/And the star-spangled banner, in triumph doth wave/ O'er the land of the free and the home of the brave."*[7]

The vast majority of Americans—a people who sing their national anthem and wave their flag to a degree unrivaled in the Western world—know nothing of Key's third verse, and those who do surely take relief that we do not sing about hirelings and slaves at baseball games. But in actuality, that is exactly what we do when we engage in our rituals of civic life.[8] When we sing of the ramparts that David Dillon and Cato Hughes built, when we flock by the millions to the Smithsonian's National Museum of American History to observe the painstaking conservation work on the Fort McHenry flag, when we quiz immigrants about the American economy in order to test their readiness for citizenship, we are in fact recognizing the centrality of hirelings and slaves to whatever claims this nation can make to being the land of the free and the home of the brave.

T he publication of this book offers the opportunity to thank the many people who participated in its making. My ideas and arguments have developed over fifteen years of conversations with teachers, students, and colleagues. Over an even longer period, I have had the support and love of my parents, Saul and Barbara Rockman, to whom this book is dedicated. Tara Nummedal has requested me to spare readers the sappy acknowledgment she deserves.

I received financial support for this project from the Department of History at the University of California, Davis; Occidental College; Brown University; and the Program in Early American Economy and Society at the Library Company of Philadelphia. PEAES director Cathy Matson has shown tremendous patience in waiting for me to finish, and I am grateful for her unflagging support. During my year in residence at the Library Company, John Van Horne, Jim Green, Connie King, Wendy Woloson, and the entire reference staff were generous with their time. Librarians and curators at the American Antiquarian Society, the Maryland State Archives, the Huntington Library, and the Maryland Historical Society treated me kindly. I owe a particular debt to Becky Gunby and Tony Roberts at the Baltimore City Archives. Thanks also to Bob Brugger, the production staff at the Johns Hopkins University Press, and Melanie Mallon. With complete generosity, Lynn Carlson, Geographic Information Systems manager at Brown University, made beautiful maps for this book.

I was not shy in contacting colleagues in search of assistance, and thanks to email, I received help from old acquaintances and total strangers alike. Bill Sutton, Stephen Whitman, Christopher Phillips, Sharon Murphy, and Jim Sidbury were generous in sharing research files with me, and Christopher Curtis, Jason Opal, Sharon Sundue, Larry Peskin, Josh Civin, and Marla Miller allowed me to learn from their works in progress. Bea Hardy, Mary Beth Corrigan, Mary Markey, John Weishampel, Robert Wright, Janice Artemel, Suni Johnson, Michael Gagnon,

Max Grivno, Bill Earle, and Jennie Levine responded to queries I posted on H-Maryland and H-Slavery. I am also grateful to James Kabala, Dorothy Tegeler, Rebecca Lasky, Henry Hoyle, Cryn Johannson, and Tara Schuster for research assistance. Charles Postel, Frank Towers, Jessica Elfenbein, Josh Greenberg, Bridget Ford, Kathleen DuVal, Herb Sloan, Jonathan Earle, and Thomas Hilbink provided necessary encouragement along the way.

Commentators and audiences at numerous conferences and seminars made invaluable suggestions for strengthening the research. I offer particular thanks to Lois Carr, Lorena Walsh, Ruth Herndon, Leslie Harris, Douglas Egerton, Bill Rankin, and Dan Rood for their insights. I benefited from the opportunity to discuss my work at the McNeil Center for Early American Studies; the PEAES seminar at the Library Company of Philadelphia; the Washington, D.C., Early American seminar; the SHEAR conference; the Brandeis University Department of History; the Center for the Study of Race and Ethnicity in America at Brown University; and the Harvard University seminar on the Political Economy of Modern Capitalism.

I am very fortunate to have had such inspirational and supportive teachers. Choosing the graduate program at UC-Davis was perhaps the smartest thing I ever did. The History Department in the 1990s featured an intellectual community and a nonhierarchical culture that I have yet to see replicated elsewhere. I got a lesson in humility from such demanding teachers as David Brody, Karen Halttunen, Clarence Walker, and the late Paul Goodman. Because I performed so unimpressively during my first year, they were eager to dump me off on the new guy, Alan Taylor. Failure has never been better rewarded! Alan taught me to write more, to speak less, and to let the research do the talking. I hope to be as generous a mentor to my graduate students as Alan has been to me.

My colleagues at Occidental College and Brown University have been supportive of this project over its long gestation. For their encouragement, I would like to thank Lynn Dumenil, Norman Cohen, Nina Gelbart, David Axeen, Ted Mitchell, Marla Stone, Michael Vorenberg, Amy Remensnyder, Elliott Gorn, James N. Green, Patricia Ybarra, Nancy Jacobs, and Phil Gould. Steven Lubar offered me a space to write at the John Nicholas Brown Center and shared my enthusiasm for early republic dredging. Robert Self, Mark Swislocki, Naoko Shibusawa, Vazira F-Y Zamindar, Deborah Cohen, Tom Silfen, and Jim Egan improved several chapters with their comments. Two people I have never met, Deborah Valenze and Tim Hitchcock, kindly offered suggestions on draft chapters. Hilary Moss, Lydia Pecker, Mary Ryan, and Peter Wood deserve particular mention for reading the entire manuscript. Jim Campbell offered the most generous reading imaginable and an unforgettable conversation to match. The most sustained critical engagement with the book—and also the most fun—came from a writing group that included Jane Kamensky, Jennifer Roberts, Michael Willrich, Steven Biel, Jonathan Hansen, Daniel Sharfstein, and Conevary Valencius. These folks got me to the finish line, and Seth Cotlar, Leslie Dunlap, Konstantin Dierks, and Sarah Knott pulled me across.

Over the course of writing this book, my undergraduate students have been an inspiration. Whether they have known it or not, people like (and this is an incomplete list) Aliza Narva, Caitlin O'Connor, Christopher Snyder, Paul Lakin, Heather Owen, Sarah Lehmann, Rachael Bedard, Kate Osborn, Jeremy Chase, Matthew Swetnam, Ethan Ris, Alexa Rosenberg, Peiling Li, Sarah Bowman, Karen Kudelko, Liz Sperber, David Krakow, Olivia Geiger, Clara Long, and Lydia Pecker have been my interlocutors in thinking through the problems of class, capitalism, and slavery in American history.

The issues in this book brought me to Baltimore as a historian, but I had been there many times before with my family. My grandparents Morris "Jeff" Rockman and Celia Novick Rockman had both grown up in Baltimore and married there in 1938. They bought a house on Copley Road in Ashburton, and raised my uncle and father (City College H.S. '60). When I arrived in Baltimore to do research in the mid-1990s, my grandfather had already passed away, but I had many opportunities to see my grandmother and to take her grocery shopping, to the public library, or out for an occasional crabcake. It has now been several years since her passing, and I am grateful that this book allows me to reestablish my connection to a place she held dear.

AHR	*American Historical Review*
American	*Baltimore American and Commercial Daily Advertiser*
BAAB	Baltimore Almshouse Admissions Book, ms. 1866.1, Maryland Historical Society Library
BCA	Baltimore City Archives, Baltimore, Md. Although the collection is organized according to record groups, each document has a unique itemization number. Hence, citations contain year and item number (e.g. BCA, 1824:319)
Genius	*Genius of Universal Emancipation*
JAH	*Journal of American History*
JER	*Journal of the Early Republic*
JSH	*Journal of Southern History*
Labor	*Labor: Studies in the Working-Class History of the Americas*
Laws	Session Laws of Maryland, 1785–1840, printed annually by various publishers as *Laws of Maryland Made and Passed at a Session of Assembly* . . . ; *Laws Made and Passed by the General Assembly of the State of Maryland* . . . ; *Laws Made and Passed by the State of Maryland* . . .
LH	*Labor History*
Mayors' Msgs.	*Annual Messages of the Mayors of Baltimore, 1797–1830* (Baltimore: Office of Legislative Reference, n.d.)
MHM	*Maryland Historical Magazine*
MHS	Maryland Historical Society Library, Baltimore, Md.
MSA	Maryland State Archives, Annapolis, Md.
Niles	*Niles' Weekly Register*
OIEAHC	Omohundro Institute of Early American History and Culture

Ordinances	Baltimore Ordinances, 1797–1841, printed annually by various publishers as *Ordinances of the Corporation of the City of Baltimore . . .* or *Ordinances and Resolutions of the Mayor and City Council of Baltimore . . .*
Pardons	Governor and Council (Pardon Papers), 1790–1836, s1061, Maryland State Archives
Patriot	*Baltimore Patriot & Evening Advertiser* (1815–1817); *Baltimore Patriot & Mercantile Advertiser* (1817–1834)
Post	*Baltimore Evening Post*
RSPP	Race and Slavery Petitions Project. Loren Schweninger, ed., *Race, Slavery, and Free Blacks*, Series II: Petitions to Southern County Courts, 1775–1867. Part B: Maryland. (Bethesda, Md.: Lexis-Nexis Microfilms, 2002–)
WMQ	*William and Mary Quarterly*

NOTES

Introduction

1. BCA, 1829:612. "The scavengers should now be often in the streets—filth and nuisance should not be suffered to lie until the atmosphere becomes contaminated with unwholesome effluvia, and the health of the people endangered" wrote "A Tax Payer" (likely T. W. Griffith) in *Patriot*, July 8, 1822. For manure as a municipal concern, see *Ordinances*, 1826.15; *Mayors' Msgs.*, 1830; "Street Manure Account" in *Ordinances*, 1837 (Baltimore: Lucas & Deaver, 1837), app. 21; BCA, 1820:188–197, 1824:195, 1837:938a, 1837:939; *Patriot*, April 17, 1822. For the importance of manure to early agricultural production, see Steven Stoll, *Larding the Lean Earth: Soil and Society in Nineteenth-Century America* (New York: Hill and Wang, 2002); Liam Brunt, "Where There's Muck, There's Brass: The Market for Manure in the Industrial Revolution," *Economic History Review* 60 (May 2007): 333–372.

2. BCA, 1829:612. Two of the petitioning street scrapers, John Thompson and Charles Burns, indicated that they had been picking up manure since 1819. Burns would still be at it in 1836, as would John Hickman, another signatory of the 1829 petition. See BCA, 1836:529, 1837:790. The street scrapers' 75¢ daily wage did not increase until 1836 (*Ordinances*, 1836.40). But even for workers on the ostensibly secure municipal payroll, budget shortfalls caused hardship. By the end of 1836, the Board of Health could pay only 87¢ per day and afford to hire men for four days per week. See *Ordinances*, 1837, app. 10, 11, 21. On petitioning as political action within a broader "culture of beseeching and begging," see Dietlind Hüchtker, "Strategies and Tactics: The Politics of Subsistence in Berlin, 1770–1850," *International Review of Social History* 49 (2004): 437; Lex Heerma van Voss, ed., *Petitions in Social History*, International Review of Social History Supplements 9 (Cambridge: Cambridge University Press, 2001).

3. On "living poor," see Billy G. Smith, ed., *Down and Out in Early America* (University Park: Pennsylvania State University Press, 2004), xviii. *American*, January 8, 1805.

4. On the extent of poverty and privation in early America, see Ruth Wallis Herndon, *Unwelcome Americans: Living on the Margin in Early New England* (Philadelphia: University of Pennsylvania Press, 2001); Simon P. Newman, *Embodied History: The Lives of the Poor in Early Philadelphia* (Philadelphia: University of Pennsylvania Press, 2003); Billy G. Smith, *The "Lower Sort": Philadelphia's Laboring People, 1750–1800* (Ithaca, N.Y.: Cornell University

Press, 1990); Billy G. Smith, *Life in Early Philadelphia: Documents from the Revolutionary and Early National Periods* (University Park: Pennsylvania State University Press, 1995); Carla Gardina Pestana and Sharon V. Salinger, eds., *Inequality in Early America* (Hanover, N.H.: University Press of New England, 1999); Stephan Thernstrom, *Poverty and Progress: Social Mobility in a Nineteenth Century City* (Cambridge, Mass.: Harvard University Press, 1964); Gary B. Nash, *The Urban Crucible: Social Change, Political Consciousness, and the Origins of the American Revolution* (Cambridge, Mass.: Harvard University Press, 1979); Christine Stansell, *City of Women: Sex and Class in New York, 1789–1860* (New York: Alfred A. Knopf, 1986); Lee Soltow, *Distribution of Wealth and Income in the United States in 1798* (Pittsburgh: University of Pittsburgh Press, 1989); Peter Way, *Common Labour: Workers and the Digging of North American Canals, 1780–1860* (New York: Cambridge University Press, 1993); Thomas J. Humphrey, *Land and Liberty: Hudson Valley Riots in the Age of Revolution* (DeKalb: University of Northern Illinois Press, 2004); Shane White, *Somewhat More Independent: The End of Slavery in New York City, 1770–1810* (Athens: University of Georgia Press, 1991); Graham Russell Hodges, *Root and Branch: African Americans in New York and East Jersey, 1613–1863* (Chapel Hill: University of North Carolina Press, 1999); Leslie M. Harris, *In the Shadow of Slavery: African Americans in New York City, 1626–1863* (Chicago: University of Chicago Press, 2003). For slavery as "enforced poverty," see Jon Butler, *Becoming America: The Revolution before 1776* (Cambridge, Mass.: Harvard University Press, 2000), 88; and Philip D. Morgan, "The Poor: Slaves in Early America," in *Slavery in the Development of the Americas*, eds. David Eltis, Frank D. Lewis, and Kenneth L. Sokoloff (New York: Cambridge University Press, 2004), 288–323.

5. The dominant historiography for the post-Revolutionary era—especially that written for a broader audience—has depicted a dynamic nation of strivers in which political democratization and economic prosperity went hand-in-hand. See Gordon S. Wood, *The Radicalism of the American Revolution* (New York: Knopf, 1992); Joyce Appleby, *Inheriting the Revolution: The First Generation of Americans* (Cambridge, Mass.: Harvard University Press, 2000); Walter A. McDougall, *Freedom Just Around the Corner: A New American History, 1585–1828* (New York: Harper Collins, 2004); Daniel Walker Howe, *What Hath God Wrought: The Transformation of America, 1815–1848* (New York: Oxford University Press, 2007).

6. In many ways, this was the challenge posed by Edmund S. Morgan, *American Slavery–American Freedom: The Ordeal of Colonial Virginia* (New York: W. W. Norton, 1975), and reformulated by David Brion Davis, "Looking at Slavery from Broader Perspectives," *AHR* 105 (April 2000): 452–466. On the capacity of different modes of historical inquiry to meet that challenge, see Nathan I. Huggins, "The Deforming Mirror of Truth: Slavery and the Master Narrative of American History," *Radical History Review* 49 (1991): 25–48; Mark P. Leone, "A Historical Archaeology of Capitalism," *American Anthropologist* 97 (June 1995): 251–268; and Fred Wilson, *Mining the Museum: An Installation*, ed. by Lisa G. Corrin (Baltimore: Contemporary; New York: New Press, 1994).

7. Studies of early American labor that situate such a broad range of workers in a broader political economy are few but include David Montgomery, "The Working Classes of the Pre-Industrial American City, 1780–1830," *LH* 9 (Winter 1968): 3–22; Jacqueline Jones, *American Work: Four Centuries of Black and White Labor* (New York: W. W. Norton,

1998); and Peter Linebaugh and Marcus Rediker, *The Many-Headed Hydra: Sailors, Slaves, Commoners, and the Hidden History of the Revolutionary Atlantic* (Boston: Beacon Press, 2000). On the extension of the Cotton South and the persistence of slavery in the Upper South, see Steven Deyle, *Carry Me Back: The Domestic Slave Trade in American Life* (New York: Oxford University Press, 2005). On the global political economy of capitalism, see Eric R. Wolf, *Europe and the People without History* (1982; repr., Berkeley: University of California Press, 1997).

8. In contrast to an older scholarship that described wage relations as the defining feature of capitalist economies, recent efforts have tried to situate multiple modes of deploying social labor (waged, nonwaged, coerced, family, and others) within the same broader capitalist system. The goal is not to collapse the differences between, say, slavery and wage labor (nor to equate the lived experience of enslavement with that of earning wages), but to identify the larger process of social change that accompanied the integration of the global economy in the early modern period. In any given setting, the local configuration of market relations invariably complicates such dichotomies as free/unfree and family/nonfamily labor, in ways Dale W. Tomich has called "simultaneously constitutive of the global system and a particular manifestation of its processes." See Tomich, *Through the Prism of Slavery: Labor, Capital, and World Economy* (Lanham, Md.: Rowman and Littlefield, 2004), 53; Robert J. Steinfeld and Stanley L. Engerman, "Labor—Free or Coerced? A Historical Reassessment of Differences and Similarities," in *Free and Unfree Labor: The Debate Continues*, eds. Tom Brass and Marcel van der Linden (Bern: Peter Lang, 1997), 107–126; Jan de Vries, "The Industrial Revolution and the Industrious Revolution," *Journal of Economic History* 54 (June 1994): 249–270. Scholars of the early republic United States have used "human commodification" as an organizing concept. See David Waldstreicher, "The Vexed Story of Human Commodification Told by Benjamin Franklin and Venture Smith," *JER* 24 (summer 2004): 268–278; Amy Dru Stanley, "Wages, Sin, and Slavery: Some Thoughts on Free Will and Commodity Relations," *JER* 24 (summer 2004): 279–288; Stephanie Smallwood, "Commodified Freedom: Interrogating the Limits of Anti-Slavery Ideology in the Early Republic," *JER* 24 (summer 2004): 289–298; Walter Johnson, "The Pedestal and the Veil: Rethinking the Capitalism/Slavery Question," *JER* 24 (summer 2004): 299–308.

9. For histories of early republic economic change, see Paul A. Gilje, ed., *Wages of Independence: Capitalism in the Early Republic* (Madison, Wis.: Madison House, 1997); Paul E. Johnson, "The Market Revolution," in *The Encyclopedia of American Social History*, eds. Mary K. Cayton, Elliott J. Gorn, and Peter W. Williams (New York: Charles Scribner's Sons, 1993), 1:545–560; Edward Pessen, "The Egalitarian Myth and the American Social Reality: Wealth, Mobility, and Equality in the 'Era of the Common Man,'" *AHR* 76 (October 1971): 989–1034; Charles Sellers, *The Market Revolution: Jacksonian America, 1815–1846* (New York: Oxford University Press, 1991); Richard L. Bushman, "Markets and Composite Farms in Early America," *WMQ* 55 (July 1998): 351–374; Naomi R. Lamoreaux, "Rethinking the Transition to Capitalism in the Early American Northeast," *JAH* 90 (September 2003): 437–461; Daniel Vickers, "Competency and Competition: Economic Culture in Early America," *WMQ* 47 (January 1990): 3–29; John Lauritz Larson, *Internal Improvement: National Public Works and the Promise of Popular Government in the Early United States* (Chapel Hill: University of North

Carolina Press, 2001); Carol Sheriff, *The Artificial River: The Erie Canal and the Paradox of Progress, 1817–1862* (New York: Hill and Wang, 1996); Morton J. Horwitz, *The Transformation of American Law, 1780–1860* (Cambridge: Harvard University Press, 1977); Ann Fabian, *Card Sharps and Bucket Shops: Gambling in Nineteenth-Century America* (New York: Routledge, 1999); Scott A. Sandage, *Born Losers: A History of Failure in America* (Cambridge, Mass.: Harvard University Press, 2005).

10. On markets and power, see Michael Merrill, "Putting 'Capitalism' in Its Place: A Review of Recent Literature," *WMQ* 52 (April 1995): 315–326; Mary Jo Maynes, "Unthinking Teleologies: Markets, Theories, Histories," *Social Science History* 30 (spring 2006): 1–13; William M. Reddy, *Money and Liberty in Modern Europe: A Critique of Historical Understanding* (New York: Cambridge University Press, 1987); Deborah M. Valenze observes that the rise of possessive individualism went hand-in-hand with the rise in the number of possessed individuals. See Valenze, *The Social Life of Money in the English Past* (New York: Cambridge University Press, 2006), 27.

11. Carolyn Merchant, *Ecological Revolutions: Nature, Gender, and Science in New England* (Chapel Hill: University of North Carolina Press, 1989), 149–270; Gunther Peck, *Reinventing Free Labor: Padrones and Immigrant Workers in the North American West, 1880–1930* (New York: Cambridge University Press, 2000). On the halting development of wage labor within capitalist societies more generally, see William M. Reddy, *The Rise of Market Culture: The Textile Trade and French Society, 1750–1900* (New York: Cambridge University Press, 1984).

12. Joseph Schumpeter, *Capitalism, Socialism, and Democracy* (1942), as quoted in de Vries, "Industrial Revolution and the Industrious Revolution," 265. On the benefits accruing to capitalist economies from workers lacking meaningful market freedom, see Jeanne Boydston, *Home and Work: Housework, Wages, and the Ideology of Labor in the Early Republic* (New York: Oxford University Press, 1990); Elaine Forman Crane, *Ebb Tide in New England: Women, Seaports, and Social Change, 1630–1800* (Boston: Northeastern University Press, 1998); Claudia Goldin and Kenneth Sokoloff, "Women, Children, and Industrialization in the Early Republic: Evidence from the Manufacturing Censuses," *Journal of Economic History* 42 (December 1982): 741–774; Charles B. Dew, *Bond of Iron: Master and Slave at Buffalo Forge* (New York: W. W. Norton, 1994); T. Stephen Whitman, "Industrial Slavery at the Margin: The Maryland Chemical Works," *JSH* 59 (February 1993): 31–62; John Bezis-Selfa, "A Tale of Two Ironworks: Slavery, Free Labor, Work, and Resistance in the Early Republic," *WMQ* 56 (October 1999): 677–700; Tina Sheller, "Freemen, Servants, and Slaves: Artisans and the Craft Structure of Revolutionary Baltimore Town," in *American Artisans: Crafting Social Identity, 1750–1850*, eds. Howard B. Rock, Paul A. Gilje, and Robert Asher (Baltimore: Johns Hopkins University Press, 1995), 17–32; James Sidbury, "Slave Artisans in Richmond, Virginia, 1780–1810," in Rock, Gilje, and Asher, *American Artisans*, 48–62.

13. Richard Parkinson, *The Experienced Farmer's Tour in America* (London: G&J Robinson, 1805), 27. For overviews of the nineteenth-century debates on the productivity of slavery, see Eric Foner, *Free Soil, Free Labor, Free Men: The Ideology of the Republican Party Before the Civil War* (New York: Oxford University Press, 1970), 11–72; Seymour Drescher, *The Mighty Experiment: Free Labor versus Slavery in British Emancipation* (New York: Oxford University Press, 2002); Robert W. Fogel, *Without Consent or Contract: The Rise and Fall of American Slavery* (New York: W. W. Norton, 1989), 60–113. The relationship of plantation

slavery to capitalism has been a classic historiographical debate, one summarized in Douglas Egerton, "Markets Without a Market Revolution: Southern Planters and Capitalism," *JER* 16 (summer 1996): 207–221. On slavery's viability in urban settings, see Richard C. Wade, *Slavery in the Cities: The South, 1820–1860* (New York: Oxford University Press, 1964); Robert S. Starobin, *Industrial Slavery in the Old South* (New York: Oxford University Press, 1970); Claudia Dale Goldin, *Urban Slavery in the American South, 1820–1860: A Quantitative History* (Chicago: University of Chicago Press, 1976).

14. On slavery as a property regime, see Gavin Wright, *Slavery and American Economic Development* (Baton Rouge: Louisiana State University Press, 2006); Jennifer L. Morgan, *Laboring Women: Reproduction and Gender in New World Slavery* (Philadelphia: University of Pennsylvania Press, 2004); Walter Johnson, ed., *The Chattel Principle: The Internal Slave Trade in the Americas* (New Haven, Conn.: Yale University Press, 2004); James L. Huston, *Calculating the Value of the Union: Slavery, Property Rights, and the Economic Origins of the Civil War* (Chapel Hill: University of North Carolina Press, 2003). The economic historian Robert Wright (in personal correspondence with the author, 2007) suggests that the persistence of slavery owed to "path dependency," or the simple fact that it is difficult to break radically from the past—a point made vivid to economic historians in Paul A. David, "Clio and the Economics of QWERTY," *American Economic Review* 75 (May 1985): 332–337.

15. On the "cultural work" of slavery, see Walter Johnson, *Soul By Soul: Life Inside the Antebellum Slave Market* (Cambridge, Mass.: Harvard University Press, 1999); Jonathan Daniel Wells, *The Origins of the Southern Middle Class, 1800–1861* (Chapel Hill: University of North Carolina Press, 2004); Kirsten E. Wood, *Masterful Women: Slaveholding Widows from the American Revolution through the Civil War* (Chapel Hill: University of North Carolina Press, 2004); Michele Gillespie, *Free Labor in an Unfree World: White Artisans in Slaveholding Georgia, 1789–1860* (Athens: University of Georgia Press, 2000); Timothy J. Lockley, *Lines in the Sand: Race and Class in Lowcountry Georgia, 1750–1860* (Athens: University of Georgia Press, 2001).

16. Wolf, *Europe and the People without History*, 379–380. Barbara Fields makes clear that Baltimore was not "at any time in its history a slave city." As she explains, "Where slave and free workers are volatile substitutes for one another on the market, there slavery has become an attribute of individuals, not any longer of the system that organizes their labor." See Barbara Jeanne Fields, *Slavery and Freedom on the Middle Ground: Maryland during the Nineteenth Century* (New Haven, Conn.: Yale University Press, 1985), 48, 52.

17. David Montgomery, *Citizen Worker: The Experience of Workers with Democracy and Free Labor during the Nineteenth Century* (New York: Cambridge University Press, 1993), 50; Amy Dru Stanley, *From Bondage to Contract: Wage Labor, Marriage, and the Market in the Age of Slave Emancipation* (New York: Cambridge University Press, 1998); Robert J. Steinfeld, *The Invention of Free Labor: The Employment Relation in English and American Law and Culture, 1350–1870* (Chapel Hill: University of North Carolina Press, 1991); Robert J. Steinfeld, *Coercion, Contract, and Free Labor in the Nineteenth Century* (New York: Cambridge University Press, 2001); Christopher L. Tomlins, *Law, Labor, and Ideology in the Early American Republic* (New York: Cambridge University Press, 1993); Karen Orren, *Belated Feudalism: Labor, the Law, and Liberal Development in the United States* (New York: Cambridge University Press, 1991); Richard B. Morris, "The Measure of Bondage in the Slave States," *Mississippi*

Valley Historical Review 41 (September 1954): 219–240; Richard B. Morris, "Labor Controls in Maryland in the Nineteenth Century," *JSH* 14 (August 1948): 385–400.

18. On class as an operative category in early American history, see Ronald Schultz, "A Class Society? The Nature of Inequality in Early America," in Pestana and Salinger, *Inequality in Early America*, 203–221; John Ashworth, "Class in American History: Issues and a Case Study," in *The State of U.S. History*, ed. Melvyn Stokes (Oxford: Berg, 2002), 367–386; Greg Nobles, "Class," in *A Companion to Colonial America*, ed. Daniel Vickers (Malden, Mass.: Blackwell Publishers, 2003), 259–287; Christopher Tomlins, "Why Wait for Industrialism? Work, Legal Culture, and the Example of Early America: An Historiographical Argument," *LH* 40 (1999): 5–34; Seth Rockman, "The Contours of Class in the Early Republic City," *Labor* 1 (winter 2004): 93–109; Simon Middleton and Billy G. Smith, eds., *Class Matters: Early North America and the Atlantic World* (Philadelphia: University of Pennsylvania Press, 2008).

19. Because artisans formed mutual aid societies and unions, waged strikes, and published their own newspapers, they were among the most vocal figures left "silent" in older historical scholarship. Their recovery began with E. P. Thompson, *The Making of the English Working Class* (New York: Pantheon 1968); Herbert Gutman, *Work, Culture, and Society in Industrializing America: Essays in American Working-Class and Social History* (New York: Alfred A. Knopf, 1976); Alan Dawley, *Class and Community: The Industrial Revolution in Lynn* (Cambridge, Mass.: Harvard University Press, 1979); Howard B. Rock, *Artisans of the New Republic: The Tradesmen of New York City in the Age of Jefferson* (New York: New York University Press, 1979); Sean Wilentz, *Chants Democratic: New York City and the Rise of the American Working Class, 1788–1850* (New York: Oxford University Press, 1984); Ronald Schultz, *The Republic of Labor: Philadelphia Artisans and the Politics of Class, 1720–1830* (New York: Oxford University Press, 1993); Donna J. Rilling, *Making Houses, Crafting Capitalism: Master Builders in Early Philadelphia, 1790–1850* (Philadelphia: University of Pennsylvania Press, 2000); Gregory L. Kaster, "Labour's True Man: Organised Workingmen and the Language of Manliness in the USA, 1827–1877," *Gender and History* 13 (April 2001): 24–64; Joshua R. Greenberg, *Advocating the Man: Masculinity, Organized Labor, and the Household in New York, 1800–1840* (New York: Columbia University Press, www.gutenberg-e.org, 2006). For an overview, see Richard Stott, "Artisans and Capitalist Development," *JER* 16 (spring 1996): 257–271. For Baltimore specifically, see Charles G. Steffen, *The Mechanics of Baltimore: Workers and Politics in the Age of Revolution, 1763–1812* (Urbana: University of Illinois Press, 1984); William R. Sutton, *Journeymen for Jesus: Evangelical Artisans Confront Capitalism in Jacksonian Baltimore* (University Park: Pennsylvania State University Press, 1998).

20. For labor history that decenters white male artisans, see Marcus Rediker, *Between the Devil and the Deep Blue Sea: Merchant Seamen, Pirates, and the Anglo-American Maritime World, 1700–1750* (New York: Cambridge University Press, 1987), and "The Revenge of Crispus Attucks; or, The Atlantic Challenge to American Labor History," *Labor* 1 (winter 2004): 35–46; Thomas Dublin, *Transforming Women's Work: New England Lives in the Industrial Revolution* (Ithaca, N.Y.: Cornell University Press, 1994); Way, *Common Labour;* Richard B. Stott, *Workers in the Metropolis: Class, Ethnicity, and Youth in Antebellum New York City* (Ithaca, N.Y.: Cornell University Press, 1990); Amy Bridges, "Becoming American: The Working

Classes in the United States before the Civil War," in *Working-Class Formation: Nineteenth-Century Patterns in Western Europe and the United States*, eds. Ira Katznelson and Aristide R. Zolberg (Princeton, N.J.: Princeton University Press, 1986), 157–196. For Baltimore in particular, see Elizabeth Fee, Linda Shopes, and Linda Zeidman, eds., *The Baltimore Book: New Views of Local History* (Philadelphia, Pa.: Temple University Press, 1991). For feminist critiques of labor history, see Sonya O. Rose, "Class Formation and the Quintessential Worker," in *Reworking Class*, ed. John R. Hall (Ithaca, N.Y.: Cornell University Press, 1997), 133–166; Alice Kessler-Harris, "Treating the Male as 'Other': Redefining the Parameters of Labor History," *LH* 34 (spring/summer 1993): 190–204; Peter Winn and Thomas Miller Klubock, eds., "Labor History after the Gender Turn," special issue of *International Labor and Working-Class History* 63 (spring 2003): 1–121; Stansell, *City of Women*; Jeanne Boydston, "The Woman Who Wasn't There: Women's Market Labor and the Transition to Capitalism in the United States," *JER* 16 (summer 1996): 183–206; Marla R. Miller, *The Needle's Eye: Women and Work in the Age of Revolution* (Amherst: University of Massachusetts Press, 2006).

21. For scholarship that deromanticizes working-class politics (or at least questions the relationship of those politics to a broader agenda of human liberation), see Peter Way, "Evil Humors and Ardent Spirits: The Rough Culture of Canal Construction Laborers," *JAH* 79 (March 1993): 1398–1401; David R. Roediger, *The Wages of Whiteness: Race and the Making of the American Working Class* (New York: Verso, 1991); Richard B. Stott, ed., *The History of My Own Times, by William Otter, Sen. . . . .* (Ithaca, N.Y.: Cornell University Press, 1995); Matthew E. Mason, "'The Hands Here Are Disposed to Be Turbulent': Unrest Among the Irish Trackmen of the Baltimore and Ohio Railroad, 1829–1851," *LH* 39 (August 1998): 253–272; Paul E. Johnson, *Sam Patch, the Famous Jumper* (New York: Hill and Wang, 2003); Paul A. Gilje, *Liberty on the Waterfront: American Maritime Culture in the Age of Revolution* (Philadelphia: University of Pennsylvania Press, 2004); Emma Christopher, *Slave Ship Sailors and Their Captive Cargos, 1730–1807* (New York: Cambridge University Press, 2006).

22. Whether or not these historians self-identify as labor historians, their studies (among many others) have expanded the cast of workers in early American history: David S. Cecelski, *The Waterman's Song: Slavery and Freedom in Maritime North Carolina* (Chapel Hill: University of North Carolina Press, 2001); W. Jeffrey Bolster, "'To Feel Like a Man': Black Seamen in the Northern States, 1800–1860," *JAH* 76 (1990): 1173–1199; Paul A. Gilje and Howard B. Rock, "'Sweep O! Sweep O!': African-American Chimney Sweeps and Citizenship in the New Nation," *WMQ* 51 (July 1994): 507–535; Timothy J. Gilfoyle, *City of Eros: New York City, Prostitution, and the Commercialization of Sex, 1790–1920* (New York: Norton, 1992); Tera W. Hunter, *To 'Joy My Freedom: Southern Black Women's Lives and Labors after the Civil War* (Cambridge, Mass.: Harvard University Press, 1997); Sharla M. Fett, *Working Cures: Healing, Health, and Power on Southern Slave Plantations* (Chapel Hill: University of North Carolina Press, 2002); Christine Daniels, "'WANTED: A Blacksmith who understands Plantation Work': Artisans in Maryland, 1700–1810," *WMQ* 50 (October 1993): 743–767; Robert Olwell, "'Loose, Idle and Disorderly': Slave Women in the Eighteenth-Century Charleston Marketplace," in *More than Chattel: Black Women and Slavery in the Americas*, eds. David Barry Gaspar and Darlene Clark Hine (Bloomington: Indiana University Press, 1996), 97–110.

23. On categories of difference as mutually constitutive and simultaneous, see Julie Greene, Bruce Laurie, and Eric Arnesen, eds., *Labor Histories: Class, Politics, and Working-Class Experience* (Urbana: University of Illinois Press, 1998); Eileen Boris and Angelique Janssens, eds., *Complicating Categories: Gender, Class, Race, and Ethnicity* (Cambridge: Cambridge University Press, 1999); David Roediger, "Interchange: The Practice of History," *JAH* 90 (September 2003): 576–611; James Sidbury, *Ploughshares into Swords: Race, Rebellion, and Identity in Gabriel's Virginia, 1730–1810* (New York: Cambridge University Press, 1997), 5 (for the helpful notion of "crosscutting identities"). In a recent forum, Ava Baron and Eileen Boris have called for labor historians to "recuperate class analysis after intersectionality." See "In Response: Dichotomous Thinking and the Objects of History; or, Why Bodies Matter Again," *Labor* 4 (summer 2007): 63.

24. On cultural expression at the center of working people's experiences, albeit often with the effect of generating antagonisms among workers, see Roediger, *Wages of Whiteness*; Eric Lott, *Love and Theft: Blackface Minstrelsy and the American Working Class* (New York: Oxford University Press, 1993); Tyler Anbinder, *Five Points: The 19th-Century New York City Neighborhood That Invented Tap Dance, Stole Elections, and Became the World's Most Notorious Slum* (New York: Free Press, 2001); Shane White, *Stories of Freedom in Black New York* (Cambridge, Mass.: Harvard University Press, 2002); Stansell, *City of Women*. Alongside class formation, historians must also search for what Louise Tilly has called "class transformation," or the material circumstances, competing social relations, and contingencies that mediated—and sometimes precluded—class politics. See Louise Tilly, *Politics and Class in Milan, 1881–1901* (New York: Oxford University Press, 1992), 11–12. The definition of class as a consciousness, identity, and politics that percolates from lived experience is primarily associated with E. P. Thompson, in *Making of the English Working Class*; "The Moral Economy of the English Crowd in the Eighteenth Century," *Past and Present* 50 (1971): 76–131; "Eighteenth-Century English Society: Class Struggle without Class?" *Social History* 3 (1978): 133–165; *Customs in Common: Studies in Traditional Popular Culture* (New York: New Press, 1991).

25. On the way in which focusing on identities has come at the expense of explaining broader social processes, see Alice Kessler-Harris, "The Wages of Patriarchy: Some Thoughts about the Continuing Relevance of Class and Gender," *Labor* 3 (fall 2006): 12. On the perils of making the search for agency into the engine of social history, see Walter Johnson, "On Agency," *Journal of Social History* 37 (fall 2003): 113–124; Susan E. O'Donovan, *Becoming Free in the Cotton South* (Cambridge, Mass.: Harvard University Press, 2007). For systemic understandings of power within capitalism, see Wallace Clement and John Myles, *Relations of Ruling: Class and Gender in Postindustrial Societies* (Montreal: McGill-Queen's University Press, 1994); Evelyn Nakano Glenn, *Unequal Freedom: How Race and Gender Shaped American Citizenship and Labor* (Cambridge, Mass.: Harvard University Press, 2002); and especially, Gerda Lerner, "Rethinking the Paradigm," in *Why History Matters: Life and Thought* (New York: Oxford University Press, 1997), 146–184.

26. Peter Way has been at the forefront of calling for a more materialist and "Malthusian" labor history. See "Evil Humors and Ardent Spirits"; and "Labour's Love Lost: Observations on the Historiography of Class and Ethnicity in the Nineteenth Century," *Journal*

of American Studies 28 (April 1994): 1–22. Simon Newman and Susan Klepp have taken up this call in their contributions to B. G. Smith, *Down and Out*. John Stuart Mill, *Principles of Political Economy*, as quoted in Jonathan A. Glickstein, "The World's 'Dirty Work' and the Wages that 'Sweeten' It: Labor's 'Extrinsic Rewards' in Antebellum Society," in *Moral Problems in American Life: New Perspectives on Cultural History*, eds. Karen Halttunen and Lewis Perry (Ithaca, N.Y.: Cornell University Press, 1998), 78–79.

27. For various facets of Baltimore's history and leading figures, see J. Thomas Scharf, *History of Baltimore City and County, From the Earliest Period to the Present Day: Including Biographical Sketches of their Representative Men* (Philadelphia, Pa.: L. H. Everts, 1881); Whitman H. Ridgway, *Community Leadership in Maryland, 1790–1840: A Comparative Analysis of Power in Society* (Chapel Hill: University of North Carolina Press, 1979); Stuart Weems Bruchey, *Robert Oliver, Merchant of Baltimore, 1783–1819* (Baltimore: Johns Hopkins University Press, 1956); Frank A. Cassell, *Merchant Congressman in the Young Republic: Samuel Smith of Maryland, 1752–1839* (Madison: University of Wisconsin Press, 1971); Edwin J. Perkins, *Financing Anglo-American Trade: The House of Brown, 1800–1880* (Cambridge, Mass.: Harvard University Press, 1975); Eric Robert Papenfuse, *The Evils of Necessity: Robert Goodloe Harper and the Moral Dilemma of Slavery* (Philadelphia, Pa.: American Philosophical Society, 1997); William S. McFeely, *Frederick Douglass* (New York: Norton, 1991); Dickson J. Preston, *Young Frederick Douglass: The Maryland Years* (Baltimore: Johns Hopkins University Press, 1980).

28. Leroy Graham, *Baltimore, the Nineteenth Century Black Capital* (Washington, D.C.: University Press of America, 1982). See also T. Stephen Whitman, *The Price of Freedom: Slavery and Manumission in Baltimore and Early National Maryland* (Lexington: University Press of Kentucky, 1997); Christopher Phillips, *Freedom's Port: The African American Community of Baltimore, 1790–1860* (Urbana: University of Illinois Press, 1997); Diane Batts Morrow, *Persons of Color and Religious at the Same Time: The Oblate Sisters of Providence, 1828–1860* (Chapel Hill: University of North Carolina Press, 2002).

29. Frederick Douglass, *Narrative of the Life of Frederick Douglass, An American Slave* (1845; repr., Boston: Bedford Books, 2003); Fields, *Slavery and Freedom*. Rethinking race and region in American history, several recent studies have situated Baltimore in a comparative framework. Stephanie Cole, "Servants and Slaves: Domestic Service in the Border Cities, 1800–1850" (Ph.D. diss., University of Florida, 1994); Amy S. Greenberg, *Cause for Alarm: The Volunteer Fire Department in the Nineteenth-Century City* (Princeton, N.J.: Princeton University Press, 1998); Camilla Townsend, *Tales of Two Cities: Race and Economic Culture in Early Republican North and South America: Guayaquil, Ecuador, and Baltimore, Maryland* (Austin: University of Texas Press, 2000); Frank Towers, *The Urban South and the Coming of the Civil War* (Charlottesville: University of Virginia Press, 2004); Hilary J. Moss, "Opportunity and Opposition: The African-American Struggle for Education in New Haven, Baltimore, and Boston, 1825–1855" (Ph.D. diss., Brandeis University, 2004); Mariana Libanio de Rezende Dantas, "Black Townsmen: A Comparative Study of Persons of African Origin and Descent in Slavery and Freedom in Baltimore, Maryland, and Sabara, Minas Gerais, 1750–1810" (Ph.D. diss., Johns Hopkins University, 2004).

30. For demographic figures, see Leonard P. Curry, *The Free Black in Urban America,*

1800–1850: The Shadow of the Dream (Chicago: University of Chicago Press, 1981). On Northern race formation and violence, see Joanne Pope Melish, *Disowning Slavery: Gradual Emancipation and "Race" in New England, 1780–1860* (Ithaca, N.Y.: Cornell University Press, 1998); David Waldstreicher, *In the Midst of Perpetual Fetes: The Making of American Nationalism, 1776–1820* (Chapel Hill: University of North Carolina Press, OIEAHC, 1997), esp. chapter 6; John Wood Sweet, *Bodies Politic: Negotiating Race in the American North, 1730–1830* (Baltimore: Johns Hopkins University Press, 2003); Michael A. Morrison and James Brewer Stewart, eds., *Race and the Early Republic: Racial Consciousness and Nation-Building in the Early Republic* (Lanham, Md.: Rowman and Littlefield, 2002); Roediger, *Wages of Whiteness*; Noel Ignatiev, *How the Irish Became White* (New York: Routledge, 1995). On historicizing whiteness, see Eric Arnesen, "Whiteness and the Historians' Imagination," *International Labor and Working-Class History* 60 (fall 2001): 3–32; Peter Kolchin, "Whiteness Studies: The New History of Race in America," *JAH* 89 (June 2002): 154–173.

31. Ira Berlin and Herbert G. Gutman, "Natives and Immigrants, Free Men and Slaves: Urban Workingmen in the Antebellum American South," *AHR* 88 (December 1983): 1175–1200. On the idea of "many Souths," see Peter Kolchin, *A Sphinx on the American Land: The Nineteenth-Century South in Comparative Perspective* (Baton Rouge: Lousiana State University Press, 2003). For the varieties of slavery, see Ira Berlin, *Generations of Captivity: A History of African-American Slaves* (Cambridge, Mass.: Harvard University Press, 2003).

32. Comparative citations appear throughout the following chapters. Key references include Olwen H. Hufton, *The Poor of Eighteenth-Century France, 1750–1789* (Oxford: Clarendon Press, 1974); Gareth Stedman Jones, *Outcast London: A Study of the Relationship Between Classes in Victorian Society* (Oxford: Clarendon Press, 1971); Maud Pember Reeves, *Round About a Pound a Week* (1913; repr., London: Virago, 1979); R. Douglas Cope, *The Limits of Racial Domination: Plebeian Society in Colonial Mexico City, 1660–1720* (Madison: University of Wisconsin Press, 1994). On social welfare in a broader Western context, see chapter 7 for more extensive citations. For specific examples offered here, see Joel F. Harrington, "Escape from the Great Confinement: The Genealogy of a German Workhouse," *Journal of Modern History* 71 (June 1999): 308–345; Isabel Dos Guimaraes Sa, "Assistance to the Poor on a Royal Model: The Example of the Misericordias in the Portuguese Empire from the Sixteenth to the Eighteenth Century," *Confraternitas* 13 (spring 2002): 3–14; Catharina Lis, *Social Change and the Labouring Poor: Antwerp, 1770–1860* (New Haven, Conn.: Yale University Press, 1986); Silvia M. Arrom, *Containing the Poor: The Mexico City Poor House, 1774–1871* (Durham, N.C.: Duke University Press, 2000).

33. Allan Sekula, *Fish Story* (Dusseldorf: Richter Verlag, 1995), 32 (quote); Barbara Ehrenreich, *Nickel and Dimed: On (Not) Getting By in America* (New York: Metropolitan Books, 2001); David K. Shipler, *The Working Poor: Invisible in America* (New York: Knopf, 2004); Jon Gertner, "What is a Living Wage?" *New York Times Magazine*, January 15, 2006; Matt Fellows, *From Poverty, Opportunity: Putting the Market to Work for Lower Income Families*, Brookings Institution Metropolitan Policy Program report, July 2006; Katherine S. Newman, *Chutes and Ladders: Navigating the Low-Wage Labor Market* (New York: Russell Sage Foundation; Cambridge, Mass.: Harvard University Press, 2006); Sudhir Alladi Venkatesh, *Off the Books: The Underground Economy of the Urban Poor* (Cambridge, Mass.: Harvard University Press, 2006).

Chapter 1 · Coming to Work in the City

1. The epigraph to this chapter is from *A Detailed and Correct Account of the Grand Civic Procession in the City of Baltimore, on the Fourth of July, 1828; In Honor of the Day and in Commemoration of the Commencement of the Baltimore and Ohio Rail Road* (Baltimore: Thomas Murphy, 1828), 42.

2. *Niles*, September 19, 1812, June 27, 1818, June 12, 1819. For general overviews of Baltimore's growth, see Sherry H. Olson, *Baltimore: The Building of an American City*, 2nd ed. (Baltimore: Johns Hopkins University Press, 1997); Gary L. Browne, *Baltimore in the Nation, 1789–1861* (Chapel Hill: University of North Carolina Press, 1980); Richard Smith Chew, "The Measure of Independence: From the American Revolution to the Market Revolution in the Mid-Atlantic" (Ph.D. diss., College of William and Mary, 2002); Rhoda M. Dorsey, "Comment: Baltimore Foreign Trade," in *The Growth of the Seaport Cities, 1790–1825*, proceedings of a conference sponsored by the Eleutherian Mills-Hagley Foundation, March 17–19, 1966, ed. David T. Gilchrist (Charlottesville: University Press of Virginia, 1967), 62–67; Clarence P. Gould, "The Economic Causes of the Rise of Baltimore," in *Essays in Colonial History Presented to Charles McLean Andrews by His Students* (New Haven, Conn.: Yale University Press, 1930), 225–251. On the origins of Baltimore's commercial men, see Charles G. Steffen, *From Gentlemen to Townsmen: The Gentry of Baltimore County, Maryland, 1660–1776* (Lexington: University Press of Kentucky, 1993); Whitman H. Ridgway, *Community Leadership in Maryland, 1790–1840: A Comparative Analysis of Power in Society* (Chapel Hill: University of North Carolina Press, 1979).

3. *Baltimore Express*, March 4, 1837.

4. Carol Sheriff, *The Artificial River: The Erie Canal and the Paradox of Progress, 1817–1862* (New York: Hill and Wang, 1996), passim.

5. *Patriot*, July 7, 1828. For Baltimore merchants, see Stuart W. Bruchey, *Robert Oliver, Merchant of Baltimore, 1783–1819* (Baltimore: Johns Hopkins University Press, 1956); Frank A. Cassell, *Merchant Congressman in the Young Republic: Samuel Smith of Maryland, 1752–1839* (Madison: University of Wisconsin Press, 1971); John Bosley Yellott, Jr., "Jeremiah Yellott—Revolutionary-War Privateersman and Baltimore Philanthropist," *MHM* 86 (summer 1991): 176–187; Frederick C. Leiner, "The Baltimore Merchants' Warships: *Maryland* and *Patapsco* in the Quasi-War with France," *MHM* 88 (fall 1993): 262; Edwin J. Perkins, *Financing Anglo-American Trade: The House of Brown, 1800–1880* (Cambridge, Mass.: Harvard University Press, 1975).

6. Efforts to situate working people at the center of Baltimore's history include Elizabeth Fee, Linda Shopes, and Linda Zeidman, eds., *The Baltimore Book: New Views of Local History* (Philadelphia, Pa.: Temple University Press, 1991); Charles G. Steffen, *The Mechanics of Baltimore: Workers and Politics in the Age of Revolution, 1763–1812* (Urbana: University of Illinois Press, 1984); William R. Sutton, *Journeymen for Jesus: Evangelical Artisans Confront Capitalism in Jacksonian Baltimore* (University Park: Pennsylvania State University Press, 1998); Frank Towers, *The Urban South and the Coming of the Civil War* (Charlottesville: University of Virginia Press, 2004). For Gladman, see *Patriot*, August 30, 1828.

7. Adam Smith, *Inquiry into the Nature and Causes of the Wealth of Nations*, ed. Edwin Cannan (Chicago: University of Chicago Press, 1976), 1:5, 34.

8. Jacob M. Price, "Economic Function and the Growth of American Port Towns in the Eighteenth Century," *Perspectives in American History* 8 (1974): 123–186; Sherry H. Olson, "Baltimore Imitates the Spider," *Annals of the Association of American Geographers* 69 (Dec. 1979): 557–574; Sherry H. Olson, "Urban Metabolism and Morphogenesis," *Urban Geography* 3 (1982): 87–109.

9. While a "staples" pattern of development makes some sense for Baltimore, the city differed from earlier urban centers insofar as it never played host to a colonial or state government, and local merchants faced little competition from a rival political elite. The drawback was that the state's political elite in Annapolis attempted to keep Baltimore on a short leash. They resisted calls for municipal independence until the end of the 1790s. Even after Baltimore elected its first mayor and city council in 1797, Annapolis left county judges in control of the city's legal system and refused Baltimore proportional representation in the house of delegates. For the entire antebellum period, Baltimore elected as many legislators as did counties with only a fraction of its population. On staples-driven development, see John J. McCusker and Russell R. Menard, *The Economy of British America, 1607–1789* (Chapel Hill: University of North Carolina Press, OIEAHC, 1985), 5–34; Franklin Knight and Elizabeth Leis, *Atlantic Port Cities: Economy, Culture, and Society in the Atlantic World, 1650–1850* (Knoxville: University of Tennessee Press, 1991); Carville Earle and Ronald Hoffman, "Staple Crops and Urban Development in the Eighteenth-Century South," *Perspectives in American History* 10 (1976): 47–51; David Goldfield, "The Urban South: A Regional Framework," *AHR* 86 (December 1981): 1009–1034. For the centrality of venting agricultural surplus to republican political economy, see Drew R. McCoy, *The Elusive Republic: Political Economy in Jeffersonian America* (Chapel Hill: University of North Carolina Press, OIEAHC, 1980).

10. Fielding Lucas, Jr., *Picture of Baltimore, Containing a Description of all Objects of Interest in the City* . . . (Baltimore: Fielding Lucas, Jr., 1832), 23.

11. Thomas Paine, *Common Sense*, in *The Complete Writings of Thomas Paine*, ed. Philip Foner (New York: Citadel Press, 1969), 1:18; Paul G. E. Clemens, *The Atlantic Economy and Colonial Maryland's Eastern Shore: From Tobacco to Grain* (Ithaca, N.Y.: Cornell University Press, 1980), 204–222; Jo N. Hays, "Overlapping Hinterlands: York, Philadelphia, and Baltimore, 1800–1860," *Pennsylvania Magazine of History and Biography* 116 (July 1992): 295–321; Lois Green Carr and Lorena Walsh, "Economic Diversification and Labor Organization in the Chesapeake, 1650–1820," in *Work and Labor in Early America*, ed. Stephen Innes (Chapel Hill: University of North Carolina Press, OIEAHC, 1988), 144–188. Peace in Europe after 1815 hindered Baltimore's trade to the Caribbean and curtailed the privateering opportunities behind many local fortunes. The English novelist Thomas Hamilton jabbed that frustrated Baltimore merchants in the 1820s were drinking toasts to "A bloody war in Europe!" and recalling "the good old times, when people in Europe cut each other's throats." Thomas Hamilton, *Men and Manners in America* (Edinburgh: W. Blackwood, 1833), 2:17.

12. Charles Varle, *A Complete View of Baltimore, with a Statistical Sketch* . . . (Baltimore: Samuel Young, 1833), 70, 95–104; Chew, "Measure of Independence," 117, 119–182; G. Terry

Sharrer, "The Merchant-Millers: Baltimore's Flour Milling Industry, 1783–1860," *Agricultural History* 56 (January 1982): 138–150; Browne, *Baltimore in the Nation*, 28.

13. *Niles*, August 19, 1815, January 29, 1825 (for data 1798–1824). Technological innovations, especially Oliver Evans's grain elevator and hopper boy at Ellicott's Mills, lowered production costs and helped make Baltimore even more attractive to market-oriented farmers. See Neal A. Brooks and Eric G. Rockel, *A History of Baltimore County* (Towson, Md.: Friends of the Towson Library, 1979), 185; Varle, *View of Baltimore*, 68–70.

14. Chew, "Measure of Independence," 150; W. Jeffrey Bolster, *Black Jacks: African American Seamen in the Age of Sail* (Cambridge, Mass.: Harvard University Press, 1997), 236; Varle, *View of Baltimore*, 68.

15. Mary Ellen Hayward and Charles Belfoure, *The Baltimore Rowhouse* (New York: Princeton Architectural Press, 1999), 7–29; Richard M. Bernard, "A Portrait of Baltimore in 1800: Economic and Occupational Patterns in an Early American City," *MHM* 69 (winter 1974): 347; Bernard L. Herman, *Town House: Architecture and Material Life in the Early American City, 1780–1830* (Chapel Hill: University of North Carolina Press, OIEAHC, 2005), 193–230; Carole Shammas, "The Space Problem in Early United States Cities," *WMQ* 57 (July 2000): 505–542; Carole Shammas, "The Housing Stock of the Early United States: Refinement Meets Migration," *WMQ* 64 (July 2007): 549–590. For house construction rates, see *Ordinances*, 1834 (Baltimore: James Lucas & E. K. Deaver, 1834), app. 4; *Ordinances*, 1835 (Baltimore: Lucas & Deaver, 1835), app. 4; *Ordinances*, 1836 (Baltimore: Lucas & Deaver, 1836), app. 4.

16. Olson, *Baltimore*, ch. 1–4; BCA, 1813:457. For the $600,000 figure, see *Ordinances*, 1836, app. 10.

17. On the international reputation of Baltimore shipbuilders, see John M. Duncan, *Travels through Part of the United States and Canada in 1818 and 1819* (New York: W. B. Gilley, 1823), 1:226. For Baltimore manufacturing, see *Niles*, June 7, 1817, April 26, 1828; Varle, *View of Baltimore*, 84–88, 95–104; Edward K. Muller and Paul A. Groves, "The Emergence of Industrial Districts in Mid-Nineteenth Century Baltimore," *Geographical Review* 69 (April 1979): 159–178. The 1810 federal manufacturing census located twenty-four different industries operating in Baltimore City, producing nearly $2 million in merchandise. See Tench Coxe, *A Statement of the Arts and Manufactures of the United States for the Year 1810* (Philadelphia, Pa.: A. J. Cornman, Jr., 1814), 79–87. The 1833 survey of American manufacturing conducted by Secretary of the Treasury Louis McLane apparently skipped Baltimore, much to the detriment of future scholars. On deskilling as a crucial facet of early industrialization, see Sean Wilentz, *Chants Democratic: New York City and the Rise of the American Working Class, 1788–1850* (New York: Oxford University Press, 1984), 105; Christine Stansell, *City of Women: Sex and Class in New York, 1789–1860* (New York: Alfred A. Knopf, 1986), 105–129; Michael Zakim, "A Ready-Made Business: The Birth of the Clothing Industry in America," *Business History Review* 73 (spring 1999): 61–90; Steffen, *Mechanics of Baltimore*, passim.

18. *Patriot*, October 21, 1826; Brooks and Rockel, *Baltimore County*, 190–191; Richard W. Griffin, "An Origin of the Industrial Revolution in Maryland: The Textile Industry, 1789–1826," *MHM* 61 (March 1966): 24–36; D. Randall Beirne, "Hampden-Woodberry: The Mill Village in an Urban Setting," *MHM* 77 (spring 1982): 6–26; Varle, *View of Baltimore*, 84;

Lawrence A. Peskin, *Manufacturing Revolution: The Intellectual Origins of Early American Industry* (Baltimore: Johns Hopkins University Press, 2003).

19. *Niles*, November 20, 1813, January 17, 1818, May 8, 1819; *American*, February 13, 1808; *Report of the Secretary of State, of Such Articles Manufactured in the United States as Would Be Liable to Duties if Imported from Foreign Countries* . . . (Washington, D.C.: Gales and Seaton, 1824), 108; Browne, *Baltimore in the Nation*, 55, 80, 86.

20. Brooks and Rockel, *Baltimore County*, 205–219; Matthew E. Mason, "'The Hands Here Are Disposed to Be Turbulent': Unrest Among the Irish Trackmen of the Baltimore and Ohio Railroad, 1829–1851," *LH* 39 (August 1998): 253–272. For rural-urban connections in a developing economy, see Kenryu Hashikawa, "Rural Entrepreneurship in New Jersey during the Early Republic" (Ph.D. diss., Columbia University, 2002).

21. William Mitchell to Ebenezer T. Warren, February 20, 1813, Vaughan Family Papers, Warren Correspondence, series 6, Massachusetts Historical Society; *Patriot*, December 15, 1828.

22. Shammas, "Space Problem," 509; *Warner & Hanna's Plan of the City and Environs of Baltimore* (Baltimore: Charles Varle, 1801); Edward C. Papenfuse and Joseph M. Coale III, eds., *The Hammond-Harwood House Atlas of Historical Maps of Maryland, 1608–1908* (Baltimore: Johns Hopkins University Press, 1982).

23. Richard Oestreicher, "The Counted and the Uncounted: The Occupational Structure of Early American Cities," *Journal of Social History* 28 (winter 1994): 351. For the percentage of white households with taxable property, see Terry D. Bilhartz, *Urban Religion and the Second Great Awakening: Church and Society in Early National Baltimore* (Rutherford, N.J.: Fairleigh Dickinson University Press, 1986), 13. For the 1796 directory, see Lawrence A. Peskin, "Fells Point: Baltimore's Pre-Industrial Suburb," *MHM* 97 (summer 2002): 172. For the 1810 directory, see Browne, *Baltimore in the Nation*, 61. Richard Bernard's "Portrait of Baltimore in 1800" glosses over mariners, seamstresses, and other day laborers because they so rarely appeared in his sample from directory and tax records.

24. *Niles*, June 1, 1816, June 12, 1819; "A Native Baltimorean" to the *Maryland Gazette* (November 1812), T. W. Griffith Scrapbook, MHS, ms. 412.1; Archibald Hawkins, *The Life and Times of Hon. Elijah Stansbury, An "Old Defender" and Ex-Mayor of Baltimore* . . . (Baltimore: John Murphy & Co., 1874), 81. The classic study of working-class transience is Stephan Thernstrom, *Poverty and Progress: Social Mobility in a Nineteenth Century City* (Cambridge, Mass.: Harvard University Press, 1964), which availed itself of the more substantive census data for Newburyport, Massachusetts, in the period 1850–1880. For a semiskilled worker's transience, see Richard B. Stott, ed., *History of My Own Times, or the Life and Adventures of William Otter, Sen.* . . . (Ithaca, N.Y.: Cornell University Press, 1995).

25. The methodology for this calculation comes from Oestreicher, "Counted and Uncounted," 357. The *Federal Census of 1800*, Baltimore City, counted 5,699 white males and 4,544 white females ages sixteen to forty-four. Oestreicher provides a labor participation rate of 0.885 for white men and 0.25 for white women, which yields 6,180 white workers. The 1800 census grouped all free African Americans together (2,771). Using the closest available figures for the age and sex of free people of color (the *Federal Census of 1820*) and a higher labor participation rate for black women, the number of free black workers can be estimated between 900 and 1,000. Finally, the 1800 census counted 2,843 slaves in Balti-

more, but made no distinction by age or sex. Using 1820 data once again (when 54 percent of enslaved African Americans were ages fourteen to forty-four), the figure for 1800 is 1,535. In sum, the *Federal Census of 1800* found approximately 8,700 working men and women in Baltimore. Because the 1800 census lumped all whites older than forty-five into a single undifferentiated category that included centenarians and those only half as old, it is impossible to know the number of older workers in the city. In her work on the female labor participation rate in 1830s Massachusetts, Margaret S. Coleman suggests that Oestreicher's 0.25 multiplier for white women might be too low for an urban center like Baltimore. Coleman estimates a rate closer to 0.45 for adult women performing nonagricultural wage labor. See Coleman, "Female Labor Supply During Early Industrialization: Women's Labor Force Participation in Historical Perspective," in *Gender and Political Economy: Incorporating Diversity into Theory and Policy*, eds. Ellen Mutari, Heather Boushey, and William Fraher IV (Armonk, N.Y.: M. E. Sharpe, 1997), 42–60. Data for 1802 comes from Cornelius W. Stafford, *The Baltimore Directory for 1802* (Baltimore: John W. Butler, 1802).

26. Baltimore County Court (Certificates of Freedom), 1806–1816, MSA, c-290-1; Baltimore County Register of Wills (Certificates of Freedom), 1805–1830, MSA, c-289-1; Christopher Phillips, *Freedom's Port: The African American Community of Baltimore, 1790–1860* (Urbana: University of Illinois Press, 1997), 71.

27. BAAB, April 8, 1826 (Guigar), October 14, 1824 (Bates), April 27, 1825 (Christian). The Almshouse Admission Book contains nativity information for 1,617 men, women, and children, or 86 percent of all admitted between May 1823 and May 1826. Those figures reveal 1,111 native-born Americans, including 842 Marylanders; and 506 immigrants, including 295 born in Ireland.

28. Steven Sarson, "Distribution of Wealth in Prince George's County, Maryland, 1800–1820," *Journal of Economic History* 60 (September 2000): 847–855; Steven Sarson, "Landlessness and Tenancy in Early National Prince George's County, Maryland," *WMQ* 57 (July 2000): 569–598; Steven Sarson, "'Objects of Distress': Inequality and Poverty in Early Nineteenth-Century Prince George's County," *MHM* 96 (summer 2001): 141–162; Christine Daniels, "'Getting His (or Her) Livelihood': Free Workers in Slave Anglo-America, 1675–1810," *Agricultural History* 71 (spring 1997): 125–162; Paul G. E. Clemens and Lucy Simler, "Rural Labor and the Farm Household in Chester County, Pennsylvania, 1750–1820," in *Work and Labor in Early America*, ed. Stephen Innes (Chapel Hill: University of North Carolina Press, OIEAHC, 1988), 106–143; Peskin, "Fells Point," 167–169. On the shift of Maryland's population, see Barbara Jeanne Fields, *Slavery and Freedom on the Middle Ground: Maryland during the Nineteenth Century* (New Haven, Conn.: Yale University Press, 1985), 13.

29. Tyler Anbinder has argued that poverty in the United States compared favorably to poverty in Europe. See *Five Points: The 19th-Century New York City Neighborhood That Invented Tap Dance, Stole Elections, and Became the World's Most Notorious Slum* (New York: Free Press, 2001), 111. Camilla Townsend contends that opportunity abounded in Baltimore relative to Guayaquil, Ecuador, in *Tales of Two Cities: Race and Economic Culture in Early Republican North and South America: Guayaquil, Ecuador, and Baltimore, Maryland* (Austin: University of Texas Press, 2000), 45.

30. *Niles*, December 2, 1815, November 7, 1829. The comparison to England was a stan-

dard for American political economists. See Willard Phillips, *A Manual of Political Economy with Particular Reference to the Institutions, Resources and Condition of the United States* (Boston: Hilliard, Gray, Little, and Wilkins, 1828), 126–162; Henry C. Carey, *Essay on the Rate of Wages: With an Examination of the Causes of the Differences in the Condition of the Labouring Population throughout the World* (Philadelphia, Pa.: Carey, Lea, and Blanchard, 1835), 145, 190, 223–231.

31. John Melish, *Information and Advice to Emigrants to the United States . . .* (Philadelphia, Pa.: John Melish, 1819), 89, 91; Mathew Carey, *Reflections on the Subject of Emigration from Europe, with a View to Settlement in the United States . . .* (Philadelphia, Pa.: H. C. Carey and I. Lea, 1826). Interestingly, European travelers in the United States frequently presented a more cautious assessment to their countrymen. "Upon the whole, America appears to me to be a most proper place for the use to which it was first appropriated, namely, the reception of convicts," observed Richard Parkinson, *The Experienced Farmer's Tour in America* (London: G&J Robinson, 1805), 489; see also *A Letter on the Present State of the Labouring Classes in America: With an Account of the Wages Given to Weavers, Warpers, Over-Lookers, Carders, Spinners, Masons, Brick-layers, Carpenters, Machine Makers, Smiths, Boot & Shoe Makers, Dyers, Tailors, Labourers, Cooks, Servants, Prices of Provisions, &c. By an intelligent Emigrant at Philadelphia* (Bury: John Kay, 1827).

32. *Maryland Journal*, May 25, 1792 (ship *John*), October 11, 1791 (German redemptioners for sale), February 12, 1793 (Sechtling and Rosabower), April 26, 1793 (Healy), July 16, 1793 (Markle). On the vitality of this trade through the 1810s, see *Laws*, 1817.226; *American*, August 6, 10, 12, 25, September 20, October 8, 1819; *Niles*, August 2, 1817, December 2, 1818. On redemptioners and indentured servants, see Aaron Fogleman, "From Slaves, Convicts, and Servants to Free Passengers: The Transformation of Immigration in the Era of the American Revolution," *JAH* 85 (June 1998): 43–76; Farley Grubb, "The End of European Immigrant Servitude in the United States: An Economic Analysis of Market Collapse, 1772–1835," *Journal of Economic History* 54 (December 1994): 794–825; Farley Grubb, "The Disappearance of Organized Markets for European Immigrant Servants in the United States: Five Popular Explanations Reexamined," *Social Science History* 18 (spring 1994): 1–30.

33. *Niles*, October 16, 1819; Shamrock Society of New York, *Hints to Emigrants from Europe, who Intend to Make a Permanent Residence in the United States* (New York: Van Winkle & Wiley, 1816), 8, 10. In 1834, Patrick O'Kelly suggested that the emigrant should "seek, on his arrival at Liverpool, or at any other seaport, a vessel bound for Baltimore, in preference to any other port in the United States, because from here he will be able to bend his course either for the Ohio, Indiana, Tennessee, Illinois, or the Missouri, &c." See O'Kelly, *Advice and Guide to Emigrants going to the United States of America* (Dublin: William Folds, 1834), 74; John Woods, *Two Years' Residence in the Settlement on the English Prairie, in the Illinois Country, United States . . .* (London: Longman, Hurst, Rees, Orme, and Browne, 1822), 24. On railroad and canal labor, see Peter Way, *Common Labour: Workers and the Digging of North American Canals, 1780–1860* (New York: Cambridge University Press, 1993); Mason, "Irish Trackmen."

34. BCA, 1830:564 (Martin quote), 1831:1304, 1833:364 (Hunt quote), 1833:753, 1833:1167, 1834:1045, 1839:658; *Baltimore Express*, July 15, 1837. Anxiety about "pauper dumping" had animated moral reformers for several decades. See *The Second Annual Report of the Man-*

agers of the Society for the Prevention of Pauperism, in the City of New-York . . . (New York: E. Conrad, 1820), 18–26; *Niles*, September 18, 1819.

35. *Laws*, 1832.303, 1833.177, and 1834.84. Counting immigrants was particularly informal before the 1820s. In an obvious undercount, the 1820 federal census found only 1,369 "Foreigners not Naturalized" in Baltimore. Court records never reported more than a few dozen naturalizations a year. Statistical accounts include *Niles*, August 2, 1817, August 1, 1818; William J. Bromwell, *History of Immigration to the United States . . . 1819 to 1855* (1856; repr., New York: Augustus Kelley, 1969); R. S. Fisher, *Gazetteer of the State of Maryland* . . . (New York: J. H. Colton, 1852), 29. One scholar has argued that Baltimore's large black population discouraged immigrants from coming to the city, but there is no contemporary evidence for this before the 1840s. Among others, Hezekiah Niles, the leading proponent of European emigration to Baltimore, voiced no such concern. Cf. D. Randall Beirne, "The Impact of Black Labor on European Immigration into Baltimore's Oldtown, 1790–1910," *MHM* 83 (winter 1988): 331–345. Nor did European guidebooks discourage potential immigrants from coming to Baltimore on grounds of the city's large black population. See Richard L. Bland, "The Handbook of Traugott Bromme: A Nineteenth Century German Immigrant," *MHM* 98 (spring 2003): 73–77.

36. BCA, 1834:1045. Inspecting every foreign vessel arriving between May 1 and October 31 each year, Martin witnessed 40,973 immigrant arrivals from 1827 through 1834. Martin's figures miss those who arrived during the nonquarantine months. Martin also suspected that shady ship captains discharged their sick European passengers before arriving at the Baltimore lazaretto for inspection. See *Ordinances*, 1833 (Baltimore: Sands & Neilson, 1833), app. 20.

37. *Laws*, 1833.303; Petition of the Hibernian Society of Baltimore, reprinted in *Niles*, May 23, 1818; Woods, *Two Years' Residence*, 31. For prominence of Irish merchants in 1790s Baltimore, see Isaac Weld, Jr., *Travels through the States of North America . . . 1795, 1796, and 1797* (London: J. Stockdale, 1799), 26. Although Irish immigration was most intense during the famine period of 1846–1854, approximately 850,000 Irish arrived in the United States between 1815 and 1845. See Beirne, "Baltimore's Oldtown," 336.

38. On religious, regional, and political affiliations transplanted from Ireland, see Mason, "Irish Trackmen"; "Proceedings of the Maryland House of Delegates," December 24, 1812, reprinted in *Niles*, January 23, 1813. In terms of imported rivalries during the 1812 riots, Presbyterian merchants likely filled the ranks of the Orangemen, who sided with the Federalists in their opposition to President Madison's maritime policies toward Britain. Whether or not the United Irishmen had organizational roots in Baltimore, their affinity for "democracy" allied them with the fiercely Republican crowd that instigated the riot by storming a Federalist press. For the general history of the riots, see Paul A. Gilje, "The Baltimore Riots of 1812 and the Breakdown of the Anglo-American Mob Tradition," *Journal of Social History* 13 (fall 1979): 547–564.

39. *Niles*, April 27, 1833; BCA, 1837:417, 1837:1089, 1837:1488.

40. BCA, 1839:649, 1834:607. The city council declined to print the laws in German. Terry Bilhartz estimated that one-tenth of Baltimore residents spoke German in 1790. See Bilhartz, *Urban Religion*, 123.

41. BCA, 1835:1206, 1836:2065, 1837:938a, 1838:238. Among the 817 inmates who

passed through the Baltimore almshouse between May 1837 and May 1838 were 282 immigrants (including 165 Irish born, 63 German born, and 24 English born). At the end of 1839, the almshouse trustees commented that of "strangers" in the institution, "a large proportion consists of German emigrants, the number of whom are constantly increasing." See *Ordinances, 1840* (Baltimore: Joseph Robinson, 1840), app. 94.

42. Frederick Douglass, *Narrative of the Life of Frederick Douglass, An American Slave, Written by Himself,* ed. David W. Blight (1845; repr., Boston: Bedford Books, 2003), 61.

43. Carville Earle, "A Staple Interpretation of Slavery and Free Labor," *Geographical Review* 68 (January 1978): 51–65; Bayly E. Marks, "Skilled Blacks in Antebellum St. Mary's County, Maryland," *JSH* 53 (November 1987): 537–563; Christine Daniels, "Alternative Workers in a Slave Economy: Kent County Maryland" (Ph.D. diss., Johns Hopkins University, 1990); Jessica Millward, "'A Choice Parcel of Country Born': African Americans and the Transition of Freedom in Maryland, 1770–1840" (Ph.D. diss., UCLA, 2003).

44. C. Phillips, *Freedom's Port,* 57–74; Leonard P. Curry, *The Free Black in Urban America, 1800–1850: The Shadow of the Dream* (Chicago: University of Chicago Press, 1981), 250; Historical Census Browser, retrieved September 9, 2007, from the University of Virginia, Geospatial and Statistical Data Center http://fisher.lib.virginia.edu/collections/stats/histcensus/index.html.

45. Steven Deyle, *Carry Me Back: The Domestic Slave Trade in American Life* (New York: Oxford University Press, 2005), 289; Michael Tadman, *Speculators and Slaves: Masters, Traders, and Slaves in the Old South* (Madison: University of Wisconsin Press, 1989), 12; John Hope Franklin and Loren Schweninger, *Runaway Slaves: Rebels on the Plantation* (New York: Oxford University Press, 1999), ch. 6; C. Phillips, *Freedom's Port,* 66–72.

46. *Patriot,* September 12, 1816 (Watt), April 21, 1819 (Betty), September 16, 1834 (Ben Johnson).

47. *Post,* October 26, 1809 (Robin); *Patriot,* January 1, 1834 (Pompey); *American,* February 24, 1817 (Joshua Sullivan); Barbara Wallace, "'Fair Daughters of Africa': African American Women in Baltimore, 1790–1860" (Ph.D. diss., UCLA, 2001), 222, 252 (for the 1835 arrest of Susan Scott, a free black woman, for sheltering a runaway); BCA, 1823:523 (Abednego). Rural slaveowners regularly advertised in Baltimore for their lost property. In 1793, for example, the *Maryland Journal* carried only eight advertisements for city slaves fleeing local masters, but over fifty for slaves absconding from rural plantation districts.

48. *Maryland Journal,* December 22, 1789 (Dawson), April 2, 1790 (Lancaster), May 28, 1793 (Mary); *Patriot,* January 4, 13, March 18, May 23, June 25, October 13, December 26, 1834. On runaway slaves and self-making, see David Waldstreicher, "Reading the Runaways: Self-Fashioning, Print Culture, and Confidence in Slavery in the Eighteenth-Century Mid-Atlantic," *WMQ* 56 (April 1999): 243–272.

49. For Volunbrun, see Shane White, *Somewhat More Independent: The End of Slavery in New York City, 1770–1810* (Athens: University of Georgia Press, 1991), 144–45; T. Stephen Whitman, *The Price of Freedom: Slavery and Manumission in Baltimore and Early National Maryland* (Lexington: University Press of Kentucky, 1997), 23. *Laws,* 1792.56, reads, "Whereas derangements in the government of France, and some of the French West-India islands, have induced several inhabitants of the said islands to take refuge in this state." For Rattoone, see Baltimore County Court (Miscellaneous Court Papers), 1801–1802, MSA,

CI-28: "I Elijah D. Rattoone do hereby certify that I arrived here from New York on or about the first day of August last and that I brought with me one negro male slave aged about 18 years and who was born in my father's family in the state of New Jersey and who has been with me ever since leaving that State, in the city and vicinity of New York and which slave I mean to keep for my own use and not for sale . . . September 3, 1802."

50. Whitman, *Price of Freedom*, 10, 16; Wallace, "Fair Daughters of Africa," 21; BCA, Tax Assessors Notebooks, Rg4, s2, 1824, Ward 8. Another Fells Point ropemaker, Col. Benjamin Rollins, did not own four of the six slaves living in his house.

51. James A. McMillin, *The Final Victims: Foreign Slave Trade to North America, 1783–1810* (Columbia: University of South Carolina Press, 2004), CD-ROM database; Hugh Thomas, *The Slave Trade: The Story of the Atlantic Slave Trade, 1440–1870* (New York: Simon & Schuster, 1997), 568–572; "Speech of Senator William Smith of South Carolina, December 1820," *Annals of Congress*, Senate, 16th Cong., 2nd sess., 73–77; Leroy Graham, *Baltimore, the Nineteenth Century Black Capital* (Washington D.C.: University Press of America, 1982), 57. For Tyson's allegations, see "The Protection Society of Maryland," *Christian Disciple* (September 1818): 266. For non-English slaves in the city, see *Maryland Journal*, November 6, 1792 (Quash, "a Guinea Negro, and though a long time in this country, speaks very bad English"), June 25, 1793 (Ambrose, "A French Negro Man . . . speaks but very little English"), July 9, 1794 (Sterling, "a Guinea Negro, and notwithstanding he came into this country young, retains the Negro dialect"); *Post*, January 10, 1809 ("a Negro Boy (African born) named John . . . speaks both English and French").

52. *Boston Repertory*, quoted in Browne, *Baltimore in the Nation*, 254n13; *Niles*, September 12, 1812 (Philadelphia quote), June 12, 1819; "A Native Baltimorean" to the *Maryland Gazette* (November 1812), Griffith Scrapbook.

53. *Niles*, October 9, 1816. During the Panic of 1819, Niles did lament the arrival of so many immigrants: "Hundreds, perhaps, we might say thousands of them, will be incumbrances on us during the ensuing winter; for many tens of thousands of our own people, accustomed to sustain themselves by their labor, will be out of employment, unless some extraordinary event shall take place." But as usual, Niles advocated protections for American industry as a remedy. See *Niles*, September 18, 1819.

54. Browne, *Baltimore in the Nation*, passim; Dorsey, "Baltimore Foreign Trade," 62–67.

55. "Memorial to the Honorable the Senate and House of Representatives of the United States in Congress Assembled, The Memorial of the Subscribers, citizens of Baltimore," U.S. Senate, 14th Cong., 2nd sess., February 22, 1817, *New American State Papers* 6, Manufactures, 1:459–465.

56. Gary Nash, "The Failure of Female Factory Labor in Colonial Boston," *LH* 20 (1979): 165; Eric G. Nellis, "Misreading the Signs: Industrial Imitation, Poverty, and the Social Order in Colonial Boston," *New England Quarterly* 59 (December 1986): 486–507; Laurel T. Ulrich, "Sheep in the Parlor, Wheels on the Common: Pastoralism and Poverty in Eighteenth-Century Boston," in *Inequality in Early America*, eds. Carla G. Pestana and Sharon V. Salinger (Hanover, N.H.: University Press of New England, 1999), 182–200; Alexander Hamilton, *Report on Manufactures* (1791), as quoted in Jacqueline Jones, *American Work: Four Centuries of Black and White Labor* (New York: W. W. Norton, 1998), 161; Brian Green-

berg, "The Political Economy of Early America: Tench Coxe, George Logan, and the Cordwainers' Conspiracy Trial," paper presented at the Program in Early American Economy
and Society Inaugural Conference, Library Company of Philadelphia, April 2001.

57. *Niles*, June 7, 1817.

58. Children under fifteen composed 42 percent of the city's white population, 36 percent of the enslaved population, and 33 percent of the free black population.

59. Wallace, "Fair Daughters of Africa," 38–49; T. Stephen Whitman, "Orphans in City
and Countryside in Nineteenth-Century Maryland," in *Children Bound to Labor: Pauper Apprenticeship in Early America*, eds. John E. Murray and Ruth Wallis Herndon (Ithaca, N.Y.:
Cornell University Press, forthcoming).

60. *American*, August 21, 1804, February 26, 1817; *Patriot*, December 4, 1824.

61. *Niles*, June 7, 1817.

62. In 1810, the city contained 9,660 white men and 7,683 white women ages sixteen
to forty-four. On the sex ratio in early republic cities, see Shammas, "Space Problem," 534.

63. Wallace, "Fair Daughters of Africa," 22–49. On the presumption that womanhood
did not protect all women from labor, see *American*, February 23, 1805. On the potential of
white women workers in the American South, see Thomas P. Jones, *An Address on the
Progress of Manufacturers and Internal Improvements, in the United States; and particularly,
On the Advantages to be Derived from the Employment of Slaves in the Manufacturing of Cotton and Other Goods. Delivered in the Hall of the Franklin Institute, November 6, 1827* (Philadelphia, Pa.: Judah Dobson, 1827), 17.

64. C. Phillips, *Freedom's Port*, 83–113; undated newspaper clipping, Griffith Scrapbook.

65. James T. Campbell, *Middle Passages: African American Journeys to Africa, 1787–2005*
(New York: Penguin, 2006), 43–45; *Report of the Committee on the Coloured Population, of
Answers of the President of the Colonization Society of Maryland, in Obedience to the Order
Adopted By the House of Delegates, on the 4th January, 1841* (Annapolis: n.p., 1841); Robert
Goodloe Harper, *A Letter from Gen. Harper, of Maryland, to Elias B. Caldwell, Esq., Secretary
of the American Society for Colonizing the Free People of Colour, in the United States, with Their
Own Consent* (Baltimore: E. J. Cole, 1818). Bruce L. Mouser has argued that Baltimore col-
onizationists like Elisha Tyson were less concerned about creating an exclusively white city
and instead considered Liberia an opportunity for a capable segment of the free black population to succeed in ways impossible in the United States. See Mouser, "Baltimore's African
Experiment, 1822–1827," *Journal of Negro History* 80 (summer 1995): 114. In contrast,
Stephen Whitman, *Price of Freedom*, ch. 6, stresses the white-supremacist logic of colonization. See also Richard L. Hall, *On Afric's Shore: A History of Maryland in Liberia* (Baltimore: Maryland Historical Society, 2004).

66. On the carters' petition, see *Genius*, January 12, 19, April 26, 1828; [Thomas Pinck-
ney], *Reflections Occasioned by the Late Disturbances in Charleston. By Achates* (Charleston:
A. E. Miller, 1822). Within the literature of the Maryland State Colonization Society, an argument in favor of replacing black labor with white labor appeared once in 1832 in *Colonization of the Free Colored Population of Maryland, and of Such Slaves as May Hereafter Become Free . . .* (Baltimore: Managers Appointed by the State of Maryland, 1832), 3. Baltimore
employers remained unsympathetic toward disgruntled white workers. See Jeffrey R.

Brackett, *The Negro in Maryland: A Study of the Institution of Slavery* (Baltimore: Johns Hopkins University, 1889), 209–210; Frank Towers, "Job Busting at Baltimore Shipyards: Racial Violence in the Civil War–Era South," *JSH* 66 (May 2000): 221–256.

67. Whitman, *Price of Freedom*, 8–32; Anita Aidt Guy, "The Maryland Abolition Society and the Promotion of the Ideals of the New Nation," *MHM* 84 (winter 1989): 342–349. One early Baltimore abolitionist did contend that free workers would prove more productive than slaves, who "have no inducement, no incentive to be industrious." See George Buchanan, *An Oration upon the Moral and Political Evil of Slavery. Delivered at a Public Meeting of the Maryland Society for the Promoting the Abolition of Slavery . . . July 4, 1791* (Baltimore: Philip Edwards, 1793), 16.

68. Peskin, *Manufacturing Revolution*, ch. 10.

69. "Slave labour employed in manufactures . . . [Signed] Hamilton, Philadelphia, Oct. 2, 1827," Library of Congress Rare Book and Special Collections Division, Printed Ephemera Collection, portfolio 153, folder 3; T. P. Jones, *Address on the Progress of Manufactures*, 3–16.

70. As American protectionists argued for harmony of interests among employers and workers, urban mechanics increasingly thought they had more to fear from American capitalists than from British imports, hence the rise of the Workingmen's parties in the late 1820s. Seth Luther decried *"national* glory, *national* wealth" as propaganda to mask labor exploitation. Luther, *An Address to the Working Men of New England, on the State of Education, and On the Condition of the Producing Classes in Europe and America . . .* , 2nd ed. (New York: George H. Evans, 1833), 16–17.

71. Linda K. Kerber, *No Constitutional Right to Be Ladies: Women and the Obligation of Citizenship* (New York: Hill and Wang, 1998), 51. Robert J. Steinfeld explains the "jurisdictional" notion of labor as community property in *The Invention of Free Labor: The Employment Relation in English and American Law and Culture, 1350–1870* (Chapel Hill: University of North Carolina Press, 1991), ch. 3.

72. The Virginian St. George Tucker captured this sentiment perfectly when he argued that society's "interests require the exertions of every individual in some mode or other; and those who have not wherewith to support themselves honestly without corporeal labour, whatever be their complexion, ought to be compelled to labour." See *A Dissertation on Slavery: With a Proposal for the Gradual Abolition of It, in the State of Virginia* (Philadelphia, Pa.: Mathew Carey, 1796), 102. The language of Baltimore's vagrancy statute first appeared in *Laws*, 1793.57, §23, followed by 1804.96. A further revision—this one assigning vagrants to the new penitentiary—appeared as 1811.212. On the journeymen's strike, see Steffen, *Mechanics of Baltimore*, 222–223.

Chapter 2 · A Job for a Working Man

1. BCA, 1812:650; *American*, July 15, 1819; Robert Beaty, *The Trial of Robert Beaty, (Who was Tarred and Feathered,) on an Indictment of Perjury* (Baltimore: n.p., 1809). Beaty, who had defected from the British Navy, reportedly called Thomas Jefferson "a French influenced jack ass" in the presence of his new Baltimore co-workers. His diatribes in fall 1808 also denounced Americans as "a set of rebels, and the offspring of convicts, transported for thiev-

ing, murder and treason." Beaty "declared he was a Tory, and gloried in the appellation." Interestingly, the state brought charges of disorderly conduct against the eight men responsible for tarring and feathering him, and sentenced them to three months of jail time. In seeking a pardon from the governor, the men explained that "an honest and ardent love for our country" compelled them "to fix a stigma on an insolent foreigner whose daily conversation was a standing reproach on the country of his refuge." See Pardons, s1061-12, folder 81, s1061-14, folder 35.

2. BCA, Early Records of Baltimore [Rg2, s1], 1795, 1:14–22.

3. "The Condition of the Coloured Population of the City of Baltimore," *Baltimore Literary and Religious Magazine* 4 (April 1838): 175.

4. T. Stephen Whitman, *The Price of Freedom: Slavery and Manumission in Baltimore and Early National Maryland* (Lexington: University Press of Kentucky, 1997), 167–169; *Post*, June 17, 28, July 15, 1809.

5. These names are culled from the September 9, 1809, payroll provided by contractor Christian Baum to the city commissioners. See BCA, 1809:236. For similar payrolls, see BCA, 1798:176, 1807:151, 1810:674, 1816:226, 1819:178, 1835:1237, 1837:790.

6. *Post*, September 22, 1809; BCA, 1809:236. Equillo, James Richardson, and Aaron Bunton appear on payrolls labeled "Paid for Extra Hands for Pumping . . . September 21, 1809" and "Paid for Extra Labourers for Pumping . . . September 25, 1809." However, each man appeared in other payrolls from the New Bridge, both before and after the September call for extra labor at the pumps.

7. Graham Russell Hodges, *New York City Cartmen, 1667–1850* (New York: New York University Press, 1985). For an explicit comparison of occupational exclusion in Baltimore and New York, see E. A. Andrews, *Slavery and the Domestic Slave-Trade in the United States. In a Series of Letters Addressed to the Executive Committee of the American Union for the Relief and Improvement of the Colored Race* (Boston: Light & Stearns, 1836), 51.

8. For free black occupations based on city directories, see Christopher Phillips, *Freedom's Port: The African American Community of Baltimore, 1790–1860* (Urbana: University of Illinois Press, 1997), 111. On skilled slaves coming from the Maryland countryside to Baltimore, see Bayly E. Marks, "Skilled Blacks in Antebellum St. Mary's County, Maryland," *JSH* 53 (November 1987): 537–563; Christine Daniels, "Alternative Workers in a Slave Economy: Kent County Maryland" (Ph.D. diss., Johns Hopkins University, 1990). Most black craftsmen in Baltimore remained in slavery (too valuable to manumit), and most free black men had lacked access in their youth to the craft apprenticeships governing access to well-paying trades in the city.

9. A near majority of white men listed in city directories claimed craft occupations, while the largest single category of free black men was "laborer." See Charles G. Steffen, *The Mechanics of Baltimore: Workers and Politics in the Age of Revolution, 1763–1812* (Urbana: University of Illinois Press, 1984), 13; Phillips, *Freedom's Port*, 111.

10. Baltimore's orphan's court, the legal institution that handled apprenticeships (even for children who had two parents), made little effort to procure craft training for black boys. Moreover, for black apprentices, the court typically stipulated lower education requirements, such as shorter schooling terms or reading without writing and math skills. By 1817, Maryland law allowed masters to deny black apprentices education altogether in exchange for

supplementing freedom dues with $30 cash. During the 1810s, free black children made up 6 percent of child apprentices in the city, a rate disproportionately low relative to their share of the city's overall population. About half of those bindings were voluntary on the part of free black parents; the other half were court ordered in response to parents' death or poverty (real or presumed). Aspiring free black craftsmen also had fewer opportunities to accumulate the necessary capital to purchase tools and materials because they were devoting most of their earnings to buying loved ones out of slavery. See Whitman, *Price of Freedom*, 28–30, 187n80; Stephanie Cole, "Servants and Slaves: Domestic Service in the Border Cities, 1800–1850" (Ph.D. diss., University of Florida, 1994), 156–169.

11. The number of free African American men working as domestic servants is difficult to obtain. Fifteen black waiters appeared in *Baltimore Directory for 1817–1818* (Baltimore: James Kennedy, 1817). Census data (after 1820) can reveal the number of adult free black men living within white households, potentially an indication of domestic service. In the commercialized sixth and seventh wards of the city, historian Barbara Wallace found 99 adult black men (of 245 black males total) living in white-headed households. See Wallace, "'Fair Daughters of Africa': African American Women in Baltimore, 1790–1860" (Ph.D. diss., UCLA, 2001), 55. References to black men as domestic servants appear in *Baltimore Literary and Religious Magazine* 4 (April 1838): 175.

12. *American*, July 12, 1804 ("attentive"); *Post*, August 5 ("a situation"), October 13 ("active"), 1809. For another example, see *Maryland Gazette*, February 24, 1792: "Wants Employment, by the Month or Year, A Free Negro Man, well qualified to serve in the capacity of a Waiter or House-Servant."

13. Wages for male domestic service are very hard to identify, but Hezekiah Niles included the figure of $12 for a "man-servant" in an essay chastising the profligate spending patterns of wealthy families in the face of economic collapse. See "Domestic Economy!," *Niles*, July 24, 1819. The *Federal Census of 1810*, Baltimore City, listed several James Richardsons, free men of color, in the seventh, eighth, and ninth wards.

14. Unlike other Southern cities like Charleston and New Orleans, the bulk of free people of color in Baltimore were not of mixed-raced ancestry, nor did they compose a kind of "middle class" between wealthy whites and enslaved African Americans. As Christopher Phillips has demonstrated, the bulk of free blacks in Baltimore were born into rural slavery and field labor, dark skinned, unskilled, poor, and less attuned to the mores of urban middle-class respectability. See Phillips, *Freedom's Port*, 63.

15. Shipboard labor had long promised black men a workplace somewhat removed from the indignities of racism on shore. To enforce racial divisions among the crew seemed counterproductive to the collective labor requirements of an oceangoing vessel and unnecessary within the rigid hierarchy that ran from the captain to the green hand. See W. Jeffrey Bolster, *Black Jacks: African American Seamen in the Age of Sail* (Cambridge, Mass.: Harvard University Press, 1997), 68–101, 190–214. For black sailors on the *Warren* voyage, see *David Hoffman vs. Peter Gold*, Court of Appeals of Maryland, 8 G&J 79, 1836; *Lyde Goodwin vs. Samuel Keavin*, Baltimore County Orphans Court, May 11, 1832, *RSPP*, 20983209. These two cases turned on ownership of the estates of the two black sailors. As the cases were adjudicated, a serious point of contention was whether the sailors were enslaved or free; no one could remember or prove it decisively. Daniel Cooper "always acted as a free man." For

the Charleston antiwhooping law, see *Masters of Vessels as well as others therein concerned . . . Port Regulations* (Charleston: n.p., 1827), Library of Congress, Rare Book and Special Collections Division, Printed Ephemera Collection, portfolio 172, folder 36.

16. *Maryland Journal,* July 27, 1792.

17. *Post,* March 28 ("coloured person"), April 11 ("middle-aged"), June 7 ("German"), August 8 ("active and able"), 1809.

18. *Post,* March 6 (Levering), June 13 ("one hundred"), 1809.

19. BCA, Early Records of Baltimore, 1795–1797, 1:1–22, 2:75.

20. Thomas Brown ran as a Federalist and called on voters to "choose one Man of Colour to represent so many hundreds of poor Blacks as inhabit this town, as well as the several thousands in the different parts of the state." See Phillips, *Freedom's Port,* 83; *Maryland Gazette,* February 3, 1794; Steffen, *Mechanics of Baltimore,* 131. For the declining prospects of free people of color, see Jeffrey R. Brackett, *The Negro in Maryland: A Study of the Institution of Slavery* (Baltimore: Johns Hopkins University, 1889); Ira Berlin, *Slaves without Masters: The Free Negro in the Antebellum South* (New York: Pantheon Books, 1974); Barbara Jeanne Fields, *Slavery and Freedom on the Middle Ground: Maryland during the Nineteenth Century* (New Haven, Conn.: Yale University Press, 1984). For a more promising account, see T. Stephen Whitman, *Challenging Slavery in the Chesapeake: Black and White Resistance to Human Bondage, 1775–1865* (Baltimore: Maryland Historical Society, 2007).

21. On the problem of wage labor in republican political thought, see David R. Roediger, *The Wages of Whiteness: Race and the Making of the American Working Class* (New York: Verso, 1991); Drew R. McCoy, *The Elusive Republic: Political Economy in Jeffersonian America* (Chapel Hill: University of North Carolina Press, OIEAHC, 1980).

22. Cornelius William Stafford, *Baltimore Directory for 1802* (Baltimore: John W. Butler, 1802) located 103 households headed by "labourers" among 4,100 total households. Bunton did not appear in the *Federal Census of 1810* for Baltimore City, but was listed as "Bunting" in William Fry, *Baltimore Directory for 1810* (Baltimore: G. Dobbin and Murphy, 1810), 41.

23. "Constitution and By-Laws of the Union Society of Journeymen Cordwainers of the City and Precincts of Baltimore, April 21, 1806," Baltimore County Court (Court Papers Exhibits), 1806–1809, MSA, c-313-5. Steffen, *Mechanics of Baltimore,* 222–223; Robert J. Steinfeld, "The *Philadelphia Cordwainers'* Case of 1806: The Struggle over Alternative Legal Constructions of a Free Market in Labor," in *Labor Law in America: Historical and Critical Essays,* eds. Christopher L. Tomlins and Andrew J. King (Baltimore: Johns Hopkins University Press, 1992), 20–43.

24. Carole Shammas, "The Space Problem in Early United States Cities," *WMQ* 57 (July 2000): 531–534; Steven Sarson, "'Objects of Distress': Inequality and Poverty in Early Nineteenth-Century Prince George's County," *MHM* 96 (summer 2001): 141–62; Steven Sarson, "Landlessness and Tenancy in Early National Prince George's County, Maryland," *WMQ* 57 (July 2000): 569–598; Paul E. Johnson, *Sam Patch, the Famous Jumper* (New York: Hill and Wang, 2003); Thomas Humphrey, "Poverty and Politics in the Hudson River Valley," in *Down and Out in Early America,* ed. Billy G. Smith (University Park: Pennsylvania State University Press, 2004), 235–61; Paul G. E. Clemens and Lucy Simler, "Rural Labor and the Farm Household in Chester County, Pennsylvania, 1750–1820," in *Work and Labor in Early America,* ed. Stephen Innes (Chapel Hill: University of North Carolina Press,

OIEAHC, 1988), 106–143; Donald R. Adams, Jr., "Prices and Wages in Maryland, 1750–1850," *Journal of Economic History* 46 (September 1986): 625–645.

25. Michael Meranze, *Laboratories of Virtue: Punishment, Revolution, and Authority in Philadelphia, 1760–1835* (Chapel Hill: University of North Carolina Press, OIEAHC, 1996); Wallace Shugg, *A Monument to Good Intentions: The Story of the Maryland Penitentiary, 1804–1995* (Baltimore: Maryland Historical Society, 2000), 3; *Niles*, November 30, 1811; 1802 Grand Jury Report, Baltimore County Court (Miscellaneous Court Papers) 1801–1802, MSA, c-1-28.

26. On "drowning cell," see Simon Schama, *The Embarrassment of Riches: An Interpretation of Dutch Culture in the Golden Age* (New York: Knopf, 1987), 2. For shipboard labor and wages, see Marcus Rediker, *Between the Devil and the Deep Blue Sea: Merchant Seamen, Pirates, and the Anglo-American Maritime World, 1700–1750* (New York: Cambridge University Press, 1987); Paul A. Gilje, *Liberty on the Waterfront: American Maritime Culture in the Age of Revolution* (Philadelphia: University of Pennsylvania Press, 2004).

27. Richard Parkinson, *The Experienced Farmer's Tour in America* (London: G&J Robinson, 1805), 18.

28. *Post*, August 8, 1809 ("active"); BCA, 1805:201 and 1812:650 (privy cleaners); *Baltimore Weekly Prices Current*, January 1, 1807 (newspaper carriers). For a listing of "Free Householders of Colour, with their Residences and Occupations," see *Baltimore Directory for 1817–1818* (Baltimore: James Kennedy, 1817), 212–222.

29. On the broader relationship of race and labor in early America, see Jacqueline Jones, *American Work: Four Centuries of Black and White Labor* (New York: W. W. Norton, 1998); Evelyn Nakano Glenn, *Unequal Freedom: How Race and Gender Shaped American Citizenship and Labor* (Cambridge, Mass.: Harvard University Press, 2002), 56–92.

30. *Votes and Proceedings of the House of Delegates of the State of Maryland, November Session, 1808* (Annapolis: Frederick Green, 1809), 75. The November session voted to delay consideration until the following session, but the petition does not appear in the subsequent minutes. White carters and draymen sought to exclude African American rivals again in 1828. See BCA, 1828:425; *Genius*, January 12, 1828.

31. *Post*, May 30 (Niles), May 31 (Levering), August 8 ("understands") 1809. For land holdings of the Goldsmith (often Gouldsmith) family, see Land Papers, 1795–1818, MHS, ms. 1960. The Goldsmith household appeared in the *Federal Census of 1810*, Baltimore City, as two white adults over forty-five, two white females ages sixteen to twenty-six, and five slaves. While the *Federal Census of 1810*, Baltimore City, lists the Goldsmiths among the waterfront residences of the city's leading merchants, Fry's *Baltimore Directory for 1810* places the Goldsmiths at 17 Front Street in Old Town. The reason for the discrepancy is unclear.

32. Whitman, *Price of Freedom*, 14; *Maryland Journal*, February 10, 1794; *Post*, July 14, 1809. On slave hiring, see Jonathan D. Martin, *Divided Mastery: Slave Hiring in the American South* (Cambridge, Mass.: Harvard University Press, 2004); Sarah S. Hughes, "Slaves for Hire: The Allocation of Black Labor in Elizabeth City County, Virginia, 1782–1810," *WMQ* 35 (April 1978): 260–286.

33. On slave property as a legacy left to widows and children, see Kirsten E. Wood, *Masterful Women: Slaveholding Widows from the American Revolution through the Civil War* (Chapel Hill: University of North Carolina Press, 2004), passim; Jennifer L. Morgan, *Laboring*

Women: Reproduction and Gender in New World Slavery (Philadelphia: University of Pennsylvania Press, 2004), 69–106; Whitman, *Price of Freedom*, 15.

34. Derochbrune petition, July 27, 1803, *RSPP*, 20980306.

35. Martin, *Divided Mastery*; Achsah Owings petition, February 9, 1813, *RSPP*, 20981308; Eleanor Dall petition, May 28, 1814, *RSPP*, 20981406; Mary C. Spence petition, November 15, 1826, *RSPP*, 20982615. The wages that came from hiring out could accumulate to substantial amounts. In 1838, Ann Lamb was due to inherit a portion of the Abraham Woodward estate but sued the estate's administrators for not including the earnings of eight or nine slaves over the intervening six years. See *George Lamb vs. Ann D. Woodward*, March 29, 1838, *RSPP*, 20983807.

36. *Post*, June 17, 1809 (Hewett), August 5, 1816 (Mary); Whitman, *Price of Freedom*, 61–92; Frederick Douglass, *Narrative of the Life of Frederick Douglass, An American Slave, Written by Himself*, ed. David W. Blight (1845; repr., Boston: Bedford Books, 2003) 64–65.

37. Whitman, *Price of Freedom*, 93–118.

38. Ibid., 98–118; *Laws*, 1796.67, 1804.90, 1817.112, 1833.224.

39. Whitman, *Price of Freedom*, 24, 183n53; Shawn A. Cole, "Capitalism and Freedom: Slavery and Manumission in Louisiana, 1725–1820," *Journal of Economic History* (December 2005): 1008–1027; *Post*, June 15 ("mulatto Girl"), July 6 ("Negro Boy"), 1809.

40. *Post*, June 19, 1809.

41. Steven Deyle, *Carry Me Back: The Domestic Slave Trade in American Life* (New York: Oxford University Press, 2005), 40–46; *Baltimore Telegraphe*, January 30, 1804; John Parrish, *Remarks on the Slavery of the Black People; Addressed to the Citizens of the United States . . .* (Philadelphia, Pa.: Kimber, Conrad, & Co., 1806), 11, 20–21.

42. For the 1813 tax list, see BCA, Tax Assessors Notebooks, Rg4, s2; Whitman, *Price of Freedom*, 181n28–9.

43. On slave sale prices, see Whitman, *Price of Freedom*, 175–177.

44. The recent historiography of slavery has focused on constrained choices. See Joshua Rothman, *Notorious in the Neighborhood: Sex and Families Across the Color Line in Virginia, 1787–1861* (Chapel Hill: University of North Carolina Press, 2003); Sharla M. Fett, *Working Cures: Healing, Health, and Power on Southern Slave Plantations* (Chapel Hill: University of North Carolina Press, 2002); Stephanie M. H. Camp, *Closer to Freedom: Enslaved Women and Everyday Resistance in the Plantation South* (Chapel Hill: University of North Carolina Press, 2004). On running away and leverage, see John Hope Franklin and Loren Schweninger, *Runaway Slaves: Rebels on the Plantation* (New York: Oxford University Press, 1999).

45. For Goldsmith slaves, see BCA, Tax Assessors Notebooks, Rg4, s2, 1813 (Sarah Goldsmith, Pitt Street). The September 21, 1809, payroll at New Bridge lists an Equilo Johnston, but this is the only record to list a possible surname.

46. Chattel Records, November 27, 1811 (Cole), July 10, 1812 (Ackerman), MHS, ms 2865. Baltimore County Court (Miscellaneous Court Papers) 1807, MSA, c-1-32 (Haynes as Hayes).

47. Whitman, *Price of Freedom*, 73–74.

48. Ibid.

49. *Post*, January 10, 1809 (John); *American*, December 22, 1818 (Duppin). Douglass, *Narrative*, 106; Douglas R. Egerton, "Slaves to the Marketplace: Economic Liberty and Black Rebelliousness in the Atlantic World," *JER* 26 (winter 2006): 617–639.

50. *Mechanics' Gazette and Merchants' Daily Advertiser*, September 13, 1815 (de Volunbrun); *American*, July 21, 1819 (Chambers).

51. Whitman, *Price of Freedom*, 11, 15; Douglass, *Narrative*, 106.

52. *Post*, November 18, 1816; *Patriot*, April 22, 1816 (Cole), July 23, 1816 ("out of city"), November 2, 1816 ("liberty"), October 11, 1816 ("consent"). In 1817, Maryland made it illegal to sell term slaves out of the state, at which point sale advertisements for term slaves no longer needed to mention an explicit restriction on such sales. But of those mentioning restrictions in 1816, nineteen were selling slaves-for-life, while twelve offered term slaves.

53. Whitman, *Price of Freedom*, 175–176; *Post*, April 11, 1809; Gwendolyn Midlo Hall, ed., *Afro-Louisiana History and Genealogy, 1718–1820*, retrieved November 2005, www.ibiblio .org/laslave/index.html.

54. Glenn, *Unequal Freedom*, 56–92.

55. Jonathan A. Glickstein has explored the competition of free and enslaved workers as a problem in antebellum political economy in *American Exceptionalism, American Anxiety: Wages, Competition, and Degraded Labor in the Antebellum United States* (Charlottesville: University of Virginia Press, 2002). On turnover costs as a consideration for employers choosing between free and unfree workers, see Christopher Hanes, "Turnover Costs and the Distribution of Slave Labor in Anglo-America," *Journal of Economic History* 56 (June 1996): 307–329.

56. Fields, *Slavery and Freedom on the Middle Ground*, 52, describes these multiple forms of labor as "volatile substitutes for one another."

57. BCA, 1798:150, 1798:216 (reprinted as "Brickmaking in Baltimore, 1798," *Journal of the Society of Architectural Historians* 18 (March 1959): 33–34).

58. Christopher T. George, "Mirage of Freedom: African-Americans in the War of 1812," *MHM* 91 (winter 1996): 427–450; BCA, 1814:468, 1814:477, 1814:502, 1814:527. See also Wallace, "Fair Daughters of Africa," 206–208.

59. Whitman, *Price of Freedom*, 16–23, 167–174.

60. Steffen, *Mechanics of Baltimore*, 32. For apprenticeship laws, see *Laws*, 1794.45, 1808.54, 1818.189. Baltimore County Court (Court Papers Exhibits), 1806–1809, MSA, c-313-5. For 6¢ runaway advertisements, see *Post*, October 26, 1809 (Ingram); *Patriot*, May 30, July 9, September 5, October 8, December 22, 1816. For 1¢, see *Patriot*, September 7, 1816.

61. For Camp, see Whitman, *Price of Freedom*, 25–26.

62. On the Maryland Chemical Works, see Whitman, *Price of Freedom*, 33–60. Mixed labor had a longer history in Maryland: Charles Steffen, "The Pre-Industrial Iron Worker: Northampton Iron Works, 1780–1820," *LH* 20 (1979): 87–110; R. Kent Lancaster, "Chattel Slavery at Hampton/Northampton, Baltimore County," *MHM* 95 (winter 2000): 409–427, and "Almost Chattel: The Lives of Indentured Servants at Hampton/Northampton," *MHM* 94 (fall 1999): 341–363.

63. On canal labor, see Peter Way, *Common Labour: Workers and the Digging of North American Canals, 1780–1860* (New York: Cambridge University Press, 1993); *Patriot*, March

1, 1826; Robert J. Steinfeld, *The Invention of Free Labor* (New York: Cambridge University Press, 1991), 166–172, 189–195.

64. On wage rates, see Adams, "Prices and Wages in Maryland"; Richard Smith Chew, "The Measure of Independence: From the American Revolution to the Market Revolution in the Mid-Atlantic" (Ph.D. diss., College of William and Mary, 2002), 370–371.

65. *Patriot*, March 1, 1826; Steffen, "Pre-Industrial Iron Worker"; Whitman, *Price of Freedom*, 45.

66. BCA, Early Records of Baltimore, 1795, 1:14–22; *Niles*, May 22, 1819.

67. *Patriot*, November 3, 1815 (Baum obituary), April 21, 1821 (Samuel insolvency); Samuel Jackson, *Baltimore Directory, corrected up to June 1819* (Baltimore: Richard J. Matchett, 1819).

68. *Patriot*, June 18, 1834 (parody); *Baltimore Gazette and Daily Advertiser*, April 22, 1833 ("good hand").

69. William Goldsmith died with several outstanding debts that Sarah first had to settle before living off the labor of her slaves. See *Rachel Ayers vs. Sarah Gouldsmith et al.*, Chancery Court Papers, Queen Anne County, MSA, s512-1-35. See also BCA, Tax Assessors Notebooks, 1818 (Sarah Gouldsmith, widow, Pitt Street).

70. *Patriot*, February 13, 1826 (Sarah obituary); Joseph R. Foard petition, March 3, 1827, RSPP, 20982706.

71. This reconstruction involves certain conjecture. Elisha and Lucy were the only two adult slaves in Elizabeth Goldsmith's household and were roughly the same age; but whether they parented the baby Equillo is a guess. Likewise, the control of slave parents over children's names was irregular. Evidence from city assessments suggests that Lucy had known Equillo since before 1810. Elisha became a slave to the Goldsmith family between 1810 and 1818, most likely after William had died. This suggests that Lucy and Elisha were not siblings. Both would have known Equillo for ten to twenty years before he was sold away after 1827.

Chapter 3 · Dredging and Drudgery

1. *Mechanics' Gazette and Merchants' Daily Advertiser*, April 27, 1815. For sailors' wages, see Articles of Agreement for 1800 voyage of brig *William*, Library of Congress, Printed Ephemera Collection, portfolio 28, folder 32d; Lemuel Chandler (Baltimore) to Tillinghast, Gorton & Tillinghast (Providence), March 25, 1812, Tillinghast Family Papers, John Carter Brown Library; Paul A. Gilje, *Liberty on the Waterfront: American Maritime Culture in the Age of Revolution* (Philadelphia: University of Pennsylvania Press, 2004), 20–21. For agricultural wages, see Donald R. Adams, Jr., "Prices and Wages in Maryland, 1750–1850," *Journal of Economic History* 46 (September 1986): 625–645; Christine Daniels, "'Getting His (or Her) Livelihood': Free Workers in Slave Anglo-America, 1675–1810," *Agricultural History* 71 (spring 1997): 125–162.

2. Joseph Tuckerman, "Who are the Poor?" [c. 1830], in *Joseph Tuckerman on the Elevation of the Poor*, ed. E. E. Hale (Boston: Roberts Bros., 1874), 65. John Melish, *Information and Advice to Emigrants to the United States . . .* (Philadelphia, Pa.: John Melish, 1819), 90. Similar celebrations of American opportunity appeared in the Shamrock Society of New

York's *Hints to Emigrants from Europe, who Intend to Make a Permanent Residence in the United States* (New York: Van Winkle and Wiley, 1816).

3. *Baltimore Directory for 1804* (Baltimore: Warner and Hanna, 1804), 95–96. Cornelius William Stafford, *Baltimore Directory for 1802* (Baltimore: John W. Butler, 1802), included just over one hundred white laborers in a city with upwards of seven thousand working-age men. The *Baltimore Directory for 1817–1818* (Baltimore: James Kennedy, 1817) listed sixty-eight African American laborers. Richard Matchett's *Baltimore Directory for 1827–1828* (Baltimore: Matchett, 1827) included 201 African American laborers and 205 white laborers for a city that had tripled in population since 1800.

4. The payrolls are scattered throughout the Baltimore City Archives. See City Register (1808), RG32, S1, box 1, items 174–176; City Commissioners Papers (1808), RG3, S1, box 10, item 173; City Commissioners Papers (1809), RG3, S1, box 12, item 236; Bills and Vouchers (1810), RG41, S3, box 1, item 676(2); Bureau of Harbors (1811), RG39, S2, box 3, items 573–612; Bills and Vouchers (1812), RG41, S3, box 1, item 733; Bureau of Harbors (1813), RG39, S2, box 3, item 548; Bureau of Harbors (1814), RG39, S2, box 3, item 130; Bureau of Harbors (1815), RG39, S2, box 4, item 235; Bureau of Harbors (1817), RG39, S2, box 4; Bills and Vouchers (1818), RG41, S3, box 4, item 984; Bills and Vouchers (1819), RG41, S3, boxes 5 and 6, item 712; City Commissioners Papers (1819) RG3, S1, box 25, item 178.

5. Peter Way, "Evil Humors and Ardent Spirits: The Rough Culture of Canal Construction Laborers," *JAH* 79 (March 1993): 1397–1428. For early republic labor history, see Bruce Laurie, *Artisans into Workers: Labor in Nineteenth-Century America* (New York: Hill and Wang, 1989); Mary H. Blewett, *Men, Women, and Work: Class, Gender, and Protest in the New England Shoe Industry, 1780–1910* (Urbana: University of Illinois Press, 1988); Thomas Dublin, *Women at Work: The Transformation of Work and Community in Lowell, Massachusetts, 1826–1860* (New York: Columbia University Press, 1979).

6. BCA, 1813:457. On the environmental history of Baltimore harbor, see Theodore Steinberg, *Down to Earth: Nature's Role in American History* (New York: Oxford University Press, 2002), 74.

7. *Mayors' Msgs.*, 95 (1823).

8. William Priest, *Travels in the United States of America, commencing in the year 1793 and ending in 1797* . . . (London: J. Johnson, 1802), 78–79; BCA, 1801:214, 1809:464.

9. Thomas W. Griffith, *Annals of Baltimore*, second edition (Baltimore: W. Wooddy, 1833), 18–20.

10. *Niles*, August 16, 1817; Sherry H. Olson, *Baltimore: The Building of an American City*, 2nd ed. (Baltimore: Johns Hopkins University Press, 1997), 50, 55, 82.

11. Griffith, *Annals of Baltimore*, 288; Olson, *Baltimore*, 38, 55.

12. William Darlington, "Journalissimo of a Peregrination to the city of Baltimore; performed in the year *domini* 1803," William Darlington Papers, New-York Historical Society.

13. *Maryland Journal*, December 1, 1789, quoted in Dennis Rankin Clark, "Baltimore, 1729–1829: The Genesis of a Community" (Ph.D. diss., Catholic University, 1976), 174.

14. *Mayors' Msgs.*, 73–74 (1821), 110–111 (1825).

15. *Barron et al. v. Mayor and City Council of Baltimore*, 32 U.S. 243 (1833); Christopher M. Curtis, "A Question of 'Great Importance': Nullification, Slavery, and the Marshall Court's

Decision in *Barron v. Baltimore* (1833)," paper presented at the Institute for Constitutional Studies, June 2005.

16. *Maryland Journal and Baltimore Advertiser*, March 20, 1790. *Laws*, 1788.24, 1793. 57; Robert C. Keith, *Baltimore Harbor: A Picture History* (Baltimore: Ocean World Publishing, 1982), 64. On dredging and harbor improvement elsewhere, see Nancy S. Seasholes, *Gaining Ground: A History of Landmaking in Boston* (Cambridge, Mass.: MIT Press, 2003). For the harbor labor of Barbary captives, see *Salem Gazette*, November 11, 1794; Gary E. Wilson, "American Hostages in Moslem Nations, 1784–1796: The Public Response," *JER* 2 (summer 1982): 132; Paul Baepler, *White Slaves, African Masters: An Anthology of American Barbary Captivity Narratives* (Chicago: University of Chicago Press, 1999).

17. *Maryland Journal*, December 20, 1791, March 20, June 26, 1792, March 17, 1794; BCA, Early Records of Baltimore, Rg2, s1, book 1.

18. *Maryland Journal*, March 17, 1791; BCA, 1792:7, 1800:292, 1802:288; Priest, *Travels*, 82–3; [James Calhoun], "Prudent Laws and Wise Regulations: Three Early Baltimore Mayor's Messages, 1797–1799," *MHM* 78 (winter 1983): 278–286.

19. *Mayors' Msgs.*, 1802; Darlington, "Journalissimo." The federal government issued fourteen dredging patents between 1793 and 1836; six went to Baltimore inventors. For efforts to develop a steam-powered mudmachine in Philadelphia, see Steven Lubar, "Was This America's First Steamboat, Locomotive, and Car?" *Invention and Technology Magazine* 21 (spring 2006): 16–24.

20. BCA, 1806:156, 1806:181, 1806:209, 1806:221–222, 1807:260, 1808:292.

21. It is difficult to ascertain more about McDonald because Fells Point was home to a second Alexander McDonald, a merchant and a "gentleman" according to directories and tax lists. However, many other municipal records did not distinguish the McDonalds by occupation, making it impossible to determine which one owned certain properties. I am using the spelling of McDonald that appeared in his own hand, although other records alternate between MacDonald, McDonnel, and McDonnald. The earliest directory entry for McDonald was in 1810, when he lived by the waterfront near Harford Run on Granby Street. By 1817, Alexander McDonald had moved to Ann Street, a block from a stinking inlet on the east side of Fells Point. Petitioners had complained in 1798 that "there is an acre of filthy matter exposed to the heat of the sun" during low tide [BCA, 1798: 156]. Samuel Jackson, *Baltimore Directory, corrected up to June 1819* (Baltimore: Richard J. Matchett) listed McDonald about a block away, on Happy Alley near Alisanna. Despite McDonald's high annual earnings (over $400 every year, over $600 in most), he did not accumulate significant wealth. In 1818, his property amounted to $255, putting him in the 60th percentile of wealth-holders in eastern Baltimore. He owned two improved lots, $10 worth of furniture, and 5 ounces of silver plate. By 1823, he had also acquired a cow (BCA, Tax Assessors Notebooks, Rg4, s2, 1818 and 1823). His job as superintendent did not necessarily bring him respect. A disgruntled waterfront property owner wrote to the city council in 1812, complaining of "Your hireling Macdonald," which surely constituted a slur in early republic parlance (BCA, 1812:270).

22. McDonald's erratic spelling is a critical problem in the records. Names appeared with a fair amount of latitude on the payrolls. One week's Hugh Coffee became Hugh Coffield the next, and Hugh Caughea the week after. The surnames Jordon, Gordon, and

Gordwin were interchangeable, as were Johnson and Johnston, McHenny and Mikelhenny, McKay and McCoy, and Sterling, Stallings, Stailer, and Stallion. The records contain many other uncertainties. For example, in 1819 Alex McCurdy appeared one week and Angus McCurdy worked the following. Was this a lone man whose name McDonald had simply mistaken, or were Angus and Alex McCurdy two distinct men? Alternatively, was Lewis French actually Lewis French, or a Frenchman named Lewis? McDonald may have identified workers—especially those who remained on the job for only a week or two—by markers other than a surname. But because the payrolls are a lengthy series, it is possible to search for patterns and clarification over time.

23. Only one other time in the next decade did McDonald use piece rates, and that was during an exceptionally busy project in the summer of 1817, when he needed extra carters and scowmen.

24. For Baltimore payrolls with wages at $1 (or 7s 6p) per day, see BCA, 1799:176, 1801:147, 1809:236, 1814:892. During the final week of digging in 1809, the base rate was $1.04, but the standard wage returned to $1.12½ for the 1810 season.

25. Peter Way, *Common Labour: Workers and the Digging of North American Canals, 1780–1869* (New York: Cambridge University Press, 1993), 27–37, 275–76; Adams, "Prices and Wages in Maryland," 625–645; Daniels, "Getting His (or Her) Livelyhood," 125–162.

26. The mudmachine payroll for 1815 included 103 different men, more than in any other year.

27. A charity plea from 1805 explicitly mentioned the workers on the mudmachine among those "thrown out of employment by the stoppage of our navigation [due to ice] and other causes incident to the time of year." The writer added that "it is not entirely for the worthless part of the community that it is proposed to raise money." *American*, January 8, 1805.

28. On transience in the early republic, see the life story of Big Bill Otter in Richard B. Stott, ed., *History of My Own Times, or the Life and Adventures of William Otter, Sen. . . .* (Ithaca, N.Y.: Cornell University Press, 1995); Craig T. Friend, ed., *The Buzzel About Kentuck: Settling the Promised Land* (Lexington: University Press of Kentucky, 1999); Paul E. Johnson, *A Shopkeeper's Millennium: Society and Revivals in Rochester, New York, 1815–1837* (New York: Hill and Wang, 1978). John Woods, *Two Years' Residence in the Settlement on the English Prairie, in the Illinois Country, United States . . .* (London: Longman, Hurst, Rees, Orme, and Browne, 1822), 24.

29. *Patriot*, August, 26, 1818; BCA, 1815:385 (Zacharie), 1821:484 (Whitten). Zacharie was the hapless inventor who had first contacted the city council concerning his mudmachines in 1791. Hoping to get funding to develop a new crane in 1817, Zacharie opened his plea to the city council with this lament: "Your petitioner, Citizen of Baltimore since thirty three years, has invented here twelve different machines, and for the want of means has not had the luck of putting a single one into execution" (BCA, 1817:243). A recipient of several patents, Zacharie received the blessings of the port wardens, but the city council instead patronized another inventor, Samuel Davis (*Ordinances*, 1817.4, 1817.49). Later in 1817, Zacharie applied to become a port warden. He had recently served as a public wood measurer, and in his estimation, "no man in that office did his duty better than I did." He was especially eager to supervise public works as a port warden: "few men in that branche of

the office would be better calculated than I think I would be, being born a natural mechanick and fond of being where there is plenty hands at work and my ingenuity might (in some case) be of public utility." Zacharie concluded that he needed the job because he had six sons, and "I have not the means to give them education, and on their account, I beg of you the birth to enable me to give them good learning before I bind them to some trade" (BCA, 1817:307). Sadly, an appointment did not follow.

30. BCA, 1806:221, 1814:482, 1814:892; Bureau of Harbors, Rg39, s2, box 4, August 9, 1817. Contractors occasionally passed other charges on to the city. Christian Baum charged the city for $7.31 worth of bread and cheese on September 21, 1809 (BCA: 1809:236). On alcohol and labor, see W. J. Rorabaugh, *The Alcoholic Republic: An American Tradition* (New York: Oxford University Press, 1979). Considering the prevalence of drinking among unskilled laborers in early America, not to mention the high concentration of taverns in Fells Point, it seems unlikely that McDonald could have wholly excluded alcohol from the workday; he may have instituted a "bring your own" policy.

31. Joseph Pickering, *Emigration or No Emigration: Being the Narrative of the Author . . .* (London: Longmans, Reese Orme, Brown, and Greene, 1830), 22; Patrick Hanks and Flavia Hodges, *A Dictionary of Surnames* (New York: Oxford University Press, 1988); *San Francisco Examiner*, March 15, 1998, D-7, for an extensive list of the county-by-county origins of Irish names.

32. Pickering, *Emigration*, 22; for McDonald, see *Federal Census of 1820*, Baltimore City, Ward 1, p. 17; for War of 1812 records, see BCA, 1814:129, 1814:892; F. Edward Wright, *Maryland Militia: War of 1812*, vol. 2 (Silver Spring, Md.: Family Line Publications, 1979); for Archibald Smith's penitentiary record, see Pardons, s1061-16, folder 47; BAAB, June 23, 1823, June 22, 1825, January 2, 1826; William J. Bromwell, *History of Immigration to the United States . . . 1819 to 1855* (1856; repr., New York: Augustus Kelly, 1969). Unfortunately, further success in tracking nativity is nearly impossible. Baltimore port officials did not collect immigrant passenger lists in the 1800s and 1810s, and standard social history sources like tax lists and directories either ignored the issue of nativity or listed only household head (something that most mudmachine workers were not). The *Federal Census of 1820* category of "foreigners not naturalized" was erratically applied and tallied only 1,359 such people in the entire city (whereas port records tabulate nearly that many immigrants landing in 1820 alone). Few poor immigrants underwent the formal naturalizations recorded in court dockets.

33. Was the Hugh Coffee who worked on the mudmachine for 144 days in 1815 the same Hugh Coffin listed in that year's directory as a laborer on Ross Street? Potentially, but not definitely: John Coffee, Patrick Caughy, Bernard Caughy, Susannah Coffee, and Richard Coffee all lived in Baltimore too. Any one of them could have had a son Hugh who labored on the mudmachine. Because only the names of householders appeared in the directories, a dependent named Hugh Coffee would remain undiscovered. If these were the same men, then Hugh Coffee was the most wealthy mudmachine employee in the tax records. His Ross Street (Ward 10) property was assessed at $195 in 1818.

34. In addition to city directories (1799–1837), tax lists (BCA, Tax Assessors Notebooks, Rg2, s4, 1813, 1818, 1823, 1836), and federal census rolls (1790–1840), I searched several lengthy runs of public records, including BAAB; Baltimore County Court (Certificates of

Freedom), 1806–1816, MSA, c290-1; Baltimore County Register of Wills (Certificates of Freedom), 1806–1816, MSA, c289-1; Baltimore County Court (Miscellaneous Court Papers), 1790–1826, MSA, c-1; Maryland Penitentiary Prisoners Record, 1811–1840, MSA, s275-1 (courtesy of Stephen Whitman's computer file). One promising source for gauging the economic viability of manual laborers is the recently acquired Baltimore Savings Bank records at the Maryland State Archives. Although the bank opened in 1818, the first records that list patrons' holdings do not begin until 1824. The only mudmachine employee from 1808–1819 who had an account open in 1824 was Alexander Mikelhenny, who had earned $157 in 1811. As of October 1824, Mikelhenny's account held $28.74. Three years later, his assets had climbed to $42.68. See Special Collections (First Fidelity Bank Collection) Account Book 1824–1826, MSA, sc4313-9-223.

35. *Maryland Journal,* October 18, 1793. What evidence suggests this is the same Michael Gorman? As I will describe in coming paragraphs, the mudmachine Gorman was Irish born and in his fifties in the early 1820s, which corresponds to the twenty-one-year-old Irish-born runaway in 1793. On the other hand, there were other Gormans in Baltimore, including a prosperous carpenter named Michael, living in Fells Point in 1804. However, that Michael Gorman fell out of the records immediately, leaving only the scowman and laborer Michael Gorman by 1810.

36. BCA, 1812:642.

37. BCA, 1812:892, Tax Assessors Notebooks, 1818, p. 130.

38. BCA, Tax Assessors Notebooks, 1823, Ward 1; BAAB, June 13, 23, 1823. The *Federal Census of 1820,* Baltimore City, Ward 1, p. 19, located a Michael Gormeron (age between twenty-six and forty-five) living in Fells Point in a household containing two boys under sixteen and an adult woman. The *Federal Census of 1830,* Baltimore City, Ward 1, p. 51, located a different Michael Gorman, in his twenties, whose household included a boy younger than ten, a girl between fifteen and twenty, a young woman, and a young man in their twenties; at this time, the mudmachinist Michael Gorman was in the almshouse.

39. BCA, 1817:278, 1817:627. John Otterson (Auterson) appeared in the city directories for 1804 and 1814, but not 1807 or 1812, nor did the household appear in the 1813 assessment list. Jane Otterson was not listed as an almshouse resident in Baltimore 1823–1826, nor were there any Ottersons or Autersons in the *Federal Census of 1820* for the entire state of Maryland. Thanks to Stephanie Cole for looking and Stephen Whitman for finding David Otterson's indenture in their respective databases of apprentices. The original records are Baltimore County Register of Wills (Indentures), 1794–1830, MSA, c337.

40. The Stallings were not models of success. See chapter 7.

41. Other workers who entered the public record (as prisoners or almshouse residents) were between their late twenties and forties when they labored on the mudmachine. See BAAB, February 23, 1824 (David Dillon, on the payroll in 1818 and 1819), January 2, 1826 (Dicky Stallings, on the payroll between 1813 and 1818), June 25, 1825 (John Watson, on the payroll in 1818 and 1819). Archibald Smith was twenty-five when he started on the mudmachine and thirty when he entered the penitentiary in 1814; see Pardons, s1061-16, folder 47. According to the *Federal Census of 1820,* Baltimore City, p. 322, Jesse Bunch (employee 1815–1819) was over forty-five years old.

42. *Federal Census of 1820,* Baltimore City, Ward 1, p. 16. Twelve of the men boarding

in McDonald's household were between twenty-six and forty-five years old. For similar strategies of labor recruiting, see Gunther Peck, *Reinventing Free Labor: Padrones and Immigrant Workers in the North American West, 1880–1930* (New York: Cambridge University Press, 2000). Pardons, s1061-16, folder 47.

43. *The House that Jack Built* (Baltimore: n.p. [1818]), Library of Congress, Printed Ephemera Collection, portfolio 30, Folder 15a; *American*, September 4, 1818.

44. *American*, April 5, 1816; *Patriot*, June 24, 1816.

45. On African American naming practices in Baltimore, see Christopher Phillips, *Freedom's Port: The African American Community of Baltimore, 1790–1860* (Urbana: University of Illinois Press, 1997), 86–91.

46. Several idiosyncrasies in the payrolls raise more possibility that black workers found jobs on the mudmachine. Recall that McDonald occasionally took a few weeks to master the names of his employees. On May 24, 1813, one of the mudmachine's newest employees was David Black, who stayed on the payroll until June 27. The following week David Black did not return, but his replacement was a David Garrett. Were these two actually the same person? Was David Garrett listed as David Black until McDonald managed to learn his name? If so, was McDonald's choice of Black as a nickname an indicator of race? The payrolls for 1813 also included Cyrous Black and Cyrous Parker, as well as Peter Black and Peter Buthes. The two Peters never appeared in the same week, but appear on the payrolls in sequential weeks; the same was true of the two Cyrouses. Unfortunately, no other records confirm Garrett, Parker, and Buthes as African Americans. There were both black and white Parkers, Garretts, and Buethes (Booths) in the records for Baltimore, but none matched to the names Cyrous, Peter, or David. I initially suspected that Cyrous Parker was a rented slave (perhaps Cyrous being a form of the African name Osirus). Two Parkers in the *Federal Census of 1810* owned slaves, but none named Cyrous (names listed in BCA, Tax Assessors Notebooks). Parker, Garrett, and Buthes were diligent employees: Buthes missed fewer than five days in seventeen weeks of labor, while Parker and Garrett each earned over $169 for the year. Parker and Garrett returned in 1814, and each garnered over $120 before the British invasion closed the operation in August; only three other men logged more days during the abbreviated season.

47. I can offer other reasons to suspect these workers were African American. Because the Howards were one of Maryland's largest slaveholding families in the eighteenth century, their surname stuck to a large segment of Maryland's free black population in the nineteenth century. There was a white Henry Howard living in Fells Point in 1815, listed as a mariner (but not as a laborer as were other mudmachine employees). George Washington was a name that some black Marylanders appropriated for themselves after becoming free. The three Washingtons listed in the census and directory records were Lawrence and Elias, both white and clerks at the Custom House, and free black Charles Washington, who ran a downtown cookshop. In 1810, there were several white Boyces in Baltimore, including several Fells Point slaveholders. By 1819, the only Boyces in the directory were free blacks, Cato and Perry. Sutton Boyce appeared on an 1816 payroll for another public construction site next to Negro Congo and Negro James. Still, the other workers on that payroll had nondescript names and may well have been white (BCA, 1816:226). Sutton certainly stood out as a fairly unusual name, but the Boyce with the most distinct

name was Prettyman, a white slaveholder. There were too many Andersons to investigate, and no Sebastons to trace.

48. Enness appeared as a free black householder in the *Federal Census of 1810*, living on the south side of the basin. His home on Federal Hill's Honey Alley was assessed at $40 in 1813, and the taxman added the word "coloured" to the record. BCA, Tax Assessors Notebooks, 1813 (Annis); *Baltimore Directory, corrected up to June 1819* identified "Enniss" as an African American laborer. The *Federal Census of 1820* showed his residence on Honey Alley.

49. *American*, April 5, 1816.

50. BCA, 1830:144; *Mayors' Msgs.*, 95 (1823), 110 (1825), 123 (1826), 132 (1827), 141 (1828), 154 (1829), 170 (1830).

51. Griffith regularly published pseudonymous editorials in Baltimore newspapers. He kept the clippings in a scrapbook but neglected to date many of them. He probably published this plan in the early 1820s, writing as A BALTIMOREAN and OGLETHORPE. See T. W. Griffith Scrapbook, MHS, ms. 412.1. A committee of visitors to the Maryland Penitentiary in 1818 called for more effective punishments, such as "the practice and example of other and older countries, where [convicts] are employed on board the hulks in deepening and cleaning the docks and harbors, &c." See *American*, December 10, 1818.

52. *Patriot*, August 21, 1822

53. For technological innovations, see BCA, 1821:445, 1821:580; *Ordinances*, 1817.4; *Patriot*, February 7, 1817; *Niles*, November 8, 1817. Samuel Davis had received patents for his mudmachines in 1817 and 1818. His supporters called him "a man of great mechanical genius," and the city advanced Davis $500 to put the machine into operation. For days of employment, see BCA, 1826:1383, 1830:144.

54. For the 1827 payrolls, see BCA, Rg39, s2, box 5, item 305; BCA, 1826:1383. Donald Adams's study of agricultural wages in Maryland shows a dip in the mid-1820s, but his series on food prices is less conclusive. See Adams, "Prices and Wages in Maryland." Gary Browne notes that monthly wages for ordinary seamen shipping out of Baltimore dropped nearly 50 percent from an 1814 high to an 1829 low. See Gary L. Browne, *Baltimore in the Nation, 1789–1861* (Chapel Hill: University of North Carolina Press, 1980), 268n15. For wages at the Maryland Chemical Works, see T. Stephen Whitman, *The Price of Freedom: Slavery and Manumission in Baltimore and Early National Maryland* (Lexington: University Press of Kentucky, 1997), 40. For additional mudmachine records, see BCA, 1830:144, 1827:115–117 (Castello), 1828:180.

55. In a petition to the mayor and city council, Whitten complained that his wages of 90¢ per day had been "a mere support for his family." As a result of his injury, Whitten had "become indebted for the necessaries of life," as well as for "the Doctor's bill." He requested the city's leaders "to grant him some relief as in your wisdom and kindness you may see fit." But whereas the council had come to the aid of Jane Otterson when her husband, John, was killed on the mudmachine in 1816, they now decided "the prayer of the petitioner ought not be granted." Whitten did manage to recover his health, and his family remained intact through the 1820s, growing to include two new children. BCA, 1821:484, 1821:623; *Federal Census of 1820*, Baltimore City, Ward 2, p. 56.

56. *Baltimore Directory for 1827–1828* (Baltimore: Matchett, 1827).

57. BCA, 1834:461, 1834:773.

58. For 1830s labor militancy in Baltimore, see William R. Sutton, *Journeymen for Je-sus: Evangelical Artisans Confront Capitalism in Jacksonian Baltimore* (University Park: Penn-sylvania State University Press, 1998), 28, 131–166; John R. Commons, *History of Labour in the United States*, vol. 1 (New York: Macmillan Company, 1936), 358, 473, 478. On the bread-winning aspirations of working men elsewhere, see Joshua R. Greenberg, *Advocating the Man: Masculinity, Organized Labor, and the Household in New York, 1800–1840* (New York: Columbia University Press, www.gutenberg-e.org, 2006.)

59. BCA, 1838:515. The problem of silting remained intense. In 1836, the city petitioned the U.S. Congress for funding to sustain "the constant use of a dredging machine worked by a steam-engine and requiring the assistance of a number of labourers." See *Ordinances*, 1836.58.

Chapter 4 · A Job for a Working Woman

1. BCA, 1816:327. None of the four women—Mary Waddle, Sarah Devier, Sarah Isburn, and Johanna Hutson—appeared in the tax records, which indicates that they possessed less than $40 of real and personal property. The women's petition shared the same rhetorical device as a speech given by the 1819 valedictorian of the New York African School: "What are my prospects? To what shall I turn my hand? Shall I be a mechanic? No one will em-ploy me; white boys won't work with me. Shall I be a merchant? No one will have me in his office; white clerks won't associate with me. Drudgery and servitude, then, are my prospective portion." Quoted in Philip S. Foner, *The History of Black Americans* (Westport, Conn.: Greenwood Press, 1975), 1:523. On market regulation in the early republic, see He-len Tangires, *Public Markets and Civic Culture in Nineteenth-Century America* (Baltimore: Johns Hopkins University Press, 2003); William J. Novak, *The People's Welfare: Law and Regulation in Nineteenth-Century America* (Chapel Hill: University of North Carolina Press, 1996).

2. Merry E. Wiesner, *Women and Gender in Early Modern Europe*, 2nd ed. (New York: Cambridge University Press, 2000), 106; *American*, February 23, 1805. On the ideological construction of women's labor, see Sonya O. Rose, *Limited Livelihoods: Gender and Class in Nineteenth-Century England* (Berkeley: University of California Press, 1992); Deborah M. Valenze, *The First Industrial Woman* (New York: Oxford University Press, 1995); William M. Reddy, *The Rise of Market Culture: The Textile Trade and French Society, 1750–1900* (New York: Cambridge University Press, 1984); Marla R. Miller, "Gender, Artisanry, and Craft Tradition in Early New England: The View Through the Eye of a Needle," *WMQ* 60 (Oc-tober 2003): 743–776; Michael Zakim, *Ready-Made Democracy: A History of Men's Dress in the American Republic, 1760–1860* (Chicago: University of Chicago Press, 2003).

3. Claudia Goldin and Kenneth Sokoloff, "Women, Children, and Industrialization in the Early Republic: Evidence from the Manufacturing Censuses," *Journal of Economic His-tory* 42 (December 1982): 741–774; Margaret S. Coleman, "Female Labor Supply During Early Industrialization: Women's Labor Force Participation in Historical Perspective," in *Gen-der and Political Economy: Incorporating Diversity into Theory and Policy*, eds. Ellen Mutari, Heather Boushey, and William Fraher IV (Armonk, N.Y.: M. E. Sharpe, 1997), 42–60;

Thomas Dublin, *Transforming Women's Work: New England Lives in the Industrial Revolution* (Ithaca, N.Y.: Cornell University Press, 1994); Joan M. Jensen, *Loosening the Bonds: Mid-Atlantic Farm Women, 1750–1850* (New Haven, Conn.: Yale University Press, 1986).

4. Wiesner, *Women and Gender*, 102; Elaine Forman Crane, *Ebb Tide in New England: Women, Seaports, and Social Change, 1630–1800* (Boston: Northeastern University Press, 1998), 102; Karin Wulf, "Gender and the Political Economy of Poor Relief in Colonial Philadelphia," in *Down and Out in Early America*, ed. Billy G. Smith (University Park: Pennsylvania State University Press, 2004), 163–188; Ellen Hartigan-O'Connor, "'She Said She Did Not Know Money': Urban Women and Atlantic Markets in the Revolutionary Era," *Early American Studies* 4 (fall 2006): 322–352; Sheryllynne Haggerty, "'Miss Fan can tun her han!': Women, Work, and Income Opportunities in Eighteenth-Century British Atlantic Port Cities," paper presented to the Harvard International Seminar on the History of the Atlantic World, Cambridge, Mass., August 2005; Jeanne Boydston, *Home and Work: Housework, Wages, and the Ideology of Labor in the Early Republic* (New York: Oxford University Press, 1990); Peter Linebaugh and Marcus Rediker, *The Many-Headed Hydra: Sailors, Slaves, Commoners, and the Hidden History of the Revolutionary Atlantic* (Boston: Beacon, 2000), 42. On women's reproductive labor theorized in more recent contexts, see Evelyn Nakano Glenn, "From Servitude to Service Work: Historical Continuities in the Racial Division of Paid Reproductive Labor," *Signs* 18 (autumn 1992): 1–43; Eileen Boris, "From Gender to Racialized Gender: Laboring Bodies that Matter," *International Labor and Working-Class History* 63 (spring 2003): 9–13; Laura Tabili, "Dislodging the Center/Complicating the Dialectic: What Gender and Race Have Done to the Study of Labor," *International Labor and Working-Class History* 63 (spring 2003): 14–20.

5. *Patriot*, October 11, 1816.

6. Bernard L. Herman, *Town House: Architecture and Material Life in the Early American City, 1780–1830* (Chapel Hill: University of North Carolina Press, OIEAHC, 2005), 119–154; Carole Shammas, "The Space Problem in Early United States Cities," *WMQ* 57 (July 2000): 516, 519–521.

7. *Patriot*, November 18, 1834.

8. *Post*, April 18 ("satisfactory"), September 21 ("unquestionable"), 1809. The latter ad ran for over one month, suggesting that such a girl was difficult to find in Baltimore. Useful discussions of domestic service in Baltimore include Anya Jabour, "Between Mistress and Slave: Elizabeth Wirt's White Housekeepers, 1808–1825," in *Beyond Image and Convention: Explorations in Southern Women's History*, eds. Janet L. Coryell, Martha H. Swain, Sandra Gioia Treadway, and Elizabeth Hayes Turner (Columbia: University of Missouri Press, 1998), 28–52; Stephanie Cole, "Servants and Slaves: Domestic Service in the Border Cities, 1800–1850" (Ph.D. diss., University of Florida, 1994). Studies focusing on other localities include David M. Katzman, *Seven Days a Week: Women and Domestic Service in Industrializing America* (New York: Oxford University Press, 1978); Daniel Southerland, *Americans and their Servants: Domestic Service in the United States, 1800–1920* (Baton Rouge: Louisiana State University Press, 1981); Faye E. Dudden, *Serving Women: Household Service in Nineteenth-Century America* (Middletown, Conn.: Wesleyan University Press, 1983); Christine Stansell, *City of Women: Sex and Class in New York, 1789–1860* (New York: Alfred A.

Knopf, 1986), 155–168; Carol Lasser, "The Domestic Balance of Power: Relations between Mistress and Maid in Nineteenth-Century New England," *LH* 28 (winter 1987): 5–22; Elizabeth L. O'Leary, *At Beck and Call: The Representation of Domestic Servants in Nineteenth-Century American Painting* (Washington D.C.: Smithsonian Institution Press, 1996).

9. Tim Meldrum, *Domestic Service and Gender, 1660–1750: Life and Work in the London Household* (Harlow, England: Longman, 2000), 52–53.

10. Laurel Thatcher Ulrich, "Martha Ballard and Her Girls: Women's Work in Eighteenth-Century Maine," in *Work and Labor in Early America*, ed. Stephen Innes (Chapel Hill: University of North Carolina Press, OIEAHC, 1988), 70–105. Faye Dudden, *Serving Women*, 5, makes a distinction between the exchange of girls' labor within communities ("help") and the impersonal urban service economy ("domestics").

11. *First Annual Report of the Society for the Encouragement of Faithful Domestic Servants in New York* (New York: D. Fanshaw, 1826), 4. The founders of this institution drew on models from 1810s London but knew of a British Society for the Encouragement of Servants that had been founded in 1793.

12. Meldrum, *Domestic Service and Gender*, 3.

13. On republicanism and servitude, see David R. Roediger, *The Wages of Whiteness: Race and the Making of the American Working Class* (New York: Verso, 1991), 47.

14. Coleman, "Female Labor Supply," 52; *First Report of the Board of Managers of the Society for the Encouragement of Faithful Domestics* (Philadelphia, Pa.: Mifflin & Parry, 1830) offered the questionable figure that 18,000 of Philadelphia's 28,000 households employed at least one domestic.

15. Stephanie Cole, "Servants and Slaves," 204.

16. *Maryland Journal*, December 30, 1794. Because census and tax records for Baltimore did not identify white indentured servants, it remains unclear how householders combined different types of laborers (enslaved black women and apprenticed white girls, for example) under the same roof; nor is it possible to determine the total number of unfree domestic servants in the city.

17. *Maryland Journal*, November 22, 1791 ("Irish"), August 20 ("Negro"), November 22 ("Black"), 1793.

18. *Maryland Journal*, January 4 ("spinner"), 18 ("two years"), 29 ("three years"), 1793. For ship *Hope*, see *Maryland Journal*, March 5, 1793. For earlier ship arrivals, see *Maryland Journal*, August 18, 1789, October 11, 1791, May 22, 25, 1792. For Mint and Birmingham, see *Maryland Journal*, January 15, February 3, 1793. Stephanie Cole calculated that nine of ten domestic service job advertisements in Baltimore newspapers between 1800 and 1830 implicitly or explicitly referred to black women. See Stephanie Cole, "Servants and Slaves," 62.

19. Stephanie Cole, "Servants and Slaves," 295, 297; *Maryland Journal*, June 22, 1792; October 25, 1793. T. Stephen Whitman's data indicates that the number of apprenticed females in Baltimore was small—an average of fifty-three girls annually in the period between 1800 and 1840. See Whitman, "Orphans in City and Countryside in Nineteenth-Century Maryland," in *Children Bound to Labor: Pauper Apprenticeship in Early America*, eds. John E. Murray and Ruth Wallis Herndon (Ithaca, N.Y.: Cornell University Press, forthcoming).

20. *American*, December 16, 1805.

21. The *Federal Census of 1800* found 44 percent of Baltimore's white population younger than fifteen, in comparison to New York, 42 percent; Philadelphia, 38 percent; and Boston, 38 percent. Census data republished in *The Growth of the Seaport Cities, 1790–1825*, proceedings of a conference sponsored by the Eleutherian Mills-Hagley Foundation, March 17–19, 1966, ed. David T. Gilchrist (Charlottesville: University Press of Virginia, 1967), 34.

22. Female Society of the Second Presbyterian Church of Philadelphia to Philip Milledoler, November 9, 1802, Milledoler Collection, New-York Historical Society, Misc. Mss., box 1; *Federal Gazette*, January 25, 1804 (snowballs).

23. *A Brief Account of the Female Humane Association Charity School of the City of Baltimore* (Baltimore: Warner and Hanna, 1803), 3–5.

24. *A Brief Statement of the Proceedings and Present Condition of the Female Humane Association Charity School* (Baltimore: Dobbin and Murphy, 1807); *Baltimore Telegraphe*, January 7, 1804, February 19, 1805; *Post*, June 15, 1809; *American*, May 2, 1808; *A Report of the Orphaline Charity School of Baltimore* (1819) in Jonas R. Rappaport Collection, MSA, sc731. An ecumenical organization, the school attracted patrons and students from across religious lines. Among the first fifty-three graduates were nineteen Roman Catholics, sixteen English Protestants, nine members of German Reformed churches, six Methodists, and three Baptists. The trustees hoped to bind children out to families of the same religion but succeeded only half the time.

25. Stephanie Cole, "'A White Woman, of Middle Age, Would Be Preferred': Children's Nurses in the Old South," in *Neither Lady Nor Slave: Working Women of the Old South,*" eds. Susanna Delfino and Michele Gillespie (Chapel Hill: University of North Carolina Press, 2002), 86. For more on Cushing, see Stephanie Cole, "Servants and Slaves," 113, 212.

26. A study of persistence rates among urban slaves poses a number of technical challenges but could be executed using city tax records from 1813, 1823, and 1836 (for which there is a stand-alone listing of 192 slaves belonging to 104 owners in two specific wards). See BCA, Tax Assessors Notebooks, Rg4, s2. Federal census data from Barbara Wallace, "'Fair Daughters of Africa': African American Women in Baltimore, 1790–1860" (Ph.D. diss., UCLA, 2001), 22. The category of "working age" corresponds to the three age brackets ranging from ten to fifty-four.

27. *American*, March 3, 1817; Wallace, "Fair Daughters of Africa," 18–19, 92, 310; T. Stephen Whitman, *The Price of Freedom: Slavery and Manumission in Baltimore and Early National Maryland* (Lexington: University Press of Kentucky, 1997), 14–15, 18–22, 180n23; *Patriot*, July 14, 1834; Petition of Margaret P. Hanna, Baltimore County Orphans Court, February 18, 1826, *RSPP*, 20982610.

28. *Post*, January 4, 1809. Thomas Hamilton, *Men and Manners in America* (Edinburgh: W. Blackwood, 1833), 2:7–8.

29. Whitman, *Price of Freedom*, 14; *American*, June 28, July 15, 1819; *Beverly Dowling v. Sophia Bland and Austin Woolfolk*, Baltimore City Court, October 1835, *RSPP*, 20983515; *Thomas Anderson v. Rebecca Garrett et al.*, Court of Appeals of Maryland, 1850, 9 Gill 120. See also Keith C. Barton, "'Good Cooks and Washers': Slave Hiring, Domestic Labor, and the Market in Bourbon County, Kentucky," *JAH* 84 (September 1997): 436–460.

30. Whitman, *Price of Freedom*, 110–118.

31. For redemptioners, see *American*, August 10, 1819. For apprentices, see Stephanie

Cole, "Servants and Slaves," app. B; Whitman, "Orphans in City and Countryside." For early term slave ads, see *American*, August 15, 1804, October 30, 1805.

32. *Post*, June 19, 1809; Whitman, *Price of Freedom*, 175; *American*, December 18, 1818.

33. Adrienne Davis, "'Don't Let Nobody Bother Yo' Principle': The Sexual Economy of American Slavery," in *Sister Circle: Black Women and Work*, eds. Sharon Harley and the Black Women and Work Collective (New Brunswick, N.J.: Rutgers University Press, 2002), 119. For further discussion of the centrality of black women's reproductive capacities to the wealth and aspirations of white slaveholders, see Jennifer L. Morgan, *Laboring Women: Reproduction and Gender in New World Slavery* (Philadelphia: University of Pennsylvania Press, 2004); Edward Baptist, "'Cuffy,' 'Fancy Maids,' and 'One-Eyed Men': Rape, Commodification, and the Domestic Slave Trade in the United States," *AHR* 106 (December 2001): 1619–1650; Walter Johnson, *Soul by Soul: Life Inside the Antebellum Slave Market* (Cambridge, Mass.: Harvard University Press, 1999).

34. Whitman, *Price of Freedom*, 17, 93–118, 121–122, 177. Most owners did not offer delayed manumissions to the children of female term slaves (121–122). Some slaveholders preferred their enslaved domestics not to have young children, presumably to avoid incurring extra mouths to feed or from fear that an enslaved woman might become distracted from her responsibilities to her owner's family. A Baltimore slaveholder in 1838 complained when her domestic gave birth to another child. Harriet Shriver called the situation "disagreeable and troublesome," lamenting, "we now expect nothing less than one every couple of years if we keep her." Some advertisers sought female slaves "without incumbrance" but were willing to accept a woman with children if she happened to be an able cook. See Stephanie Cole, "Servants and Slaves," 207.

35. The percentage of term slaves among the total enslaved population in Baltimore is unclear. Whitman, *Price of Freedom*, 17, 24, 115, 208fn75. In the working-class wards of eastern Baltimore (Wards 1–4) in 1823, 193 white families owned a single slave. At least 119 of these families owned a black female between the ages of ten and thirty-five. See BCA, Tax Assessors Notebooks, 1823.

36. Wallace, "Fair Daughters of Africa," 39–42, 86. In 1820, Baltimore contained 1,373 enslaved women and 3,280 free black women (in comparison to 1,016 enslaved men and 2,013 free black men) in the fourteen to forty-four age bracket.

37. Wallace, "Fair Daughters of Africa," 50–54. For 1820, Wallace counted 1,183 (of the city's 3,280) free black women ages fourteen to forty-four living in white households. The percentage of working-age free black women residing in white households remained at 33 percent for the 1830 and 1840 censuses (although the age brackets expanded to include free black girls and women ten to fifty-four years old). For analysis on the neighborhood level, Wallace picked Wards 6 and 7, where 71 percent (330 of 463) of free black adult women resided in white households in 1820. By 1840, that figure still stood at 65 percent (766 of 1,175). Wallace is clear that most of these women were not living in white households as boarders or renters, but as servants, because these households contained few free black males of companionate age or free black children. On the enslaved origins of Baltimore's free black population, see Christopher Phillips, *Freedom's Port: The African American Community of Baltimore, 1790–1860* (Urbana: University of Illinois Press, 1997), 57–82. For Caw, see Baltimore County Court (Certificates of Freedom), 1806–1816, MSA, c290-1.

38. *Niles*, October 15, 1831; *Patriot*, November 18, 1828 ("situations"); *American*, July 15, 1819 ("Europe"); *Baltimore Gazette and Daily Advertiser*, July 10, 1833 ("American"); *Patriot*, March 19, June 4, August 13, November 17, December 11, 1834.

39. *Post*, April 18, May 2, 1809; *Patriot*, August 13 ("children"), November 17 ("cooking"), 1834; Mathew Carey, *A Plea for the Poor, Particularly Females. An Inquiry How Far the Charges Alleged Against Them of Improvidence, Idleness, and Dissipation, are Founded in Truth*, 7th ed. (Philadelphia, Pa.: L. R. Bailey, 1837), 9.

40. For Nancy Hignan's almshouse admission warrant, see Baltimore County Trustees of the Poor, Ground Rent Record, 1810–1819, MSA, c332-1, loose insert; Maryland Penitentiary Prisoners Record, 1811–1840, MSA, s275-1 (courtesy of Stephen Whitman's computer data file). Some prescriptive literature suggested that a white domestic servant in New England might work from eighteen until thirty-eight. See [Sarah Savage], *Advice to a Young Woman at Service; in a Letter from a Friend. By the Author of James Talbot* (Boston: John B. Russell, 1823), 26.

41. *Maryland Journal*, February 14, 1794; *Baltimore Gazette*, July 10, 1833; *Patriot*, October 29, 1816, July 19, 1830, December 20, 1834.

42. Stephanie Cole, "Servants and Slaves," ch. 1; Wallace, "Fair Daughters of Africa," 93; Stephanie Cole, "Children's Nurses," 92; *Patriot*, January 17, 1834.

43. *Baltimore Whig*, July 2, 1810. Faye Dudden located a New York intelligence office in operation in 1786. See Dudden, *Serving Women*, 274n28; Charles Varle, *A Complete View of Baltimore, with a Statistical Sketch* . . . (Baltimore: Samuel Young, 1833), 82; *American*, May 11, 1820, October 26, 1833. Wallace, "Fair Daughters of Africa," 118, located one African American woman whose occupation appeared as "Intelligence Office" in *Matchett's Baltimore Directory, Corrected up to 1831*.

44. Scott A. Sandage, *Born Losers: A History of Failure in America* (Cambridge, Mass.: Harvard University Press, 2005), 99–128; Herman Freudenberger and Jonathan B. Pritchett, "The Domestic United States Slave Trade: New Evidence," *Journal of Interdisciplinary History* 21 (winter 1991): 447–477.

45. On misogyny and violence against women in the early republic, see Patricia Cline Cohen, *The Murder of Helen Jewett: The Life and Death of a Prostitute in Nineteenth-Century New York* (New York: Alfred A. Knopf, 1998); Victoria E. Bynum, *Unruly Women: The Politics of Social and Sexual Control in the Old South* (Chapel Hill: University of North Carolina Press, 1992); Stansell, *City of Women*; Sharon Block, *Rape and Sexual Power in Early America* (Chapel Hill: University of North Carolina Press, OIEAHC, 2006); Clare A. Lyons, *Sex among the Rabble: An Intimate History of Gender and Power in the Age of Revolution, Philadelphia, 1730–1830* (Chapel Hill: University of North Carolina Press, OIEAHC, 2006); Christine Daniels and Michael V. Kennedy, eds., *Over the Threshold: Intimate Violence in Early America* (New York: Routledge, 1999).

46. Pardons, s1061-12, folder 32 (Bowyer), s1061-16, folder 64 (Potter), s1061-26, folder 91 (Lewis), s1061-7, folder 36 (Duffy), s1061-14, folder 19 (Decoursey), s1061-19, folder 56 (Davis). On the Davis ducking, see *American*, December 3, 1818. For a Georgia woman facing this early modern punishment, see *Niles*, November 2, 1811; and a Philadelphia woman in *Niles*, November 13, 1824. In 1830, William Cranch, chief justice of the U.S. Circuit Court of the District of Columbia, upheld the "common scold" law but declared the

ducking penalty illegitimate. See Robert J. Steinfeld, *The Invention of Free Labor: The Employment Relation in English and American Law and Culture, 1350–1870* (New York: Cambridge University Press, 1991), 176.

47. Baltimore County Court (Miscellaneous Court Papers), 1809–1810, MSA, c1-34, folder 498 (Bryden-Butcher).

48. Pardons, s1061-5, folder 2 (Potter), folder 13 (Brady), folder 54 (Walton), folder 79 (Nann). It is worth noting that character was a criterion for male domestic servants also, and that in criminal proceedings, employers offered character testimony. In 1836, for example, James Spiers described his free black servant John Chambers as "always very honest, sober, and attentive." Interestingly, Chambers was not relieved from a four-year sentence for stealing. See Pardons, s1061-38, folder 43.

49. [Savage], *Advice to a Young Woman at Service*, 10–11. In this account, "Susan," who repented in the almshouse, was redeemed by her old mistress and "restored to her service, in which she has been the last ten years." Catharine Beecher, *Letters to Persons who are Engaged in Domestic Service* (New York: Leavitt & Trow, 1842), 86. For an overview, see Barbara Ryan, *Love, Wages, Slavery: The Literature of Servitude in the United States* (Urbana: University of Illinois Press, 2006).

50. Catharine Maria Sedgwick, *Live and Let Live; or, Domestic Service Illustrated* (New York: Harper & Brothers, 1837), v; Mrs. John Farrar [Eliza Farrar], *The Young Ladies' Friend* (Boston: American Stationers' Company, 1836), 245.

51. *American*, December 29, 1820. This piece was signed "Community" but used phrasing common to Griffith's other public addresses. *Baltimore Clipper*, October 22, 1839; *Patriot*, August 1, 1831. Sophia May to Abigail May, December 2, 1806, Sophia May Letters, 1800–1812, Mss., American Antiquarian Society, Worcester, Mass.

52. *American*, January 9, 1821; *Patriot*, August 1, 1831.

53. On surveillance in New York, see John Pintard, response to New York Society for the Encouragement of Faithful Domestic Servants circular, February 11, 1828, New-York Historical Society, Misc. Mss.; *Patriot*, April 25, 1822; *Post*, April 18, May 2, 1809; *Maryland Journal*, March 31, September 24, 1794 (wet nurses). On the demand for almshouse wet nurses, see BCA, 1838:324.

54. Robert Goodloe Harper, *A Letter from Gen. Harper, of Maryland, to Elias B. Caldwell, Esq., Secretary of the American Society for Colonizing the Free People of Colour, in the United States, with Their Own Consent* (Baltimore: E. J. Cole, 1818), 4–10; *Niles*, September 14, 1822; T. W. Griffith, undated newspaper clipping [likely 1817], T. W. Griffith Scrapbook, MHS, ms. 412.2; *American*, October 30, November 6, 1833.

55. Joan M. Jensen and Sue Davidson, eds., *A Needle, A Bobbin, A Strike: Women Needleworkers in America* (Philadelphia, Pa.: Temple University Press, 1984), 9.

56. With 1,886 total entries between 1823–1826, the BAAB contained 625 women ages seventeen and over. Of these women, 370 were listed with skill information. Constituting 87 of the 370, African American women were present in this cohort at the same rate that they appeared in the total almshouse population and in the city's at-large female population.

57. BAAB, May 22, 1823 (Abigail Anderson), July 1, 1824 (Rachel Wilson), November 16, 1825 (Kitty Davis), and April 22, 1825 (Betsy Pepper). Another institutionalized group

of women suggests that white women were more likely to have greater sewing experience: the 454 Baltimore women who served time in the Maryland Penitentiary between 1811 and 1830. The warden recorded the skills of all arriving inmates, and as at the almshouse, left no record of the criteria he used. "Seamstresses" accounted for nineteen percent of white women (31/160), but only four percent of black women (11/294). However, 50 percent of black women in the prison had experience spinning (148/294), compared with 38 percent of white women (61/160). The number of women with only housekeeping skills was roughly equal (16 percent of white women; 19 percent of black women). Penitentiary records also show the labor women performed inside the institution: 85 percent of white women were engaged in some aspect of yarn and cloth making and sewing, as were 74 percent of black women. Proportionately, more black women spun and more white women sewed. Nine white women were the only inmates engaged in hat making, but there were seven black female weavers to the one white female weaver. See Maryland Penitentiary Prisoners Record, MSA (courtesy of Stephen Whitman's computer data file).

58. Gloria Seaman Allen, "Slaves as Textile Artisans: Documentary Evidence for the Chesapeake Region," *Uncoverings: The Research Papers of the American Quilt Study Group* 22 (2001): 1–36; Gloria Seaman Allen, "Threads of Bondage: Chesapeake Slave Women and Plantation Cloth Production, 1750–1850" (Ph.D. diss., George Washington University, 2000).

59. We will never know about the abilities of the vast majority of free black women who did not enter the institution. The almshouse records are surely skewed toward the most marginal members of society. However, if the black women and white women in the institution were equal in other regards (as likely to be pregnant, sick, or new to Baltimore), then the discrepancy in household skills points to one way that race did structure the labor market for domestic workers. On situation-wanted ads, see Stephanie Cole, "Servants and Slaves," 88; *Post*, November 18, 27, 1809; *Patriot*, August 29, 1816. On the shifting nature of enslaved women's plantation labor, see Carole Shammas, "Black Women's Work and the Evolution of Plantation Society in Virginia," *LH* 26 (1985): 5–28.

60. *Post*, November 18, 1809. For Louisiana records, see Gwendolyn Midlo Hall, ed., *Afro-Louisiana History and Genealogy, 1718–1820*, retrieved November 2005, www.ibiblio.org/laslave/index.html.

61. For Chloe, see Stephanie Cole, "Servants and Slaves," 93; *American*, August 4, 1805; *Patriot*, August 21, 1816.

62. Griffith, undated newspaper clipping [likely 1817], Griffith Scrapbook.

63. Pardons, s1061-16, folder 20 (Crawford); *American*, March 18, 1816.

64. *Trial of John Graham at Baltimore County Criminal Court . . .* (Baltimore: Fryer and Clark, 1804), 33; Pardons, s1061-14, folder 13 (O'Donnell); *Jane Lyons v. John Lyons*, August 1844, Baltimore County Court, RSPP, 20984401. See also James D. Rice, "Laying Claim to Elizabeth Shoemaker: Family Violence on the Baltimore Waterfront, 1808–1812," in Daniels and Kennedy, *Over the Threshold*, 185–201; Stephanie Cole, "Keeping the Peace: Domestic Assault and Private Prosecution in Antebellum Baltimore," in Daniels and Kennedy, *Over the Threshold*, 148–172; Lyons, *Sex among the Rabble*, 232–235.

65. William Logan Fisher, *Pauperism and Crime* (Philadelphia, Pa.: W. L. Fisher, 1831), 48.

66. *Post*, October 6, 1809; *Mechanics' Gazette and Merchants' Daily Advertiser*, June 29,

1815; *Patriot*, September 16, 1834. On enslaved women in manufacturing, see Whitman, *Price of Freedom*, 18–23; Midori Takagi, *"Rearing Wolves to Our Own Destruction": Slavery in Richmond, Virginia, 1782–1865* (Charlottesville: University Press of Virginia, 1999), 26–28.

67. *Patriot*, October 26, 1831.

68. Robert Olwell, "'Loose, Idle and Disorderly': Slave Women in the Eighteenth-Century Charleston Marketplace," in *More than Chattel: Black Women and Slavery in the Americas*, eds. David Gaspar and Darlene Clark Hine (Bloomington: Indiana University Press, 1996), 97–110; Betty Wood, *Women's Work, Men's Work: The Informal Slave Economies of Lowcountry Georgia* (Athens: University of Georgia Press, 1995); Richard Parkinson, *The Experienced Farmer's Tour in America* (London: G & J Robinson, 1805), 433–34; Phillips, *Freedom's Port*, 110, 203. In various "nuisance" complaints, white petitioners to the city council left plenty of indication that African Americans congregated in Baltimore's marketplaces but little evidence of black women as marketers themselves. See BCA, 1805:206a, 1823:515, 1824:831.

69. BCA, 1838:1283.

70. *Ordinances*, 1797.16, 1805.21, 1807.20, 1816.12; 1819.8, 1820.15, 1823.15, 1824.17, and 1826.38. For complaints by established marketers or public officials, see BCA, 1816:467, 1823:241, 1824:338, 1824:423–444, 1824:831. Interestingly, the men who petitioned against female hucksters used the same language of family need as the women peddlers. For example, the cedar coopers described themselves as "totally dependent on their occupation and industry for support for their families" (1824:427).

71. BCA, 1812:547.
72. BCA, 1827:484.
73. BCA, 1831:615.
74. BCA, 1812:547.
75. BCA, 1816:326–327, 1816:467.
76. BCA, 1827:484.
77. *Patriot*, May 15, 1828.
78. BCA, 1830:1006.
79. Pardons, s1061-17, folder 117; BCA, 1832:1091, 1833:390.

80. [William Darlington], "Journalissimo of a Peregrination to the city of Baltimore: performed in the year *domini* 1803," William Darlington Papers, New-York Historical Society. For an overview of the sex trade, see Timothy J. Gilfoyle, *City of Eros: New York City, Prostitution, and the Commercialization of Sex, 1790–1920* (New York: W. W. Norton, 1992), ch. 3. On rape and enslaved women, see this chapter's note 33.

81. BCA, Tax Assessors Notebooks, for Baltimore east of Jones Falls (Wards 7 and 8) contained six free women of color in 1813; nineteen in 1818 (Wards 7, 8, and 9); and twenty-four in 1823 (Wards 1, 2, 3, and 4). Surprisingly, these women rarely appeared in the city directories; none who owned property in 1813 or 1818 appeared in the *Baltimore Directory for 1817–1818* (Baltimore: James Kennedy, 1817). Two laundresses, Fanny Page and Catherine Waters, appeared in the *Baltimore Directory for 1819* (Baltimore: Samuel Jackson, 1819). Of the twenty-four property-owning women in 1823, nine (including six laundresses) appeared in R. J. Matchett, *Baltimore Directory for 1824* (Baltimore: Matchett, 1824). The fail-

ure to match black female property holders between directories and tax records is curious. Potentially, more of the city's African American laundresses lived on the west side of Baltimore, as did Rachel Coale. Black laundresses were not absent in east Baltimore, however, and ten of the forty-six African-American laundresses in the *Directory for 1817–1818* resided east of Jones Falls. Moreover, an 1817 petition against black laundresses (discussed below) focused on Harford Run in east Baltimore. For directory data, see Wallace, "Fair Daughters of Africa," 108–119. See also Loren Schweninger, "Property Owning Free African-American Women in the South, 1800–1870," *Journal of Women's History* 1 (1990): 13–44.

82. BCA, 1817:253. In the eighteenth century, enslaved women in the West Indies developed a distinct style of washing that struck European observers such as Moreau de Saint-Méry as sexual. The migration of several hundred slave and free women from Saint Domingue after 1793 brought many of those cultural expressions to Baltimore. See David Geggus, "Slave and Free Colored Women in Saint Domingue," in *More than Chattel*, 259–278; Phillips, *Freedom's Port*, 72–3. See also Tera W. Hunter, *To 'Joy My Freedom: Southern Black Women's Lives and Labors after the Civil War* (Cambridge, Mass.: Harvard University Press, 1997), 44–73. On the control of family labor as a key route to black property ownership, see Dylan Penningroth, "Slavery, Freedom, and Social Claims to Property among African Americans in Liberty County, Georgia, 1850–1880," *JAH* 84 (September 1997): 405–435.

83. *Southern Pioneer and Gospel Visitor*, January 3, 1835.

Chapter 5 · The Living Wage

1. *American*, September 23, 1833, February 23, 1805 ("bound for life"). On the tension between women as universal workers and gendered subjects in the nineteenth century, see Michael Zakim, *Ready-Made Democracy: A History of Men's Dress in the American Republic, 1760–1860* (Chicago: University of Chicago Press, 2003), 157–184; Mari Jo Buhle, "Needlewomen and the Vicissitudes of Modern Life: A Study of Middle-Class Construction in the Antebellum North," in *Visible Women: New Essays on American Activism*, ed. Nancy A. Hewitt and Suzanne Lebsock (Urbana: University of Illinois Press, 1993), 145–165; Jeanne Boydston, "The Woman Who Wasn't There," *JER* 16 (summer 1996): 183–206; Christine Stansell, *City of Women: Sex and Class in New York, 1789–1860* (New York: Alfred A. Knopf, 1986), 105–129; Dietlind Hüchtker, "Strategies and Tactics: The Politics of Subsistence in Berlin, 1770–1850," *International Review of Social History* 49 (2004): 435–453.

2. On slop work (which had originally referred to cheap clothing produced for sailors and soldiers), see Zakim, *Ready-Made Democracy*, 43–44. On the range of skills involved in clothing production, see Marla R. Miller, *The Needle's Eye: Women and Work in the Age of Revolution* (Amherst: University of Massachusetts Press, 2006); Joan M. Jensen, "Needlework as Art, Craft, and Livelihood before 1900," in *A Needle, A Bobbin, A Strike: Women Needleworkers in America*, ed. Joan M. Jensen and Sue Davidson (Philadelphia, Pa.: Temple University Press, 1984), 1–19; Ava Baron and Susan E. Klepp, "'If I Didn't Have My Sewing Machine . . .': Women and Sewing Machine Technology," in Jensen and Davidson, *A Needle, A Bobbin, A Strike*, 20–59. For the reorganization of clothing production in Baltimore,

see Charles G. Steffen, *The Mechanics of Baltimore: Workers and Politics in the Age of Revolution, 1763–1812* (Urbana: University of Illinois Press, 1984), 118; Philip Kahn, Jr., *A Stitch in Time: The Four Seasons of Baltimore's Needle Trades* (Baltimore: Maryland Historical Society, 1989), 3–9.

3. Amy Dru Stanley, *From Bondage to Contract: Wages, Labor, Marriage, and the Market in the Age of Slave Emancipation* (New York: Cambridge University Press, 1998), 144–147; Deborah Valenze, *The First Industrial Woman* (New York: Oxford University Press, 1995); Rachel G. Fuchs, *Gender and Poverty in Nineteenth-Century Europe* (New York: Cambridge University Press, 2005).

4. Sonya O. Rose, *Limited Livelihoods: Gender and Class in Nineteenth-Century England* (Berkeley: University of California Press, 1992); Anna Clark, *The Struggle for the Breeches: Gender and the Making of the British Working Class* (Berkeley: University of California Press, 1995); Joan Wallach Scott, *Gender and the Politics of History* (New York: Columbia University Press, 1988), 53–90; William M. Reddy, *The Rise of Market Culture: The Textile Trade and French Society, 1750–1900* (New York: Cambridge University Press, 1984); Margaret S. Coleman, "Low Wages, Labor Shortage, Wage and Labor Structures, and Poverty: 1810–1840 in the Northeastern United States" (Ph.D. diss., New School for Social Research, 1996).

5. *American*, February 23, 1805.

6. On the "problem" of the autonomous adult woman, see Karin A. Wulf, *Not All Wives: Women of Colonial Philadelphia* (Ithaca, N.Y.: Cornell University Press, 2000); Judith M. Bennett and Amy M. Froide, eds., *Singlewomen in the European Past, 1250–1800* (Philadelphia: University of Pennsylvania Press, 1999); Bridget Hill, *Women Alone: Spinsters in England, 1660–1850* (New Haven, Conn.: Yale University Press, 2001); Olwen H. Hufton, "Women without Men: Widows and Spinsters in Britain and France in the Eighteenth Century," *Journal of Family History* 9 (winter 1984): 355–376.

7. *Federal Census of 1810*, Baltimore City, Wards 7 and 8. Women constituted 20 percent of householders in these two wards in the *Federal Census of 1820*. The overall rate of female householding in Baltimore varied by source, date, and neighborhood. Women headed 10 percent of Baltimore households listed in the *Federal Census of 1790*; 8.5 percent in Cornelius W. Stafford, *Baltimore Directory for 1802* (Baltimore: John W. Butler, 1802); 13 percent in *Baltimore Directory for 1817–1818* (Baltimore: James Kennedy, 1817). From directory data, Baltimore had a lower rate of female householding than Philadelphia. See Claudia Goldin, "The Economic Status of Women in the Early Republic: Quantitative Evidence," *Journal of Interdisciplinary History* 16 (winter 1986): 375–404. These findings may be an artifact of the flawed nature of directories in general, or the proclivities of Baltimore's directory compilers in particular. See also Daniel Scott Smith, "Female Householding in Late Eighteenth-Century America and the Problem of Poverty," *Journal of Social History* 28 (fall 1994): 83–107; Richard Oestreicher, "The Counted and the Uncounted: The Occupational Structure of Early American Cities," *Journal of Social History* 28 (winter 1994): 351–361.

8. Tax records typically undercount the number of female householders, owing both to women's poverty and to the willingness of assessors to provide ad hoc abatements for poor women with dependent children. See Karin A. Wulf, "Assessing Gender: Taxation and the Evaluation of Economic Viability in Late Colonial Philadelphia," *Pennsylvania Magazine of History and Biography* 121 (July 1997): 203–235. In the working-class district east of

Jones Falls, women headed 14 percent of assessed households in 1813 and 11 percent in 1818. Both figures are lower than the tallies of the nearest federal census. Widows made up the largest subgroup of taxed women: 56 of 229 women were listed explicitly as widows in the 1818 assessment (although the assessor's notations were irregular). See BCA, Tax Assessors Notebooks, Rg4, s2, 1813 (Wards 7 and 8), 1818 (Wards 7, 8, and 9).

9. Women most frequently appeared in city directories with no occupational designation, or as "gentlewoman" or "widow." This was the case for 57 percent of women appearing in Kennedy, *Baltimore Directory for 1817–1818*. In that volume, 996 women (930 white, 66 African American) accounted for 13 percent of the 7,770 total entries. Entries for 426 of the 996 women listed occupations. The largest categories for white women were seamstress (95 women), boardinghouse keeper (67 women), and grocer (43 women); for free women of color, laundress (46 women), cookshop keeper (4 women), and midwife (2 women).

10. Maryland Penitentiary Prisoners Record, 1811–1840, MSA, s275-1 (courtesy of Stephen Whitman's computer data file). Of the forty-two Baltimore seamstresses, twenty-seven had been arrested as vagrants. BAAB, May 2, 1826 (O'Brion). In its three years of detailed entries (1823–1826), the BAAB listed occupational data for 370 of 625 adult women.

11. BCA, 1816:327 (hucksters); *American*, July 13, 1804 (Paul), April 21, 1819 (charity schools).

12. *American*, January 8, 1805 (seasonal unemployment); *Federal Gazette*, February 8, 1804 (no labor); *Post*, January 7, 1809 (mayor).

13. On state-sponsored work as a means of relieving female poverty, see Gary B. Nash, "Poverty and Poor Relief in Pre-Revolutionary Philadelphia," *WMQ* 33 (January 1976): 3–30; Eric G. Nellis, "Misreading the Signs: Industrial Imitation, Poverty, and the Social Order in Colonial Boston," *New England Quarterly* 59 (December 1986): 486–507; Laurel Thatcher Ulrich, "Sheep in the Parlor, Wheels on the Common: Pastoralism and Poverty in Eighteenth-Century Boston" in *Inequality in Early America*, eds. Carla G. Pestana and Sharon V. Salinger (Hanover: University Press of New England, 1999), 182–200; Lawrence A. Peskin, *Manufacturing Revolution: The Intellectual Origins of Early American Industry* (Baltimore: Johns Hopkins University Press, 2003), 35–40; Drew R. McCoy, *The Elusive Republic: Political Economy in Jeffersonian America* (Chapel Hill: University of North Carolina Press, OIEAHC, 1980), 115–119.

14. For Rumford and the School of Industry, see *Federal Gazette*, January 30, February 8, 1804; *American*, August 21, 1804, January 25, December 16, 1805. For the Benevolent Society, see. *American*, February 23, March 16, April 6, 1805. For the Aimwell, see BCA, 1811:562–572.

15. "READY MADE LABOURERS' & NEGROES' TROUSERS" read an advertisement in the *Baltimore Telegraph and Mercantile Advertiser*, January 27, 1815. In a pamphlet meant to discourage immigration to the United States, Joseph Pickering reported, "Great quantities of fine linen shirts made up in Baltimore for the South American market: women getting only 1s each for their making. The South American trade benefits the States much and the enterprising inhabitants promptly avail themselves of its advantages." Pickering, *Emigration or No Emigration: Being the Narrative of the Author . . .* (London: Longmans, Reese, Orme, Brown, and Greene, 1830), 25. On the allocation of plantation labor, see Jensen and Davidson, *A Needle, A Bobbin, A Strike*, 9.

16. Steffen, *Mechanics of Baltimore*, 118. On labor conflict in the clothing trade, see Christine Stansell, "The Origins of the Sweatshop: Women and Early Industrialization in New York City," in *Working-Class America: Essays on Labor, Community, and American Society,* eds. Michael H. Frisch and Daniel J. Walkowitz (Urbana: University of Illinois Press, 1983), 78–103; Zakim, *Ready-Made Democracy*, 134–149.

17. *American,* February 23, 1805; BCA, 1823:236; *Niles,* July 26, 1823; E. L. Finley, *An Address Delivered by Request of the Managers of the Humane Impartial Society, at their Annual Meeting, Held on the 24th January 1831 . . .* (Baltimore: Lucas & Deaver, 1831), 7.

18. *Patriot,* November 16, 1815.

19. As discussed in chapter 4, there may have been a needle-skills deficit among free women of color in Baltimore. Charles Keenan's *Baltimore Directory for 1822 and '23* listed 231 free black women with occupations: 10 were seamstresses (as opposed to 194 laundresses). Richard Matchett's *Baltimore Directory, Corrected up to 1831* listed 289 black women with occupations: no seamstresses, 2 mantua makers, and 250 washerwomen and laundresses. *Matchett's Baltimore Directory for 1840–1841* included 526 black women with occupations, but only 14 seamstresses and 1 milliner. See Barbara Wallace, "'Fair Daughters of Africa': African American Women in Baltimore, 1790–1860" (Ph.D. diss., University of California, Los Angeles, 2001), 116–119.

20. Peskin, *Manufacturing Revolution,* 106; *Patriot,* June 7, 1826. On silkworms more generally, see David Rossell, "The Culture of Silk: Markets, Households, and the Meaning of an Antebellum Agricultural Movement" (Ph.D. diss., State University of New York—Buffalo, 2001); Thomas P. Jones, *An Address on the Progress of Manufactures and Internal Improvement, in the United States; and particularly, On the Advantages to be Derived from the Employment of Slaves in the Manufacturing of Cotton and Other Goods. Delivered in the Hall of the Franklin Institute, November 6, 1827* (Philadelphia, Pa.: Judah Dobson, 1827), 17. For women's textile labor within European developmental schemes, see Mary Jo Maynes, "In Search of Arachne's Daughters: European Girls, Economic Development, and the Textile Trade, 1750–1880," in *Secret Gardens, Satanic Mills: Placing Girls in European History,* eds. Mary Jo Maynes, Birgitte Søland, and Christine Benninghaus (Bloomington: Indiana University Press, 2005), 40–42.

21. *Niles,* July 26, 1823.

22. *Niles,* July 24, 1819. Wages paid to domestic servants are not readily available in the records. One Baltimore householder, Mrs. John D'Arcy, paid her female cook and washerwomen $5 or $6 per month in 1834. See Stephanie Cole, "Servants and Slaves: Domestic Service in the Border Cities, 1800–1850" (Ph.D. diss., University of Florida, 1994), 258.

23. BCA, 1823:236; *Patriot,* November 20, 1828.

24. David R. Roediger, *The Wages of Whiteness: Race and the Making of the American Working Class* (New York: Verso, 1991), 43–92; Edward Pessen, *Most Uncommon Jacksonians: The Radical Leaders of the Early Labor Movement* (Albany: State University of New York Press, 1967); Sean Wilentz, *Chants Democratic: New York City and the Rise of the American Working Class, 1788–1850* (New York: Oxford University Press, 1984); Ronald Schultz, *The Republic of Labor: Philadelphia Artisans and the Politics of Class, 1720–1830* (New York: Oxford University Press, 1993); Bruce Laurie, *Artisans into Workers: Labor in Nineteenth-Century America* (New York: Hill and Wang, 1989).

25. Joshua Greenberg, "'Powerful—Very Powerful is the Parental Feeling': Fatherhood, Domestic Politics, and the New York City Working Men's Party," *Early American Studies* 2 (spring 2004): 192–227; Stanley, *From Bondage to Contract*, 138–174.

26. Steven Mintz, *Moralists and Modernizers: America's Pre-Civil War Reformers* (Baltimore: Johns Hopkins University Press, 1995), 11. Even the prophet Matthias denounced the exploitation of seamstresses. See Paul E. Johnson and Sean Wilentz, *The Kingdom of Matthias: A Story of Sex and Salvation in 19th-Century America* (New York: Oxford University Press, 1994), 94. A man claiming to be Matthias came through Baltimore in 1836 but was not warmly received. "If, under any circumstances, it were justifiable for individuals to take the law into their own hands, and mete out the deserved punishment, here is a case which calls for its exercise," declared the Fells Point newspaper *Eastern Express*, December 27, 1836.

27. Mathew Carey, *Miscellaneous Essays* (Philadelphia, Pa.: Carey and Hart, 1830), 352; "Thoughts on Infant Schools, respectfully submitted to the Liberal and Human of both Sexes. Philadelphia, June 18, 1827," in Carey, *Miscellaneous Essays*, 311; "Essays on the Public Charities in Philadelphia . . ." in Carey, *Miscellaneous Essays*, 172.

28. Carey, *Miscellaneous Essays*, 194, 154. The language of "grinding the faces of the poor" comes from the book of Isaiah 3:15. On Carey, face grinding, and "Christian socioeconomic ethics," see William R. Sutton, *Journeymen for Jesus: Evangelical Artisans Confront Capitalism in Jacksonian Baltimore* (University Park: Pennsylvania State University Press, 1998), 24, passim.

29. Carey, *Miscellaneous Essays*, 190, 154, 194.

30. "Report on Female Wages. Philadelphia, March 25, 1829," in Carey, *Miscellaneous Essays*, 268, 270.

31. "Public Charities in Philadelphia," in Carey, *Miscellaneous Essays*, 159. The secretary of New York's United Tailoresses Society, Louise Mitchell, gave a forceful speech during the 1831 strike, declaring "for we are, literally, *slaves*." Auditors in Baltimore would have had a better sense of literal slavery. For Mitchell's speech, see Nancy Cott, Jeanne Boydston, Ann Braude, Lori D. Ginzberg, Molly Ladd-Taylor, eds., *Root of Bitterness: Documents of the Social History of American Women*, 2nd ed. (Boston: Northeastern University Press, 1996), 121.

32. Joseph Tuckerman, *An Essay on the Wages Paid to Females for their Labour; in the Form of a Letter From a Gentleman in Boston to his Friend in Philadelphia* (Philadelphia, Pa.: Carey & Hart, 1830), ii.

33. Ibid., 35, 38–42. On Tuckerman, see Jonathan A. Glickstein, "The World's 'Dirty Work' and the Wages that 'Sweeten' It: Labor's 'Extrinsic Rewards' in Antebellum Society," in *Moral Problems in American Life: New Perspectives on Cultural History*, edited by Karen Halttunen and Lewis Perry (Ithaca, N.Y.: Cornell University Press, 1998), 59–80.

34. Tuckerman, *Wages Paid to Females*, quotes on 25, 27, 29, 42.

35. *To the Public. Baltimore, May 10, 1830* (Baltimore: n.p., 1830), American Antiquarian Society, Worcester, Mass.

36. Ibid.

37. Carey, "To the Ladies who have undertaken to establish a House of Industry in New York [May 11, 1830]," in *Miscellaneous Essays*, 279.

38. [Mathew Carey], *A Plea for the Poor, Particularly Females. An Inquiry How Far the Charges Alleged Against them of Improvidence, Idleness, and Dissipation, are Founded in Truth,* 7th ed. (Philadelphia, Pa.: L. R. Bailey, 1837), 6–7. The Library Company of Philadelphia has the June 1830 Philadelphia handbill, as well as a similar one that circulated in New York in April 1830, a month before Baltimore's.

39. Mathew Carey, *Address to the Wealthy of the Land, Ladies as well as Gentlemen, on the Character, Conduct, Situation, and Prospects, of those whose Sole Dependence for Subsistence, is on the Labour of their Hands* (Philadelphia, Pa.: Wm. F. Geddes, 1831), ii; BCA, 1830:447; *Explanation of the Views of the Society for Employing the Poor; with the Constitution and By-Laws* . . . (Boston: n.p., 1820), 4; *First Report of the Provident Society for the Employment of the Poor, Presented at the Meeting, January 11, 1825* (Philadelphia, Pa.: L. R. Bailey, 1825), 7. In the 1830s, some women's philanthropy groups did seek to raise wages paid to working women. See Susan P. Benson, "Business Heads and Sympathizing Hearts: The Women of the Providence Employment Society, 1837–1858," *Journal of Social History* 12 (winter 1978): 302–312.

40. Carey, "To the Ladies," 279–281; Carey, "Address submitted for consideration to, and adopted by the Board of Managers of the Impartial Humane Society of Baltimore [May 15, 1830]," in *Miscellaneous Essays,* 283; Fielding Lucas, Jr., *Picture of Baltimore, Containing a Description of all Objects of Interest in the City* . . . (Baltimore: Fielding Lucas, Jr., 1832), 157; Carey, *Address to the Wealthy,* 16.

41. *Patriot,* August 11, 1829; Finley, *Address,* quotes on 5–9 (emphasis in original). Finley (1794–1839) was a man of the new republic. As a very young lawyer in 1818, he participated in a notable capital trial for the mail robbers Lewis Hare and John Alexander. In 1824, he traveled with the Baltimore delegation to meet Lafayette and bring the Revolutionary War hero back to the city. In addition to giving the 1829 address for the Baltimore & Susquehanna Railroad, he also delivered addresses (later published) for the Sunday School Union in 1830 and the Young Men's Preachers Aid Society in 1831. Finley became linked with Hezekiah Niles in 1831, when Niles campaigned as a Workingmen/National Republican for the Maryland House of Delegates. In one newspaper announcement of a joint appearance of the two men, Finley was called "the friend of the working-men" (*Patriot,* September 2, 1831). Seemingly at odds with that friendship, Finley became president of the Baltimore & Port Deposit Railroad in May 1833, and the following summer he led a unit of the Baltimore militia to suppress rioting Irish workers on the Baltimore and Washington Railroad. In 1835, Finley lost property in the riots pertaining to a banking scandal in Baltimore.

42. Finley, *Address.* Lawrence B. Glickman argues that the claim to the living wage emerged in post–Civil War period of labor unrest. Amy Dru Stanley finds the concern in eighteenth-century political economy. Either way, the term *living wages* itself has a distinct history from the concept itself, and I cannot locate an earlier usage, although the antithesis— starvation wages—does appear. See Glickman, *A Living Wage: American Workers and the Making of Consumer Society* (Ithaca, N.Y.: Cornell University Press, 1997); Stanley, *From Bondage to Contract,* 144–147.

43. *Acts Incorporating the Impartial Humane Society of the City of Baltimore* . . . (Baltimore: Thomas Murphy, 1830), 9. On the concept of the living wage as a family wage, see Stanley, *From Bondage to Contract,* 144–147.

44. Finley, *Address*, 9; *Patriot*, September 13, 1830; *American*, September 20, 1833. For 1830s labor militancy in Baltimore, see Sutton, *Journeymen for Jesus*, 28, 131–166; John R. Commons, *History of Labour in the United States*, vol. 1 (New York: Macmillan Company, 1936), 358, 473, 478. Little is known of the women at the forefront of Female Union Society of Tailoresses and Sempstresses, as the organization would come to be known that fall. The two women who convened the Fells Point meeting, Eleanora Wherett and Mary T. Ennis, did not appear in city directories, nor did the women who headed the Baltimore meeting, Susannah L. Stansbury and Hannah Moran. Stansbury and Moran assumed the leadership of the Female Union Society, and their names appeared numerous times in the city newspapers during the fall.

45. *Baltimore Republican*, September 14, 1833.

46. On women in public in the 1820s and 1830s, see Lori Ginzberg, "'The Hearts of Your Readers Will Shudder': Fanny Wright, Infidelity, and American Freethought," *American Quarterly* 46 (June 1994): 195–226; Mary Hershberger, "Mobilizing Women, Anticipating Abolition: The Struggle Against Indian Removal in the 1830s," *JAH* 86 (June 1999): 15–40.

47. "Petition of a Number of Widows, Orphans, and Families of New Manchester, NJ in Behalf of Domestic Manufacturing, February 5, 1816," U.S. Senate, 14th Cong., 1st sess., *New American State Papers* 6, Manufactures, 1:439.

48. Mary H. Blewett, *We Will Rise in Our Might: Workingwomen's Voices from Nineteenth-Century New England* (Ithaca, N.Y.: Cornell University Press, 1991), 37–38; Stansell, *City of Women*, 130–154; *Artisan*, September 26, 1833, as quoted in Teresa Anne Murphy, *Ten Hours' Labor: Religion, Reform, and Gender in Early New England* (Ithaca, N.Y.: Cornell University Press, 1992), 52.

49. *New York Daily Sentinel*, March 3 and June 25, 1831, as cited in Cott et al., *Root of Bitterness*, 118–122.

50. *American*, September 7, 1833. Interestingly, the editors did not include Carey's original 1831 dedication of the *Address* to the women of Baltimore's Humane Impartial Society. The subsequent essays of the *Address* appeared in the *American* on September 11, 16, 23, October 1, 2, 4, 7, 1833.

51. *American*, September 20, 1833.

52. *American*, September 20, 23, 30, 1833.

53. *American*, September 23, 30, October 3, 1833.

54. *American*, October 3, 4, 19, 26, 1833; *Baltimore Republican*, October 23, 1833.

55. *American*, November 20, 1833.

56. *American*, October 26, 1833.

57. *Niles*, October 31, 1835.

58. *Mechanic's Banner and Workingmen's Shield*, March 29, 1834. On New England labor unrest, see Blewett, *We Will Rise*, 38–48; Thomas Dublin, *Women at Work: The Transformation of Work and Community in Lowell, Massachusetts, 1826–1860* (New York: Columbia University Press, 1979), 86–107.

59. *Baltimore Saturday Visitor*, March 15, 1834; *The Experiment* [Baltimore], July 23, August 23, 1834; *Patriot*, September 25, 1834; *American*, October 17, 1834; *Baltimore Republican*, November 6, 1834. Weishampel was the printer of the *Experiment*, Baltimore's first

320	*Notes to Pages 154–158*

penny daily, whose short run lasted for the summer months of 1834. On Ladies' Deposi-
tories, see Buhle, "Needlewomen and Modern Life," 157–158.

60. *Patriot*, September 25, 1834; *American*, October 4, 1834; *Baltimore Republican*, January 3, 1835. The Humane Impartial Society advertised to patrons, "Ladies and gentlemen
who intend to go to the Springs this Summer, will find it to their advantage to call at the
office of this Society, where they can obtain any article of clothing that they may require
ready made." *Patriot*, August 13, 1834.

61. *Baltimore Republican*, January 15, June 8, October 16, 1835; *Fell's Point News-letter
and Mercantile Advertiser*, August 14, October 16, 1835. Weishampel put those seventy-five
subscriptions to good use, deploying them in the section of the *Fell's Point News-letter* called
"Variety. Begged—Borrowed—Stolen." Generally speaking, fund-raising for this kind of
philanthropy was difficult. Baltimore residents almost instantly raised $5,700 to aid sur-
vivors of a fire in Fayettesville (*Patriot*, July 1, 1831), but organizations like the Humane Impartial Society were still grateful to James Creighton for a donation of $22.62 from a char-
ity exhibition of the "Grand Moral Painting of Adam and Eve" (*Patriot*, May 22, 1834).

62. *Baltimore Republican*, April 24, 28, 1835.

63. *Baltimore Republican*, June 8, 1835.

64. *Fell's Point News-letter*, August 21, 1835.

65. David Grimsted, "Democratic Rioting: A Case Study of the Baltimore Bank Mob of
1835," in *Insights and Parallels: Problems and Issues of American Social History*, ed. William L.
O'Neill (Minneapolis: Burgess Publishing Company, 1973), 125–191; BCA, 1835:327; Pardons, S1061-38, folders 70–75.

66. *Fell's Point News-letter*, August 21, October 9, 1835; *Baltimore Republican*, September 14, 1835.

67. *Baltimore Republican*, September 14, 1835; *Fell's Point News-letter*, August 21, October 16, 1835.

68. *Niles*, October 31, 1835; *Fell's Point News-letter*, March 12, 1836.

69. Zakim, *Ready-Made Democracy*, 3.

Chapter 6 · The Hard Work of Being Poor

1. Olwen H. Hufton, *The Poor of Eighteenth-Century France, 1750–1789* (Oxford: Clarendon Press, 1974); Rachel G. Fuchs, *Gender and Poverty in Nineteenth-Century Europe* (New
York: Cambridge University Press, 2005), 14; Bettina Bradbury, *Working Families: Age, Gender, and Daily Survival in Industrializing Montreal* (Toronto: McClelland & Stewart Inc., 1993);
Steven King and Alannah Tomkins, eds., *The Poor in England, 1700–1850: An Economy of
Makeshifts* (Manchester, U.K.: Manchester University Press, 2003); Jeanne Boydston, *Home
and Work: Housework, Wages, and the Ideology of Labor in the Early Republic* (New York: Oxford University Press, 1990), 128–141; Pamela Sharpe, *Adapting to Capitalism: Working Women
in the English Economy, 1700–1850* (New York: St. Martin's Press, 1996); Anna Clark, *The
Struggle for the Breeches: Gender and the Making of the British Working Class* (Berkeley: University of California Press, 1995), 25–41, 63–87; Sonya O. Rose, *Limited Livelihoods: Gender
and Class in Nineteenth-Century England* (Berkeley: University of California Press, 1992), 76–

101; Christine Stansell, *City of Women: Sex and Class in New York, 1789–1860* (New York: Alfred A. Knopf, 1986), 193–216; Ellen Ross, *Love and Toil: Motherhood in Outcast London, 1870–1918* (New York: Oxford University Press, 1993); Dietlind Hüchtker, "Strategies and Tactics: The Politics of Subsistence in Berlin, 1770–1850," *International Review of Social History* 49 (2004): 435–453. On delayed gratification and self-exploitation in early modern capitalism, see Jan de Vries, "The Industrial Revolution and the Industrious Revolution," *Journal of Economic History* 54 (June 1994): 249–270; John Bezis-Selfa, *Forging America: Ironworkers, Adventurers, and the Industrious Revolution* (Ithaca, N.Y.: Cornell University Press, 2004).

2. Brevitt to father, May 12, 1806, Joseph Brevitt Letterbook, MHS, ms. 137; John Melish, *Information and Advice to Emigrants to the United States . . .* (Philadelphia, Pa.: John Melish, 1819), 90–91; BCA, 1827:1114.

3. For the new language of improvidence in the early republic discourse on poverty, see Bruce Dorsey, *Reforming Men and Women: Gender in the Antebellum City* (Ithaca, N.Y.: Cornell University Press, 2002), 50–89; Seth Rockman, *Welfare Reform in the Early Republic: A Brief History with Documents* (Boston: Bedford Books, 2003), 1–33.

4. Pardons, s1061-25, folder 92.

5. Bettina Bradbury draws explicit attention to the inequalities of gender and age in working-class households: "The complementarity of the roles of husbands and wives, sons and daughters, should not blind us to their inequality. Power and rights were not evenly distributed within any families at this time. In working-class families wage dependency locked wives and children to husbands in a relationship that was at once mutual and complementary, yet hierarchical and dependent." On the most material level, such inequalities revealed themselves in the daily caloric intake of adult men relative to women and children. See Bradbury, *Working Families*, 220.

6. On households as a mode of pooling resources to meet subsistence needs, see Robert Jutte, *Poverty and Deviance in Early Modern Europe* (New York: Cambridge University Press, 1994), 83–99; Peter Laslett, *Household and Family in Past Time* (Cambridge: Cambridge University Press, 1972); Boydston, *Home and Work*, 30–42. On overlapping modes of patriarchal authority, see Gerda Lerner, "Rethinking the Paradigm," in *Why History Matters: Life and Thought* (New York: Oxford University Press, 1997), 146–184.

7. BCA, 1827:1001 (Bayly), 1830:1062 (Stimson), 1832:1092 (Langley).

8. Pardons, s1061-15, folder 22 (King), s1061-25, folder 92 (Johnson). The Johnson petition attested to the power of elite patrons to assist common men and women in trouble with the law. Johnson told the court that he could "perduse as good a carracter as any man in my situation by Gentlemen that I have worked for." None other than Revolutionary War hero and Maryland senator Samuel Smith wrote to recommend Johnson as a "sober honest and industrious man" for the nine months they had been acquainted. On the ideology of male breadwinning elsewhere, see Joshua R. Greenberg, *Advocating the Man: Masculinity, Organized Labor, and the Household in New York, 1800–1840* (New York, Columbia University Press, www.gutenberg-e.org, 2006), ch. 5.

9. *American*, January 8, 1805; Boydston, *Home and Work*, 128–141; John Colvin, *The Baltimore Weekly Magazine, Complete in One Volume . . .* (Baltimore: William Pechin, 1801), December 20, 1800.

10. *Ordinances, 1833* (Baltimore: Sands & Neilson, 1833), app. 52. On the connection between sea and shore and the gender dynamics of maritime families, see Margaret S. Creighton and Lisa Norling, eds., *Iron Men, Wooden Women: Gender and Seafaring in the Atlantic World, 1700–1920* (Baltimore: Johns Hopkins University Press, 1996).

11. Baltimore County Court (Chattel Records) 1813–1814, MSA, c298-4, pp. 47, 509; Maryland Penitentiary Prisoners Record, 1811–1840, MSA, s275-1, November 25, 1817; BAAB, June 22, 1823.

12. *Ordinances, 1833*, app. 52; Pardons, s1061-9, folder 50 (White).

13. Pardons, s1061-16, folder 69 (Grace); s1061-13, folder 2 (Woolen). Woolen received character testimonials from such leading Baltimore citizens as Jesse Tyson, Levi Hollingsworth, Thomas W. Griffith, and Samuel Byrnes, who reported that Woolen "was in my employ as a Labourer for several years previous . . . he always conducted Himself orderly & I considered Him one of the best Labourers at the mills." For Overfield, see *American*, December 22, 1818. Owen Allen, the owner of the stolen watches, described Overfield as a "most refined villain" with "a morose dark countenance" who "can turn his hand almost to any thing: is a quarrier at times, carpenter and wheelwright."

14. Pardons, s1061-31, folder 18 (Thompson); BAAB, March 2, 1825 (Halloway).

15. *Fifth Annual Report of the Maryland State Temperance Society* (Baltimore: n.p., 1836), 6.

16. BAAB, July 2, 1825 (McCormick); Pardons, s1061-5, folder 82 (Alexander).

17. *Federal Census of 1810*, Baltimore City. Of the 563 households in Ward 8, seventy-eight were headed by women. However, to tabulate working-class female-headed households, I reduced that number by eliminating the sixteen slaveholding white women whose livelihoods owed to their ability to rent out enslaved workers, as well as another ten women who appeared as substantial property holders in the 1813 City Assessment. Thus, I was left with fifty-two female-headed households presumably "reliant upon their own industry."

18. *Federal Census of 1820*, Wards 1, 2, and 3 (formerly Wards 7, 8, and 9 before the 1818 renumbering; see William G. Lefurgy, "Baltimore's Wards, 1797–1978: A Guide," *MHM* 75 [June 1980]: 145–153). For the 1818 tax data, see BCA, Tax Assessors Notebooks, Rg4, s2. In Wards 7, 8, and 9 (covering all of Baltimore east of Jones Falls), the median assessment for women was $160, in contrast to the $210 median for male householders.

19. Baltimore County Court (Miscellaneous Court Papers) 1807, MSA, c-1-32 (Guy); Chattel Records, 1811–1812, MHS, ms 2865, November 27, 1811 (Cole); Barbara Wallace, "'Fair Daughters of Africa': African American Women in Baltimore, 1790–1860" (Ph.D. diss., UCLA, 2001), 207–208 (Blake). Christopher Phillips has located the success of Baltimore's black community in the prevalence of "male-headed and two-parent" households and the eagerness of African American Baltimore residents to define freedom through traditional family norms. See Christopher Phillips, *Freedom's Port: The African American Community of Baltimore, 1790–1860* (Urbana: University of Illinois Press, 1997), 93. Wallace qualifies this perspective in "Fair Daughters of Africa," 38–80. For demographic comparisons with other cities, see Suzanne Lebsock, *The Free Women of Petersburg: Status and Culture in a Southern Town, 1784–1860* (New York: W. W. Norton, 1984), 100; James Sidbury, *Ploughshares into Swords: Race, Rebellion, and Identity in Gabriel's Virginia, 1730–1810* (New York: Cambridge University Press, 1998), 224; Gary B. Nash, *Forging Freedom: The Forma-*

tion of Philadelphia's Black Community, 1720–1840 (Cambridge, Mass.: Harvard University Press, 1988), 162; Shane White, *Somewhat More Independent: The End of Slavery in New York City, 1770–1810* (Athens: University of Georgia Press, 1991), 163.

20. Pardons, s1061-31, folders 84 and 110. In seeking a pardon, Denny reported that his family "tho Coloured have ever endeavored to deport themselves in such a way as to avoid offence to any." While incarcerated, Denny also accrued daily prison maintenance charges of 20¢ per day. Although he received a pardon in May 1830, he was still imprisoned at the end of July for inability to pay those fees. As his supporters reported to the court, Denny worked himself to exhaustion to make up the fees. He sawed 200 cords of wood while incarcerated—until his clothes wore out.

21. Wallace, "Fair Daughters of Africa," 38–80

22. Wallace, "Fair Daughters of Africa," 207–208; *Thomas Anderson v. Rebecca Garrett et al.*, Court of Appeals of Maryland, 9 Gill 120, June 1850.

23. Wallace, "Fair Daughters of Africa," 38–80; Pardons, s1061-7, folder 35 (Hill).

24. Disorderly boys figured prominently in the annual addresses of Baltimore mayors and in newspaper accounts of urban life. *Federal Gazette*, January 25, 1804; *Patriot*, June 11, 1816, January 16, 1822; *American*, May 9, 1816, January 9, 1819, July 3, 1819; *Baltimore Daily Transcript*, March 10, 1836; [Baltimore] *Eastern Express*, November 11, 1836; *Baltimore Express*, April 22, 1837. The *Patriot* celebrated Christmas 1826 for "the almost entire absence of the firing of squibs, crackers, and guns, and mobs of noisy boys and negroes, which have heretofore been so annoying to our citizens, on the eve and the day of any festival" (December 26, 1826). For petitions to the city council complaining of disorderly boys, see BCA, 1824:375, 1831:421, 1831:455, 1831:477, 1833:367, 1833:679, 1835:690, 1835:859, 1837:435, 1837:438a. For mayor's speeches, see BCA, 1816:461, 1818:619, 1824:375; *Ordinances*, 1818.23, 1820.20.

25. *American*, August 21, 1804; *Eastern Express*, January 6, 1837. On demography of childbearing, see Wallace, "Fair Daughters of Africa," 44–51.

26. *Post*, July 14, August 16, 1809; *Mechanics' Gazette and Merchants' Daily Advertiser*, June 29, 1815; T. Stephen Whitman, *The Price of Freedom: Slavery and Manumission in Baltimore and Early National Maryland* (Lexington: University Press of Kentucky, 1997), 182n82–83.

27. BCA, 1830:494 (Wells); Pardons, s1061-14, folder 1 (Williamson), s1061-26, folder 36 (Cunningham).

28. T. Stephen Whitman, "Orphans in City and Countryside in Nineteenth-Century Maryland," in *Children Bound to Labor: Pauper Apprenticeship in Early America*, eds. John E. Murray and Ruth Wallis Herndon (Ithaca, N.Y.: Cornell University Press, forthcoming); T. Stephen Whitman, "Manumission and Apprenticeship in Maryland, 1770–1870," *MHM* 101 (spring 2006): 55–71.

29. Fuchs, *Gender and Poverty*, 43–68; Clare A. Lyons, *Sex among the Rabble: An Intimate History of Gender and Power in the Age of Revolution, Philadelphia, 1730–1830* (Chapel Hill: University of North Carolina Press, OIEAHC, 2006), 186–236; Susan E. Klepp, "Revolutionary Bodies: Women and the Fertility Transition in the Mid-Atlantic Region, 1760–1820," *JAH* 85 (December 1998): 910–945.

30. Indemnities for illegitimate children were filed in Baltimore County courts, which

leaves unclear how many cases originated in the rural areas surrounding Baltimore and how many originated in the city. I generated a database of 121 indemnities between 1805 and 1812, but the records provided very little other information in terms of residence or occupation. See Baltimore County Court (Miscellaneous Court Papers) 1805–1812, MSA, c1-30 to c1-37.

31. On working-class mortality in early republic cities, see Simon Newman, "Dead Bodies: Poverty and Death in Early National Philadelphia," in *Down and Out in Early America*, ed. Billy G. Smith (University Park: Pennsylvania State University Press, 2004), 41–62; Susan E. Klepp, "Malthusian Miseries and the Working Poor in Philadelphia, 1780–1830: Gender and Infant Mortality," in B. G. Smith, *Down and Out in Early America*, 63–92. For contemporary statistics, see Nathaniel Niles, Jr., and John D. Russ, *Medical Statistics; or a Comparative View of the Mortality in New-York, Philadelphia, Baltimore, and Boston* . . . (New York: Elam Bliss, 1827), 4–10; Baltimore City Health Department, *The First Thirty-Five Annual Reports, 1815–1849* (Baltimore: City of Baltimore, 1953); *Niles*, January 16, 1819; *Patriot*, January 8, 1822. For a critique of these records, see *American*, September 5, 1818. For almshouse data, the BAAB (1823–1826) included 206 children under five, of whom 66 died in the institution. For the buried twins, see *Patriot*, July 1, 1823. Newspapers featured regular announcements of children's deaths, such as the African American twelve-year-old who died from a locust sting (*Patriot*, June 12, 1834).

32. *Baltimore Literary and Religious Magazine* 3 (June 1837): 276–280.

33. Douglas F. Stickle, "Death and Class in Baltimore: The Yellow Fever Epidemic of 1800," *MHM* 74 (September 1979): 282–299; *American*, December 9, 1819 ("reduced to beggary").

34. John Weatherburn Collection, ms. 44, letterbook 119, November 20, 1803, Milton S. Eisenhower Library, Special Collections, The Johns Hopkins University; James Smith, *The Additional Number to the Letters of Humanitas* . . . (Baltimore: n.p., 1801); David M. Reese, *Observations on the Epidemic of 1819, as it Prevailed in a Part of the City of Baltimore* . . . (Baltimore: John D. Toy, 1819); *A Series of Letters and other Documents relating to the Late Epidemic of Yellow Fever* . . . (Baltimore: William Warner, 1820); *An Appeal to the Citizens of Baltimore and its Vicinity, by the Board of Directors of the Baltimore Second Dispensary* . . . (Baltimore: B. Lundy, 1827), 4 ("proportion of the poor"); For Diffenderffer's records, see BCA, 1827:334, 1828:314

35. Fuchs, *Gender and Poverty*, 5; Pardons, s1061-6, folder 45 (Cardiffe).

36. *Patriot*, January 4 (Kemp), 16 (burned child), 25 (Warren Factory), 1834; *Beverly Dowling vs. Sophia Bland and Austin Woolfolk*, October 1835, *RSPP*, 20983515 (especially James O. Law to Sophia Bland, June 1834, and Sophia Law to Captain Mayo, June 1834).

37. *American*, October 14, 1819. The Baltimore almshouse was not able to purchase wood wholesale for less than $5 a cord in the 1810s. See Baltimore County Trustees of the Poor (Proceedings), 1806–1818, MSA, c402-1.

38. On the range of currencies in Baltimore, see Denwood N. Kelly, Armand M. Shank, Jr., and Thomas S. Gordon, "A Catalogue of Maryland's Paper Money, 1790–1865," in *Money and Banking in Maryland* (Baltimore: Maryland Historical Society, 1996). See also Stuart R. Bruchey and Eleanor S. Bruchey, "A Brief History of Commercial Banking in the Old Line State," in *Money and Banking in Maryland*. For working-class criticism of paper

money, see Benjamin Davies, *The Bank Torpedo; or, Bank Notes Proved to be a Robbery on the Public, and the Real Cause of the Distresses of the Poor* (New York: McCarty and White, 1810); J. R. Greenberg, *Advocating the Man*, ch. 3.

39. Paul A. Gilje and Howard B. Rock, *Keepers of the Revolution: New Yorkers at Work in the Early Republic* (Ithaca, N.Y.: Cornell University Press, 1993), 104 (reprinted from *American Citizen*, April 10, 1809); Mathew Carey, *Address to the Wealthy of the Land, Ladies as well as Gentlemen, on the Character, Conduct, Situation, and Prospects, of those whose Sole Dependence for Subsistence, is on the Labour of their Hands* (Philadelphia, Pa.: Wm. F. Geddes, 1831), 5–6; *To the Public, Baltimore May 10, 1830* (Baltimore: n.p., 1830). For wintertime disbursements, see BCA, 1810:541; [Baltimore] *Journal of the Times*, December 26, 1818 (also included sugar and tea among items distributed to needy families); *American*, February 5, 1819 ("the necessaries of life, as wood, flour, tea, sugar, &c.").

40. Richard Chew found that a day laborer's $1 wage in 1802 was worth only 68¢ in 1814. Even mudmachinists who saw wage increases in the 1810s nonetheless saw their real wages decline. See Richard Smith Chew, "The Measure of Independence: From the American Revolution to the Market Revolution in the Mid-Atlantic" (Ph.D. diss., College of William and Mary, 2002), 370–371.

41. On the moral economy and market regulation, see Ruth Bogin, "Petitioning the New Moral Economy of Post-Revolutionary America," *WMQ* 45 (July 1988): 391–425; Barbara Clark Smith, "Food Rioters and the American Revolution," *WMQ* 51 (January 1994): 3–38; William J. Novak, *The People's Welfare: Law and Regulation in Nineteenth-Century America* (Chapel Hill: University of North Carolina Press, 1996), 95–105; Helen Tangires, *Public Markets and Civic Culture in Nineteenth-Century America* (Baltimore: Johns Hopkins University Press, 2003); Roger Horowitz, Jeffrey M. Pilcher, and Sydney Watts, "Meat for the Multitudes: Market Culture in Paris, New York City and Mexico City over the Long Nineteenth Century," *AHR* 109 (October 2004): 1055–1083.

42. For Baltimore's key marketing regulations, see *Ordinances*, 1797.16, 1805.21, 1816.12, and 1826.38. For candles and meat, see BCA, 1823:241, 1824:337.

43. Baltimore's 1802 bread assize differed from those enforced in New York and other cities by fixing the weight but not the price. Elsewhere, the weight of legal loaves changed with wholesale price of flour. In New York, for instance, a 1-shilling loaf might weigh 40 ounces one month and 35 ounces the next. New York abandoned its assize in 1821. See Howard B. Rock, *Artisans of the New Republic: The Tradesmen of New York City in the Age of Jefferson* (New York: New York University Press, 1979), ch. 7. Baltimore's 1792 bread assize was similar to New York's and set six prices for loaves, the weight of which would vary with the price of flour. See *Maryland Journal*, June 22, 1792. The 1802 assize required bakers to stamp their last names on each loaf and instituted a $20 fine for anyone who shall "adulterate or mix any improper or unwholesome ingredient in the flour whereof such bread is made." See *Ordinances*, 1802.31; *Mayors' Msgs.*, 1802 (Calhoun quote). Subsequent revisions tinkered with the enforcement mechanism or fines but did not alter the fundamental premise of the law. See *Ordinances*, 1808.56 and 1824.10. The 1826 and 1828 laws lowered minimum weights and ultimately allowed prices to fluctuate with the wholesale price of flour. See *Ordinances*, 1826.36 and 1828.7. Throughout the entire period, bakers complained that they could not survive on the price set by the assize and custom, and that they had been

singled out among tradesmen as being untrustworthy. For petitions and legislative debates, see BCA, 1803:219, 1808:179, 1808:206, 1809:343 (Evans quote), 1817:359, 1820:317, 1820:495, 1824:347; *Mayors' Msgs.*, 1803, 1808, 1817. For other discussion of the issue, see *American*, October 5, 1805, July 31, 1819; *Niles*, December 15, 1821.

44. *Patriot*, September 16, 1824; BCA, 1824:348, 1826:418, 1827:418, 1828:419.

45. See the "Public Notice" printed in *American*, March 9, 1808. During the 1780s and early 1790s, the state assembly and its appointees, the Special Commissioners for Baltimoretown, passed enclosure laws that made the streets, lanes, and alleys the only remaining "commons." See *Maryland Journal*, June 8, 1792.

46. *Ordinances*, 1797.15, 1801.27, 1807.29, 1812.20, 1816.21, 1826.14; BCA, 1803:288, 1807:348, 1810:535, 1824:409; *Late Epidemic of Yellow Fever*, 57.

47. *Late Epidemic of Yellow Fever*, 66; *Ordinances*, 1821.23; *Patriot*, February 27, 1822; BCA, 1825:420, 1826:343; [Providence, RI] *Ladies Museum*, October 8, 1825, 44. Baltimore temporarily shut the urban range in 1826 but reopened it from April to December (*Ordinances*, 1831.10). A Connecticut visitor in 1835 was distressed to find two pigs sleeping in a schoolhouse but remarked, "these animals act as licensed scavengers in the streets of 'monumental city,' and are particularly active in the neighborhood of the markets." E. A. Andrews, *Slavery and the Domestic Slave-Trade in the United States. In a Series of Letters Addressed to the Executive Committee of the American Union for the Relief and Improvement of the Colored Race* (Boston: Light & Stearns, 1836), 87–88.

48. *Patriot*, November 23, 1826; BCA, 1828:631; *Ordinances*, 1836 (Baltimore: Lucas & Deaver, 1836), app. 8.

49. For constipation, see BCA, 1827:333, 1828:314. For other diets, see Douglas G. Carroll, Jr., and Blanche D. Coll, "The Baltimore Almshouse: An Early History," *MHM* 66 (summer 1991): 151; Lorena S. Walsh, "Feeding the Eighteenth-Century Town Folk, or, Whence the Beef?" *Colonial Williamsburg Interpretor* 21 (2000). Ascertaining food prices in the market is tricky. Many historians have used published "Price Currents," but these reflect wholesale not retail prices. European visitors commented on the costs of victuals in the market but invariably converted values to fluctuating English currency. Hezekiah Niles created a food budget in 1815 that specified 6¢/lb. for meat and 2.5¢/lb. for bread, even as he must have been aware that the price of a loaf of bread was nearly twice as high. See *Niles*, December 2, 1815. Other sources for food prices include Donald R. Adams, Jr., "Prices and Wages in Maryland, 1750–1850," *Journal of Economic History* 46 (September 1986): 625–45; *American*, July 31, 1819; Francis Baily, *Journal of a Tour in Unsettled Parts of North America in 1796 and 1797* . . . (London: Baily Bros., 1856), 106; Joseph Pickering, *Emigration or No Emigration: Being the Narrative of the Author* . . . (London: Longmans, Reese, Orme, Brown, and Greene, 1830), 10; Richard Parkinson, *The Experienced Farmer's Tour in America* (London: G&J Robinson, 1805), 561. Annual reports from the Baltimore almshouse estimated the market value of produce raised on the poor farm. In 1827, a bushel of potatoes was valued at 50¢, a bushel of onions at $1, a bushel of string beans at 66¢, and a bushel of parsnips at 50¢. See BCA, 1827:1114. For Lawson, see BCA, 1816:467.

50. *Niles*, December 2, 1815. Niles allocated only three-quarters a pound of bread per day per person. Historians have subsequently reconstructed the diets of the urban poor and found daily bread consumption above one pound. Billy Smith set the daily ration of bread

at 1.31 pounds for poor Philadelphians at the end of the eighteenth century. In pegging the price of bread to the cost of a bushel of wheat, Niles assumed that poor families purchased in bulk (at $1.50 per bushel) and that they possessed the appropriate equipment and fuel for baking. More commonly, Baltimore's poor purchased bread at market, paying a consistent 12½¢ for a three-pound loaf. Billy Smith elaborates a sophisticated methodology for calculating working-class diets, one which I did not have the resources to reproduce specifically for Baltimore. See Billy G. Smith, *The "Lower Sort": Philadelphia's Laboring People, 1750–1800* (Ithaca, N.Y.: Cornell University Press, 1990), 95–103. On the cost of food in penal institutions, see *Report of the Visitors of the Jail of Baltimore City and County* (Baltimore: n.p., [1839]); *Baltimore Penitentiary Unroofed: or the Penitentiary System Illustrated, in a Letter to the Philadelphia Society for Ameliorating the Miseries of Public Prisons* (Philadelphia, Pa.: n.p., 1831), 26. On wintertime food relief, see *American*, June 11, 1805 (This report tallied 800 families *not including* those in Fells Point and a second neighborhood. My estimate of 1,000 households includes these two districts in the total), February 17, 24, 1817; BCA, 1810:540. For soup houses, *American*, January 22, April 22, 1805, October 21, 28, 1819, March 22, December 28, 1820; BCA, 1821:913.

51. For the frozen harbor, see John Weatherburn Letterbook, March 23, 1805, entry 123; *American*, February 22, 1805; *Patriot*, January 29, 1816; *Jefferson Reformer and Baltimore Daily Advertiser*, March 11, 1836. On wintertime wood relief, see *Baltimore Telegraphe*, January 19, 1805; *Baltimore Telegraph and Mercantile Advertiser*, February 2, 1815 ("hundreds"); *Patriot*, December 7, 1831; BCA, 1808:261, 1810:540, 1822:237, 1827:504. "I use the word 'perish' with due deliberation, and a full conviction of its appropriate application to the case, however revolting it may seem to the reader," declared Mathew Carey (*Address to the Wealthy*, ix). On wood banks, see *Maryland Gazette*, June 13, 1794; BCA, 1808:213; *Circular. Fuel Savings Society, for the Benefit of the Poor* (Philadelphia, Pa.: n.p., 1821); *Constitution of the Society for the Relief of the Destitute, and for Supplying Poor Families with Cheap Fuel in the City of New York, with an Address Recommending the Society to Public Patronage* (New York: William A. Mercein, 1827).

52. *Patriot*, September 25, 1828; *American*, February 5, 1805.

53. E. L. Finley, *An Address Delivered by Request of the Managers of the Humane Impartial Society, at their Annual Meeting, Held on the 24th January 1831* . . . (Baltimore: Lucas & Deaver, 1831), 7; Charles G. Steffen, *The Mechanics of Baltimore: Workers and Politics in the Age of Revolution, 1763–1812* (Urbana: University of Illinois Press, 1984), 23, found that absentee landlords owned nearly 50 percent of Fells Point property in 1783. For the nineteenth century, I used BCA, Tax Assessors Notebooks, Rg4, s2, to compile the entire run of assessments for Wards 7 and 8 (1813); Wards 7, 8, and 9 (1818); and the renumbered Wards 1 through 4 (1823). Because the wards were redrawn and the boundaries of the city expanded, these wards were not coterminous but covered the bulk of Baltimore east of Jones Falls. In 1813, the median taxable wealth in Fells Point and Old Town was $250, well below the $336 figure for the city as a whole (Whitman, *Price of Freedom*, 17). The bottom half of taxpayers possessed 13 percent of the neighborhood's property in 1813, and only 11 percent a decade later. That statistic actually obscures the extent of poverty in Fells Point because it does not include the majority of householders who fell below the $40 assessment minimum. Taking into account those too poor to tax, the inequality was more striking: one half of Fells

Point families collectively owned a piddling 3 to 5 percent of the neighborhood's wealth. In sum, eastern Baltimore had a higher concentration of poor residents than other neighborhoods, and its poor residents tended to live in deeper poverty than did the poor elsewhere in the city. In 1813, some of the absentee owners in Fells Point included General Samuel Smith, Judge Nicholas Brice, merchant Cumberland Dugan, and gentleman William Patterson. By 1823, the richest tenth of property holders in Fells Point possessed 66 percent of the neighborhood's total wealth.

54. Mary Ellen Hayward and Charles Belfoure, *The Baltimore Rowhouse* (New York: Princeton Architectural Press, 1999), 8–45, esp. 20–21; Bernard L. Herman, *Town House: Architecture and Material Life in the Early American City, 1780–1830* (Chapel Hill: University of North Carolina Press, OIEAHC, 2005), 193–195; Carole Shammas, "The Housing Stock of the Early United States: Refinement Meets Migration," *WMQ* 64 (July 2007): 549–590. Baltimore's story is akin to that of Philadelphia and New York, as told in Donna J. Rilling, *Making Houses, Crafting Capitalism: Builders in Philadelphia, 1790–1850* (Philadelphia: University of Pennsylvania Press, 2001), and Elizabeth Blackmar, *Manhattan for Rent, 1785–1850* (Ithaca, N.Y.: Cornell University Press, 1989).

55. For a Happy Alley plat containing such residents as Richard Janes, an African American, and Widow Welsh, see BCA, 1802:94. On Moving Day, see Blackmar, *Manhattan for Rent*, 213–216.

56. *Patriot*, October 23, 1822; BCA, 1820:360; *Rules and By-laws of the Baltimore General Dispensary* . . . (Baltimore: Sower and Cole, 1803); *Address to the Citizens of Baltimore and its Vicinity, Containing a Concise Account of the Baltimore General Dispensary* . . . (Baltimore: Benjamin Edes, 1812); *American*, June 14, 1805; BCA, 1824:862, 1827:333, 1828:314. For Mary Newton's records, see Baltimore General Dispensary Case Records, 1801–1805, December 27, 28, 1804, January 2, 1805, CMS, Archive/Library, Medical & Chirurgical Faculty of Maryland, Baltimore.

57. BCA, 1820:360 ("these poor people"), 1828:371 ("most in need"), 1830:425, 1834:394. For Whitten, see BCA, 1821:484, 1821:623.

58. For wintertime clothing distribution, see *Baltimore Telegraphe*, January 16, 19, 30 ("clad by the bounty"), 1805; BCA, 1810:541, 1811:562–572. For shoes and clothing expenses of day laborers, see Carey, *Address to the Wealthy*, 5. For thefts, see Baltimore City Court of Oyer and Terminer and Gaol Delivery (Docket and Minutes), MSA, c183-3 (1807–1808), c183-6 (1810), c183-8 (1813), c183-9 (1816).

59. Whitman, "Manumission and Apprenticeship," 57.

60. Whitman, *Price of Freedom*, 51–53.

61. *Beverly Dowling vs. Sophia Bland and Austin Woolfolk*, RSPP, 20983515 (especially James O. Law to Sophia Bland, October 26, 1833); *Bland and Woolfolk vs. Negro Beverly Dowling*, Court of Appeals of Maryland, 9 G&J 19, June 1837.

62. Whitman, *Price of Freedom*, 90, 98, and ch. 5; Phillips, *Freedom's Port*, 46–52, 91–96. For evidence of purchasing family members, see Baltimore County Court (Chattel Records), MSA, c298-3 (1800–1801), c298-4 (1813–1814); Chattel Records, 1785–1788, 1811–1812, MHS, ms 2865.

63. BCA, 1827:419. See also Stansell, *City of Women*, 193–216; Boydston, *Home and Work*, 128.

64. BCA, 1831:1774, 1833:743 ("relic"), 1835:739. The annual *Report of the Visiters [sic] and Governors of the Jail of Baltimore County* (published within each year's *Ordinances of the Mayor and City Council of Baltimore . . .*) contained the best data on imprisoned debtors. After 1832, many debtors got out of jail more speedily once creditors became responsible for the cost of board in prison. *Laws*, 1830.155, prohibited debt imprisonment for amounts less than $30, but that law was repealed by 1832 (1832.142). On debt imprisonment more generally, see Bruce H. Mann, *Republic of Debtors: Bankruptcy in the Age of American Independence* (Cambridge, Mass.: Harvard University Press, 2002).

65. Pawning should have left an extensive paper trail, because Baltimore's municipal ordinance required all items to be recorded in a broker's account book and all customers to receive a certificate; yet such artifacts remain hidden. For critiques of pawning in other cities, see *The Second Annual Report of the Managers of the Society for the Prevention of Pauperism, in the City of New-York . . .* (New York: E. Conrad, 1820), 11; James Mease, *On the Utility of Public Loan Offices & Saving Funds, Established by City Authorities* (United States: n.p., 1836). See also Wendy Woloson, "In Hock: Pawning in Early America," *JER* 27 (spring 2007): 35–81; *Ordinances*, 1828.22.

66. Charles Varle, *A Complete View of Baltimore, with a Statistical Sketch . . .* (Baltimore: Samuel Young, 1833), 83; *American*, October 10 (Millem), October 15 (Eytinge), 1833; *Patriot*, September 1, 1834 (Eytinge sale). BCA, 1819:467, 1832:577, 1832:1170 (Millem's license application). On the meaning of respectable goods in working-class homes, see Herman, *Town House*, 193–230.

67. Pardons, s1061-15, folder 11 (Cruse).

68. Pardons, s1061-25, folders 22 and 87 (Barnett). For hucksters and peddlers who stole from foyers, see *Patriot*, September 11, 1829, January 26, 1830

69. *Post*, February 20, 1809; BCA, 1805:206a, 1819:467, 1823:515, 1824:831.

70. Pardons, s1061-35, folder 13 (Crowl), s1061-12, folder 53 (Tate). Caleb Dougherty participated in a murderous jailbreak in 1808 and died on the gallows (*American*, March 17, April 20, 1808). For cases of white storekeepers fencing goods for African Americans, see also Pardons, s1061-12, folder 17, s1061-31, folder 3.

71. Pardons, s1061-28, folder 38 (Holmes). For other cases, see s1061-37, folder 2; BCA, 1827:655–656. For watchmen's livelihoods, see chapter 8.

72. For license lists and fines, see Baltimore County Court (Miscellaneous Court Papers) 1801–1802, MSA, c1-28, folder 428; Baltimore City Court of Oyer and Terminer and Gaol Delivery (Docket and Minutes), MSA, c183-6 (1810), c183-9 (1816); BCA: Early Records of Baltimore (1795), Rg2 s1, I, item 28; also 1799:188, 1805:384, 1807:360. Pardons, s1061-14, folder 16 (Johnson), s1061-28, folder 73 (Bryan), s1061-29, folder 3 (Good).

73. BCA, 1803:288 (offal), 1824:482 (scrap metal); Pardons, s1061-30, folder 15 (Zwigler).

74. Pardons, s1061-6, folder 24 (Harnett), s1061-29, folder 90 (Nevit).

75. Carey, *Address to the Wealthy*, 2. For the public relief system in Baltimore, see chapter 7. In 1818, the Baltimore Humane Society distributed $515 in supplies to over 150 households. *Journal of the Times*, December 26, 1818. BCA, 1810:540–541, 1811:562–572.

76. W. Ray Luce, "The Cohen Brothers: From Lotteries to Banking," *MHM* 68 (fall 1973): 288–308; *Cohen's Lottery Gazette*, 1820–1824; *Patriot*, December 22, 1834. On gambling, see Pardons, s1061-26, folders 17, 19; *Mayors' Msgs.*, 1803; *American*, December 10, 1818.

77. *Patriot*, December 2, 1834; *Matchett's Baltimore Directory for 1831* (Baltimore: R. J. Matchett, 1831), front material; *Matchett's Baltimore Directory for 1833* (Baltimore: R. J. Matchett, 1833), front material; Pardons, s1061-26, folder 17. On gambling, economic rationality, and the working class, see Ann Fabian, *Card Sharps and Bucket Shops: Gambling in Nineteenth-Century America* (1990; repr., New York: Routledge, 1999).

78. *American*, February 17, 1817 ("accidental contingencies").

79. *American*, December 22, 1818 ("time of need"), August 11, 1819 ("port of Economy"), May 9, 16, 23, 30, 1820; *The Savings Bank of Baltimore* . . . [1818], MHS, Broadsides Collection.

80. First Fidelity Bank Collection, Account Book 1824–1826, MSA, sc4313-9-223, and Signature Book 1818–1853, sc4313-3-59; Peter Lester Payne and Lance Edwin Davis, *The Savings Bank of Baltimore, 1818–1866: A Historical and Analytical Study* (Baltimore: Johns Hopkins Press, 1956), 58–64. See also Michael Nash, "Research Note: Searching for Working-Class Philadelphia in the Records of the Philadelphia Saving Fund Society," *Journal of Social History* 29 (spring 1996): 683–687.

81. *Documents Relative to Savings Banks, Intemperance, and Lotteries. Published by Order of the Society for the Prevention of Pauperism, in the City of New York* (New York: E. Conrad, 1819), 8 ("luxury and dress"); *American*, January 8, 1805 ("meaner offices"), February 3, 1820 ("whiskey"). For the Baltimore Temperance Society, see *Patriot*, October 9, 1829; *The Constitution and Address of the Baltimore Temperance Society* (Baltimore: J. D. Toy, 1830).

82. *Colonization of the Free Colored Population of Maryland, and of Such Slaves as May Hereafter Become Free* . . . (Baltimore: Managers Appointed by the State of Maryland, 1832), 4.

Chapter 7 · The Consequence of Failure

1. For mudmachine payrolls (with Dicky and Zachariah both listed as Stailor), see chapter 3. *Baltimore Directory for 1817–1818* (Baltimore: James Kennedy, 1817) shows Richard, nailer, Eden and Dulany, Old Town; Zachariah, laborer, Caroline St., Fells Point. *Baltimore Directory, Corrected up to June 1819* (Baltimore: Richard J. Matchett, 1819) shows Richard, nailer, Apple Alley; no listing for Zachariah. *Federal Census of 1820*, Baltimore City, Ward 2, p. 92, shows Zachariah's household containing two girls under ten, a man between sixteen and twenty-six (presumably Zachariah), a woman between sixteen and twenty-six (presumably the mother of the two girls), and a man and a woman between the ages of twenty-six and forty-five (potentially Richard and Nelly, since no separate listing appeared for Richard). Data on ages, family relations, and history comes from BAAB, June 25, 1825 (Zachariah), January 1, 1826 (Richard), January 6, 1826 (Zachariah).

2. On the "commonwealth" tradition that established public responsibility for the needy, see Kathleen D. McCarthy, *American Creed: Philanthropy and the Rise of Civil Society, 1700–1865* (Chicago: University of Chicago Press, 2003). For surveys of early American public relief, see Michael B. Katz, *In the Shadow of the Poorhouse: A Social History of Welfare in America* (New York: Basic Books, 1986); Walter I. Trattner, *From Poor Law to Welfare State: A History of Social Welfare in America*, 3rd ed. (New York: Free Press, 1984). For a model of connecting almshouse regimes to political regimes, see Silvia M. Arrom, *Containing the Poor: The Mexico City Poor House, 1774–1871* (Durham, N.C.: Duke University Press, 2000). For

the history of the Baltimore Almshouse, see J. Thomas Scharf, *The Chronicles of Baltimore* . . . (Baltimore: Turnbull Brothers, 1874), 72–75; Charles Varle, *A Complete View of Baltimore, with a Statistical Sketch* . . . (Baltimore: Samuel Young, 1833), 90; *Acts of the General Assembly of Maryland, Relating to the Poor of Baltimore City and County* . . . (Baltimore: John D. Toy, 1830). For the key acts, see *Laws*, 1773.30, 1816.201, 1817.87, 1818.122, 1822.167.

3. BCA, 1826:1094.

4. *Patriot*, January 29, 1834.

5. For carting paupers to the almshouse, see BCA, 1829:1718, 1837:789. BAAB, June 22, 1825 (Stallings). The admissions book recorded information on tobacco use, but tabulated data on this subject did not appear in the institution's annual reports.

6. BCA: 1830:543. Baltimore's taxpayers supported the almshouse through a special levy of 75¢ per $100 of assessable property. Insofar as property holders paid only $2.30 per $100 to fund every other operation of the municipal government, the poor tax was not inconsequential. For poor tax, see BCA, 1817:268a; *Ordinances*, 1820.21, 1821.20, 1822.26, 1823.5, 1824.8, 1825.9; *Niles*, September 6, 1823. The 1823 City Assessment located $3,311,134 in assessable property in Baltimore's twelve wards, yielding poor tax revenue of $24,833. The 1824 almshouse budget was $23,971. See BCA, 1824:495, Tax Assessors Notebooks, Rg4, s2, 1823.

7. For overviews of these competing interpretative traditions, see Mark Colvin, *Penitentiaries, Reformatories, and Chain Gangs: Social Theory and the History of Punishment in Nineteenth-Century America* (Boston: St. Martins, 1997); David Garland, *Punishment and Modern Society: A Study in Social Theory* (Chicago: University of Chicago Press, 1990); David Garland, *Punishment and Welfare: A History of Penal Strategies* (Brookfield, Vt.: Gower, 1985).

8. BCA, 1826:1094, 1827:1040. Susanna Rowson's *Charlotte Temple. A Tale of Truth* (orig. 1791) appeared in a 1794 American edition and became the blockbuster novel of the early republic. Not to spoil the ending, but Zachariah Stallings's question came from the penultimate page of the novel. See the ninth American edition published by Mathew Carey in 1812, p. 135. By the 1820s, Charlotte's story was a familiar cross-class cultural reference. From a far wider range of sources, variants of the expression "to die in the street" were common in Anglo-American culture.

9. For the simultaneity of social processes, see Marco H. D. van Leeuwen, "Logic of Charity: Poor Relief in Preindustrial Europe," *Journal of Interdisciplinary History* 24 (spring 1994): 589–613; Pieter Spierenburg, "Punishment, Power, and History: Foucault and Elias," *Social Science History* 28 (winter 2004): 607–636; Peter Mandler, ed., *The Uses of Charity: The Poor on Relief in the Nineteenth-Century Metropolis* (Philadelphia: University of Pennsylvania Press, 1989).

10. Even as the early republic witnessed the emergence of a more impersonal and instrumental philanthropy, charity remained a crucial cultural expression, especially for members of a new Northern middle class and Southern elites invested in the hierarchical relationships of patronage. See Robert A. Gross, "Giving in America: From Charity to Philanthropy," in *Charity, Philanthropy, and Civility in American History*, eds. Lawrence J. Friedman and Mark D. McGarvie (New York: Cambridge University Press, 2003), 29–48. For "personalism" in Southern charity, see Suzanne Lebsock, *The Free Women of Petersburg: Status and Culture in a Southern Town, 1784–1860* (New York: W. W. Norton, 1984). For benevolence

as an articulation of class and social identity, see Lori D. Ginzberg, *Women and the Work of Benevolence: Morality, Politics, and Class in the 19th-Century United States* (New Haven, Conn.: Yale University Press, 1990); Conrad Edick Wright, *The Transformation of Charity in Postrevolutionary New England* (Boston: Northeastern University Press, 1992); Bruce Dorsey, *Reforming Men and Women: Gender in the Antebellum City* (Ithaca, N.Y.: Cornell University Press, 2002).

11. The institutional regime of surveillance, compulsory labor, and physical punishment was designed to inculcate self-reliance while discouraging workers from relying on public relief in the first place. The almshouse also repaired broken workers, sheltered the surplus workforce during slack times, allowed employers to pay minimal wages without fearing that their laborers would starve, and provided enough of a safety net to dissuade the desperate from using violence when food ran short. The relationship of social welfare practices to social discipline—especially serving the interests of liberal capitalist regimes—draws from both Foucaultian and Marxist traditions: Michel Foucault, *Discipline and Punish: The Birth of the Prison*, trans. Alan Sheridan (New York: Pantheon Books, 1978); Michael Ignatieff, *A Just Measure of Pain: The Penitentiary in the Industrial Revolution* (New York: Pantheon Books, 1978); Michael Meranze, *Laboratories of Virtue: Punishment, Revolution, and Authority in Philadelphia, 1760–1835* (Chapel Hill: University of North Carolina Press, OIEAHC, 1996); Simon P. Newman, *Embodied History: The Lives of the Poor in Early Philadelphia* (Philadelphia: University of Pennsylvania Press, 2003). On the role of disciplinary institutions in regulating labor markets, see Rosalind P. Petchesky, "At Hard Labor: Penal Confinement and Production in Nineteenth-Century America," in *Crime and Capitalism: Readings in Marxist Criminology*, ed. David F. Greenberg (Philadelphia, Pa.: Temple University Press, 1993), 595–611. On the disciplinary aspects of institutions generally, see David J. Rothman, *The Discovery of the Asylum: Social Order and Disorder in the New Republic* (Boston: Little, Brown, 1971); John K. Alexander, *Render Them Submissive: Responses to Poverty in Philadelphia, 1760–1800* (Amherst: University of Massachusetts Press, 1980).

12. For work stressing the agency of the poor, see Tim Hitchcock, *Down and Out in Eighteenth-Century London* (London: Hambleton & London, 2004); Ruth Wallis Herndon, *Unwelcome Americans: Living on the Margin in Early New England* (Philadelphia: University of Pennsylvania Press, 2001); Anne Winter, "'Vagrancy' as an Adaptive Strategy: The Duchy of Brabant, 1767–1776," *International Review of Social History* 49 (August 2004): 249–277; David R. Green, "Pauper Protests: Power and Resistance in Early Nineteenth-Century London Workhouses," *Social History* 31 (May 2006): 137–159; Monique Bourque, "Populating the Poorhouse: A Reassessment of Poor Relief in the Antebellum Delaware Valley," *Pennsylvania History* 70 (2003): 397–432; Bourque, "Poor Relief 'Without Violating the Rights of Humanity': Almshouse Administration in the Philadelphia Region, 1790–1860," in *Down and Out in Early America*, ed. Billy G. Smith (University Park: Pennsylvania State University Press, 2004): 189–212.

13. Baltimore County Court (Miscellaneous Court Papers), 1784, MSA, c1-9, folder 164, item 402; *Baltimore Telegraphe*, February 29, 1804; BAAB, January 2 (Trefant), 3 (Cain and Sharp), 1826.

14. James Smith, *The Additional Number to the Letters of Humanitas . . .* (Baltimore: n.p., 1801), 43; *Patriot*, January 15, 1823; *Niles*, July 26, 1823. See also July 24, August 7, 1819, De-

cember 16, 1820, May 17, September 6, 1823; Gary Browne, "Baltimore and the Panic of 1819," in *Law, Society, and Politics in Early Maryland,* eds. Aubrey C. Land, Lois Green Carr, and Edward C. Papenfuse (Baltimore: Johns Hopkins University Press, 1977), 212–227.

15. For almshouse populations data, see BAAB for 1814–1826, and trustees' annual reports as follows: BCA, 1824:495, 1825:189, 1827:1114–1115, 1828:284, 1829:1718, 1830:624, 1831:1313, 1833:743, 1833:1113, 1834:1099, 1834:2516, 1835:1206, 1836:2065, 1837:938a, 1838:223–239; *Ordinances,* 1839 (Baltimore: John D. Toy, 1839), app. 29; *Ordinances, 1840* (Baltimore: Joseph Robinson, 1840), app. 92; *Minutes of the Trustees of the Poor for Baltimore City and County, 1833–1842,* BCA, microfilm reel 397.

16. On badges as a shaming mechanism, see Steve Hindle, "Dependency, Shame, and Belonging: Badging the Deserving Poor, c. 1550–1750," *Cultural and Social History* 1 (2004): 6–35; *American,* February 8, 1811, cited in Dennis Rankin Clark, "Baltimore, 1729–1829: The Genesis of a Community" (Ph.D. diss., Catholic University, 1976), 290–291; *By-Laws of the Trustees and Rules for the Government of the Poor-House of Baltimore County* (Baltimore: P & RW Edes, 1818).

17. *By-Laws of the Trustees*; Douglas G. Carroll, Jr., and Blanche D. Coll, "The Baltimore Almshouse: An Early History," *MHM* 66 (summer 1971): 135–52; Katherine A. Harvey, "Practicing Medicine at the Baltimore Almshouse, 1828–1850," *MHM* 74 (September 1979): 223–237; *Mayors' Msgs.,* 1825.

18. *By-Laws of the Trustees.*

19. BCA, 1829:1718; *Patriot,* January 15, 1823.

20. BCA, 1830:624, 1831:1313. Despite narrower opportunities for economic self-sufficiency, women may have had superior access to private charity (especially through women-directed voluntary organizations) and could thus avoid the almshouse. See Priscilla Ferguson Clement, "Nineteenth-Century Welfare Policy, Programs, and Poor Women: Philadelphia as a Case Study," *Feminist Studies* 18 (spring 1992): 35–58. For women's benevolence in Baltimore, see *A Brief Account of the Female Humane Association Charity School, of the City of Baltimore* (Baltimore: Warner and Hanna, 1803); *The Constitution of the Baltimore Female Association for the Relief of Distressed Objects* (Baltimore: Warner and Hanna, 1808); BCA, 1811:562–572 (Aimwell Society), 1827:504 (Female Indigent Sick Society); *Acts Incorporating the Impartial Humane Society of the City of Baltimore* . . . (Baltimore: Thomas Murphy, 1830); *Southern Pioneer and Gospel Visitor,* January 18, 1834 (Samaritan Society). For elsewhere, see Anne Boylan, *The Origins of Women's Activism: New York and Boston, 1797–1840* (Chapel Hill: University of North Carolina Press, 2002).

21. *American,* February 17, 1817; *Emerald and Baltimore Literary Gazette,* May 31, 1828.

22. On railroad and canal workers in the almshouse, see BCA, 1828:284, 1829:1718, 1830:624; *Document 11 Accompanying the Executive Message to the Legislature, December 31, 1829: Report respecting the Chesapeake and Ohio Canal* (Annapolis: J. Hughes, 1829); For European immigrants, see BCA, 1829:1718.

23. *Report of a Committee Appointed by the Guardians for the Relief and Employment of the Poor of Philadelphia, &c., to Visit the Almshouses of Baltimore, New York, Boston, and Salem, November 1833* (Philadelphia, Pa.: Wm. F. Geddes, 1834), 39–40; Baltimore County Trustees of the Poor (Proceedings), 1806–1818, MSA, c402-1, November 22, 1813, February 5, 1814; BCA, 1824:495, 1827:1114, 1829:1718; C. J. Jeronimus, ed., *Travels by His Highness Duke Bern-*

hard of Saxe-Weimar-Eisenach through North America in the Years 1825 and 1826, trans. William Jeronimus (Lanham, Md.: University Press of America, 2001), 224. Accommodations for Catholic inmates became a controversial issue in 1840, when the almshouse keeper sued the fiercely anti-Catholic Robert J. Breckinridge for libel. See Breckinridge, *Papism in the XIX. Century, in the United States . . .* (Baltimore: David Owen and Son, 1841).

24. BCA, 1826:1094, 1831:1774 (jail report), 1834:2516. After a cholera outbreak at the almshouse in 1832, "extra clothing [was] distributed as rewards among those whose conduct had been exemplary during that trying time." See *Ordinances,* 1834 (Baltimore: Lucas & Deaver, 1834), 39.

25. Baltimore Almshouse Medical Records, 1833–1837, MHS, ms. 2474; Harvey, "Practicing Medicine"; BAAB, July 8, 1824 (Every). Case records were frequently published in *American Journal of the Medical Sciences,* beginning with vol. 3 (1828).

26. BAAB, April 18, June 24, 1825 (Reland); July 7, October 16, 1823 (Jonqua); July 15, August 14, 1825 (Myers). For "white" mothers, see September 9 (Letty Bounds), October 25 ("Negro" daughter Pamela Barnes), 1823. When new mothers did try to withhold the fathers' names, administrators included notes in the institution's birth records: February 8 (Henry Martin "illegitimate son of Mary Martin and John Martin, chair maker"), March 26 ("son of Mary Coffman, who says she is a married woman"), 1824. Departing from a lax regime of public support for children born out of wedlock, Philadelphia began forcing poor women in the 1820s to deliver in the almshouse if they hoped to receive out-relief later. Baltimore did not offer regular out-relief payments to new mothers, and pregnant women there voluntarily used the almshouse. See Clare A. Lyons, *Sex among the Rabble: An Intimate History of Gender and Power in the Age of Revolution, Philadelphia, 1730–1830* (Chapel Hill: University of North Carolina Press, OIEAHC, 2006), 261–266, 360–380.

27. BAAB, March 13 (Tight), July 12 (Fields), 1824, July 25 (Hogg), August 22 (Monday), 1825, February 15 (Carson), April 20 (Choherty), 1826; BCA, 1838:324; *Patriot,* January 15, 1823.

28. Baltimore County Trustees of the Poor (Ground Rent Records), 1810–1819, MSA, c332-1, loose insert (Hignan); BAAB, January 5 (Collins), September 10 (Haskins), 1825.

29. BCA, 1828:284; *Laws,* 1793, ch. 45; BAAB, December 30, 1825 (Tagert). See note 15 for annual reports containing the number of children bound out annually. For wealthy Baltimore families, the almshouse served as an asylum for disabled children. Sally Bowen, the insane daughter of a propertied Fells Point widow, spent more than a decade in the institution, where she received a monthly delivery of clothing and superior food from her mother's estate. See Bowen Account Book, MHS, ms. 85.

30. Baltimore County Trustees of the Poor (Proceedings), 1806–1818, MSA, c402-1, passim (for indentures to Brevitt, Nicholas, and Gonet); BAAB, May 22, 1824 (Gonet, as Garnet), January 4, 1826 (Stallings); *By-Laws of the Trustees.* For the larger context of apprenticed child labor in the early republic, see Ruth Wallis Herndon and John E. Murray, eds., *Children Bound to Labor: Pauper Apprenticeship in Early America* (Ithaca, N.Y.: Cornell University Press, forthcoming).

31. Carroll and Coll, "Baltimore Almshouse," 141 (Griffith).

32. BCA, 1826:1094, 1829:1718; BAAB, January 2, 1826 (Stallings).

33. BCA, 1831:395.

34. *Patriot*, January, 15, 1823; BCA, 1827:1114, 1829:1718, 1830:624, 1831:1313; [Baltimore] *Eastern Express*, October 28, 1836 ("too promiscuous").

35. *Acts . . . Relating to the Poor*, 48; Carroll and Coll, "Baltimore Almshouse," 150.

36. Baltimore County Trustees of the Poor (Proceedings), MSA, c402-1, August 1, 1816 (Lucy); BAAB, January 22 (Lane), October 23 (Bristo), 1824, January 20 (Sacks), January 30 (Johnson), March 30 (Hutchins), September 8 (Hazard), December 29 (Webster), 1825. For its three years (1823–1826) of detailed data, the Almshouse Admissions Book contained the names of 364 African American inmates. Of those inmates, 178 died in the institution. Visitors Alexis de Tocqueville and Gustave de Beaumont both drew attention to a particular African American inmate—a man made insane by the haunting perception that notorious Baltimore slave trader Austin Woolfolk was ripping off his skin in order to eat. See Beaumont, *Marie, or Slavery in the United States*, trans. Barbara Chapman (1835; repr., Baltimore: Johns Hopkins University Press, 1999), 46; Alexis de Tocqueville, *Journey to America*, ed. J. P. Mayer, trans. George Lawrence (Westport, Conn.: Greenwood Press, 1981), 159.

37. BCA, 1834:1099; BAAB, July 24, 1823, October 10, 1824, August 6, 1825 (Stallings), June 1, 1820, April 17, May 30, June 9, October 4, 1821, February 11, March 29, December 31, 1822, June 20, December 20, 1823, January 28, June 3, 1824, March 10, August 10, 1825, April 13, 1826 (Evans); *Patriot*, January 15, 1823.

38. BAAB, 1823–1826. White men ages twenty-one to sixty accounted for 561 of the 1,886 detailed admissions records for this period.

39. BAAB, June 9, 1824 (Volk), January 25 (McIntire), February 3 (Volk), 12 (Loring), 1825; February 22, 1826 (Volk). For Volk, see also BCA, 1805:384, 1818:167, 1820:265.

40. BAAB, December 24, 1825 (Drummond), March 27, 1826 (Kinman). The 1826 annual report attributed 554 of 739 admissions over the previous year to alcohol (whether "intemperance" or injuries "received whilst the parties were in a state of intoxication"). See BCA, 1827:1114, 1826:1094, 1828:284. On the class dimensions of the early republic medicalization of alcohol use, see Matthew Warner Osborn, "Diseased Imaginations: Constructing Delirium Tremens in Philadelphia, 1813–1832," *Social History of Medicine* 19 (August 2006): 191–208.

41. *American*, January 22, 1805; BCA, 1809:466. On the shifting terrain of individual and civic benevolence, especially through the eighteenth-century language of liberality, see J. M. Opal, "The Labors of Liberality: Christian Benevolence and National Prejudice in the American Founding," *JAH* 94 (March 2008): 1082–1107; Philip Hamburger, "Liberality," *Texas Law Review* 78 (May 2000): 1215–1285.

42. Josiah Quincy, *Report of the Massachusetts General Court's Committee on the Pauper Laws of this Commonwealth* [1821], reprinted in *The Almshouse Experience: Collected Reports* (New York: Arno Press, 1971), 5. For a range of 1810s publications, see *The Philanthropist: Or, Institutions of Benevolence, By a Pennsylvanian* (Philadelphia, Pa.: Isaac Peirce, 1813); *Miscellaneous Remarks on the Police of Boston; as Respects Paupers; Alms and Work House . . .* (Boston: Cummings and Hilliard, 1814); *Report of the Library Committee of the Pennsylvania Society for the Promotion of Public Economy* (Philadelphia, Pa.: Merritt, 1817); *Report of a Committee on the Subject of Pauperism* (New York: Samuel Wood & Sons, 1818); *The First Annual Report of the Managers of the Society for the Prevention of Pauperism in the City of New-York . . .* (New York: J. Seymour, 1818); Josiah Quincy, *Report of the Committee on the Subject of Pau-*

perism and a House of Industry in the Town of Boston (Boston: n.p., 1821). For an overview of this debate, see Seth Rockman, *Welfare Reform in the Early Republic: A Brief History with Documents* (Boston: Bedford Books, 2003), 1–33; B. Dorsey, *Reforming Men and Women*, 50–89; S. D. Kimmel, "Sentimental Police: Struggles for 'Sound Policy and Economy' Amidst the Torpor of Philanthropy in Mathew Carey's Philadelphia," *Early American Studies* 3 (spring 2005): 164–226.

43. Annual wintertime fund-raising for the poor had less relationship to Christmas than it does today. Beyond the changing cultural meanings of Christmas, another explanation is more straightforward: the wintertime needs of the poor in Baltimore did not generally become urgent until late January or February, and most ad hoc relief efforts began then. For wintertime relief, see BCA, 1798:232b, 1800:297, 1801:263, 1808:261, 1809:466, 1810:540; *Maryland Journal*, February 10, 1792; *Baltimore Telegraphe*, January 30, 1804; *Federal Gazette*, February 8, 1804; "Poor of Baltimore in Acct. with Andrew Buchanan, January 1805," Andrew Buchanan Collection, MHS, ms. 1555; *American*, January 14, 31, February 5, June 11, 1805; Thorowgood Smith broadside, [1808], insert, Thomas W. Griffith Scrapbook, MHS, ms. 412.1; BCA, 1810:445 (Johnson quote), 1817:268a ("much harrassed"); *American*, February 26, 1817 ("no doubt"). Blanche D. Coll, "The Baltimore Society for the Prevention of Pauperism, 1820–1822," *AHR* 61 (October 1955): 77–87. For a thorough discussion of wintertime relief, see Seth Rockman, "Work, Wages, and Welfare at Baltimore's School of Industry," *MHM* 102 (spring 2007): 572–607.

44. *American*, February 20, 1817; *Patriot*, January 15, 1823. A contemporary newspaper editorial noted the importance of Malthus's writing in Baltimore's public debate on poor relief. See *Patriot*, January 12, 1822.

45. *Patriot*, January 15, 1823. Officials in other American cities also clung to the underlying premises of public relief. "[T]he experience of England under the operation of her poor laws, have led some of her most distinguished statesmen and writers on public economy to denounce all public, or compulsory provision for the poor," noted Boston's Josiah Quincy, but neither he nor his peers in other American cities thought this a wise path to follow. See Quincy, *Report of the Massachusetts General Court's Committee . . .* , 5.

46. Thomas Haskell located the origins of modern sympathy in the market relations of the eighteenth century. See "Capitalism and the Origins of the Humanitarian Sensibility," in *The Antislavery Debate: Capitalism and Abolitionism as a Problem in Historical Interpretation*, ed. Thomas Bender (Berkeley: University of California Press, 1992), 107–160. Elizabeth Clark countered that in the nineteenth century, "ministers not merchants" were at the forefront of compassion. See "'The Sacred Rights of the Weak': Pain, Sympathy, and the Culture of Individual Rights in Antebellum America," *JAH* 82 (September 1995): 463–493. For foundational scholarship on sensibility, see G. J. Barker-Benfield, *The Culture of Sensibility: Sex and Society in Eighteenth-Century Britain* (Chicago: University of Chicago Press, 1992); Karen Halttunen, "Humanitarianism and the Pornography of Pain in Anglo-American Culture," *AHR* 100 (April 1995): 303–334; Sarah Knott, "Sensibility and the American War for Independence," *AHR* 109 (February 2004): 19–40.

47. Terry D. Bilhartz, *Urban Religion and the Second Great Awakening: Church and Society in Early National Baltimore* (Rutherford, N.J.: Farleigh-Dickinson University Press, 1986), 13–14; *American*, February 17, 22, 1817.

48. *Baltimore Telegraph and Mercantile Advertiser*, February 2, 1815; *Baltimore Telegraphe*, February 8, 1805 (Richardson); *American*, February 12, 1807; *Patriot*, September 17, October 4, 1824. On voyeurism within poor relief, see Halttunen, "Humanitarianism and the Pornography of Pain"; Seth Koven, *Slumming: Sexual and Social Politics in Victorian Britain* (Princeton, N.J.: Princeton University Press, 2004).

49. T. H. Poppleton, *Plan of the City of Baltimore*, 1823, MHS; George Wilson Pierson, *Tocqueville in America* (1938; repr., Baltimore: Johns Hopkins University Press, 1996), 493, 516; Cornelius William Stafford, *Baltimore Directory for 1803* (Baltimore: John W. Butler, 1803), 75.

50. *Baltimore Telegraphe*, January 30, 1804, January 30, 1805; BCA, 1809:466, 1811:461; *Laws*, 1818.122.

51. Carroll and Coll, "Baltimore Almshouse," 149.

52. Ibid. On the issue of violence and the dispossessed, see Camilla Townsend, *Tales of Two Cities: Race and Economic Culture in Early Republican North and South America: Guayaquil, Ecuador, and Baltimore, Maryland* (Austin: University of Texas Press, 2000). Mark P. Leone argues that Baltimore's panoptic architecture served to minimize the chance of violent uprisings. See Leone, "A Historical Archaeology of Capitalism," *American Anthropologist* 97 (June 1995): 257–260.

53. Whitman H. Ridgway, *Community Leadership in Maryland, 1790–1840: A Comparative Analysis of Power in Society* (Chapel Hill, University of North Carolina Press, 1979), 215–240; Joshua Civin, "Civic Experiments: Community-Building in Baltimore and Liverpool, 1785–1835" (Ph.D. in progress, Oxford University); *American*, August 21, 1804, January 14, 1805. By the late 1820s, almshouse appointments were clearly in the realm of political patronage. Mayor Small reportedly offered John Schunck an appointment as a trustee in exchange for electoral support. Schunck turned down the position and its $2 weekly salary because "it would cost me more than 2 dollars to go out that distance [to the almshouse], weekly, and return." See *Patriot*, October 18, 1828.

54. *Patriot*, April 5, 1823, January 26, 1824. By the start of the 1830s, Baltimore had more than three dozen benevolent organizations. See Varle, *View of Baltimore*, 44–45.

55. *Report of the Committee appointed by the Board of Guardians of the Poor of the City and Districts of Philadelphia, to visit the Cities of Baltimore, New-York, Providence, Boston, and Salem* . . . (Philadelphia, Pa.: Samuel Parker, 1827), 6. On the articulation of class through social welfare, see Ginzberg, *Women and the Work of Benevolence*; B. Dorsey, *Reforming Men and Women*; Christine Stansell, *City of Women: Sex and Class in New York, 1789–1860* (New York: Alfred A. Knopf, 1986).

56. *Baltimore Morning Chronicle*, January 27, April 15, 1820; Baltimore County Court (Miscellaneous Court Papers) 1801–1802, MSA c1-28, folder 428; *A Series of Letters and other Documents relating to the Late Epidemic of Yellow Fever* . . . (Baltimore: William Warner, 1820), 135; *Mayors' Msgs.*, 1817; *American*, March 9, 1816. Baltimore residents learned of the 1824 arrest of a man in Hartford, Connecticut, who had been soliciting alms up and down the eastern seaboard. During his stop in Baltimore, he "appeared to be quite helpless, but the muscles of his face not keeping time with the twitching of his limbs, and limping, and apparently crippled gait of his tongue, he did not excite much sympathy." But his act had passed muster in New York and Hartford, where he had acquired $85 in donations. When he en-

countered the overseer of the workhouse in Hartford, "all at once his limbs resumed unusual strength, and he ran like a deer down State Street" before being apprehended and incarcerated for forty days. *Patriot,* July 6, 1824.

57. Count Rumford [Benjamin Thompson], "An Account of an Establishment for the
Poor at Munich," in *Collected Works of Count Rumford,* volume 5, *Public Institutions,* ed. San-
born C. Brown (Cambridge, Mass.: Belknap Press of Harvard University Press, 1970), 1–
98, quotes on 13 and 35. For Rumford, see Sandra Sherman, *Imagining Poverty: Quantifi-
cation and the Decline of Paternalism* (Columbus: Ohio State University Press, 2001),
141–215; Jayme A. Sokolow, "Count Rumford and Late Enlightenment Science, Technology, and Reform," *The Eighteenth Century* 21 (winter 1980): 67–86; Charles Guzzetta, "Jefferson, Rumford, and the Problem of Poverty," *Midwest Quarterly* 26 (1985): 343–356.

58. *Baltimore Telegraphe,* February 10, 13, 1804; Baltimore Library Company Record
Books, box 5, MHS, ms. 80; Rumford, "Of the Fundamental Principles on which General
Establishments for the Relief of the Poor May Be Formed in All Countries," in Brown, *Col-
lected Works of Count Rumford,* 99–165, quote on 146; *American,* Aug. 21, 22, 1804.

59. *American,* August 21, 1804.

60. Rumford, "Fundamental Principles" in Brown, *Collected Works of Count Rumford,*
118 ("kind usage"), 127 ("force"), 157 ("expulsion"). *American,* August 22, 1804.

61. *American,* August 21 ("good habits" and "real addition"), 22 ("proper means"), 1804;
Rumford, "Poor at Munich," in Brown, *Collected Works of Count Rumford,* 62.

62. BCA, 1810:445, 1811:414, 1816:481; *Mayors' Msgs.,* 1811.

63. *Laws,* 1793.57, 1804.96, 1811.212, 1818.169; BCA, 1812:549. The records of the Maryland Penitentiary reflect the strident enforcement of this law. Between 1812 and 1819, 186
men and women spent a year in the institution as vagrants. The typical convicted vagrant
was a white woman in her late twenties who had been born in Maryland, but not in Baltimore itself. Although the 1811 statute scrapped language on prostitutes, 75 percent of those
convicted were women. Maryland Penitentiary Prisoners Record, 1811–1840, MSA, s275-1.
For vagrancy as a surrogate for prosecuting prostitution, see also Priscilla Clement, "The
Transformation of the Wandering Poor in Nineteenth-Century Philadelphia," in *Walking
to Work: Tramps in America, 1790–1935,* ed. Eric H. Monkkonen (Lincoln: University of Ne-
braska Press, 1984), 56–84.

64. *Laws,* 1814.116; *American,* January 19, February 22, March 5, 1817.

65. *Mayors' Msgs.,* 1817.

66. *American,* February 3, 20, 24, 1817, August 1, 1818, February 5, 1819.

67. *Morning Chronicle,* April 15, 1820; *American,* March 9, 1820, January 12, 1822; *Patriot,* January 12, 1822; Coll, "Baltimore Society"; [Anon.], *To the Citizens of Baltimore* (Baltimore: T. Maund, 1822). The SPP was not met with uniform admiration. One critic called
its program "an *Inquisition,* more disgusting, and not less degrading and oppressive than
that which for centuries kept Spain and Portugal in one continued night of darkness and
terror." See [Anon.], *A Warning to the Citizens of Baltimore* (Baltimore: n.p., 1821).

68. On Thomas's railroad career, see James D. Dilts, *The Great Road: The Building of
the Baltimore and Ohio, the Nation's First Railroad, 1828–1853* (Stanford, Ca.: Stanford University Press, 1993), 36–48. *Report of the Committee appointed by the Board of Guardians
of the Poor,* 26; Artemas Simonds, *Boston Common Council—No. 15, 1835, Report on Alms-*

houses and Pauperism (Boston: J. H. Eastburn, 1835), 20–26 (quote on 26). French visitor Gustave de Beaumont celebrated the Baltimore almshouse and its superior mode of public charity in *Marie*, a literary companion to Tocqueville's *Democracy in America*. In New York and Boston, the poor "live upon alms, degrading themselves and ruining society," but Baltimore—and here Beaumont was mistaken—was different: "Since assistance can be refused to the poor, no one feigns poverty, being sure of the disgrace without being sure of the relief." See *Marie*, 43.

69. *Report of the Committee Appointed at a Town Meeting of the Citizens of the City and County of Philadelphia, on the 23rd of July, 1827* . . . (Philadelphia, Pa.: Clark & Raser, 1827), 7; Carroll and Coll, "Baltimore Almshouse," 148; BCA, 1824:494. Baltimore County Trustees of the Poor (Pension Record), 1817–1819, MSA, c397-1; Baltimore County Trustees of the Poor (Proceedings), MSA, c402-1, June 15, 1814 (Keighler), May 6, 1816 (Pessener); Baltimore County Levy Court (Daybook), MSA, c320-1, March 1, 1817 (Hetty Peirce).

70. BCA, 1827:1114 ("melancholy"), 1829:1718 (intemperance, House of Refuge), 1830:624 ("degrading"); *Ordinances*, 1840, 24 ("alien").

71. Stephen Allen, *Reports on the Stepping or Discipline Mill, at the New York Penitentiary* . . . (New York: Van Pelt and Spear, 1823); James Hardie, *The History of the Tread-Mill: Containing an Account of its Origin, Construction, Operation, Effects* . . . (New York: Samuel Marks, 1824); *Niles*, November 9, 1822; *Patriot*, November 15, 1822; David H. Shayt, "Stairway to Redemption: America's Encounter with the British Prison Treadmill," *Technology & Culture* 30 (October 1989): 908–938; *Acts* . . . *Relating to the Poor*, 45–47; BCA, 1826:380a.

72. *Report of a Committee* . . . *to Visit the Almshouses*, 10; Meranze, *Laboratories of Virtue*, 312–313 (Philadelphia's Eastern State Penitentiary acquired the shower bath in the 1830s); Punishment and Death, thematic issue, *Radical History Review* 96 (Fall 2006): cover image and preface. In 1836, the trustees further decided that returned runaways would sport a patch on their right shoulder marked with the letters "PB"—a punishment that had been largely dormant since it became Maryland law in 1773. See Minutes of the Trustees of the Poor for Baltimore City, April 3, 1836, BCA, microfilm reel 397.

73. BCA, 1827:1114, 1828:284. Baltimore's almshouse had several other advantages over those in other cities. Its large farm contained stands of trees that could be harvested for heating, which was a major expense of institutions elsewhere. On paupers seeking jail over the almshouse, see BCA, 1831:1774. On early republic penal labor, see Larry Goldsmith, "'To Profit By His Skill and to Traffic on His Crime': Prison Labor in Early 19th-Century Massachusetts," *LH* 40 (1999): 439–457; Jonathan A. Glickstein, *American Exceptionalism, American Anxiety: Wages, Competition, and Degraded Labor in the Antebellum United States* (Charlottesville: University of Virginia Press, 2002), 163–182.

74. *Report of the Committee appointed by the Board of Guardians of the Poor*, 21–22; Simonds, *Report on Almshouses and Pauperism*, 57. The farm grew produce worth $6,589 in 1835–1836. Most was consumed on-site, but market sales brought in $334.71. See BCA, 1836:2065. On declining per capita expenditures, see BCA, 1827:1114, 1831:1313.

75. For benevolent discipline, see *American*, February 3, 1820. On striving and failure in early republic capitalism, see Scott A. Sandage, *Born Losers: A History of Failure in America* (Cambridge, Mass.: Harvard University Press, 2005).

76. The moralization of poverty and its conceptualization as social deviance runs

through the early modern period. Pieter Spierenburg, *The Prison Experience: Disciplinary Institutions and their Inmates in Early Modern Europe* (New Brunswick: Rutgers University Press, 1991); Robert Jutte, *Poverty and Deviance in Early Modern Europe* (New York: Cambridge University Press, 1994); Joel F. Harrington, "Escape from the Great Confinement: The Genealogy of a German Workhouse," *Journal of Modern History* 71 (June 1999): 308–345; Marjorie K. McIntosh, "Poverty, Charity, and Coercion in Elizabethan England," *Journal of Interdisciplinary History* 35 (winter 2005): 457–479.

77. BCA, 1827:1114. For "tough love," see Jonathan A. Glickstein, "Pressures from Below: Pauperism, Chattel Slavery, and the Ideological Construction of Free Market Labor Incentives in Antebellum America," *Radical History Review* 69 (1997): 116.

Chapter 8 · The Market's Grasp

1. [James Kent], "A New Yorker in Maryland, 1793 and 1821," *MHM* 47 (June 1952): 139; Francis Baily, *Journal of a Tour in Unsettled Parts of North America in 1796 and 1797* ... (London: Baily Bros., 1856), 104–105.

2. William N. Blane, *Travels through the United States and Canada* ... (London: Baldwin and Co., 1828), 33; *Freedom's Journal* [New York], August 15, 1828; Garrison to Harriet Farnham Horton, May 12, 1830, in *Letters of William Lloyd Garrison*, ed. Walter M. Merrill (Cambridge, Mass.: Belknap Press of Harvard University Press, 1971), 1:92. See also William Lloyd Garrison, *A Brief Sketch of the Trial of William Lloyd Garrison, for an Alleged Libel on Francis Todd, of Newburyport, Mass.* (Boston: Garrison and Knapp, 1834).

3. *Baltimore Clipper*, October 19, 1839.

4. Barbara Jeanne Fields, *Slavery and Freedom on the Middle Ground: Maryland during the Nineteenth Century* (New Haven, Conn.: Yale University Press, 1986), 1–22, 40–62; Richard C. Wade, *Slavery in the Cities: The South, 1820–1860* (New York: Oxford University Press, 1964), 325 (population figures). E. A. Andrews, *Slavery and the Domestic Slave-Trade in the United States. In a Series of Letters Addressed to the Executive Committee of the American Union for the Relief and Improvement of the Colored Race* (Boston: Light & Stearns, 1836), 53.

5. There is not yet longitudinal research that can determine the number of people experiencing slavery over a given decade, but assuredly that number would be several times higher than the number identified in the federal census, especially as mobility (sales, runaways, reassignments) limited the overlap between two successive enumerations.

6. Walter Johnson, "Introduction: The Future Store," in *The Chattel Principle: Internal Slave Trades in the Americas*, ed. Walter Johnson (New Haven, Conn.: Yale University Press, 2004), 1–31. On slavery as property more broadly, see Gavin Wright, *Slavery and American Economic Development* (Baton Rouge: Louisiana State University Press, 2006).

7. For the tax regime of slavery in Maryland, see T. Stephen Whitman, *The Price of Freedom: Slavery and Manumission in Baltimore and Early National Maryland* (Lexington: University Press of Kentucky, 1997), 181n29; Robin L. Einhorn, *American Taxation, American Slavery* (Chicago: University of Chicago Press, 2006), 207–250. The question of whether early republic banks made loans explicitly on slaves has been at the center of recent municipal disclosure ordinances that require present-day corporations (e.g., Wachovia, JP Mor-

gan/Chase, PNC Bank, Bank of America) to investigate the actions of their antebellum-era predecessors. While there is evidence of loans written against slaves as collateral, it is possible that the fungibility of slaves made such explicit contracts unnecessary.

8. Robert Gilmor Journal, 1806–1807, South Caroliniana Library, University of South Carolina, Manuscripts Collections, accessed February 16, 2007, at www.sc.edu/library/socar/uscs/1998/gilmor98.html.

9. *Patriot*, April 15, 1816 ("all sorts and sizes"), May 27, 1816 (Walker's), June 7, 1816 (Fowler's), April 19, 1817 (Marriot's), September 27, 1834 (Arkansas); Andrews, *Slavery and the Domestic Slave-Trade*, 77–78. For denunciations of Baltimore's role in the domestic slave trade, see John Parrish, *Remarks on the Slavery of the Black People; Addressed to the Citizens of the United States . . .* (Philadelphia, Pa.: Kimber, Conrad, & Co., 1806), 11, 20, 21; Daniel Coker, *A Dialogue between a Virginian and an African Minister . . .* (Baltimore: Benjamin Edes, 1810), 12–14; *Christian Disciple* 6 (September 1818): 262; [John S. Tyson], *Life of Elisha Tyson, the Philanthropist. By a Citizen of Baltimore* (Baltimore: B. Lundy, 1825), 7–11; *Minutes of an Adjourned Session of the American Convention for Promoting the Abolition of Slavery, and Improving the Condition of the African Race, Convened at Baltimore, on the twenty-fifth of October, 1826* (Baltimore: Benjamin Lundy, 1826), 29; *Minutes of the Twentieth Session of the American Convention for Promoting the Abolition of Slavery, and Improving the Condition of the African Race, Convened at Philadelphia, on the second of October, 1827* (Baltimore: Benjamin Lundy, 1827), 49–50.

10. Steven Deyle, *Carry Me Back: The Domestic Slave Trade in American Life* (New York: Oxford University Press, 2005), 98–100; Robert H. Gudmestad, *A Troublesome Commerce: The Transformation of the Interstate Slave Trade* (Baton Rouge: Louisiana State University Press, 2003), 25–32; William Calderhead, "The Role of the Professional Slave Trader in a Slave Economy: Austin Woolfolk, A Case Study," *Civil War History* 23 (September 1977): 195–211; *Patriot*, December 27, 1815; *American*, May 23, 1825; *Minutes of the Adjourned Session of the Twentieth Biennial American Convention for Promoting the Abolition of Slavery and Improving the Condition of the African Race, held at Baltimore, Nov. 1828* (Philadelphia, Pa.: Samuel Parker, 1828), 24. In 1826, a contingent of Woolfolk slaves led a shipboard insurrection on route to New Orleans. The leader of the *Decatur* insurrection, William Bowser, was tried in New York and executed on Ellis Island in the presence of Woolfolk. See Eric Robert Taylor, *If We Must Die: Shipboard Insurrections in the Era of the Atlantic Slave Trade* (Baton Rouge: Louisiana State University Press, 2006), 147–150; *Niles*, May 20, 1826.

11. *Niles*, July 19, 1817; Gudmestad, *Troublesome Commerce*, 78–80; *Mayors' Msgs.*, 1821. In 1818, a city grand jury denounced "the infamous traffic in human flesh," especially as higher prices sparked "the cupidity of needy and unprincipled adventurers" and provoked "violence of every hue and grade." See *American*, December 10, 1818.

12. BCA, 1821:558; Andrews, *Slavery and the Domestic Slave-Trade*, 80. On kidnapping, see [Tyson], *Life of Elisha Tyson*, 10–12; *Minutes of the Twentieth Session . . . 1827*, 49. On slavery and the gothic, see Karen Halttunen, "Humanitarianism and the Pornography of Pain in Anglo-American Culture," *AHR* 100 (April 1995): 303–334.

13. Tocqueville called the man "one of the most beautiful Negroes I have ever seen, and

he is in the prime of life." See Alexis de Tocqueville, *Journey to America*, ed. J. P. Mayer, trans. George Lawrence (Westport, Conn.: Greenwood Press, 1981), 159–160; Gustave de Beaumont, *Marie, or Slavery in the United States*, trans. Barbara Chapman (Baltimore: Johns Hopkins University Press, 1999), 45–46. For slave suicides, see *Niles*, May 19, 1821 (a man "cut his own throat and died at the moment when he was about to be delivered over to the blood-merchant"); "The Protection Society of Maryland," *Christian Disciple* 6 (1818): 264–265; [Tyson], *Life of Elisha Tyson*, 95–96. For slavery as terror, see Saidiya V. Hartman, *Scenes of Subjection: Terror, Slavery, and Self-Making in Nineteenth-Century America* (New York: Oxford University Press, 1997).

14. Gudmestad, *Troublesome Commerce*, 79.

15. Whitman, *Price of Freedom*, 78; *Patriot*, January 1, 1834 (Pompey), January 3, 1834 (Bennett); Calderhead, "Professional Slave Trader," 204.

16. Pardons, s1061-19, folder 29 (Quay). For the Tyson ruse, see BCA, 1827:656. By some accounts, Woolfolk and other professional traders turned kidnappers into the authorities to bolster the legitimacy of their own much-maligned business practices. See Gudmestad, *Troublesome Commerce*, 164. Initially runaway term slaves had their terms extended but became subject to sale out of state in 1833. See *Laws*, 1804.90, 1833.224.

17. *Minutes of an Adjourned Session . . . 1826*, 29.

18. Garrison in *Boston Courier*, August 12, 1828, reprinted in Merrill, *Letters of William Lloyd Garrison*, 67; *Patriot*, August 9, 1822 (Lewis).

19. *Patriot*, January 1 (Johnson), June 22 (Bauseman and Callahan), 1822, April 11, 1829 (Norfolk); Pardons, s1061-22, folder 84 (Shipley); Andrews, *Slavery and the Domestic Slave-Trade*, 181. For the Protection Society, see *Patriot*, November 19, 1816 (advertisement); *Christian Disciple* 6 (September 1818): 261–267; [Tyson], *Life of Elisha Tyson*, 100. For earlier efforts, such as the Maryland Society for Promoting the Gradual Abolition of Slavery, and the Relief of Free Negroes and Others Unlawfully Held in Bondage, see *Maryland Gazette*, October 11, 1791; Anita Aidt Guy, "The Maryland Abolition Society and the Promotion of the Ideals of the New Nation," *MHM* 84 (winter 1989): 342–349; *American*, August 6, 1807. Institutional efforts were halting. When the Abolition Society of Sussex County, Delaware, contacted Hezekiah Niles in search of a Baltimore abolition society in 1809, Niles replied, "I am sorry to say we have no such society—and, that while we struggle so manfully to preserve the liberties of WHITE men, no provision exists to ameliorate the condition of the unfortunate NEGRO." See *Post*, November 13, 1809. For the Baltimore Society for the Protection of Free People of Color (founded 1827), see *Minutes of the Adjourned Session . . . Nov. 1828*, 53. Between 1812 and 1832, only twenty-seven Marylanders served prison terms for kidnapping or "negro stealing." See *Report of William Crawford, Esq., on the Penitentiaries of the United States, Addressed to His Majesty's Principal Secretary of State for the Home Department* (London: Home Office, 1835), 99; Maryland Penitentiary Prisoners Record, 1811–1840, MSA, s275-1 (courtesy of Stephen Whitman's computer data file). In addition to the twenty-seven people serving time, another nine Marylanders received pardons or dismissals before their cases came to trial.

20. *Fennell et al. v. Ogden*, RSPP, 20982705, 20982708, 20982710, 20982711, 20982713. The Fennell suit was joined by Benjamin Gorsuch, whose family Ogden also attempted to reclaim. A similar incident appears in Andrews, *Slavery and the Domestic Slave-Trade*, 182.

21. *Minutes of the Twentieth Session . . . 1827,* 50.

22. *Niles,* June 13, 1835. For Niles's denunciations of the interregional slave trade, see *Niles,* July 19, 1817, September 14, 1822.

23. For free-labor ideology and the recasting of wage labor as freedom itself, see Jonathan A. Glickstein, *Concepts of Free Labor in Antebellum America* (New Haven, Conn.: Yale University Press, 1991); Amy Dru Stanley, *From Bondage to Contract: Wage Labor, Marriage, and the Market in the Age of Slave Emancipation* (New York: Cambridge University Press, 1998); David R. Roediger, *The Wages of Whiteness: Race and the Making of the American Working Class* (New York: Verso, 1991).

24. Richard Gabriel Stone, *Hezekiah Niles as an Economist* (Baltimore: The Johns Hopkins Press, 1933); Lawrence A. Peskin, *Manufacturing Revolution: The Intellectual Origins of Early American Industry* (Baltimore: Johns Hopkins University Press, 2003), 207–222.

25. Daniel Raymond, *The Elements of Political Economy,* 2nd ed., (Baltimore: Fielding Lucus, Jr., 1823), 2 vols. For commentary, see Donald E. Frey, "The Puritan Roots of Daniel Raymond's Economics," *History of Political Economy* 32 (fall 2000): 607–629; Paul K. Conkin, *Prophets of Prosperity: America's First Political Economists* (Bloomington: Indiana University Press, 1980), 77–107.

26. For the legal history of free labor, see Robert J. Steinfeld, *The Invention of Free Labor: The Employment Relation in English and American Law and Culture, 1350–1870* (Chapel Hill: University of North Carolina Press, 1991) and *Coercion, Contract, and Free Labor in the Nineteenth Century* (New York: Cambridge University Press, 2001); Karen Orren, *Belated Feudalism: Labor, the Law, and Liberal Development in the United States* (New York: Cambridge University Press, 1991); Peter Karsten, "'Bottomed on Justice': A Reappraisal of Critical Legal Studies Scholarship Concerning Breeches of Labor Contracts by Quitting or Firing in Britain and the U.S., 1630–1880," *American Journal of Legal History* 34 (July 1990): 213–261; Christopher Tomlins, *Law, Labor, and Ideology in the Early American Republic* (New York: Cambridge University Press, 1993); Jeffrey S. Kahana, "Master and Servant in the Early Republic, 1780–1830," *JER* 20 (spring 2000): 27–57; James D. Schmidt, *Free to Work: Labor Law, Emancipation, and Reconstruction, 1815–1880* (Athens: University of Georgia Press, 1998).

27. Steinfeld, *Invention of Free Labor,* 166–172, 189–195; Richard B. Morris, "Labor Controls in Maryland in the Nineteenth Century," *JSH* 14 (August 1948): 385–400.

28. For this broader read on antebellum culture, see Steven Mintz, *Moralists and Modernizers: America's Pre-Civil War Reformers* (Baltimore: Johns Hopkins University Press, 1995); Scott A. Sandage, *Born Losers: A History of Failure in America* (Cambridge, Mass.: Harvard University Press, 2005). On evangelical culture and reform in Baltimore, see Terry D. Bilhartz, *Urban Religion and the Second Great Awakening: Church and Society in Early National Baltimore* (Rutherford, N.J.: Fairleigh Dickinson University Press, 1986); *Constitution and Address of the Baltimore Temperance Society* (Baltimore: J. D. Toy, 1830); *Fifth Annual Report of the Maryland State Temperance Society* (Baltimore: n.p., 1836); John H. B. Latrobe, *Manual Labor School. Address on the Subject of a Manual Labor School* (Baltimore: John D. Toy, 1840). On public schools, see Tina Sheller, "The Origins of Public Education in Baltimore, 1825–1829," *History of Education Quarterly* 22 (spring 1982): 23–43. For House of Refuge, see *Patriot,* November 19, 25, December 9, 1830.

29. Charles G. Steffen, *The Mechanics of Baltimore: Workers and Politics in the Age of Rev-*

olution, 1763–1812 (Urbana: University of Illinois Press, 1984); William R. Sutton, *Journeymen for Jesus: Evangelical Artisans Confront Capitalism in Jacksonian Baltimore* (University Park: Pennsylvania State Press University, 1998). On the broader cultural significance of negotiating time and pay, see Richard Biernacki, *The Fabrication of Labor: Germany and Britain, 1640–1914* (Berkeley: University of California Press, 1995); David R. Roediger and Philip S. Foner, *Our Own Time: A History of American Labor and the Working Day* (New York: Greenwood Press, 1989), 1–43.

30. For Niles's campaign, see "To the Working Men . . . ," [1831], MHS, Broadside Collection; *Patriot*, September 2, 3, 1831.

31. William J. Bromwell, *History of Immigration to the United States . . . 1819 to 1855* (1856; repr., New York: Augustus Kelly, 1969); BCA, 1834:1045 (Martin).

32. BCA, 1833:364, 1833:1167 (Baltimore petitions), 1832:1113, 1833:1099, 1834:1171–74 (almshouse figures).

33. On mobilizing labor for the B&O, see James D. Dilts, *The Great Road: The Building of the Baltimore and Ohio, the Nation's First Railroad, 1828–1853* (Stanford: Stanford University Press, 1993), 132–139, 177–184; *Document 11 Accompanying the Executive Message to the Legislature, December 31, 1829: Report respecting the Chesapeake and Ohio Canal* (Annapolis: J. Hughes, 1829); Sherry H. Olson, *Baltimore: The Building of an American City*, 2nd edition (Baltimore: Johns Hopkins University Press, 1997), 72–3.

34. *Baltimore Republican*, December 2, 1834, as cited in Dilts, *Great Road*, 180; *Niles*, June 21, November 29, December 6, 1834; *Patriot*, June 17, 18, 20, 1834; Matthew E. Mason, "'The Hands Here are Disposed to be Turbulent': Unrest Among the Irish Trackmen of the Baltimore and Ohio Railroad, 1829–1851," *LH* 39 (August 1998): 253–272.

35. For the alcohol ban, see *Fourth Annual Report, of the President and Directors, to the Stockholders of the Baltimore and Ohio Rail Road Company* (Baltimore: William Wooddy, 1830), 126–27; *Fifth Annual Report . . .* (Baltimore: William Wooddy, 1831), 113–119; *Sixth Annual Report . . .* (Baltimore: William Wooddy, 1832), 73–74.

36. *Baltimore Daily Transcript*, March 18, 1836.

37. Frederick Douglass, *Narrative of the Life of Frederick Douglass, An American Slave, Written by Himself*, ed. David W. Blight (1845; repr., Boston: Bedford Books, 2003), 47, 106–109. On Douglass in Baltimore, see Dickson J. Preston, *Young Frederick Douglass: The Maryland Years* (Baltimore: Johns Hopkins University Press, 1980); Frank Towers, "African-American Baltimore in the Era of Frederick Douglass," *ATQ: the American Transcendental Quarterly* 9 (September 1995): 165–180.

38. Douglass, *Narrative*, 67 ("urchins").

39. Preston, *Young Frederick Douglass*, 148–151.

40. *Niles*, September 14, 1822.

41. "Letter of Judge Brice," *Genius*, March 1, 1828.

42. For the contested history of the 1831 Southampton rebellion, see Kenneth S. Greenberg, ed., *Nat Turner: A Slave Rebellion in History and Memory* (New York: Oxford University Press, 2003).

43. *Freeman's Banner*, September 17, 1831; *Patriot*, October 8, 1831; *Liberator*, November 5, 1831; BCA, 1830:462–463; Sarah Katz, "Rumors of Rebellion: Fear of a Slave Uprising in Post-Nat Turner Baltimore," *MHM* 89 (fall 1994): 328–333.

44. Thomas R. Gray, *The Confessions of Nat Turner, The Leader of the Late Insurrection in Southampton, VA* (Baltimore: Lucas & Deaver, 1831), 5.

45. *Baltimore Times*, November 5, 1831.

46. *Address of the Young Men's Colonization Society, to the Young Men of Maryland* (Baltimore: John. W. Woods, 1835), 5 (quote). On earlier support for colonization in Baltimore, see, Robert Goodloe Harper, *A Letter from Gen. Harper, of Maryland, to Elias B. Caldwell, Esq. . . .* (Baltimore: E. J. Cole, 1818); Humanitas, *A New and Interesting View of Slavery* (Baltimore: n.p., 1820); *Proceedings of a Meeting of the Friends of African Colonization. Held in the City of Baltimore, on the Seventeenth of October, 1827* (Baltimore: B. Edes, 1828); *Address of the Maryland State Colonization Society, to the People of Maryland . . .* (Baltimore: Lucas & Deaver, 1831). See also Bruce L. Mouser, "Baltimore's African Experiment, 1822–1827," *Journal of Negro History* 80 (summer 1995): 113–127; Eric Robert Papenfuse, *The Evils of Necessity: Robert Goodloe Harper and the Moral Dilemma of Slavery* (Philadelphia, Pa.: American Philosophical Society, 1997); Leroy Graham, *Baltimore, the Nineteenth Century Black Capital* (Washington D.C.: University Press of America, 1982), ch. 3.

47. *Colonization of the Free Colored Population of Maryland, and of Such Slaves as May Hereafter Become Free . . .* (Baltimore: Managers Appointed by the State of Maryland, 1832), 3

48. W. McKenney, *A Brief Statement of Facts, Shewing the Origins, Progress, and Necessity of African Colonization, Addressed to the Citizens of the State of Maryland . . .* (Baltimore: John D. Toy, 1836); *Report of the Committee on Grievances and Courts of Justice, of the House of Delegates, Relative to the Colored Population of Maryland* (Annapolis: Jeremiah Hughes, 1832); "The Condition of the Coloured Population of the City of Baltimore," *Baltimore Literary and Religious Magazine* 4 (April 1838): 168–176; [P.T.], *Some Thoughts Concerning Domestic Slavery, in a letter to —— ——, Esq., of Baltimore* (Baltimore: Joseph N. Lewis, 1838).

49. For a sample of Watkins's writings, see *Genius*, January 12, 1828; *Liberator*, February 19, April 2, June 4, 1831, March 23, 1833 (quote). For a detailed overview of Watkins' career, see Graham, *Baltimore*, 93–146. George Wilson Pierson, *Tocqueville and Beaumont in America* (New York: Oxford University Press, 1938), 516. On the possibility of abolition in post-Turner Virginia, see Alison Goodyear Freehling, *Drift toward Dissolution: The Virginia Slavery Debate of 1831–1832* (Baton Rouge: Louisiana State University Press, 1982). On opposition to colonization, see also [William Lloyd Garrison], *The Maryland Scheme of Expatriation Examined. By a Friend of Liberty* (Boston: Garrison & Knapp, 1834).

50. Pierson, *Tocqueville*, 496; Harper, *Letter from Gen. Harper*, 8; John Hersey, *An Appeal to Christians on the Subject of Slavery*, 2nd ed. (Baltimore: Armstrong and Plaskitt, 1833), 88–89.

51. *Laws*, 1832.323.

52. For overviews of laws, see Jeffrey R. Brackett, *The Negro in Maryland: A Study of the Institution of Slavery* (Baltimore: Johns Hopkins Press, 1889). *Laws* 1790.9 and 1796.67 established the circumstances of legal manumission in Maryland and provided the right of freed people to remain in Maryland. The 1832 code made certain exceptions for the city of Baltimore. For instance, instead of banning all religious observances outside the direct supervision of a white minister, free people of color in the city could hold services if they had the written permission of a white minister and dispersed before 10 p.m.

53. Andrews, *Slavery and the Domestic Slave-Trade*, 36.

54. Daniel Coker, *Journal of Daniel Coker, a Descendant of Africa, From the time of Leaving New York* . . . (Baltimore: Edward J. Coale, 1820); James T. Campbell, *Middle Passages: African American Journeys to Africa, 1787–2005* (New York: Penguin, 2005), 46–53. For black rejection of colonization in Baltimore, see the writings of William Watkins as "A Colored Baltimorean" in *Liberator*, February 19, April 2, November 5, 1831, March 23, 1833, January 25, February 1, 1834, July 4, 1835. "Ching a Ring Chaw" (Baltimore: Geo. Willig, Jr., [ca. 1833]).

55. BCA, 1838:1282 (Roberts), 1838:1286 (Ford), 1838:1285 (Boudley), 1839:332 (Henson), 1839:330 (Downs), 1838:1230 (Randall).

56. BCA, 1830:1037 (Alcott), 1830:1043 (Becker), 1830:1047 (Gill), 1830:1058 (Peterson), 1830:1062 (Stimson), 1831:551 (Trego), 1832:1149 (McGlenn), 1833:431 (Donahue), 1834:275 (Herrington), 1838:1354 (Bennett).

57. For watchman salaries, see BCA, 1828:617, 1829:619, 1832:1083, 1834:540, 1836:523.

58. BCA, 1834:1202, 1836:454–455, 1838:1363. Gardner appeared as a property owner on Star Alley as early as 1809 (plat) and had his house and lot assessed at $100 in 1813 (BCA, Tax Assessors Notebooks, Rg4, s2, Ward 8). His entry in the 1835 city directory listed him as "of Health Boat," while previous and subsequent directories listed him as "laborer." Joseph Stewart, a second oarsman on the Health Department boat and resident of Shakespeare Street in Fells Point, held the position from 1826 through at least 1838. BCA, 1826:534.

59. Discussing the pre-1818 period, Stuart Blumin has called Baltimore "perhaps the most conservative of cities with respect to artisanal political participation." The practice of viva-voce voting until 1805 allowed wealthy employers and creditors to exercise a watchful eye over the electorate. Stuart M. Blumin, *The Emergence of the Middle Class: Social Experience in the American City, 1760–1900* (New York: Cambridge University Press, 1989), 63.

60. For patronage appointments, see *Patriot*, October 18, 1828; BCA, 1833:449 (Polk), 1834:290 (Threlkeld), 1838:1388 (Whig).

61. "To the Irishmen of Baltimore," September 25, 1826, MHS, Broadsides Collection.

62. *Patriot*, September 30, 1828; *Read!! Pause and Reflect. Van Buren in favor of Negroes voting, and opposed to the Poor White Man's enjoying this inestimable privilege!* (Baltimore: n.p., [1836]), Library of Congress, Printed Ephemera Collection, portfolio 30, folder 12; "Martin Van Buren voted that every free negro be entitled to vote at the polls!!" August 11, 1836, MHS, Broadside Collection; "Look On this Picture, And then on This!" [1840], MHS, Broadside, Collection. For a rare newspaper caricature of free people of color in Baltimore portrayed in dialect, see *Patriot*, July 5, 1834.

63. Pierson, *Tocqueville*, 516; *Eastern Express*, September 27, 1836. On the race war theme, see J. J. Sheed, *A Letter from a Gentleman of Baltimore, to his Friend in the State of New York, on the Subject of Slavery* (Baltimore: Sherwood & Co., 1841). On Tocqueville, Beaumont, and American racial ideology, see Laura Janara, "Brothers and Others: Tocqueville and Beaumont, U.S. Genealogy, Democracy, and Racism," *Political Theory* 32 (December 2004): 773–800.

64. BCA, 1833:391 (Armacost), 1834:195 (Howard).

65. On the failure of legal exclusion from various jobs, see Brackett, *Negro in Maryland*, 210; *Colonization of the Free Colored Population of Maryland, and of Such Slaves as May Hereafter Become Free* . . . , 3; *Baltimore Gazette and Daily Advertiser*, April 22 and July 10, 1833 (job ads).

66. Preston, *Young Frederick Douglass*, 142–156.

Conclusion

1. For historical commentary on the construction of colonial British North America and the United States as a land of unparalleled opportunity, see Stephen Innes, "Fulfilling John Smith's Vision: Work and Labor in Early America," in *Work and Labor in Early America*, ed. Stephen Innes (Chapel Hill: University of North Carolina Press, OIEAHC, 1988), 3–47; "Forum: How Revolutionary was the Revolution? A Discussion of Gordon S. Wood's *The Radicalism of the American Revolution*," *WMQ* 51 (October 1994): 677–716; David Brion Davis, "Looking at Slavery from Broader Perspectives," *AHR* 105 (April 2000): 452–466; David Waldstreicher, *Runaway America: Benjamin Franklin, Slavery, and the American Revolution* (New York: Hill and Wang, 2004). For the naturalization test, see U.S. Citizenship and Immigration Services, "Civics (History and Government) Items for the Redesigned Naturalization Test," accessed October 1, 2007, www.uscis.gov/files/nativedocuments/100q.pdf.

2. Lonn Taylor, *The Star-Spangled Banner: The Flag that Inspired the National Anthem* ([New York]: National Museum of American History, Smithsonian Institution, in association with Harry N. Brams, 2000); Irvin Molotsky, *The Flag, the Poet and the Song: The Story of the Star-Spangled Banner* (New York: Dutton, 2001).

3. A. J. Langguth, *Union 1812: The Americans Who Fought the Second War of Independence* (New York: Simon and Schuster, 2006).

4. Pickersgill's work is commemorated at the Flag House and Star-Spangled Banner Museum, located at Pickergill's Fells Point home. All quotes are taken from the Flag House and Star-Spangled Banner Museum, www.flaghouse.org, accessed September 28, 2007.

5. For a provocative discussion of the hidden social relations of textile production in general, but in the context of the flag in particular, see Char Miller, "Exhibition Review: The Star-Spangled Banner: The Flag that Inspired the National Anthem," *JAH* 87 (December 2000): 977–981. In 2002, Pickersgill was inducted into the Maryland Women's Hall of Fame, and her name is now displayed on a plaque in the Maryland State Law Library in Annapolis.

6. Christopher T. George, "Mirage of Freedom: African-Americans in the War of 1812," *MHM* 91 (winter 1996): 441 (Douglass quote); BCA, 1814:502 (Zacharie). For the mobilization of workers of color on the city's fortifications, see BCA, 1814:465, 1814:468, 1814:477, 1814:527. For individual workers, names taken from War of 1812 payrolls, BCA, 1814:129, 1814:791, 1814:801, 1814:808, 1814:819, 1814:831, 1814:837, 1814:853, 1814:856, 1814:892. Other data taken from mudmachine payrolls (see chapter 3, note 4); Christian Baum bridge (BCA, 1809:236); BAAB, February 23, 1824 (Dillon); Cornelius W. Stafford, *Baltimore Directory for 1802* (Baltimore: John W. Butler, 1802); Edward Matchett, *Baltimore Directory and Register for 1816* (Baltimore: Wanderer Office, 1816).

7. David R. Roediger, *The Wages of Whiteness: Race and the Making of the American Working Class* (New York: Verso, 1991), 44.

8. Elizabeth Olson, "Stars and Stripes Forever: Smithsonian Works to Preserve that Special Flag," *New York Times*, July 3, 2003; Julia Preston, "New Test Asks: What Does 'American' Mean?" *New York Times*, September 28, 2007. The Smithsonian's National Museum of American History places the Star-Spangled Banner at the center of its version of the American past. See http://americanhistory.si.edu/ssb.

I first became curious about the relationship of capitalism, slavery, and the American Revolution in college lecture courses with Eric Foner and Barbara Fields. Then in my first year of graduate school, I read in succession Gordon S. Wood's *The Radicalism of the American Revolution*, Charles G. Sellers's *The Market Revolution*, and Robert Fogel's *Without Consent or Contract*. In Wood's account, American independence created extraordinary opportunities for ordinary people to pursue their economic self-interest; the result was a democratic society of unparalleled freedom. For Sellers, economic development in the early republic ran counter to the democratic possibilities of the American Revolution and provoked widespread resistance to the values of the marketplace. Fogel made slavery—and by extension, exploitation—the dynamic engine of the American economy and a crucial component in the history of capitalism. The challenge of reconciling these interpretive frameworks has guided my work ever since.

For this book, the easy part was choosing Baltimore as a site of research: a new city in the new nation, a boomtown economy whose capitalist architects embraced the cultural logic of the marketplace, and a place where the number of slaves grew fourfold between 1790 and 1810. In his *Narrative*, Frederick Douglass had made the city's shipyards and alleys familiar to students of nineteenth-century American history. Still, documentation of the labor processes in the city remained difficult to find. As is true virtually everywhere, casual labor left few traces in the historical record, and the work of servants, seamstresses, mariners, and day laborers remains hidden in the archives. This explains why there are so few works in the field of labor history that address the experiences of so-called unskilled workers.

Primary Sources

For this study, four sets of sources proved indispensable. First, the array of receipts, payrolls, contracts, and petitions at the Baltimore City Archives, where virtually every scrap pertaining to city governance since 1797 has been preserved and cataloged. Because local governments took responsibility for the infrastructure of docks, roads, and bridges that facilitated commerce, municipal records can reveal the labor processes involved in building a capitalist city. In Baltimore, these records were often filed under the generic heading of Returns and Receipts. Papers belonging to the city commissioners and the port wardens also contained payrolls and other records for dredging the harbor, leveling streets, and installing curbstones. The papers of the mayor's office and the city council also provided glimpses of the daily rhythm of the urban economy through the reports of the city's appointed inspectors, wardens, masters, and overseers. In keeping elected officials apprised, municipal officers related the danger of visiting a neighborhood pump as a young domestic servant, the presumed causes and patterns of debt imprisonment, and the prevalence of secondhand markets in spoiled food. If the social history of marginal people involves piecing together fragmentary glimpses of everyday life, then municipal archives offer scholars a fantastic starting point. (I would be remiss if I did not use this opportunity to make a plea for the future of the Baltimore City Archives, currently stored in a non-climate-controlled warehouse and in risk of imminent disintegration. There are dozens of books waiting to be written out of that collection, but future scholars may soon miss their chance.)

The next sources crucial to this project were petitions, such as the one from the street scrapers who opened the book. Because petitions were intended to be persuasive, they could be formulaic and written to convey what a supplicant person *thought* a person in power wanted to hear. Nonetheless, petitions offer a chance to hear marginal people represent themselves in their own words, and if nothing else, are instructive for what they reveal about the range of plausible stories in a given culture. The Baltimore City Archives contain hundreds of petitions, including many from women who identified themselves as citizens despite being unable to vote. An even more compelling set of petitions can be found in the Maryland State Archives, cataloged as Pardon Papers (s1061). Men and women who had been indicted for or convicted of crimes petitioned the governor and council for clemency. Petitioners had been arrested for offenses ranging from vagrancy and illegal tavern keeping to slave kidnapping and murder. These files contain corroborating accounts and character testimonials, as well as counter-petitions from aggrieved neighbors and crime victims. In these petitions, slaveholders came to the defense of their slaves, domestic servants testified against their employers, and poor women explained why salvaging wood chips from the docks did not make them vagrants. For petitions where people of color narrated their own life stories, see the Maryland court cases microfilmed for the Race and Slavery Petitions Project at the University of North Carolina, Greensboro.

In many cases, marginal people enter the historical record only when they interact with the institutions of the state. To that extent, important sets of records come from such institutions as Maryland's penitentiary, Baltimore's almshouse, and the county courts. Institutional records frequently contain data pertaining to nativity, occupation, and age, as well as physical characteristics like height and skin tone. The Penitentiary Records (s275) at the Maryland State Archives make it possible to discover, for example, the characteristics shared by those convicted of vagrancy (they were overwhelmingly women). Also at the Maryland State Archives, the records of various courts centralized data on large groups of people, ranging from the children registered as apprentices to the free people of color applying for freedom certificates. These records allow a social historian to create collective portraits of groups of people otherwise under the radar. Perhaps the most important records in this study belonged to the Baltimore Almshouse, archived at the Maryland Historical Society. The Admissions Book (ms. 1866.1) contains over 1,800 detailed entries for the mid-1820s and makes it possible to see how impoverished people moved in and out of the social welfare system.

Finally, newspapers offer a vivid glimpse into the lives of marginal workers in the early republic city. A historian can mine newspapers systematically, culling all want ads or runaway slave ads for a given year, for example. Several Baltimore newspapers are widely available on microfilm (the *American*, *Niles' Weekly Register*, *Genius of Universal Emancipation*, the *Patriot*) and now appear in digitalized collections that allow full-text searching (too late for this historian, who spent the best years of his life planted in front of a microfilm machine). Equally important, newspapers published mountains of useful commentary in the forms of editorials and letters. I especially benefited from the opportunity to read several short-lived Fells Point newspapers from the 1830s in the collection of the American Antiquarian Society in Worcester, Massachusetts.

While I was working on this project, I had several dispiriting conversations with senior colleagues. When I explained I was writing about day laborers, seamstresses, and other "unskilled" people, the reply was, "That's going to be one short book!" In fact, some labor historians have declared the outright impossibility of knowing much of anything about the vast majority of workers who built early American cities. This book intends to refute that premise and to encourage social historians to return to the archives in search of people and processes long thought to be unrecoverable. The archive *is* there, but it requires a willingness to see bigger stories in smaller evidentiary fragments.

Secondary Sources

The biggest challenge for this book was finding an analytical framework to make sense of an economy where slaves like Douglass earned wages, where white people performed the bulk of degraded labor, and where employers combined diverse workers on the same job sites. I have borrowed insights from many historians working across several chronological periods and geographies, but most of this scholarship shares a grounding in *political economy,* or the premise that the rules governing economic activity emerge from law and culture. Exploring how markets are embedded in the state and in a broader range of social relations (as opposed to functioning autonomously and inherently seeking equilibrium) has become a preoccupation for historians. For a good introduction, see David Montgomery, *Citizen Worker: The Experience of Workers in the United States with Democracy and the Free Market during the Nineteenth Century* (New York: Cambridge University Press, 1993). Much recent work has taken place under the auspices of the Harvard Workshop on the Political Economy of Modern Capitalism, convened by Sven Beckert and Christine Desan, as well as through the seminars and conferences of the Program in Early American Economy and Society, directed by Cathy Matson.

The field of early republic labor history has fragmented over the last twenty-five years. The New Labor History offered an understanding of the subjective experiences of working people, but did so by depicting male artisans as universal workers. Sean Wilentz, *Chants Democratic: New York City and the Rise of the American Working Class, 1788–1850* (New York: Oxford University Press, 1984), remains the standard reference. Feminist scholars then asked what difference it made if workers were female. Christine Stansell, *City of Women: Sex and Class in New York, 1789–1860* (New York: Alfred A. Knopf, 1986), and Jeanne Boydston, *Home and Work: Housework, Wages, and the Ideology of Labor in the Early Republic* (New York: Oxford University Press, 1990), showed the centrality of women to working-class formation. Scholars in African American history then asked what difference it made if workers were people of color or slaves (albeit usually within community studies rather than studies of labor processes). See, for example, Gary B. Nash, *Forging Freedom: The Formation of Philadelphia's Black Community, 1720–1840* (Cambridge, Mass.: Harvard University Press, 1988), Shane White, *Somewhat More Independent: The End of Slavery in New York City, 1770–1810* (Athens: University of

Georgia Press, 1991), W. Jeffrey Bolster, *Black Jacks: African American Seamen in the Age of Sail* (Cambridge, Mass.: Harvard University Press, 1997), James Sidbury, *Ploughshares into Swords: Race, Rebellion, and Identity in Gabriel's Virginia, 1730–1810* (New York: Cambridge University Press, 1997), Graham Russell Hodges, *Root and Branch: African Americans in New York and East Jersey, 1613–1863* (Chapel Hill: University of North Carolina Press, 1999), and Leslie M. Harris, *In the Shadow of Slavery: African Americans in New York City, 1626–1863* (Chicago: University of Chicago Press, 2003). Other scholars brought attention back to white men, but now as racialized and gendered subjects in their own right, or as workers whose material circumstances worked against class formation: David R. Roediger, *The Wages of Whiteness: Race and the Making of the American Working Class* (New York: Verso, 1991), Peter Way, *Common Labour: Workers and the Digging of North American Canals, 1780–1860* (New York: Cambridge University Press, 1993), Paul A. Gilje, *Liberty on the Waterfront: American Maritime Culture in the Age of Revolution* (Philadelphia: University of Pennsylvania Press, 2004), and Joshua R. Greenberg, *Advocating the Man: Masculinity, Organized Labor, and the Household in New York, 1800–1840* (New York, Columbia University Press, www.gutenberg-e.org, 2006).

Not surprisingly, the center could not hold, and labor history as a field is still struggling to situate the intersectionality of race, class, and gender within a systematic understanding of social relations under capitalism. Scholarship that tries to put the pieces back together into something larger includes Jacqueline Jones, *American Work: Four Centuries of Black and White Labor* (New York: W. W. Norton, 1998), Peter Linebaugh and Marcus Rediker, *The Many-Headed Hydra: Sailors, Slaves, Commoners, and the Hidden History of the Revolutionary Atlantic* (Boston: Beacon Press, 2000), and Evelyn Nakano Glenn, *Unequal Freedom: How Race and Gender Shaped American Citizenship and Labor* (Cambridge, Mass.: Harvard University Press, 2002). An essay I found particularly useful is Gerda Lerner's "Rethinking the Paradigm" in her collection *Why History Matters: Life and Thought* (New York: Oxford University Press, 1997). For recent explorations of class in early America, see Simon Middleton and Billy G. Smith, eds., *Class Matters: Early North America and the Atlantic World* (Philadelphia: University of Pennsylvania Press, 2008). On the utility of class analysis in settings where patriarchy and slavery largely determined who worked where, I advanced several arguments in "The Contours of Class in the Early Republic City," in *Labor: Studies in Working-Class History of the Americas* 1 (winter 2004). Over the last five years, several leading journals have published forums on how multiple categories of social difference reconfigure labor history. In addition to *Labor*, see *International Labor and Working-Class History*, *Journal of Social History*, and *Social Science History*.

Four other bodies of scholarship figure prominently in this book's analysis. First, recent work in the history of American slavery has stressed the importance of the market and the underlying logic of "human commodification" within legal bondage. I have learned a great deal from Walter Johnson, *Soul by Soul: Life Inside the Antebellum Slave Market* (Cambridge, Mass.: Harvard University Press, 1999), Jennifer L. Morgan, *Laboring Women: Reproduction and Gender in New World Slavery* (Philadelphia: University of Pennsylvania Press, 2004), David Waldstreicher, *Runaway America: Benjamin Franklin, Slavery, and the American Revolution* (New York: Hill and Wang, 2004), Steven Deyle, *Carry Me Back: The Domestic Slave Trade in American Life* (New York: Oxford University Press, 2005), and Stephanie E. Smallwood, *Saltwater Slavery: A Middle Passage from Africa to American Diaspora* (Cambridge, Mass.: Harvard University Press, 2007).

Second, feminist scholarship revealed the centrality of nonmarket relationships and patriarchal ideology to economic development. Works that were especially important include Carolyn Merchant, *Ecological Revolutions: Nature, Gender, and Science in New England* (Chapel Hill: University of North Carolina Press, 1989), Sonya O. Rose, *Limited Livelihoods: Gender and Class in Nineteenth-Century England* (Berkeley: University of California Press, 1992), Deborah Valenze, *The First Industrial Woman* (New York: Oxford University Press, 1995), and Anna Clark, *The Struggle for the Breeches: Gender and the Making of the British Working Class* (Berkeley: University of California Press, 1995).

Third, recent scholarship on poverty has been especially thoughtful in its exploration of how impoverished people navigated social welfare systems. I particularly appreciate Ruth Wallis Herndon, *Unwelcome Americans: Living on the Margin in Early New England* (Philadelphia: University of Pennsylvania Press, 2001), Tim Hitchcock, *Down and Out in Eighteenth-Century London* (London: Hambledon, 2004), and the essays collected in Billy G. Smith, ed., *Down and Out in Early America* (University Park: Pennsylvania State University Press, 2004).

Finally, a trio of excellent books on Baltimore published in the 1990s helped me tremendously: T. Stephen Whitman, *The Price of Freedom: Slavery and Manumission in Baltimore and Early National Maryland* (Lexington: University Press of Kentucky, 1997), Christopher Phillips, *Freedom's Port: The African American Community of Baltimore, 1790–1860* (Urbana: University of Illinois Press, 1997), and William R. Sutton, *Journeymen for Jesus: Evangelical Artisans Confront Capitalism in Jacksonian Baltimore* (University Park: Pennsylvania State University Press, 1998).

Otterson, David, 92
Otterson, Jane, 92–93
Otterson, John, 92–93
out-relief. *See* poor relief
Overfield, Martin, 163
Owen, Thomas, 125
Owings, Achsah, 58
Owings, Elizabeth, 58
Owings, J. W., 116
Owings, Leaven, 58

Paine, Thomas, 19
Panic of 1819, 85, 96, 199, 215, 224
Panic of 1837, 174, 199, 232
Paris, 14
Parrish, John, 61
Pasture, Biddy, 162–163, 167
Pasture, Charles, 162–163
Paterson, N.J., 39
patriarchy: and women's economic opportunity,
    6, 8, 101, 118–120, 131, 133–134, 141–142, 149,
    156–157, 160; and women's sexuality, 118
Patterson, Elizabeth (Bonaparte), 108, 145, 183
Patterson, William, 145
Paul, Catherine, 136
pawning, 183, 185–187, 247
Peacock, Mrs., 183
penal labor, 55, 81–82, 96, 226–228. *See also*
    Maryland Penitentiary
Pennsylvania Society for the Encouragement
    of Public Economy, 214
Pepper, Betsy, 123
Perry (slave), 37
Pessener, Elizabeth, 225
Petersburg, Va., 166
Peterson, Martin, 253
petty marketing. *See* hucksters
Philadelphia, 19, 25, 37, 116, 170–171; African
    American households, 166; charity organiza-
    tions, 108, 146–147, 153; demography, 13, 34;
    domestic service in, 105, 108, 126; poor relief
    programs, 136, 225–228; ten-hour day, 244
philanthropy: on behalf of European immi-
    grants, 31–32; on behalf of poor children, 108–
    109; on behalf of seamstresses, 142–148, 152–
    156; and Christian charity, 216; colonization
    couched as, 41, 250; and community respon-
    sibility for poor, 190, 196–198, 213–219; and

sensibility, 216–217; and social discipline,
    108–109, 219–225, 228–229. *See also* charity
    organizations; poor relief
Phillips, Isaac, 87
Phoebe (slave), 111
Pickering, Joseph, 89
Pickersgill, Mary, 261–262
Pierce, Hetty, 225
pigs, 177–178
police. *See* watchmen
Polk, James, 255
Pompey (slave), 35, 237
poor relief: and capitalist discipline, 196–198,
    214–215, 219–229, 243; and civil society, 215–
    218, 229; clothing distribution, 182–183, 190;
    efforts to stem abuse, 217, 219–229; historical
    interpretations of, 197; less-eligibility concept,
    196, 219–229; make-work programs, 136–
    137, 221–222, 228; medical care, 181–182, 205–
    206; out-relief pensions, 190, 225–226; and
    pauper agency, 194–213; wintertime assis-
    tance, 2, 136, 174–175, 179–180, 190, 192,
    214–215. *See also* Baltimore almshouse;
    charity organizations; School of Industry
Potter, Catherine, 119
Potter, Thomas, 118
poverty: and African American households,
    166–168; and alcohol use, 164, 192, 197, 212–
    213, 215, 224; and American exceptionalism,
    2–3, 158–159, 191–193, 214, 229, 259–262;
    charity as presumed cause, 192, 214–215,
    222–225; and disease, 171–172, 182; among
    European immigrants, 32–33; inherent to
    wage labor, 1–3, 17, 44, 77, 98–99, 156, 158–
    159, 173–175, 229–230, 258; intensifying in
    1830s, 252–253; measured by almshouse
    admissions, 199–200; and political economy,
    214–219; seasonality, 179–180, 192, 202–204,
    222. *See also* working-class households
Powhatan Mills, 24, 126
Price, William, 70
Priest, William, 79, 82
privateering, 22
Procter, Margaret, 165
prostitution: accusations of, 118; brothels, 129,
    206; criminalized, 129, 223; as livelihood,
    129–130; as presumed consequence of low
    wages, 141–143, 146